P9-DEY-341

Evaluating Second Language Education

THE CAMBRIDGE APPLIED LINGUISTICS SERIES

Series editors: Michael H. Long and Jack C. Richards

This new series presents the findings of recent work in applied linguistics which are of direct relevance to language teaching and learning and of particular interest to applied linguists, researchers, language teachers, and teacher trainers.

Evaluating Second Language Education

Edited by

J. Charles Alderson
Lancaster University

Alan Beretta
Michigan State University

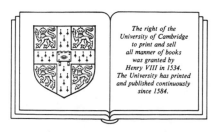

The right of the
University of Cambridge
to print and sell
all manner of books
was granted by
Henry VIII in 1534.
The University has printed
and published continuously
since 1584.

Cambridge University Press
Cambridge
New York   Port Chester
Melbourne   Sydney

Published by the Press Syndicate of the University of Cambridge
The Pitt Building, Trumpington Street, Cambridge CB2 1RP
40 West 20th Street, New York, NY 10011–4211, USA
10 Stamford Road, Oakleigh, Victoria 3166, Australia

© Cambridge University Press 1992

First published 1992

Printed in Great Britain
by Bell & Bain Ltd, Glasgow

Library of Congress cataloguing in publication data

Evaluating second language education / edited by J. Charles Alderson, Alan Beretta.
     p.   cm. – (The Cambridge applied linguistics series)
ISBN 0-521-41067-3.   ISBN 0-521-42269-8 (pbk.)
1. Education, Bilingual – Evaluation.
I. Alderson, J. Charles. II. Beretta, Alan. III. Series.
LC3719.E93   1991
371.97–dc20   91-25320 CIP

A catalogue record for this book is available from the British Library.

ISBN 0 521 41067 3 hardback
ISBN 0 521 42269 8 paperback

Copyright
The law allows a reader to make a single copy of part of a book for purposes of private
study. It does not allow the copying of entire books or the making of multiple copies of
extracts. Written permission for any such copying must always be obtained from the
publisher in advance.

CE

Contents

Contributors

J. Charles Alderson, Lancaster University, Lancaster, England
Alan Beretta, Michigan State University, East Lansing, USA
Hywel Coleman, University of Leeds, Leeds, England
Brian Lynch, University of California, Los Angeles, USA
Rosamond Mitchell, University of Southampton, Southampton, England
Adrian Palmer, University of Utah, Salt Lake City, USA
Steven Ross, University of Hawaii at Manoa, Honolulu, USA
Mike Scott, The University of Liverpool, Liverpool, England
Assia Slimani, Polytechnic of Central London, London, England

Series editors' preface

If the desire of most practitioners to professionalise language teaching were not motivation enough, increasing demands for accountability in foreign and second language education – both from those who finance such programmes and from students, the consumers – make programme evaluation of growing importance for applied linguists, administrators and language teachers. To be satisfactory, evaluations will need to be rigorous, theoretically motivated and data-based. As such, the field experiences and developing expertise among second language programme evaluators are suitable topics for inclusion in the *Cambridge Applied Linguistics Series*.

The more sophisticated study of second language acquisition and second language classroom processes of the 1970s and 1980s has placed second language programme evaluators in a better position to meet the demands for accountability. So has the increasing availability in masters level programmes of basic training in research methods and statistics. What is still often lacking, however, is much appreciation of the potential of qualitative methods in evaluation work, and of how useful a combination of second language research findings and quantitative and qualitative methods can often be.

Drs Alderson and Beretta are both seasoned programme evaluators and very aware of these issues. In *Evaluating Second Language Education*, they have provided a series of case studies which illustrate the strengths and limitations of qualitative and quantitative approaches and the frequent value of combining them. In addition, in this book, they and the other contributors have sought to document evaluation studies from the inside, in all their gory, private detail, rather than to provide more polished, but less informative, versions for the shop window. The contexts, scope and scale of the individual studies vary greatly, as does the level of success of the original projects, which were sometimes conducted in difficult circumstances. Throughout, however, this is a book written by evaluators for evaluators and for those likely to be evaluated. The stories are often not pretty, and things do not always go as planned, but we are likely to learn more from the frank accounts of what really happened and is likely to happen again than from another set of articles about how to conduct the ideal study in a laboratory setting.

Michael H. Long
Jack C. Richards

Acknowledgements

The editors would like to thank Alan Davies, Michael Long, Ron Mackay, Nina Spada, and an anonymous reviewer, who read parts or all of the manuscript and offered constructive criticism. They are grateful to students on the MA in Linguistics for English Language Teaching, Lancaster University, for their comments on some of the chapters and postscripts. Particular thanks are due to Dianne Wall, who spent innumerable hours checking and re-checking manuscript and proofs and offering valuable suggestions for improvement.

The editors and publishers would like to thank the following for permission to reproduce copyright material:
Oxford University Press for 'sample items from the five texts used in Phase 1 of the Evaluation', from A. Beretta and A. Davies, 1985, Evaluation of the Bangalore Project, *English Language Teaching Journal* vol. 38 no. 4, reprinted as Appendix 1 on pp. 265–6; and for 'CTP Teacher Implementation Categories', from A. Beretta, 1990, Implementation of the Bangalore Project, *Applied Linguistics* vol. 11, reprinted as Appendix 2 on pp. 266–7; TESOL for 'Treatment categories based on Chaudron's (1977) framework', from A. Beretta, 1989, Attention to form or meaning?: error treatment in the Bangalore project, *TESOL Quarterly* vol. 23; The British Council for Helen Boyle (Ed.), Dunford Seminar Report 1987, pp. 25 and 29–30, reprinted as Appendix A on p. 300 and Appendix B on pp. 301–2; Editora da PUC-SE for Appendices 1–10 from *The Brazilian ESP Project: an evaluation*, by M. A. A. Celani, J. L. Holmes, R. C. G. Ramos and M. R. Scott, 1988, reprinted on pp. 306–49.

Introduction

This book examines prominent theoretical and methodological issues in the evaluation of second language education. It offers a range of state-of-the-art case studies, a review of the literature showing how the field got to where it is, and practical advice on how to design and execute evaluations in the field.

As a cursory glance at publishers' lists and the contents of the major journals reveals, the discipline of second language education evaluation has been afforded relatively little attention. By contrast, in general social and educational spheres, provision is routinely made for evaluation, and this emphasis is reflected in their respective literatures. One of the most eminent behavioural scientists of the last 50 years has devoted two recent books to the subject (Cronbach 1982, Cronbach *et al.* 1980) and has called evaluation 'the liveliest frontier of American social science' (1980:13).

In second language education, there has long been dissatisfaction with evaluation which has been methodologically inflexible and uncertain or misguided as to its role. If the published literature is at all representative, it has not been a lively frontier.

This edited collection is designed as a first step in bringing the evaluation of second language education to the cutting edge.

Specifically, this book offers commentary and data intended to foster a self-reflecting attitude in researchers already involved in evaluation and to provide useful input to teacher-training programmes.

In designing the book, it was judged that what an evaluator really needs to know is how to deal with *ad hoc* investigation that appears to have no tradition that can be appealed to. Each inquiry faces apparently unique difficulties. Therefore, to present a series of cleaned-up case studies which give the impression of a smooth operation would not be helpful. Instead it was intended to present a picture of the reality that led to final reports. A range of scholars who were involved in evaluations in diverse parts of the world and whose studies focused on quite different issues were therefore asked to contribute to this book. On the grounds that at this stage of our development, the history of an evaluation is probably more important than its findings, they were asked to spell out

1

the decision points when a study took one direction rather than another, and the reasons for them.

This call for histories of evaluation processes is seen by Cronbach *et al.* as appropriate to the development of the field. They write:

> Interchanges that occur in private during the planning stages of many other evaluations would have great educative value if written up as candid case studies.
>
> (1980: 169)

> Evaluators gain much experience in the course of designing and redesigning a study. Unfortunately, little of that experience is recorded for the benefit of the evaluation community. Rarely does a research report mention the branching points where the study took one shape rather than another or explain why the final plan was preferred [...] Methods of evaluation would improve faster if evaluators more often wrote retrospective accounts of design choices [...] to consider how questions were chosen, how resources were deployed, how quality of data was controlled, and how observations were assembled for communication.
>
> (1980: 214)

The inclusion of case studies in this book has the same purpose: by documenting the histories of actual studies it is hoped to contribute to an understanding of the discipline of evaluating second language education.

The book comprises three parts:

Part I: An overview
This section examines evaluations that have been published in the second language literature and contrasts the lack of development manifested there with what has meantime been learnt in the wider field of educational evaluation.

Part II: Case studies
This section consists of eight histories of evaluation processes, all of which deal with different problems in widely divergent settings. While the focus is on how each evaluator addresses the difficulties central to each study, the findings are also included. All of the chapters have been written especially for this volume and have not appeared elsewhere. All are firmly grounded empirical inquiries rather than speculative position papers. In addition, each chapter is followed by a postscript by the editors of this volume, commenting on the chapter and linking it to the various themes that run through the book.

Part III: Guidelines for the design of evaluation projects
In this final section, the aim is to offer suggestions about how to set up and carry out evaluations in any given setting. The section attempts to

provide a balanced overview and discussion of the issues encountered in the evaluation of second language education, and calls for many sources and types of information. In doing so, this final section reflects the intention of the volume as a whole to furnish insights into the nature of evaluation in a way that is intended to provide practical guidance to would-be evaluators.

References

Cronbach, L. J. 1982. *Designing evaluations of educational and social programs.* San Francisco: Jossey-Bass.

Cronbach, L. J., S. R. Ambron, S. M. Dornbusch, R. D. Hess, R. C. Hornik, D. C. Phillips, D. F. Walker and S. S. Weiner. 1980. *Toward reform of program evaluation.* San Francisco: Jossey-Bass.

PART I

Evaluation of language education: an overview

Alan Beretta

Introduction

This chapter has two principal aims. The first is to provide a review of previous evaluation studies in foreign language teaching, so that future evaluations may be informed by past experience in the field; the second, to set the evaluation of language education within the broader framework of educational evaluation.

An overview of the history and development of the evaluation of language education since the early 1960s is presented. Although occasional studies were carried out before the 1960s, the past quarter of a century has seen a notable growth in such studies and therefore the period from the 1960s to the present will be the focus of the review. In addition, reference is also made, in the second part of the chapter, to evaluation studies and theory in education more generally. The aim is not to be exhaustive, but to characterise trends and developments in language education evaluation.

To date, very few books have appeared on the evaluation of language teaching programs in general. This compares unfavorably with the general field of educational evaluation, where dozens of titles appear annually in one publishing house alone (Sage). In the language teaching journals, evaluation studies are rarely published which do not focus on the seemingly never-ending 'methods' debate (which had wearied Sweet as long ago as 1899) or on the highly politicised bilingual programs. Yet in the educational and social spheres, specialist evaluation journals proliferate. In TESOL, the major professional organisation for English teachers, there is not even a special interest section on program evaluation. Compare this with the need felt in the American Educational Research Association (AREA) for evaluation to form its own association and hold its own conferences – the American Evaluation Association was formed in 1985 and its major topical interest group is educational evaluation. By comparison, quite clearly, in the field of second language education, there has been little attention given to evaluation.

Throughout the 1970s and into the 1980s, evaluation of language teaching programs has proceeded as if unaware of developments in educational evaluation. Almost every evaluation study that has been published has used some form of testing and quasi-experimental design regardless, often, of its usefulness in given settings (see Beretta 1986a).

Of course, there have been many evaluations which have been carried out for restricted audiences, and which have therefore not been published. For example, it is known that organisations like the British Council and the British Overseas Development Administration frequently commission applied linguists to undertake evaluations of aid-funded projects. Such evaluations are known to involve the expert visiting the project, often only briefly, and writing a report to the sponsors on their opinions of the value of work to date. However, for-your-eyes-only reports sponsored by government or government institutions are, by their very nature, rarely made available to the language education profession. Thus, it is virtually impossible to know if any of these evaluations are scholarly or disciplined studies. Any evaluation which does not attempt to make public its method of inquiry and its findings can have little to say to an academic audience, so this class of investigation is ignored here.

Some of the evaluations carried out in the language teaching field are published through official channels, and some of these (such as the work carried out at Concordia University by Mackay) bear the hallmarks that a properly trained evaluator would recognise. However, such studies, crucial though they are to the advancement of the field, have not yet been published in the major second language education outlets.

This chapter will briefly trace the short and simple annals of published second language program evaluation and set them within the framework of what has been learnt in the wider field of educational evaluation. The focus will be on the method studies, since the bilingual programs, notably the Canadian Immersion programs, have been documented elsewhere (Genesee 1983, Swain and Lapkin 1982) and until recently were almost invariably investigations solely of product and thus, for the purposes of this book, of limited methodological interest.

25 years of L2 program evaluation

It is not easy to decide where to begin a review of published L2 program evaluation. Certainly, it is barely worth considering much L2 research of any description before 1963, as Agard and Dunkel's (1948) and Carroll's (1963) reviews despondently attest. However, 1963 is a good place to start because it was an auspicious year for educational research in general and for program evaluation in particular. Campbell and Stanley's (1963) monumental treatise on research design appeared that year as did Cronbach's (1963) seminal paper on program evaluation. However,

1963 was also the year that Keating's large-scale evaluation of competing language teaching methods appeared, initiating a disillusionment with evaluation in language education that was quickly compounded by the more famous Scherer and Wertheimer (1964) and Smith (1970) studies, which also compared methods.

Keating (1963) investigated the usefulness of the language laboratory in the teaching of French. More than 5,000 students from 21 school districts participated in this much maligned study, which found that better results were achieved in classes which did not use a laboratory. Stern (1983:69) recalls that it 'caused a furore'; Freedman (1971:33) dismisses it; Smith warns that 'a careful reading of the study raises serious doubts about the validity of the research' (1970:10). Keating himself makes no claim to the contrary: 'this cannot be considered an experiment in any proper sense' (1963:24). Quite an understatement: there was no attempt to specify what kinds of treatment the experimental subjects received; we are not told to what extent use of laboratories varied, or what use, if any, was made of them at all; we know nothing about what happened in control classrooms. Again, Keating is disarmingly candid about this: 'absolutely no provision was made for central control of any kind over the independent language instruction programs going on in the various school districts' (1963:38).

The Scherer and Wertheimer (1964) study, widely known as the Colorado Project, did little to enhance the reputation of evaluation. Scherer and Wertheimer compared audiolingual and cognitive code methods of teaching German and aimed to 'draw some definite scientific conclusions about the relative merits of the two methods' (1964:12). The original plan for a tightly controlled study collapsed and a chapter of accidents ensued: a press leak motivated control students to exercise pressure to join the experimental groups (1964:24); the construction of a new language laboratory was not completed until audiolingual students were to have finished the audio phase of their training; test administration could not be simultaneous for all students because the exam halls were all booked up by other departments. Monitoring of the programs was inadequate and there were insuperable problems with program-fair testing. The results are virtually uninterpretable.

Results failed to show the expected superiority of the audiolingual method in the Pennsylvania Project (Smith 1970). However, these results are, like those of Keating (1963) and Scherer and Wertheimer (1964), extremely difficult to interpret. Distinctions between audiolingual and cognitive code methods were inadequately monitored. There was an attempt at classroom observation, but this did not allow comparison between methods as different schemes were used. Once again, the criterion measures were not program-fair. Once again, a great deal of time and money were spent, expectations were high among the academic community, and from the very beginning there was never a chance that these expectations would be fulfilled. The Pennsylvania Project signalled the end of the line for large-scale method comparisons, at least in the United States.

It is characteristic of the Pennsylvania Project and other earlier second language evaluation studies that they expected to be able to achieve such tight controls as to be in a position to contribute to theories of language learning. After all, if we knew the best way to promote the learning of languages, many other issues that an evaluation might look at would pale into insignificance. In this sense, it might be considered unfortunate that the Campbell and Stanley paper attracted so much attention from evaluators; its focus on true- and quasi-experimental design, certainly welcome in educational research in general, was less appropriate for evaluation in contexts which typically would be resistant to tight control and theory development. For instance, Scherer and Wertheimer felt able to predict a 'rigidly controlled large-scale scientific experiment which would yield clear-cut data' (1964:12). This was clearly an untenable aim for a study which was to compare audiolingual teaching with cognitive-code, in which the treatments could only be vaguely described and were extremely vaguely monitored, in which neither student nor teacher variables could be controlled, in which all manner of real-world accidents could have occurred (and did), and in which the testing, in my view, at least, could never be program-fair (cf. Beretta 1986b; but also see Bachman 1989 for a more positive view).

By and large, the fall-out from the Pennsylvania Project (Smith 1970) was that those who wished to evaluate methods, concerned at their lack of control in the field, moved to the 'laboratory', investigating aspects of methods over short durations, with at least some variables controlled. For example, Seliger (1975) and Freedman (1976) got around the problem of the teacher variable by replacing teachers with prerecorded lessons, in the process effectively precluding any possibility of external validity. Although the aim was the same – to be able to contribute to theories of language learning – these studies could not have any implications for real world practice as they had been removed from real world classroom settings to more manipulated 'laboratory' inquiries carried out over very short durations (what Eisner 1984:451 has called 'educational commando raids').

To give an idea of the nature of published second language evaluation studies, I have examined thirty-three such studies. The designs of these studies are summarised in Table 1 in terms of duration, number of subjects, whether or not there was some attempt at randomisation, the method being examined, and the strategy adopted (if any) to try to control the teacher variable.

It is evident that the duration of the studies varies considerably, from six lessons or three weeks, to four years. How long an evaluation study should last is obviously an important but difficult issue. Language learning is usually held to be a long-term task, which needs time to be effective. Even if gains are noted in the short term, they may disappear over time. However, the longer the period under study, the greater the contamination from extraneous variables, the greater the risk of drop-out, changes in the project's direction or content, and so on. Yet since evaluation is typically concerned with real-world issues rather than with laboratory effects, studies that show learning or achievement over the long term are going to be more relevant than short-term experiments. It is notable that of the studies examined, only five cover a period of one year or more. The generalisations one can arrive at from an evaluation of a few lessons are obviously very limited.

The studies examined vary greatly with respect to the number of subjects involved, ranging from a total of 21 to a massive 5,000. Most studies involve relatively small numbers of subjects, as can be seen from Table 1. If one takes further account of the design of the studies, however, then the number of subjects in any one group – experimental or control – is even smaller. Wagner and Tilney (1983) and Bushman and Madsen (1976) have only seven subjects per treatment. In cases like these, the small sample sizes call into question the appropriacy of the statistical tests used. It has clearly not been easy for evaluators in language education to gather adequate, representative samples. Nevertheless, the criticism made above of large-scale evaluations like Smith (1970) and Scherer and Wertheimer (1964) stands: the larger the scale of the evaluation, the more things can and do go wrong, and the less the control that can be exercised over events and variables. (This is not to say that all testing comparisons in field settings are wasteful; no methodology can expect to provide the full picture.)

In Table 1, fourth column, 'R' indicates whether any attempt was made to establish the initial equivalence of comparison groups through randomisation or matching procedures. It can be seen that the majority of studies did indeed attempt to match groups, although these attempts did not always result in groups that could be considered equivalent. However, one aim of randomisation is to allow one to generalise results from the sample to the population which, in theory, involves the evaluator sampling from the total population. None of the studies reviewed here would meet this criterion. Indeed, it is unlikely that any real-world evaluation would ever receive sufficient government or financial support to permit such sampling as would allow statistical generalisability. Evaluators have typically had to take whatever subjects they can get. Thus, the pursuit of statistical generalisability in evaluation is unrealistic.

TABLE I 33 METHOD EVALUATION STUDIES

Study	Duration	No.	R/NR	Method	Control of Teacher Variable
Keating 1963	1 yr	5,000	NR	AL v CC	None
Scherer and Wertheimer 1964	2 yrs	227	R	AL v CC	Give lesson plans to program teachers
Casey 1968	Ex post facto	50	NR	AL v CC	Questionnaire asking teachers which program they taught
Chastain and Woerdehoff 1968	2 semesters	99	R	AL v CC	None
Smith 1970	4 yrs	1,090	NR	AL v CC	None
Hauptman 1971	3 weeks	69	?	Gr v Sit	None
Mueller 1971	2 semesters	77	NR	AL v CC	None
Levin 1972 (i)	6 lessons	227	R	AL v CC	Recorded lessons
Levin 1972 (ii)	"	104	R	"	Recorded lessons
Levin 1972 (iii)	"	247	R	"	Recorded lessons
Levin 1972 (iv)	"	98	R	"	Recorded lessons
Levin 1972 (v)	"	170	R	"	Recorded lessons
Levin 1972 (vi)	"	57	R	"	Recorded lessons
Levin 1972 (vii)	12 lessons	577	R	"	Recorded lessons
Levin 1972 (viii)	6 lessons	235	R	"	Recorded lessons
Levin 1972 (ix)	"	152	R	"	Recorded lessons
Levin 1972 (x)	10 lessons	125	R	"	Recorded lessons
Asher 1972	32 hrs	37	NR	TPR v Reg	None
Savignon 1972	1 semester	42	NR	Comm v AL	None
Von Elek and Oskarsson 1973	10 lessons	125	R	AL v CC	Recorded lessons
Olsson 1973 (i)	6 lessons	18gps	R	AL v CC	Recorded lessons
Olsson 1973 (ii)	6 lessons	24gps	R	AL v CC	Recorded lessons
Postovsky 1974 (i)	12 weeks	50	R	TPR v Reg	Same teachers for comparison programs
Postovsky 1974 (ii)	12 weeks	48	R	TPR v Reg	Same teachers for comparison programs
Asher et al. 1974	1 semester	69	NR	TPR v Reg	None
Gary 1975	22 weeks	50	R	TPR v Reg	Same teacher for comparison programs
Bushman and Madsen 1976	10 hrs	41	NR	Sugg v Reg	Same teachers for comparison programs
Wolfe and Jones 1982	12 weeks	79	R	TPR v Reg	None
Pal 1982	12 lessons	37	R	AL v CC	None
Van Baalen 1983	1 year	80	NR	AL v CC	Questionnaire asking teachers what they taught
Thiele and Scheibner-Herzig 1983	34 lessons	43	NR	TPR v Reg	None
Wagner and Tilney 1983	5 weeks	21	R	Sugg v Reg	Recorded lessons
Beretta and Davies 1985	4 years	341	NR	Comm v Gr	None

Note: AL=Audiolingual, CC=Cognitive Code, TPR=Total Physical Response (and other approaches involving delayed starts in oral production), Sugg=Suggestopedia, Comm=Communicative method, Gr=a grammar-based method, Sit=Situational, and Reg=Regular (unspecified control).

The fifth column of Table 1 shows that all of the studies focused on some method or other: suggestopedia, total physical response, and so on.

Typically, some form of quasi-experimentation was the chosen design, and the aim was to address theoretical problems. The studies were never tightly enough controlled for this task. Indeed they could not be since they took place in real-world classrooms over time. It might reasonably be argued that the designs were quite inappropriate for the questions asked.

The sixth column shows the extent to which the evaluation studies attempted to control the teacher variable (an important element in the standardisation of treatments).

It has been widely recognised that there is a need to control the teacher variable in evaluations that aim to compare programs or to make some theoretical statement. The teacher in Program A might be more highly qualified, more enthusiastic, or may differ in any number of ways from the teacher of Program B. This could offer a rival explanation of results, detracting from the claims of the treatment program. One option is to randomly assign teachers to treatments from a pool large enough to increase confidence that differences are cancelled out. However this has never been achieved even by those who had access to large samples (e.g. Smith 1970, Keating 1963). But even if they had managed it, they could not have controlled for novelty effects: the very newness of a program could produce greater enthusiasm among experimental teachers and students. A second option is to have both programs taught by the same teacher (e.g. Postovsky 1974, Bushman and Madsen 1976), but the teacher may still be more swayed by one than the other with incalculable effects on practice; indeed the Bushman and Madsen paper acknowledges the 'appropriate temperament and excellent teaching skill' of one of the teachers who possessed the right 'philosophical persuasions' for teaching suggestopedic classes (1976:35–7). A third option is to eliminate teachers altogether and replace them with tape-recorded lessons (e.g. Levin 1972). The trouble with this is that it removes the study from the real world and does not permit generalisation beyond the confines of the inquiry. A fourth strategy has been to try to determine what went on in the classroom by asking teachers to fill out questionnaires (e.g Casey 1968, Van Baalen 1983); this strategy is rarely used because of the obvious difficulties associated with self-report.

The notion of standardisation is an important issue in program evaluation. Sometimes there is more variation within programs than between programs, and this has compromised many method comparisons. Attempts to standardise treatments (apart from controlling the teacher variable) are not included in Table 1 because most of the studies make no reference at all to such attempts. There is one exception: the lesson plans used by Scherer and Wertheimer (1964). This can be considered a partial attempt to standardise the teaching, which along with interviews and class visits may have achieved some regularity. Some researchers mention in passing that they visited some of the classes, and others may have done so without reporting it. But none of the studies attempted to monitor implementation in any principled fashion. Mostly, implementation appears to have been left to chance.

Standardisation of classroom events would be a move in the direction of control, but cannot be accomplished in the field, over time, with real teachers, and all manner of real-world intrusions. If the aim is to claim knowledge about language learning, the impossibility of standardising treatments is one more reason why this aim should be forgotten. However, the need remains to know what happened in the classroom, and so on. The way that programs are implemented is fundamental to evaluation. The most obvious way of gathering this information is through observation, and yet, of the studies in Table 1, only Smith (1970) tried to observe systematically, but he unfortunately used different instruments for the comparison groups, thus precluding comparison.

Table 1 is useful now only for reference and as a historical record. Probably, none of the studies serves as a particularly useful guide to evaluators of language education programs today. First of all, investigations of method have not produced any deeper understanding of the methods involved; second, it has yet to be shown that programs can be subject to tight controls or that comparative testing can be fair. And third, there seems no reason to expect that evaluation can aim primarily to contribute to the advancement of language learning theory. These studies are easy to criticise because we have the benefit of hindsight, but it would be a pity not to learn from them. Anyone who reads them will find that second language program evaluation has only slowly become aware of its existence as a distinct field of inquiry, of the existence of a flourishing evaluation discipline beyond the confines of applied linguistics, and consequently, of any clear sense of its role and direction. It is to evaluation research in the educational and social spheres, which Cronbach *et al.* have called the 'liveliest frontier' of the social sciences (1980:13), that we now turn for sustenance.

What has been learned in educational evaluation?

An explosion of interest in program evaluation occurred in the 1960s. Two reasons are generally offered for this. First, in the wake of the launch of Sputnik in 1957, federal funds in the US were poured into curriculum development in science, mathematics and foreign languages and, eventually, into the evaluation of these programs.

A second reason is that the 'Great Society' reforms of President Johnson in the USA led to massive compensatory education programs such as *Sesame Street, Head Start* and *Follow Through*. For purposes of accountability, evaluation of these programs was required by law (see Wolf 1987). Kerlinger cites a particular politician's demand for pay-off: 'We want N.I.E. [National Institute of Education] to show us that we are getting a bang for the bucks we are spending on educational research' (1977:8).

One of the consequences for educational researchers was that they had to develop theories and methodologies of evaluation that would meet the responsibilities thrust upon them. The major influence on evaluation thought until this time was Ralph Tyler's (1949) book *Basic principles of curriculum and instruction*.

Tyler and behavioral objectives

Basically, Tyler's approach, which has since had a tremendous influence on evaluation, involved comparing intended outcomes with actual outcomes. First of all, behavioral objectives are specified, then tests are developed which reflect all of these objectives. This kind of evaluation was used in the frequently-mentioned Eight Year Study (Smith and Tyler 1942).

It is worth noting some implications of this approach. To start with, the tests have to be sensitive to the program's aims. Therefore, standardised tests would be inadequate to the task. Second, the comparison of intended outcomes with actual outcomes does not necessitate the setting up of experimental and control groups. Third, and somewhat problematically, the process of arriving at behavioral objectives is fraught with potential misinformation.

It is worth pausing briefly to discuss the role of objectives in evaluation and to note the enduring influence that such a pragmatic approach would have on later evaluators.

Cronbach, who participated in the Eight Year Study, is informative on the issue of how objectives were teased out of the 30 schools in the inquiry:

> As matters turned out, no matter what a school's initial list of goals, each of the thirty local discussions ended with agreement on very nearly the same comprehensive set of objectives.
> A teacher who came to a meeting prepared to list the *topics* of her chemistry course – oxidisation, equilibrium, the halogens – was not allowed to stop there. Was she perhaps also concerned with her students' progress in the use and understanding of scientific method? Did her goals stop with proper use of the metric system and with successful reproduction in the laboratory of results described in the textbook? Or would she also want students

> to keep good records of observations? To find loopholes in
> arguments? To formulate scientific propositions in testable form?
> Yes, all those, and the end was not yet. The chemistry teacher
> found herself led to confess concern that students develop socially
> while in her charge ...
>
> (Cronbach *et al.* 1980: 173–4)

The problem with confining evaluation to behavioral goals is that it ignores unexpected outcomes, outcomes that are hard to define, that are remote in time, difficult to measure; it ignores changes of perception between the time that objectives are stated and the time they are tested; it encourages arbitrariness with regard to continuous outcome variables. Some examples are in order.

McIntyre and Mitchell (1983) remark that the Western Isles Bilingual Project in Scotland had as one of its aims 'to instil in pupils a sense of their own identity and to validate their physical, social and cultural environments for them' (p. 4). Since this was a long-term objective relating to a general social climate in the Western Isles, it could not be tested. Yet it would appear that the project was motivated by such a goal; in an objectives forum, it would be inadmissible evidence.

To take another example: the Bangalore Project (Prabhu 1987) rested upon an incubation hypothesis; that is, that acquisition of grammar cannot be forced but will take its own time. Since no deadlines are offered, is the goal to be tested at the end of a semester, two, three, at the end of two years, beyond the duration of the project? Again, such a goal is not readily set forth in a testable manner.

With regard to continuous outcome variables, foreign language programs are particularly susceptible. If a program aims to improve listening skills, it would be reasonable to signal approval whenever scores move along the scale in the direction that has been identified as positive. If a Tylerian evaluator were to ask whether the program has achieved its goals, he would be implying that there is a discontinuity of value on the scale, that there is a point of minimal adequacy; he would be asking for an arbitrary level (see Cronbach 1982: 221). Knowing what to measure is much easier than knowing the level it should attain.

Patton gives an example of a behavioral objective applied to reading skills: student achievement test scores in reading will increase one grade level from the beginning of the first grade to the beginning of the second grade. He comments:

> This statement is not, however, a goal statement. The goal is that
> children improve their reading. This is a statement of how that
> goal will be measured and how much improvement will be desired
> ... Confusing the (1) specification of goals with (2) their
> measurement and (3) the standard of desirability is a major
> conceptual problem in many program evaluations.   (1982: 103)

Many goals, then, are abstract, broad, long-term, unplanned, subject to changing perceptions and needs, or relate to continuous scales; as such, they resist transformation into behavioral objectives. Anderson *et al.* (1978) object that if such ineffable goals are admissible, program developers effectively put themselves beyond the reach of either corroboration or refutation: 'any program that wishes to rid itself forever of the discomforts of evaluation need only add to its list of objectives one metaphysical, obscure, or otherwise unmeasurable purpose' (p. 163). In the 1960s, suspicion of unmeasurable goals resulted in bumper stickers bearing the legend 'STAMP OUT NONBEHAVIORAL OBJECTIVES' (Atkin 1968). Richards (1984) draws attention to the fact that many currently favored language teaching methods have not yet been put to the empirical test and insists that they should first of all define their goals. Thus, it is quite clear that in spite of the shortcomings of an insistence on defining and testing objectives, many commentators continue to be influenced by Tyler's approach. While pressing for clear statements of objectives might be useful from the point of view of orienting curriculum development, there are sufficient reasons to doubt its usefulness as a recipe for evaluation.

An aspect of the Tyler approach which has been more generally found wanting is that it ignores process. What happens during the course of a program is assumed to be irrelevant. The emphasis on test outcomes diverted attention from the 'black box' of the treatment that had been received.

The development of the field

Results from the large evaluations of the 1960s were disappointing (Coleman *et al.* 1966, Cicirelli *et al.* 1969, Ball and Bogatz 1970). It became clear that evaluation was not delivering the goods and that the Tylerian style of inquiry and the Campbell and Stanley (1963) concept of experimental design were inadequate to the demands made of them. In the 1960s, a few major articles had shown how perceptions might change. Cronbach (1963) proposed an emphasis on course improvement; Stake (1967) discussed a 'countenance model' of evaluation which stressed descriptive data and the importance of value judgments; Scriven (1967) made the distinction between 'formative' and 'summative' evaluation (formative being a matter of improving ongoing programs, summative, a question of determining the effects of a program that has come to an end).

The evaluation literature then began in earnest. A number of journals appeared: *Evaluation News, Educational Evaluation and Policy Analysis, Studies in Evaluation, CEDR Quarterly, Evaluation Review, Evaluation and Program Planning, Evaluation Practice, New Directions for*

Program Evaluation and *Studies in Educational Evaluation*. In addition, the American Evaluation Association was formed.

Furthermore, for about a decade (the late 1960s to the late 1970s), a plethora of so-called models were developed. These will only be summarised here as there are many perfectly adequate reviews available (e.g. Jenkins 1976, Nevo 1983, Fraser 1984, and especially Stufflebeam and Webster 1980).

A major 'model' is Stake's (1967, 1975) 'countenance evaluation'. In this approach, there is no prearranged evaluation design. Fearing that a prespecified design could lead to narrow and rigid outcomes that may not address the needs of the stakeholding audiences, Stake recommends picking up on whatever turns up and allowing the investigation to be shaped by both the known and unfolding concerns of the stakeholders.

The countenance model involves both descriptive and judgment data. The descriptive element examines the congruence between intended and observed antecedents, transactions and outcomes. Antecedents are the conditions that exist prior to the program, transactions are questions relating to the teaching program, and outcomes (some of which are not intended) refer principally to student learning. The judgment data refer not to judgments that the evaluator makes but to the collection of others' judgments (those of parents, teachers, students, subject matter experts).

Another approach that has attracted a great deal of attention is the CIPP (Context, Input, Process and Product) of Stufflebeam *et al.* (1971). The main emphasis here is to provide information for decision-makers. The 'process' element concentrates on implementation (systematic observation, interviews, diaries, participant observation, etc.), while the 'product' determines whether or not objectives were achieved.

CIPP defines evaluation as 'the process of delineating, obtaining, and providing useful information for judging decision alternatives' (1971:43). Helping the policy-shaping community to make decisions from a number of alternatives – the CIPP model – shows an early awareness of the need for program evaluation to involve itself in the realities of policy analysis.

Context evaluation refers to the analysis of the situation (actual and desired conditions). Input evaluation is the extent to which the evaluator lends assistance in program design. Process evaluation focuses on implementation using a variety of methodologies from participant observation to interviews and rating scales. Product evaluation reports on the degree to which objectives were or were not achieved (cf. Tyler 1949).

Another model is 'discrepancy evaluation' (Provus 1971), which slightly elaborates the Tyler model, taking into account the gaps between time-tied objectives and actual performance.

Scriven (1972) proposed 'goal-free evaluation', in which the evaluator pays no attention to stated goals but examines what is actually happening, arguing that if the goals are relevant, they will show up in the classroom; the value of a program resides in the extent to which a program's *effects* are congruent with the perceived needs of the students.

As Scriven says,

> The goal-free evaluator (GFE) is a hunter out on his own and he goes over the ground very carefully, looking for signs of any kind of game, setting speculative snares when in doubt. The goals man has been given a map which supposedly shows the main game trails; it is hard for him to work quite so hard in the rest of the jungle.
>
> (1973, cited in Jenkins 1976:55)

There is a problem with goal-based evaluation that Stufflebeam (1972) has drawn attention to: GFE would be inefficient in prioritising areas for investigation. Costs in time and dollars would militate against it. For this reason, it may be better to think of it as playing a useful *supplemental* role in evaluation.

The 'adversary approach' to evaluation, developed by, among others, Owens (1973) and Wolf (1975), is based on advocacy; teams of evaluators argue opposing points of view and attempt to present a powerful case for their 'side'. Problems with this approach include its cost and the disparity in competence between adversary groups (see House, Thurston and Hand 1984).

Eisner's (1977) concept of evaluation is what he calls 'educational connoisseurship'. No quantitative data are collected; instead the evaluator observes the program in operation and writes a rich, narrative report, in which metaphorical language is encouraged. His approach is also known as the 'art criticism' model.

Connoisseurship, rooted in the arts rather than the sciences, is regarded by ethnographic evaluators (e.g. Fetterman 1988) as an important alternative to positivistic forms of inquiry. It stems from a belief that life in the classroom is a matter of a teacher's individual artistry rather than a set of behavioral laws. The aim is to re-educate perceptions of stakeholders.

The concept of 'illuminative' evaluation, espoused by Parlett and Hamilton (1978) is similar to the process element of the CIPP model (referred to above). The stress here is on multiperspective description and triangulation. No 'product' is of interest; 'process' is all. Typically, there are three stages: i) observation, ii) further inquiry, iii) explanation. In practice, these stages overlap both temporally and functionally, and go on and on until, after successive inquiries, a clearer focus is obtained. Starting as a divergent inquiry, taking on as many questions as possible, the progressive focussing converges on the issues at the heart of the evaluation.

There are numerous other approaches which have their adherents, but the above summaries represent the best-known. Many approaches consciously line up on either side of a divide; they are either qualitative (Eisner 1977; Guba 1981; Parlett and Hamilton 1978; Stake 1975) or quantitative (Campbell and Stanley 1963; Taba 1966; Tyler 1949). More recently, the perception has surfaced that no single type of evaluation can possibly do service for the wide range of programs that evaluators must address and the wide range of evaluation purposes. A more eclectic philosophy has slowly emerged which is supported by Weiss (1972), Cook and Reichardt (1979), and most authoritatively by Cronbach *et al.* (1980) and Cronbach (1982).

Once the period of intense model-building had come to an end and it had been accepted that there was no one way of doing evaluation, it was possible for the field to make a major step: the articulation of standards. For this to command general respect, the heterogeneity of evaluation needs and approaches had to be (and was) recognised in the *Standards for Evaluations of Educational Programs, Projects and Materials* (Joint Committee 1981). Widely shared principles for undertaking evaluations were laid down according to four attributes of evaluation: utility, feasibility, propriety and accuracy. The *utility* standards relate to the duty of an evaluator to find out who are the stakeholding audiences and to provide them with relevant information on time. The *feasibility* standards require evaluators to ensure that the evaluation design be workable in real world settings. The *propriety* standards demand that the evaluator behave ethically and recognise the rights of individuals who might be affected by the evaluation. Finally, the *accuracy* standards are concerned with the soundness of an evaluation, requiring that information be technically adequate and that conclusions be linked logically to the data.

Summary

The overview that has just been presented cannot do justice to the issues involved. The purpose has been to illustrate the general trends and the fact that there are now a great variety of approaches to evaluation. The concept of evaluation is still in the process of being defined, but since the sudden expansion of 20 years ago, evaluation has emerged as a distinct area of inquiry, with its own journals and its own standards.

From the behavioral objectives approach of Tyler (1949), a range of qualitative, quantitative and eclectic methodologies has given the evaluator of the 1980s a spectrum of forms of inquiry to select from as the nature of the program to be evaluated requires.

The evaluation of language education programs in the 1990s

Given the wealth of writings and experience in the evaluation of social and educational programs, what is the future for the evaluation of language education?

After a prolonged period of methodological weakness and imprudent aspiration, it is appropriate for second language program evaluation to become more familiar with the developments in educational evaluation. The second language program evaluator of the 1990s will select opportunistically from a wide range of research methodologies; he or she will devote far more attention to negotiation, understanding of policy, and report writing than heretofore; and the aim will be to provide utilisable information in the short run.

That the published second language program evaluations are so easy to criticise does not bestow any particular wisdom on the critics. Looking back, we are just later, not wiser. After all, L2 evaluation as a self-conscious discipline has only recently evolved and educational evaluation also spent a long time getting its house in order. It is time, however, for our field to attempt to give a clearer account of itself. The case studies in this volume offer a glimpse of the kinds of L2 evaluations now being undertaken worldwide (which is not to claim that they are exemplary: the whole point of the present book is that all of the authors know that they are not!).

What will the evaluators of the 1990s do that is different from their current modus operandi? The final chapter in this volume (by Alderson) discusses this issue at length and puts forward alternatives for the design of evaluation studies in language education. Here, the general trends that might be hoped for are outlined.

1 First of all, interest in the evaluation of methods will be reduced to a focus on answerable questions (i.e. none of the questions that have until recently nearly always been asked). Experimental and quasi-experimental designs will be employed only when they can best yield the information desired, and reflex appeal to them will cease; it should be stressed, however, that when comparative outcomes on tests are precisely what the policy-shaping community needs to know about, as was the case with the early Canadian immersion programs (see, for instance, Lambert and Tucker, 1972), then, in spite of known difficulties, it is appropriate to make the best of whatever tools are available. Of course, no methodological approach is flawless, but what is important is to avoid reflex use of *any* particular approach.

2 Aspirations regarding the advancement of language learning theory will be distinctly subdued – they will be secondary to the provision of user-relevant information in the short run.

3 Since it is expected that evaluation will be taken more seriously in language education in the future, it is hoped that evaluation will be considered in the design of the program, and not left until the eleventh hour.

4 The first stage of an evaluation will be a period of negotiation when client, evaluator and stakeholders aim to arrive at a coherent charter for the evaluation. If initial questions cannot be answered with the certainty envisioned by those who pose them, this would be the time for the evaluator to point out the likely nature of any findings. Deadlines must be discussed; if certain questions cannot be answered within a given time frame, it may be that other questions will be preferred; is the evaluator expected to make recommendations or simply to provide information? Who will receive a report? When will findings be made public? Above all, it will be established what *use* will be made of the findings as this will dictate the kinds of questions that are asked, the kinds of designs that are employed, and the kinds of data that are collected. Questions will be prioritised in terms of time, cost, how much will be learnt and how much leverage the findings will have on policy. When all of the issues have been thrashed out, all parties should know what they are going to get and when they are going to get it. In short, the first stage involves translating policy questions into evaluation questions.

5 The second stage of an evaluation will be the design, data collection and analysis. Since no single design can hope to address the great diversity of questions that are asked about programs, evaluators will attempt to master a variety of research methodologies, both qualitative and quantitative. The design and research methodologies adopted will be the province of the evaluator, but he or she will be influenced by the information needs and deadlines of clients.

6 The third stage is to translate findings back into the language of policy. While for academic reasons, there will always be an archive document, reports will take different forms to accommodate the different audiences specified in the initial charter. The jargon of research might be replaced for one audience by a telling anecdote, for another by a one-page executive summary, for another by a detailed examination of peripheral findings and grey areas; and so on.

In these ways, evaluation will increasingly shed light on the nature of program design, development and implementation. Reflexive evaluations, such as those reported in the following chapters, will offer insights into the nature of evaluation, and will enable future evaluations to profit from the experience gained. The evaluation of language education will be an increasingly serious, professional concern, to the benefit of everyone involved in language education.

References

Agard, F. B. and H. B. Dunkel. 1948. *An investigation of second language teaching.* Boston: Ginn and Company.

Anderson, R. B., R. G. St. Pierre, E. C. Proper and L. B. Stebbins. 1978. Pardon us, but what was the question again? A response to the critique of the Follow Through evaluation. *Harvard Educational Review* 48: 161–70.

APA (American Psychological Association). 1954. *Technical recommendations for psychological techniques and diagnostic techniques.* Washington, D. C.: Author.

APA (American Psychological Association). 1966. *Standards for educational and psychological tests and manuals.* Washington, D.C.: Author.

APA (American Psychological Association). 1985. *Standards for educational and psychological testing.* Washington, D.C.: The American Psychological Association, Inc.

Asher, J. J. 1972. Children's first language as a model for second language learning. *Modern Language Journal* 56 (3): 133–9.

Asher, J. J., J. A. Kusudo and R. de la Torre. 1974. Learning a second language through commands: the second field test. *Modern Language Journal* 58: 24–32.

Atkin, M. 1968. Behavioral objectives in curriculum design: a cautionary note. *The Science Teacher* 35: 27–30.

Bachman, L. 1989. The development and use of criterion-referenced tests of language ability in language program evaluation. In R. K. Johnson (Ed.) *The second language curriculum*, 242–58. Cambridge: Cambridge University Press.

Ball, S. and G. A. Bogatz. 1970. *The first year of Sesame Street: an evaluation.* Princeton, NJ: Educational Testing Service.

Beretta, A. 1986a. Toward a methodology of ESL program evaluation. *TESOL Quarterly* 20 (1): 144–55.

Beretta, A. 1986b. Program-fair language teaching program evaluation. *TESOL Quarterly* 20 (3): 431–44.

Beretta, A. and A. Davies. 1985. Evaluation of the Bangalore Project. *English Language Teaching Journal* 39: 121–7.

Bushman, R. W. and H. S. Madsen. 1976. A description and evaluation of suggestopedia – a new teaching methodology. In J. F. Fanselow and R. H. Crymes (Eds.) *On TESOL '76*: 29–40. Washington, D. C.: TESOL.

Campbell, D. T. and J. C. Stanley. 1963. Experimental and quasi-experimental designs for research on teaching. In N. L. Gage (Ed.) *Handbook of research on teaching*, 171–246. Chicago: Rand McNally.

Carroll, J. B. 1963. Research on teaching foreign languages. In N. L Gage (Ed.) *Handbook of research on teaching*, 1060–100. Chicago: Rand McNally.

Casey, J. B. 1968. The effectiveness of two methods of teaching English as a foreign language in some Finnish secondary schools. Unpublished report, University of Helsinki.

Chastain, K. D. and F. J. Woerdehoff. 1968. A methodological study comparing the audio-lingual habit theory and the cognitive code-learning theory. *Modern Language Journal* 52 (5): 268–79.

Cicirelli, V. G. *et al.* 1969. *The impact of Head Start: an evaluation of the effects of Head Start on children's cognitive and affective development.* Study by Westinghouse Learning Corporation and Ohio University. Washington, D.C.: Office of Economic Opportunity.

Coleman, J., E. Campbell, C. Hobson, J. McPartland, A. Mood, F. Weinfield and R. York. 1966. *Equality of educational opportunity.* Washington, D.C.: U.S. Office of Health, Education, and Welfare.

Cook, T. D. and C. S. Reichardt. 1979 (Eds.) *Qualitative and quantitative methods in evaluation research.* Beverly Hills, CA: Sage.

Cronbach, L. J. 1963. Course improvement through evaluation. *Teachers College Record* 64: 672–83.

Cronbach, L. J. 1982. *Designing evaluations of educational and social programs.* San Francisco: Jossey-Bass.

Cronbach, L. J., S. R. Ambron, S. M. Dornbusch, R. D. Hess, R. C. Hornik, D. C. Phillips, D. F. Walker and S. S. Weiner. 1980. *Toward reform of program evaluation.* San Francisco: Jossey-Bass.

Eisner, E. W. 1977. On the uses of educational connoisseurship and criticism for evaluating classroom life. *Teachers College Record* 78 (3): 345–58.

Eisner, E. W. 1979. *The educational imagination: on the design and evaluation of school programs.* New York: Macmillan.

Eisner, E. W. 1984. Can educational research inform educational practice? *Phi Delta Kappan* 65 (7): 447–52

Fetterman, D. M. 1988. Qualitative approaches to evaluating education. *Educational Research* 17: 17–23.

Fraser, B. J. 1984. Directions in curriculum evaluation. *Studies in Educational Evaluation* 10: 125–34.

Freedman, E. 1971. The road from Pennsylvania – where next in foreign language experimentation? *Audio-Visual Language Journal* 9:33–8.

Freedman, E. S. 1976. Experimentation into foreign language teaching methodology. *System* 4 (1): 12–28.

Gary, J. O. 1975. Delayed oral practice in initial stages of second language learning. In M. Burt and H. Dulay (Eds.) *On TESOL '75*: 89–95. Washington, D.C.: TESOL.

Genesee, F. 1983. Bilingual education of majority language children: the immersion experiments in review. *Applied Psycholinguistics* 4: 1–46.

Guba, E. G. 1981. The paradigm revolution in inquiry: implications for vocational research and development. Paper presented at the National Center for Research in Vocational Education Staff Development Seminar, Columbus, Ohio. (ERIC Document Reproduction Service No. ED 212 829)

Hauptman, P. C. 1971. A structural approach versus a situational approach to foreign language teaching. *Language Learning* 21 (2): 234–44.

House, E. R., P. Thurston and J. Hand. 1984. Evaluation reflections: the adversary hearing as a public forum. *Studies in Educational Evaluation* 10: 111–23.

Jenkins, D. 1976. *Curriculum evaluation.* Milton Keynes: The Open University.

Joint Committee on Standards for Educational Evaluation. 1981. *Standards for evaluations of educational programs, projects, and materials.* New York: McGraw-Hill.

Keating, R. F. 1963. *A study of the effectiveness of language laboratories.* New York: Institute of Administrative Research, Teachers College.

Kerlinger, F. N. 1977. The influence of research on education practice. *Educational Researcher* 6: 5–12.

Lambert, W. E. and G. R. Tucker 1972. *Bilingual education of children: the St. Lambert experiment.* Rowley, MA: Newbury House.

Levin, L. 1972. *Comparative studies in foreign language teaching: the GUME project.* Stockholm: Almqvist and Wiksell.

McIntyre, D. and R. Mitchell, 1983. Processes, outcomes and context of bilingual education in the Western Isles. University of Stirling, Department of Education.

Mueller, T. H. 1971. The effectiveness of two learning models: the audiolingual habit theory and the cognitive code-learning theory. In P. Pimsleur and T. Quinn (Eds.) *The psychology of second language learning*, 113–22. Cambridge: Cambridge University Press.

Nevo, D. 1983. The conceptualisation of educational evaluation: an analytical review of the literature. *Review of Educational Research* 53 (1): 117–28.

Olsson, M. 1973. Learning grammar: an experiment. *English Language Teaching* 27 (3): 266–9.

Owens, T. R. 1973. Educational evaluation by adversary proceedings. In E. R. House (Ed.) *School evaluation: the politics and the process*, 295–305. Berkeley, CA: McCutchan.

Pal, A. 1982. An applied psycholinguistic experiment in remedial teaching of English grammar. *IRAL* 20 (2): 152–60.

Parlett, M. and D. Hamilton, 1978. Evaluation as illumination: a new approach to the study of innovatory programmes. In D. Hamilton, D. Jenkins, C. King, B. MacDonald and M. Parlett (Eds.) *Beyond the numbers game.* London: Macmillan.

Patton, M. Q. 1982. *Practical evaluation.* Beverly Hills, CA: Sage.

Postovsky, V. A. 1974. Effects of delay in oral practice at the beginning of second language learning. *Modern Language Journal* 58: 229–39.

Prabhu, N. 1987. *Second language pedagogy; a perspective.* Oxford: Oxford University Press.

Provus, M. M. 1971. *Discrepancy evaluation.* Berkeley, CA: McCutchan.

Richards, J. C. 1984. The secret life of methods. *TESOL Quarterly* 18: 7–23.

Savignon, S. J. 1972. *Communicative competence: an experiment in foreign language teaching.* Philadelphia: The Center for Curriculum Development, Inc.

Scherer, G.A.C. and M. Wertheimer. 1964. *A psycholinguistic experiment in foreign language teaching.* New York: McGraw-Hill.

Scriven, M. S. 1967. The methodology of evaluation. In R. Tyler, R. Gagne and M. S. Scriven. *Perspectives of curriculum evaluation.* AREA Monograph Series on Curriculum Evaluation, No. 1. Chicago: Rand McNally.

Scriven, M. S. 1972. Prose and cons about goal-free evaluation. *Evaluation Comment* 3. Los Angeles Center for the Study of Evaluation, University of California.

Seliger, H. W. 1975. Inductive method and deductive method in language teaching: a re-examination. *IRAL* 13 (1): 1–18.

Smith, E. R. and R. W. Tyler. 1942. *Appraising and recording educational progress.* New York: Harper and Row.

Smith, P. D. 1970. *A comparison of the cognitive and audio-lingual approaches to foreign language instruction: the Pennsylvania Foreign Language Project.* Philadelphia: The Center for Curriculum Development, Inc.

Stake, R. E. 1967. The countenance of educational evaluation. *Teachers College Record* 68: 523–40.

Stake, R. E. 1975. *Evaluating the arts in education: a responsiveness approach.* Columbus, Ohio: Merrill.

Stern, H. H. 1983. *Fundamental concepts of language teaching.* Oxford: Oxford University Press.

Stufflebeam, D. L. 1972. Should or can evaluation be goal-free. *Evaluation Comment* 4 (3).

Stufflebeam, D. L., W. J. Foley, W. J. Gephart, E. G. Guba, R. L. Hammon, H. O. Merriman and M. M. Provus. 1971. *Educational evaluation and decision-making.* Ithaca, Illinois: Peacock.

Stufflebeam, D. L. and W. J. Webster. 1980. An analysis of alternative approaches to evaluation. *Educational Evaluation and Policy Analysis* 2 (3): 5–20.

Swain, M. and S. Lapkin. 1982. *Evaluating bilingual education: a Canadian case study.* Clevedon, Avon: Multilingual Matters.

Sweet, H. 1899/1964. *The practical study of languages: a guide for teachers and learners.* London: Oxford University Press.

Taba, H. 1966. Teaching strategies and cognitive functioning in elementary school children. Cooperative Research Project No. 2404, San Francisco State College.

Thiele, A. and G. Scheibner-Herzig. 1983. Listening comprehension training in teaching English to beginners. *System* 11 (3): 277–86.

Tyler, R. W. 1949. *Basic principles of curriculum and instruction.* Chicago: University of Chicago Press.

Van Baalen, T. 1983. Giving learners rules: a study into the effect of grammatical instruction with varying degrees of explicitness. *Interlanguage Studies Bulletin* 7 (1): 71–100.

Von Elek, T. and M. Oskarsson. 1973. *Teaching foreign language grammar to adults: a comparative study.* Stockholm: Almqvist and Wiksell.

Wagner, M. J. and G. Tilney. 1983. The effect of 'superlearning techniques' on vocabulary acquisition and alpha brainwave production of language learners. *TESOL Quarterly* 17 (1): 5–17.

Weiss, C. H. 1972. *Evaluation research: methods of assessing program effectiveness.* Englewood Cliffs, NJ: Prentice-Hall.

Wolf, R. L. 1975. Trial by jury: a new evaluation method, 1: the process. *Phi Delta Kappan* 56: 185–7.

Wolf, R. M. (Guest Ed.) 1987. Educational evaluation: the state of the field. Introduction. *International Journal of Educational Research* 11 (1): 3–6.

Wolfe, D. E. and G. Jones. 1982. Integrating total physical response strategy in a Level 1 Spanish class. *Foreign Language Annals* 15 (4): 273–80.

PART II
CASE STUDIES OF CURRENT PRACTICE

1 Insiders, outsiders and participatory evaluation

J. Charles Alderson and Mike Scott

Introduction

This chapter reports on the evaluation of a nation-wide project in English for Specific Purposes in Brazilian Federal Universities. The Project evaluation was designed from the beginning to involve as many as possible of the Project participants in the design, execution and interpretation of the evaluation, in an attempt to reflect the voluntary and participant-oriented nature of the ESP Project, to take account of a strong distrust of outside evaluators and externally oriented evaluations, and, perhaps above all, to carry out an evaluation that reflected as closely as possible the concerns and insights of those involved in Project implementation. The chapter presents the rationale, design, execution and results of this attempt and concludes with reflections on the problems and limitations of the evaluation and recommendations for future attempts at participatory evaluation.

A common paradigm for the conducting of formal evaluations of language education projects, particularly those funded by British aid agencies, is that of the JIJOE: the Jet-In Jet-Out Expert. Some eminent 'expert' in applied linguistics, syllabus design, methodology or a related aspect of language education is approached by an organisation like the British Council or the Overseas Development Administration (ODA), and invited to visit a project in some exotic location, for a period of up to three weeks. During that time, the expert is to familiarise him or herself with the project, its aims and objectives, its history, personnel, achievements, problems and hopes, and at the end she or he submits a report on the project, with recommendations as to the future development, abandonment or modification of the project. Its hopes and fears, its background, history and achievements or otherwise are supposedly laid bare and judgement passed by this JIJOE, who has overnight added an expertise in the project to the already impressive list of expertise. Sometimes – not always – this expert's report is followed up by other JIJOE visits, perhaps by London-based British Council or ODA officers, who in their turn become instant experts in the project, and themselves pronounce on the project and the previous expert's report. Sometimes no further visit ensues, but the report is read and commented on by London-based 'experts' – often busy officials responsible for a range of projects or indeed countries. Sometimes, in fact often, action follows: funding is cut off, reduced, increased; expatriate appointments are renewed, terminated, advertised; local project staff are sent on training courses; materials are written and published, rewritten or scrapped; old projects are abandoned, new projects are set up.

This paradigm has a long history, and is still current in language education, despite its having been superseded in other areas of education and overseas development projects. The British in particular have a love of the expert, who is thought to be objective if she or he comes from afar (i.e. the UK). And indeed there may still be some value in having outsider perspectives on projects, insofar as they can offer a relatively disinterested view of events, policies and people. Such perspectives are, however, necessarily limited, both in time and in depth of understanding of a project. However hard she or he tries, the JIJOE is unlikely to be able to conduct data-based studies of the project. If data are not already available for inspection – test results, classroom observations, reports, together with evidence, of the effect of implementing materials, syllabuses and so on – she or he is bound to rely for information upon the accounts of people in and around the project, both teachers (and, rarely, students) and advisers, as well as local and expatriate officials. She or he will have to make judgements about the reliability and validity of such accounts on the basis of his or her own very superficial knowledge of the project in question, and equally superficial experience of a range of other projects. Even if she or he has extensive experience of some other project, possibly through extended service overseas, the applicability of such experience must be tempered by the prevailing project ecology.

From the perspective of the project staff – the local and expatriate staff – the visit of such a JIJOE can be both an opportunity and a threat. The opportunity exists to convince the expert of the worthiness of the project, explaining any problems and disadvantages, and to argue for continued or expanded resources. The threat is that the outsider cannot possibly gain an adequate understanding of the background to the project, the nature of its development over time, the reason for important decisions and the likely effect of alternative decisions, the status ante, and the organic perceptions of all associated with the project. Thus she or he is quite likely to misrepresent the project or, worse, to dismiss its achievements. Although, on the whole, it is fairly rare for JIJOEs to condemn projects or recommend their termination (and it is interesting but irrelevant to this chapter to speculate on why this might be so), it remains true that most outsider evaluations on the JIJOE model are perceived by insiders as at least threatening to themselves and the future of their project, and at worst as irrelevant to the interests and perspectives of the project. A strong and understandable belief persists that outsider evaluations are influenced by outsider or external priorities and perceptions, rather than by project-internal or local priorities and perceptions. The action that results from such irrelevant evaluations must be dubious in its contribution to the furthering of the language education aims of the project.

Evaluation is itself, of course, often perceived as threatening the interests of those involved in the object of the evaluation. For this reason, on the whole, evaluation tends to be neglected in project planning and development. Only when external pressures, or the need for external assistance, dictate, do projects tend to be evaluated, and such evaluation is then perhaps necessarily perfunctory, superficial and inadequate. Yet when it is finally carried out, evaluation has a potentially powerful impact on projects, a fact which compounds the threatening nature of its activity and which adds to the vicious circle of neglect.

This chapter reports on attempts at designing and implementing a project evaluation which would directly address the above concerns. As will become clear, an external evaluation centred on a JIJOE would not have been a coherent way of evaluating the work being carried out in the Brazilian ESP Project. Instead, a participatory model, centred on insiders though benefiting from the advice of outsiders, was needed and developed. The theoretical basis for such participatory evaluation endeavours is outlined. We also discuss the claim that participatory evaluation can enhance understanding of the value or otherwise of a project, and discuss to what extent the Brazilian evaluation was able to do so.

At the time when the work reported here was undertaken, namely the mid 1980s, there was no suitable framework and there were no developed models to guide a 'participatory' evaluation in language education. The project to be evaluated was itself unique in some ways, including the number of institutions involved and type of skills emphasised. The present chapter attempts to develop a theoretical model of participatory evaluation, but it must be stated at the outset that the main motivation in attempting a participatory evaluation was interpersonal, not EFL-theoretical. In other words, it was socially important to all of those involved to work together in examining, from the inside and in detail, most facets of the Project's work. It was important not to damage that work in so doing. It was essential to look at the work from the same level in co-operation, not from above in a spirit of judgement.

The Project

In the 1970s there was considerable growth in Brazil, as in the rest of Latin America, of university EAP courses called 'Instrumental English' or 'Technical English'; it became clear to university English teachers that both a methodological foundation and teacher skills were lacking for such courses. The need was already perceived (and shown in formal needs analyses) as centring on the reading skill. Teachers from all parts of Brazil taking the M.A. in Linguistics Applied to the Teaching of Languages at the Catholic University of São Paulo (PUC–SP) were among the first to stimulate discussion of this problem.

In order to tackle this national need, a series of steps were taken. In 1978, Antonieta Celani of PUC–SP and Maurice Broughton, a British Council Visiting Lecturer there, began moves to set up a national ESP Project: contacting potential sponsors and visiting 20 of the 25 Federal Universities in Brazil. In 1979, the first national Project seminar was held, involving twelve universities, and concentrating on EAP materials writing. At the same period the Ministry of Education in Brasilia and the ODA in London agreed to provide support for the Project. The ODA contribution was administered by the British Council. Three British ESP specialists (Deyes, Holmes and Scott) were then contracted, and in November 1980 a further national seminar was held, launching a second phase of the Project.

It is important to stress that the Project grew out of perceived needs felt by teachers in classrooms (i.e. those taking the M.A. at PUC–SP in 1978). It was encouraged by theoretical developments and by international example (both illustrated by Latin American ESP meetings in Colombia, 1977 and Mexico, 1979), but did not originate in a Ministry. No one was appointed to 'run' the Project, or to compel any institution or teacher to take part in it. There was no 'fee' for joining the Project, no membership cards, and no commitment other than a willingness to take part in seminars and occasionally to organise one. Local teams chose a co-ordinator, who dealt with correspondence with São Paulo, but in most cases this post implied no institutional privileges. The structure was loose and informal. Funding was at the best of times rather uncertain, and came in fits and starts.

Both the informality and the non-authoritarian quality of the Project structure carried implications for the model of evaluation which would be appropriate. In other words, it is no accident that the evaluation model used – and defended here – is participatory, and attaches more weight to the insider than to the outsider.

The Project's aims at that time were seen as 1) materials production, 2) teacher training, and 3) the setting up of a national resource centre. One of the British specialists (the second author of this chapter) was, accordingly, contracted specifically for materials preparation.

In other ESP projects in Colombia and Malaysia, the outcome of similar priorities had been the production of high-quality course materials, which eventually became available world wide and were distributed by international publishers. However, within months of the 1980 seminar, it became apparent that a more appropriate plan in Brazil would be to invert priorities 1) and 2) so that ESP teachers would first be trained in the underlying principles and then encouraged, not to co-write a national textbook, but to write their own materials either individually or as local ESP teams.

Such a materials-writing policy may mean considerable 're-inventing the wheel', which has often been decried as wasteful, and indeed avoiding re-inventing the wheel was a standard argument for the existence of a Project. But the need to create materials in a Brazilian context rather than using materials from outside (however well written, and with whatever degree of participation in the writing) has the benefit of concentrating one's mind on what one is trying to achieve. The product may be less sophisticated, but, it was argued, the process is what really counts: teachers need to understand the materials they use. This reasoning was quite consistent with EAP ideology in the late 1970s and early 1980s.

We have seen two strands of the Project's organisational history: that it grew from 'grassroots' needs, and that the original materials writing emphasis was replaced by a teacher-training emphasis. These two development strands could apply to any project, in terms of origins and aims.

The third strand of the Project's early history was more specific to EAP practice. Before 1980 the emphasis in materials in most parts of the world was on grammar and vocabulary. Teachers argued that the first goal was to review the basic structures of English first, then work on morphology and sentence structure, illustrating these with texts. This was reflected in the materials in existence in the late 1970s and early 1980s in Brazil. After 1980 the Project co-ordinators (Antonieta Celani, Head of Project, and the three British KELTs (KELT is the acronym given to teachers contracted by the British Council to serve on overseas projects funded by ODA) worked instead on a much greater emphasis on reading strategies (Scott 1981b), using 'authentic' text (i.e. text written for the expression of ideas, not for language teaching).

It was already clear that many of the problems faced by Latin American learners relate not only to lack of foreign language knowledge but also to their reading skills (Alderson 1984). The Project at that time consciously attempted to push the pendulum away from grammar and vocabulary (Scott 1981a) and towards the teaching of reading strategies.

In view of these three decisional strands of Project development – grassroots needs and loose organisational structure, teacher training leading to materials writing, and emphasis on reading strategies – the Project had to come up with a practical structure for development. This structure was centred at first around a pattern of seminars, operating at three levels: local, regional and national.

Decisional strands		*Operational levels*
non-authoritarian management structure;	—	local seminars
teacher-training objective;	———————	regional seminars
reading strategy methodology	—	national seminars

From 1980, a pattern of local visits was set up. Any participating university could request a visit from one of the KELTs. The only requirement was that the university should meet the cost of the fare and accommodation. All the institutions in this way received at least one visit, usually for a week of workshops and discussions. As time went by and the Project grew, the numbers rose to some 45 institutions, as Federal Technical High Schools (ETFs) entered the Project from 1985 onwards.

This structure was complemented by regional seminars. Every year, a regional seminar lasting a week was held in each of three regions (North/North-East, Centre-West, and Southern) of Brazil. Teachers from participating institutions came in by bus or by plane, usually part-funded by their university or ETF. This often meant a fourteen-hour bus journey each way. ODA provided a specialist from a British university for each of these regional events.

The third level of teacher training was national seminars, held in 1979, 1980, 1983, 1986 and 1988, mostly attended by Federal University co-ordinators, with further input from visitors from Britain. Since 1987 there has also been an annual national seminar for the ETFs.

All types of seminars undoubtedly had teacher training as their main purpose. However, they were not 'courses', though they did concentrate on workshops led by the KELTs and by Head of Project. Courses proper were instituted, from 1986, when a large number of ETFs joined the Project and the Project turned its energies much more towards these schools.

Phases of the Project

The Project grew through several phases, illustrated below. The setting-up phase, 1978–80, saw the non-authoritarian management structure set up, and the first regional and national seminars.

Phase 1:	setting-up	1978–80
Phase 2:	working with the universities	1980–85
Phase 3:	ETFs enter the Project	1986
Phase 4:	withdrawal of the KELTs	1989

The third phase of the Project, involving FTFs, and the current phase (wherein the KELTs have been withdrawn and the Project operates autonomously, with main British input in the form of book donations for the resource centre and provision of visiting lecturers for seminars and courses) are outside the scope of this chapter, which relates specifically to the evaluation of work carried out in the first two phases, to 1986. The emphasis of the regional seminars has throughout the period been partly on teacher training and partly on the exchange of ideas and news. Since 1983 there has been a development of locally-organised workshops.

Topics for workshops, lectures and discussions were originally developed out of a growing 'menu' from which local co-ordinators and teachers could choose. These topics were backed up by a series of Working Papers written mainly by the KELTs, and this series, with *the ESPecialist*, the Project's 'bulletin' (which developed into a journal) provided the start of the publication effort. As local teams developed, they in turn wrote papers for publication in *the ESPecialist* and Working Papers. Likewise regional seminars always saw a number of papers contributed by local teams: in the very early days of 1981 and 1982 these were often reports on progress, but thereafter there was an increasing number of theoretical papers and reports on classroom practice. (From 1980 to 1983 out of 25 *ESPecialist* articles, ten were written by local teachers, and fourteen by the Project co-ordinators, Portuguese–English ratio 9:16. The 1986 and 1987 volumes had 37 out of 41 articles written by local teachers, Portuguese–English ratio 12:29.) These papers, then, formed the basis of the early resource centre, which grew slowly from the beginning of the Project.

From 1983 these were complemented by 'Resource Packages', containing examples of ideas for materials production, and a regular monthly Newsletter.

In the early 1980s the need for a Resource Centre became increasingly apparent, and with book donations and local teams beginning to send in their materials to PUC–SP, a resource centre was gradually formed. Now called CEPRIL (Centre for Research, Information and Resources on Reading) and housed at PUC–SP, it holds a collection of 1) many courses, units or exercises sent in by participating local teams, including a few coursebooks published by Project teams, 2) globally-published ESP materials and theoretical books, journals and articles donated by the British Council and ODA, 3) Working Papers, Resource Packages, Newsletters and *ESPecialists*, 4) two banks of authentic texts, and a bank of magazines, 5) theses of relevance to ESP and reading. CEPRIL is run by a staff consisting of a Project co-ordinator with her team of four to eight research assistants who help carry out research as well as administering the use of CEPRIL.

Finally, the Project saw increasing interest in and need for research. Too much of current ESP (and ELT generally) is based on opinion and fashion, and the Project identified three major areas which needed investigation.

The first area of research to be tackled, in line with current recommendations (e.g. Munby 1978) was needs analysis. A number of analyses were undertaken, the most formal perhaps that carried out at the Federal University of Parana in 1979–80 (Arns and Engel 1979–80): all, whatever their level of specification, showed clearly that the overwhelming need and priority, expressed by teachers and students in Brazilian universities, was to read English for their academic purposes. There is also a wish to develop the other skills, particularly the spoken skills, but the priority was for reading. Needs analysis was from the start seen as not just the collection of questionnaire data on perceived needs and wishes, but as an instrument leading straight into course design (Holmes 1981). A more recent investigation has involved the use of English by Brazilian researchers, teachers and scientists (Celani *et al.* 1988).

Second, there is always the need to understand basic processes of classroom interaction, reading practices, and student difficulties. An example is Deyes (1981) on Minimal Discourse Grammar, where the objective of the research was to find out the language components which are centrally important to appreciation of academic discourse (as opposed to sentences). Some research of this kind has been carried out particularly in formal study for MA theses, and a small but now growing amount of informal, classroom research is appearing in the pages of *the ESPecialist* and in presentations at regional and national seminars. Deyes (1985) reported on research carried out within the Project to 1983 and Scott (1985) reported on a large number of topics suggested by Project teachers, for further research.

Third, and of central relevance here, is research supporting the evaluation of classroom practice and Project strengths and weaknesses.

This latter research will be related in some detail in this chapter, but first it is useful to conclude this section by comparing the aims of the Project near the beginning with its aims in 1985 and 1986 when the evaluation reported on in this paper was planned in detail.

As stated above, the original aims were 1) materials production, 2) teacher training, and 3) the setting up of a national resource centre. By the second half of the decade they had become 1) teacher training with considerable emphasis on reading strategies, 2) publications to reinforce teacher training, 3) development of CEPRIL, the resource centre, to house the publications and the fruits of teacher training, 4) individual or team writing of materials as outcomes of teacher training, 5) a research effort, with much emphasis on evaluation to see whether the Project was achieving its goals, and 6) widening the Project to include Federal Technical High Schools. It is important to stress the inter-relationships between these six aspects: teacher training is held together by the joint roles of publications, research and materials as made nationally available by CEPRIL.

The Project's evaluation research

From 1981 there had been a preoccupation with evaluation, and the question was raised in the annual meeting of the Brazilian University Teachers of English that year as to how the Project proposed to evaluate its effects.

At that time there were two answers to the question. First, an evaluation of sorts was already under way. This was a study carried out by the educationalist Bogaard (reported in 1983) in 1981. This study used 4,032 informants in seven Federal Universities, and relied on two types of questionnaire, the first largely centred on needs (in which the importance of the reading skill and the need for 'Instrumental' English – EAP – were the main findings), and a second questionnaire aiming at student attitudes to objectives, course content, teachers' competence, the classroom environment, and a global opinion. Forty-five ESP teachers answered an almost identical questionnaire of this second type.

Bogaard's instrument was prepared prior to the start of phase two of the Project (November 1980) and though he submitted it for appreciation and alteration to that national meeting, no major changes were made to it. The main reason was that to modify the questionnaires at all would mean re-writing them almost from scratch: they were clearly oriented towards general educational goals, rather than the ESP Project's specific aims and methodologies.

Bogaard's study revealed interesting discrepancies between teacher and student perceptions of the course. He used Likert scales ranging from -3 to $+3$, and teacher opinions about the relevance and organisation of their course content was generally around $+2$, with student opinion lower, at about $+1$.

The three major problems with the Bogaard study were:
1 the study was perceived by teachers and students as external (the questionnaire was headed 'Ministry of Education')
2 it was of general educational interest and did not address central questions of ESP methodology
3 the report was tactless in separating and identifying the participating universities in relation to their 'scores'.

The second answer to the question 'how do you propose to evaluate yourselves?' was 'we haven't the time'. Neither re-structuring Bogaard's instruments nor setting up another evaluation was feasible, because the Project was so busy establishing its lines of action and setting up the network of seminars, publications, resource centre and so on, in November 1980 and for the next two or three years. There simply was not time to carry out a proper baseline study.

By 1984, however, it became possible to think of evaluating the work of the Project, in such a way as to get at a wide range of aspects of the Project's work. This view of evaluation, as a research endeavour, was visible from 1984. There had been an inspection, carried out by Henry Widdowson at the time of the 1983 National Seminar, and which made useful suggestions – but what was envisaged was much more far-reaching than an inspection.

1984 was when the Project was reaching the end of the Universities phase, and when plans were being laid for a significant expansion, with a change in direction, into the ETFs. In the planning document drafted at that time the Project co-ordinators wrote that 'evaluating the effectiveness of the National ESP Project ending in 1985 is of crucial importance for the formal research element proposed in the present project'.

When the next phase of the Project got under way, officially, in August 1985 (Scott, having left Brazil in December 1984, returned to take up the post previously held by Deyes) the first step, agreed by the Project co-ordinators and ODA, was to plan the evaluation research. To this end, a series of preliminary workshops were held in the Regional Seminars in September.

This time it was felt to be most important to try to get the information needed, without at the same time antagonising relevant parties. It would obviously be necessary to avoid tactless comparison between universities, but it was also essential to find out to what extent Project teachers wanted an evaluation, and what their feelings were about how this should be done, if at all.

The outcome of these workshops was a series of recommendations. Any Project evaluation should aim to avoid:
– exposing weaknesses in public (referring to individual teachers' or university teams' weaknesses, not those of the Project as a whole);

- being externally oriented rather than internally useful;
- standardised questionnaires not capable of reflecting the real situation;
- excessively long procedures or instruments.

It should instead:
- provide opportunities for discussion and exchanges of opinion;
- produce concrete recommendations;
- be responsive to the variety of situations in a country as diverse as Brazil;
- have a clear sense of its purpose

In November 1985 ODA funded a visit by Alderson to help plan the evaluation effort. Alderson's role was as ODA-approved evaluation consultant, but at the same time he had been a visitor to the Project (for a Regional Seminar), and was generally in sympathy with its aims. ODA appeared at the time to expect, in part, a JIJOE report, but both the Project co-ordinators and Alderson himself felt it more appropriate for him to act as a genuine consultant, i.e. providing expertise and guidance, rather than as an external evaluator. This was made clear in all reports and appears to have been accepted by ODA.

One may legitimately ask why the idea of an evaluation as *research*, and not simply as an inspection, and springing in fact from the Project itself, fell on fertile soil in ODA. Research of the other types distinguished above did not meet with much official support. It is true that there is a venerable tradition of inspections from London, so we may presume that sponsors have generally been interested in assessing 'value for money', but past history of educational projects does not suggest that such agencies have generally thought in terms of evaluation as research. It seems to us that this was because of two factors. First, managerial changes in the educational and political climate in Britain at the time, with concomitant interest in 'performance indicators' and the like, made it possible for evaluation research to be seen as useful model building as well as permitting an assessment of value for money. Second, the proposal originated in the organisation to be evaluated.

At all events, once it was made clear that Alderson would play the consultant's and not the JIJOE's role, there was no difficulty; ODA (and the British Council) continued to support a good share of the costs of the evaluation.

The aims of the evaluation

It should be clear from the previous section that there were several different aims of the planned evaluation. ODA's perspective was presumably to determine whether the British taxpayer had received 'value for money' over the years from the Project, and specifically to decide whether to fund some continuation of the Project. The Project was at a point in its history where funding was due for review, and where plans were well developed in Brazil for the possible extension of the Project from the university sector to the technical secondary and tertiary sector, for which further funding was being requested. The Project's aims, as developed during the early phases of the planning, and as represented in public documents – Alderson's *Report on Visit to Project* November 1985 and Celani *et al.* 1988 (page 10 and Appendix 1) – were eight-fold:

- to attempt to carry out an evaluation which would be participatory and informative in nature
- to help the participants – Brazilian teachers – to become more aware and self-critical, to see themselves as agents, not patients
- to help similar projects do well (or better)
- to help understand the nature of innovation by monitoring developments and guiding them by the provision of feedback
- to show how the project evaluated itself and to investigate the evaluative process
- to encourage project funders to take evaluation more seriously and to build it into the design *ab initio* of projects
- to show supporting agencies what had been achieved
- to have defences in case of possible criticism.

Before describing the Brazilian evaluation, we wish to 'put our cards on the table', so to speak. Alderson was approached by the British Council at the suggestion of Project staff, and invited to visit Brazil to undertake an evaluation consultancy for the Project. His own motives in agreeing to carry out this consultancy were:

- a professional and academic interest and involvement in evaluation, from a theoretical and practical point of view; in particular, an interest in the value or otherwise of outsider JIJOE evaluations, and a desire to demonstrate the need for and the practicability of participatory evaluations, as well as a wish to convince funding agencies of the need to take evaluation more seriously, above all to plan and provide for evaluation from the very beginning of a Project;
- an interest in the development of the Project as an example of English for Specific Purposes in a Latin-American context (he had previously worked in Mexico on a project which bore some resemblance to the Brazil Project);
- an interest in identifying the achievements of the Project, many of whose teachers had attended short in-service courses at Lancaster University, and in the implications of such (non-) achievements for the design of in-service teacher education courses in Lancaster.

It should be noted at this point that the outside consultant was not unfamiliar with the Project, because of his association with the in-service education courses that contributed to the Project, nor was he unsympathetic to its aims, philosophy of innovation and methods. More disinterested consultants, less familiar with the Project's background and development, might have conducted a very different consultancy. Indeed, it is unclear whether the British Council and the ODA were initially aware that the evaluation would not be conducted along the traditional JIJOE lines.

The role played by Scott – the other author of this chapter but of course one of a wide team involved in the evaluation – was clearly that of Insider. He had been involved in the Project in Brazil since 1980 and is still at the time of writing one of the Project co-ordinators in São Paulo. His motivation cannot be described as disinterested. He shared most of Alderson's motivations as stated above and was also concerned by the Latin-American dimension and applicability of the Brazilian endeavour, but perhaps especially felt the teacher-training motivation stated elsewhere by Alderson, in a report to ODA after their first joint planning session, in November 1985:

> the encouragement of the upcoming evaluation process is important as a major focus for research – evaluation research – where participants learn about the development of relatively valid and/or reliable procedures and instruments, the need for systematicity in collection and interpretation, and an emphasis on the practical utility of results ...

Principles of participatory evaluation

'Participatory evaluation' was not well defined at the start of the evaluation exercise. It was quite evident that Project teachers did not want anything externally imposed, having already tasted that flavour and found it unappealing. But it was not at all clear to those organising the effort what ingredients would make the research participatory, and whether they should be shaken or stirred.

Other models were not directly applicable. Although there are similarities between the methodologies being used in Brazil and, say, those of Mexico or other Latin American countries, the organisational structure of the Project was unique, involving at the time some 23 universities in an extent of territory comparable with the whole of Europe. The role of the resource centre was – as far as we knew – unusual in acting as a hub for an equally singular pattern of teacher-contact seminars. How could such a loose network be most suitably examined?

The literature on the process was not of much help, either. Few if any writers on evaluation directly address the design of participatory evaluations, although there is some discussion of its desirability. A common distinction in the literature is that of 'formative' and 'summative' evaluation, and it could be argued that the participatory evaluation being planned fitted into the mould of 'formative' evaluation. It was already clear by 1984 that the purpose of the evaluation was to inform rather than simply to sum up the value of the effort expended. The intention to make the evaluation a research project and not an inspection is evidently related to this distinction.

What is meant by 'participatory'?

Yet what, we must ask, is a 'participatory' evaluation, and in what ways could an evaluation be 'non-participatory'? We propose, therefore, lacking any better theoretical perspective, and now in hindsight, to define the term 'participatory'.

One fundamental distinction must lie between planning, on the one hand, and execution on the other. In most human endeavours there are 'managers' who decide, and 'workers' who, as their name indicates, do the work (sometimes called donkey-work). Workers are even called 'hands', in agriculture, industry or at sea, a process which reduces them rather drastically to their own appendages. (Managers may also be 'Heads', but not quite in the same sense, and they often gain a 'capital' H.) This first distinction is of use in clearing out of the way what is meant by non-participation. A participatory evaluation will involve the sharing of decisional, planning roles as well as the donkey-work amongst all involved.

Another axis, it seems to us, cuts across the first one: the distinction between 'getting involved' and 'standing apart'. To be participatory means taking an active part, and not just watching from the sidelines. In conjunction with the planning/execution distinction it means doing a fair share of the planning and a fair share of the donkey-work.

This is not yet enough. For what incentive is there for anyone to be participatory in these two ways? The third aspect, we would argue, is perhaps the most important of all: gaining benefit from the work carried out. An endeavour which pretends to be participatory because it gets everyone genuinely involved and working in the planning as well as the execution, but only provides benefits to one segment, will not succeed in being truly participatory; moreover, it will sooner or later collapse, when enough of those involved see that there is nothing in it for them. There is no benefit: the sponsor sighs or smiles, the evaluated get back to business as usual, and the report gathers dust. A formative evaluation, at least, carries the potential benefit, especially to those whose work has been evaluated, that it points to things which could be improved, and should suggest fruitful ways of changing current practice. But we would argue that a formative evaluation, if non-participatory, will not usually bring benefits to those who got evaluated, but to others. This is because the evaluees will generally be either uninterested, unable to understand, or irritated at being evaluated by outsiders.

The above clarification of principles may be useful as an assay, against which the Brazil Project evaluation can be tested. However, one caveat is in order: no evaluation is purely summative, purely formative, wholly participatory or wholly non-participatory. This was no exception.

A participatory background

The Project itself, as guided by Antonieta Celani, had always been a loose network, with plenty of give and take, and no impositions of any kind. There was a Project 'line' of belief, and of proposed methodology, and indeed some 'Rosa Luxemburgism' – by which we meant a naive supposition on the part of some teachers that the Project's line was infallible – but participants in seminars essentially attended because they wanted to, and almost always partly at their own expense.

The Head of Project was always most careful not to appear to interfere in internal affairs of individual universities. This was partly because of her sense of tact, and partly owing to the fact that PUC–SP, a private university, was not part of the same network of Federal institutions that the Project served. So whenever teachers reported personal tensions, shortages or other difficulties in their universities, the Project could not pull any official strings, and avoided trying to pull them unofficially. The furthest the Project might go would be, where local teachers were not receiving proper support from their co-ordinator, selected or elected by the Federal University, to arrange to send out two sets of publications, one to the official local co-ordinator, and a second set to another teacher.

Thus far, we may conclude that a non-participatory evaluation would have had little chance of success, the mood of the whole Project being participatory. The intention from November 1985 was to involve all parties as much as possible, but we were unsure as to how realistic that would prove in such a vast country, with all the attendent costs and difficulties of communication. In any case it became clear in the sounding and planning stages that the Project wished to take an *a priori* decision about the nature of its evaluation. A participatory evaluation would be the only type coherent with the spirit of the Project itself.

Checking participation against stages of the evaluation

In the event the degree of participation involved in the evaluation research surprised all involved. We can distinguish at least the following levels of organisation of the evaluation:

– soundings	(Reg. Seminars, Sep. 1985)
– designing the whole evaluation	(São Paulo, Nov. 1985)
– constructing the instruments	(Embu, May 1986)
– testing them out	(Brazil, June 1986)
– collecting data	(Brazil, June–Sept. 1986)
– data analysis	(Brazil, 1986–8)
– drafting the report	(São Paulo, Feb. 1988)
– reading and learning from it	(various, ever since)

It is fair to claim that at all stages the evaluation was carried out in a participatory fashion to some degree. It is also fair to point out that the degree of participation varied somewhat, and that the whole evaluation cannot be seen as purely participatory.

Let us consider these stages in terms of our three-fold definition (planning versus execution, getting involved versus standing apart, gaining versus not gaining benefit) and the main parties involved. These were the local **teachers** and **co-ordinators** in each university, the **Project Co-ordinators** in São Paulo, the **research assistants** also at CEPRIL, the external **consultant**, and **sponsors** in the UK and Brasilia.

The role of sponsors was non-participatory. They paid much of the travel costs, provided computer facilities, and helped subsidise publication, but were not even invited to participate. In a more truly participatory evaluation perhaps they should have been.

DESIGNING THE WHOLE EVALUATION

Planning was carried out mainly by Project Co-ordinators and consultant. Teachers and co-ordinators had a role in the first workshops in 1985, and were consulted after the plans were drafted. Co-ordinators and research assistants attended the Embu seminar (May 1986) when plans and instruments were finalised.

CONSTRUCTING THE INSTRUMENTS

First drafts were developed by teachers and co-ordinators in the local university teams, then re-worked over by teachers, co-ordinators, project co-ordinators, research assistants, and consultant in Embu. Final editing was done by Project Co-ordinators, and consultant immediately afterwards, with typing up by Project Co-ordinators. Individual studies were also to have been carried out by five local teams of teachers and co-ordinators, but in the event only one was done. All subsequent stages were carried out by that team (in Curitiba), with feedback from other teachers at regional seminars and consultations with Project Co-ordinators.

TESTING THEM OUT

Final drafts were tested out by teachers, co-ordinators, and Project Co-ordinators in local teams (including São Paulo). Alterations were made by Project Co-ordinators.

COLLECTING DATA

This was mostly carried out by teachers and co-ordinators in the individual universities. Project Co-ordinators took part as the São Paulo team. Research assistants collected data on CEPRIL use.

DATA ANALYSIS

Teachers, co-ordinators, Project Co-ordinators, research assistants and consultant were all involved. Consultant knew most about it, and held some sort of responsibility, besides being the guest speaker at national seminars (May 1986 and February 1988) when stages 2 and 5 were being carried out. People who attended these events – the only way of getting together – were mostly co-ordinators but also included some teachers. Data were also analysed in the interim, in regional seminars attended by teachers, co-ordinators and Project Co-ordinators, and in CEPRIL by research assistants.

DRAFTING THE REPORT

This was carried out by co-ordinators, Project Co-ordinators, research assistants and consultant. Consultant's role was to oversee, not to write. Co-ordinators and research assistants wrote preliminary drafts and Project Co-ordinators mostly were responsible for re-writing and editing these, quite considerably, and over several weeks after February 1988.

READING AND LEARNING FROM IT

This stage is still with us. Consultant and (one of the) Project Co-ordinators are responsible for this chapter, and having to go over the process again to write it. No procedures have been developed for checking into this last stage, important though it is for a formative evaluation. The evidence presented in Chapter 8 of Celani *et al.* (1988:131–2) suggests that some teachers and co-ordinators may not have felt 'ownership' of the study, which, if true, would probably suggest that they are unlikely to be carrying out this final stage fully.

PARTICIPATION SUMMARISED

	insiders				*outsiders*	
	UT	UC	PC	RA	EC	SP
designing the whole evaluation	*	*	**	*	**	
constructing the instruments	**	**	**	**	**	
testing them out	**	**	**			
collecting data	**	**	**	**		
data analysis	**	**	**	**	**	
drafting the report		**	**	**	*	
reading and learning from it	?	?	**	?	**	**

Key: * = approximate degree of involvement
? = no evidence available
UT – University Teachers
UC – University Co-ordinators (who are also UTs)
PC – São Paulo Project Co-ordinators
RA – Research Assistants in CEPRIL (stay approx. 2 years)
EC – External Consultant
SP – Sponsors
A fuller description of these stages is to be found in Celani *et al.* (1988), especially Chapter 3.

Participation, to the degree that it was found feasible, could not take place without training. For all involved it was a learning experience, but training was part and parcel of the endeavour, as indeed it is part of the Project philosophy. Does this represent a limitation of the degree of participation? As defined above, participation involves joint execution and planning, joint involvement and joint perception of benefit. We would argue that participation is not weakened by the need for training. In the Brazilian case, the training was internal, mostly provided by co-ordinators and consultant to the other sectors of those involved.

The national seminars (1986 and 1988) were clearly both training and productive sessions. The work carried out by research assistants was throughout 1986, 1987 and 1988 supervised and led by Project Co-ordinators. The co-ordinators had to learn a great deal about the process as they did it, too: this involved the intricacies of getting data into computer-processable shape, and how to train co-ordinators and research assistants to process computer printouts.

Comments from local co-ordinators and teachers, as well as from research assistants, made it quite clear that this learning experience was perceived as valuable: the Project fulfilling its teacher-training role. Indeed, it is possible that a major benefit of the evaluation was in learning how to do evaluation, which includes learning from our mistakes. The minor benefit, if the above comments on learning from the evaluation are true, was in getting the findings.

The research questions

The main questions in the design related to the following eleven major categories, developed in November 1985 and refined to May 1986.

Context
   1   Attitudes and motivation with regard to the Project
Methodology
   2 The ESP methodology or approach adopted
   3 Classroom Management
Implementation of methodology
   4 Materials
Project achievements
   5 Learning outcomes (students' learning)
   6 Impact on 'outsiders'
Teacher-training implementation
   7 In-service training
   8 Publications
   9 Research carried out by teachers
Exchange of ideas and experience
  10 The administration of the Project
  11 Resource Centre

These eleven categories developed in the November 1985 brain-storming as a view of the major aspects of the Project. The categories served as a framework for data collection and analysis. Each of the framework categories was then sub-divided into a series of questions which it was hoped the evaluation would answer. Question 2 (methodology), for example, was specified as including:

a) What do participants think the ESP Approach consists of?
b) Did the Project evolve in relation to specific Brazilian necessities or was it imposed from outside?
c) Was the approach presented as Eternal (God-given) Truth, or by rational argument, with reference to evidence?
d) Did teachers simply accept the project approach word for word or did they approach it critically and understand the underlying principles?
e) Is there perceived to be an 'ESP Approach' or a variety of personally evolved ESP approaches?
f) Is the approach appropriate according to students and teachers?
g) What resistance has the approach met up to now?

h) Do teachers understand that the principles/approach can be realised in the classroom or in materials in a variety of equally valid ways?
i) Do teachers see the difference between technique and principle? ('We've tried ESP and it doesn't work.')

The full list is too extensive to reproduce here, but it can be seen that these questions, the result of the November 1985 planning meeting in São Paulo, cover a wide and far-ranging list of research questions.

The design

The main characteristics of the research design were
1 Triangulation of source and of method. This means collecting data from a variety of informants (though employers were not included for logistical reasons), and by means of both questionnaire and interview with the main types of informant.
2 Most instruments provided information on perceptions. There were no test results or classroom observation data. This was a) because no adequate standardised test existed in the Project, and b) the expressed wishes of teachers at the September 1985 regional seminars. It would have been ironical to have damaged or destroyed the Project by evaluating it insensitively! However, the evaluation clearly over-relied on perception data.

The instruments were the following, with number of respondents:
1 a questionnaire for current ESP students   (2,066)
2 a questionnaire for ex-students of ESP   (233)
3 a long questionnaire for ESP teachers   (121)
4 a questionnaire for subject specialists   (143)
   (teachers of chemistry, sociology, etc.)
5 ESP student reports of class discussions   (121)
6 ESP teacher reports on the same discussions   (34)
7 post-questionnaire interviews with ESP teachers   (50)
8 statistics on use of CEPRIL
9 analysis of materials sent in to CEPRIL

The sample included ESP students from 20 participating universities (out of 23 nominally engaged in the Project at the time). Response rates varied across universities, but were never less than 20 per cent of the student population in any one university, and were occasionally as high as 100 per cent (PUC–SP). Given the difficulties of approaching former students, we had attempted to approach only 30 per university. The final response was rather more than one third of that target, from 17 out of the 20 universities. The response rate for ESP teachers was about 64 per cent of the estimated number, and for subject specialists, from fifteen universities, was about half the hoped-for number.

The class discussion reports came from fourteen universities, and the ESP teacher interviews from nine.

Results

Although the detailed results of the evaluation are peripheral to the central purpose of this chapter, which is to present a model of participatory evaluation, we report below the main findings in relation to the principal research question headings presented above. It will be appreciated that it is impossible within the limits of this chapter to present either the instruments used, or the compilation of responses to the instruments. Instead, we confine ourselves to reporting the main conclusions drawn from the data. The instruments, and details of the compiled data can be found in Celani *et al.* (1988).

1   *Attitudes and motivation with regard to the Project*

1 Students were moderately satisfied with the ESP course overall.
2 Few respondents believed ESP was a tool of imperialism or preparation for the consumer society.
3 Few students felt that the ESP course would actually result in increased chances of getting a better job; however, their teachers attached more practical value to a knowledge of English, especially the subject specialist teachers, and ex-students did see the ESP course as relevant to their professions.
4 Post-graduates had clearly more positive attitudes towards their ESP course overall than did undergraduates.
5 Students in homogeneous groups (in terms of subject specialism, not EFL proficiency) showed a more positive attitude to their ESP course, especially at post-graduate level.
6 At undergraduate level though not at post-graduate level, students being taught by teachers active in the Project seem to have had more positive attitudes to their ESP course.
7 Teachers and students are generally satisfied with the ESP materials in use.
8 Classroom management was not felt to be entirely satisfactory in the questionnaires but appears more favourable in the class reports. Teachers' and students' opinions differed as to the amount of opportunity for personal expression and awareness of the programme and methodology.
9 Teacher-training events and Project seminars received a favourable reaction.

10 The current Project administrative structure was felt to be appropriate.
11 The presence of British specialists was supported.
12 Project publications were felt to be useful.
13 Attitudes to research indicated some lack of interest and lack of
opportunity.
14 The relatively low use made of CEPRIL suggested some fear of
making one's own materials public until they were definitive.

2   *The ESP methodology or approach adopted*

1 Teachers and students generally agreed as to which skills were being
taught, so that all chose to mention reading comprehension as the
main skill.
2 Their perceptions of course components within this picture of an
overall one-skill course differed. There is a suggestion that teachers did
not succeed in negotiating and explaining course content.
3 The approach was not totally monolithic. A small percentage of
students were being taught oral skills.
4 About 85 per cent of teachers felt that the Project's approach was
different from what they had used previously.
5 The novelty lay in emphasis on reading strategies, awareness of
reading processes, concentration on the reading skill, lexical inference,
critical reading, developing a minimal text comprehension grammar,
and the ability to find main points in texts.
6 There is no evidence that teachers felt the Project had been imposed on
them in terms of methodology.
7 There seems to have been some uniformity in promoting a Project
approach. On the other hand, there is evidence that the Project
co-ordinating team were aware of the dangers of dogmatism.

3   *Classroom management*

1 Teachers and students notice that there is a difference between Project
and non-Project English classes.
2 Teachers and students also agree substantially on the characteristics of
an ESP class within the Project methodology.
3 In terms of classroom management, the majority of teachers identified
the main characteristics as follows:
Teacher–student relations
Class discussions
Awareness of methodology
Student participation

4 The majority of students only identified student participation as characteristic of Project classes.
5 Comparing the answers to the above two items it can be seen that students and teachers perceive classroom practices differently. Teachers appear to indicate specifically 'Project' features with more frequency than students. In addition, analysis of the materials shows little explicit evidence for negotiation of course objectives, group or individualised work, although there is evidence of open-ended discussions taking place.

4 *Materials*

1 There is little difference in the sources of texts, or in type of publication, when we compare Project and non-Project teachers. We can note a tendency for Project teachers to make more use of magazines and periodicals of general interest whilst non-Project teachers tend to make more use of texts taken from EFL textbooks.
2 As to where these texts are found, Project teachers make much more use of the Resource Centre as a source of texts compared with non-Project teachers.
3 Classroom materials usually come from teachers' private collections for both Project and non-Project teachers. We were unable to find what the sources of these personal collections were.
4 Texts are mostly chosen by the individual teacher, although Project teachers also work as a team.
5 Materials are constantly modified after being used in the classroom for the first time.
6 Project teachers tend to be more satisfied with their materials than non-Project teachers are.
7 Project and non-Project teachers differ in their reasons for modifying materials. Project teachers modify them for a variety of reasons connected with feedback from classroom use. Non-Project teachers mention the same reasons but the most important one is a habit of constantly renewing material.
8 The majority of current students and ex-students thought that the materials were interesting.
9 Students also considered the content of the texts interesting and relevant to their area of specialism.
10 Students thought that the presentation and lay-out of the texts was not entirely satisfactory.
11 Although teachers said that they may revise materials with students' opinions in mind, it is not clear if students felt that this is true.
12 Students agreed with teachers on the topics covered in materials.

13 On examining materials sent to the Resource Centre, it was seen that the majority of exercises concentrated on the teaching of reading strategies. A substantial proportion also dealt with vocabulary. In general the Project approach is reflected in the content of the materials.

5   Learning outcomes (students' learning)

1 Students appear to be learning text comprehension, and reading strategies seem to be helping considerably towards this ability.
2 Most students report that they can get the gist of a text in English, use reading strategies for this, and now read more easily and independently.
3 Teachers report considerably greater success than their students do, and somewhat different course aims and components.
4 Some students expect to learn oral skills or grammar as well as text comprehension and report some frustration in their learning outcomes, in connection with the differences between the actual and desired objectives and content of ESP courses. However, there is no relation between a wish for listening (in contrast with speaking) or the teaching of 'translation' and claimed improvement as a result of the ESP course.
5 Students who report more success in terms of learning outcomes differ from less successful ones on a variety of measures, in terms of objectives wanted or established for the ESP class, course content, classroom management, attitude to materials, and to the social role of ESP.
6 Post-graduates tend to report greater success in learning outcomes. Their aims and expectations also coincide more with their teachers'.
7 Project teachers get slightly better learning outcomes than do non-Project teachers, though only in the case of undergraduates.
8 A minority of students report improvements in their reading in Portuguese as well as in English.
9 ESP classes achieve reasonable learning outcomes even from students whose reported initial level of English was weak, though those whose English was non-existent are learning somewhat less or are less confident.

6   Impact on 'outsiders'

1 Subject specialists attach practical value to a knowledge of English; students and ex-students, however, do not seem to perceive the same value in relation to the ESP courses.

2 Subject specialist Academic Departments do not seem to have been affected by ESP courses.
3 Non-Project teachers feel that contact with the Project has been beneficial and has affected their techniques in the classroom.
4 Teachers of other foreign languages have shown interest in the activities of the Project and have often participated in them.
5 There has been a clear impact on the community, through extension courses, seminars, consultancies. This includes closer links with secondary and technical schools.
6 The impact overseas can be seen in terms of number of subscriptions to publications of the Project, letters, requests, papers given in international conferences and interchange of other publications.

7   In-service training

1 Seminars in general are seen as effectively contributing to professional development.
2 Local seminars were positively evaluated by the majority of respondents, with very few ESP teachers pointing out negative aspects.
3 Three-month courses in the UK were described as very useful or useful by all respondents.
4 A total of 50 local seminars, eighteen regional seminars and four national seminars were held in the period 1980–6, with the North/North-East region being the recipient of the greatest number of local seminars.
5 Local seminars had the greatest number of participants.
6 Scholarships for intensive courses in the UK were fairly evenly distributed per region and were awarded to 37 ESP teachers in all.
7 Visiting speakers' visits were evenly distributed per region.
8 Research assistants seem to have directly benefited from informal training led by KELTs.

8   Publications

1 The Project publications seem to have been well known by Project and non-Project teachers alike, especially *the ESPecialist*.
2 Teachers had adequate access to publications, and about a quarter of Project teachers read and discussed them as a team.
3 The number of publications was thought satisfactory.
4 Teachers felt that the influence of publications was mostly in helping prepare materials, as well as a contribution to theoretical underpinnings.
5 The commonest changes suggested to the publications were: more reports of classroom activities, and critical reviews of published materials.

6 *The ESPecialist, Working Papers, Resource Packages* were all voted 'very useful' by a majority of Project teachers. The *Newsletter* was felt less useful. The only publication which non-Project teachers were generally familiar with was *the ESPecialist*.
7 The region which contributed most to the publications (disregarding PUC–SP) was the southern region.

9   Research carried out by teachers

1 Just over half of the Project teachers reported that they had done ESP research.
2 The most commonly reported topic of research done was reading, but suggestions for research emphasised grammar and testing rather more.
3 The southern region appears to have been most involved in research.
4 Most of the research is individual and informal, carried out in the researcher's own university alone, quite often not for publication.
5 The most stated reason for not doing research was lack of time. Lack of interest and lack of confidence were rarely selected options.

10   The administration of the Project

1 There are indications that most of the ESP teachers want the Project to continue to be administered from PUC–SP, with possible regional co-ordinations and local projects integrated with the National Co-ordination.
2 The communication system is considered efficient between the National Co-ordination and local co-ordinations but inefficient between local co-ordinations.
3 There are indications that responsibility for teacher development is being taken up by Brazilians.
4 The organisation/structure of the Project seems to be satisfactory.
5 The KELTs' influence on the Project is not considered to have been excessive.

11   Resource Centre

1 Teachers report that CEPRIL meets many of their needs, and that it helps in filling the gaps which appear in their ESP courses.
2 Teachers also report that they often send their own materials to CEPRIL for comments and criticism by the KELTs.
3 The main reasons for not requesting materials from the Resource Centre are attributable to physical problems of distance, time available and funds.

4 Data seem to show that the setting up of a local resource centre would not reduce the number of requests for materials sent to CEPRIL.
5 Teachers report that the Resource Centre helps them in finding different materials from those available locally.
6 Teachers report that they usually receive material from CEPRIL in reasonable time. In the case of those who noted excessive delays this was caused by teachers requesting material which was not available or not specifying the request clearly.
7 Teachers indicate that the Resource Centre helps them keep in touch with developments in other ESP teams.
8 Resource Centre records indicate that the Resource Centre is used by far more people than the Project teachers.

The evaluation process resulted in a large amount of usable and useful data, which it is difficult to summarise briefly in a paper such as this. The interested reader is referred to Celani *et al.* (1988) for full information about the results of the questionnaire surveys, and for some data on the results of the interviews and discussions, and of the projects carried out by individual universities or research assistants at PUC–SP.

Summary of findings

Teachers and students reported general satisfaction with teaching materials in use, and with the Project approach to ESP, although the latter was more appreciated by teachers and post-graduate students than by undergraduates. Students generally considered the texts used to be relevant to their interests, and felt that their English (and particularly their reading ability) had improved as a result of their ESP classes.

Some aspects of classroom management appear not to have been entirely satisfactory. In addition, some students reported dissatisfaction with the presentation of teaching materials. Unfortunately, no direct evidence was gathered on what actually happened in Project classrooms, so it is very difficult to draw conclusions about the degree of implementation of Project ideas and 'methods'. It is, however, possible to draw inferences about classroom activities from student and teacher responses to the questionnaires, interviews and discussions. It would appear that, broadly speaking, the Project's methods were being implemented, but with varying degrees of modification. The Project's methodology for conducting ESP classes was felt to have been different from previous practice, and to have been generally beneficial, yet was not perceived to have been imposed by the Central Co-ordination of the Project (essential to the Project's participatory philosophy).

Teachers felt that the in-service training available through the Project had been very satisfactory, that the Project's infrastructure, administration and communication systems had proved adequate, that the Project's publications had been very useful, and that the Resource Centre had met many teachers' needs, and was able to supply useful materials. Nevertheless, results also suggest a disappointing rate of submission of teaching materials to the Resource Centre, for the use of other teachers and universities, and many teachers felt that they did not make as much use of the Resource Centre as they might have, because of its remoteness from their own university. Teachers also reported a disappointing lack of opportunity to engage in Project-related research, and some lack of interest in so doing.

The Project was felt by many to have had a positive impact on the wider English teaching community in Brazil. It was particularly notable that although the contribution of British expatriates was acknowledged and valued, responses to various questions suggested that Brazilian teachers and co-ordinators had begun to take on responsibility for the development and direction of the Project. Since overseas input (in the shape of expatriate advisers and associated funding) is bound to be reduced eventually, this finding is encouraging for those who believe the Project must continue beyond the end of such external assistance.

Problems of this evaluation

The heading to this section should not mislead the reader into believing that there were only problems associated with this evaluation. In fact, there were many achievements and positive outcomes. Above all, there was a remarkable degree of enthusiasm, collaboration and interest in the evaluation on the part of ESP teachers throughout the country. Over 50 teachers and research assistants attended seminars held as part of the planning, designing and analysing phases. One university conducted its own independent study (on drop-out rates), and most provided comments on the aims and planned content of the evaluation, on the draft evaluation instruments and procedures, and on the resulting data and their draft interpretation. As one result, the teachers have taken the results of the evaluation very seriously, and where negative findings resulted, have attempted to account for them, or to take them on board, rather than reject them as irrelevant or invalid. Many, if not most, of the teachers involved also seemed to learn a great deal about evaluation: how it might be planned, how data might be collected, and how results might be interpreted. It is hoped that they have gained insights into the Project as a result of the study, and have learned something of the potential and actual value of evaluation. They have also learned something about how research more generally might be conducted.

The response rates were in general encouraging, and it is possible to have a fairly high degree of confidence in the generalisability of the results. The intended triangulation of data, both through the use of different instruments and of different types of informants, worked fairly well, and allows us to claim that account has been taken of the variety of different perspectives on the Project that might be expected to exist, and thereby to have greater confidence in the results.

One consequence of the participatory nature of the evaluation was the length of time that it took to conduct the study. Autumn 1985 saw the beginnings of plans that were not finally realised as a report of the result until summer 1988. Some of the delay was due to the late delivery and operation of a computer capable of doing the required analyses of the quantitative data, but some delay was doubtless due to the need to ensure full and open consultation with all participating institutions, especially in giving feedback on plans, instruments and data, but also in trying to allow participants to take major responsibility for whole sections of instruments, trialling, draft reports, and so on.

The questionnaires show signs – perhaps inevitably – of weaknesses, despite piloting. Occasionally questions which were supposed to be repeated in different questionnaires for purposes of triangulation were repeated not entirely verbatim or else with one item missing. The questionnaires contain some items whose answers have proved uninformative. Sometimes items are repeated in different words, which reduces the levels of response overall and dilutes the respondent's opinions over more than one option. There are questions missing even in the long ESP teacher questionnaire.

The data sources were not as complete as first envisaged. Not all the promised studies were carried out. The opinions of non-Project teachers are represented by only 34 teachers who reported that they were 'not active' in the Project, and – not surprisingly – there are far too few data available from universities which were inactive in the Project, and none at all from universities which were not nominally part of the Project.

It is not clear whether all the sampling procedures were carried out adequately. As far as students are concerned the questionnaire and discussions were supposed to be done with *all* ESP students in the participating universities, and we have no clear data on how those who did respond were selected. For ex-students, the instructions were simply to find 'a minimum of 30, from a variety of areas and with a range of likely opinion', and subject specialists were supposed to be 'at least one per discipline / department'. How exactly the sample came to be in fact, is not entirely clear and never can be, as it evolved in response to the pressures and constraints of the different universities in June 1986, and many *ad hoc* decisions were taken as it proved impossible to contact one ESP group, one teacher, one subject specialist, or one ex-student.

Another problem was that quantitative data – from questionnaires – proved both easier to gather, and more amenable to analysis and summary. Although responses to the more qualitative methods were good, their open-ended nature made it more difficult to compare reports of discussions and interviews, as well as to relate to other, independently gathered information. Despite the expressed wish early in the planning process to avoid reliance on long questionnaires, the main instrument used with teachers – the questionnaire – was twelve pages long, and was feared by those who developed it to be excessive. Yet the response rate was very high on this instrument, and the evidence suggests that teachers responded thoughtfully and honestly.

The absence of direct classroom observation data is problematic, since we are forced to rely upon inferences from reports of behaviour for conclusions about the degree of implementation of the Project's ideas and philosophy. Since what people say is notoriously different from what they do, some observational data would have been very valuable, if only as corroboration.

It was also regrettable that no independent data were available of student learning. Appropriate standardised tests do not exist, and the variety of learning situations within the Project is probably so great as to preclude the use of any common instrument in all participating universities. However, it might have been possible for some at least of the universities to have devised special studies of student achievement. This weakness is related to a problem with respect to the development of language or reading tests within the Project (and in language education more generally), but the lack of test data is probably also related to a fear that it might be difficult to substantiate perceived achievement by test data. Nevertheless, some attempt at this would have been valuable.

One result of the lack of observational and test data is that the evaluation tended to rely rather too much upon reported opinions, rather than taking account of independent evidence. The triangulation went some way to dispelling worries on this score, but not entirely.

Insider–outsider roles in participatory evaluation

From the tenor of this chapter, it will be clear that it is the present authors' opinion that participatory evaluation is the most satisfactory, because it is the most complete way of carrying out evaluation. It is also evidently a more democratic way of proceeding than the JIJOE model. It necessarily involves a lot more time and effort, because of communication between all the interested parties: that is the difference between team work and individual work. In the Brazilian case, it also involved a large component of teacher training. This was not unwelcome – after all, that was the Project's major goal, as explained in *The Project*, pp. 28–33.

It has hopefully been clear from this account that the role of the outsider in the evaluation was barely evaluative: he functioned rather as an adviser on how to design, execute and interpret an evaluation. Although he commented upon the progress of the evaluation, and made relatively informal comments in various reports on the Project, its achievements, the motivation of participating teachers, the role of the KELT advisers, the functioning of the Resource Centre, and so on, he tried to avoid pronouncing upon the value of the Project in any summative sense. Thus, although he certainly commented upon the interpretations of the data, both during the February seminar, and in the drafting of the Report (Celani *et al.* 1988), he refused to be drawn into commenting upon the success of the Project. It could be argued that he thereby failed to function as an outside evaluator, and that therefore this evaluation is not an example of an Insider–Outsider Evaluation at all.

In a sense, this is true: the consultant made many suggestions with respect to the aims and the design of the evaluation. He contributed to the discussions of its content, both in general, and as enshrined in detail in the various instruments that were used. He gave his opinion on the data that resulted, advised on their analysis, and to a degree on their interpretation. However, he did not present an independent analysis, or a contrary interpretation to those reached by the Project participants. At times, some teachers found this very frustrating, and one or two expressed the view, near the beginning of the process, that the evaluation should be left to experts to design, conduct and report on. Such comments doubtless stem in part from the frustrations of the process of deciding upon appropriate instruments, or plausible interpretations of results, and partly from a genuinely held belief that 'experts' can be relied upon to deliver an objective, definitive judgement of the value of the Project. The problem is, of course, at least twofold: this depends upon the expert being objective, fully informed and sufficiently insightful as to be able to grasp all the complexities of the situation, many of which are not even known to participants, and to be able to gather and to balance conflicting evidence. But importantly, this also assumes that if the expert came up with unpalatable findings and judgements, these would be accepted by all parties. Experience shows, however, that unpalatable findings are most likely to be accepted if they have been 'discovered' by those working on a project, and if those people understand or can be helped to understand the reasons for such a state of affairs. Yet if the results of an evaluation are to have any impact, or to be in any way useful, they must be accepted by members of the project. And unpalatable outsider evaluations are simply less likely to be accepted.

What, then, is the role of the outsider to be? Is she or he to be denied any judgemental role? Do his/her judgements count? What weight are they to be given? The obvious danger is that readers of evaluations are more likely to accept the views of outsiders than of insiders, since the latter might be taken to be biased. (Needless to say, perhaps, the outsider him/herself can hardly be expected to be unbiased, but this is usually overlooked.) Is the role of the outsider simply to legitimise evaluations conducted by insiders: findings that would not be accepted by sceptics if they originated from biased insiders might be acceptable if involved outsiders agree with them? Apart from the difficulty of agreeing that such a privileged position for an outsider is possible – 'knowing' that findings are appropriate – there is clearly a difficulty for the outsider here, in that she or he appears to be being used somewhat cynically in a public relations exercise, which she or he might not wish to equate with the aims of an evaluation.

In this Project evaluation, the contribution of the outside consultant was probably to the quality of the study's design, its instruments, and to the adequacy of the interpretations of the results. As we have seen, there are aspects of the evaluation that he would have designed differently in the unlikely event that he had been in a position to conduct an independent study. (Data on classroom implementation of Project ideas, and above all, in the not unbiased view of this outsider, data on students' test performance would have contributed substantially to an understanding of the effect the Project had on students.) But such an evaluation study would have been extremely costly to design and execute, would have been a logistical nightmare, and would probably have alienated most of the teachers in the Project. Indeed, such a study, especially in the context of this particular Project, is probably only feasible if designed and conducted by insiders, albeit with outside advice.

All of which is not to deny the potential value of an outside visitor to a project, in a capacity other than that of evaluation adviser. Provided that a project has conducted a well-designed evaluation of its activities, with or without outside advice, an outsider can provide a very useful distanced view on the value of the resulting data, and the legitimacy of the interpretations that are offered in any written report. Thus, a JIJOE could certainly be of use in contributing to decisions about a project's effectiveness, but only if the project has already systematically evaluated itself. Unfortunately, such a scenario is rarely presented to visiting 'experts', and they are all too frequently expected to evaluate a project in the almost complete absence of data or reports.

Probably contrary to the funding agency's expectations, this evaluation has failed to determine whether the Project has proved to be 'value for money'. This is because such an evaluation would need to take account of factors beyond the immediate language education aims of the Project. It would, for example, need to have access to evaluations of similar projects that were known or thought to have been 'value for money'. It would need to know how 'value for money' was understood by funding agencies, what criteria they would wish to apply in arriving at such a judgement. What measures of throughput and output, to use currently fashionable economics jargon, are appropriate to apply to a nation-wide project like this? How significant is the number of teachers who have undergone in-service education at local, regional and national seminars, on short courses in São Paulo and longer courses in the UK? Is the value of such INSET to be determined by the proportion of returnees who become project co-ordinators in their local universities? Or by the proportion who go on to write textbooks, to study successfully for higher degrees? Who buy British goods in preference to US goods, or who holiday in Europe rather than locally, given the choice? What weight is to be given to the increased self-confidence of teachers, the increase in Brazilian contributions to professional journals, the increased number of specially produced teaching materials? Do these represent 'value for money' for the Project and the funding agency? Clearly, an improvement in the standard of English in participating institutions is one of the main aims of the Project, and we believe that attempts should be made to define what this means, and then to measure it. However, even if this is achieved, it will be very difficult to decide (or even to know) that any improvement that might be identified represents 'value for money', since there are no studies of similar projects against which this Project could be compared. It is in other words impossible in the current state of our knowledge about language education and its effectiveness to say whether an equivalent improvement in English could have been brought about by a cheaper project.

The upshot of the Brazilian evaluation experience is that, despite some reservations, a participatory model is both possible and rewarding. The outsider's role is as a consultant, and a co-evaluator. Insiders are the main beneficiaries. The model fits the Chinese saying: 'Tell me and I forget, show me and I remember, involve me and I learn.'

References

Alderson, J. C. 1984. Reading in a foreign language: reading problem or language problem? In J. C. Alderson and A. H. Urquhart (Eds.) *Reading in a Foreign Language*. London: Longman.

Arns, O. and G. I. Engel (Eds.) 1979–80. *A língua estrangeira instrumental: perfil das necessidades e do interesse na Universidade Federal do Paraná*. Curitiba: Federal University of Paraná.

Bogaard, L. 1983. A necessidade e eficiência do ensino de Inglês instrumental em universidades brasileiras. *The ESPecialist* 6: 10–51.

Celani, M. A. A., J. L. Holmes, R. C. G. Ramos and M. R. Scott. 1988. *The Brazilian ESP Project: an evaluation*. São Paulo: Editora de PUC–SP.

Deyes, A. 1981. Applications of discourse analysis (towards a minimum discourse grammar). *Working Papers of Brazilian ESP Project*, No. 3. São Paulo: Catholic University of São Paulo.

Deyes, A. 1985. Research within the context of the ESP Project – a register. The *ESPecialist* 11: 11–23.
Holmes, J. L. 1981. Using authentic material in an authentic way. *Lexden Papers* 2: 22–33.
Munby, J. 1978. *Communicative syllabus design*. Cambridge: Cambridge University Press.
Scott, M. R. 1981a. Teaching and unteaching coping strategies. *Working Papers of Brazilian ESP Project*, No. 1. São Paulo: Catholic University of São Paulo.
Scott, M. R. 1981b. Reading comprehension in English for Academic Purposes. *The ESPecialist*, No. 3.
Scott, M. R. 1985. Research design for EAP. The *ESPecialist*, No. 11.

Editors' postscript to Alderson and Scott

Alderson and Scott describe an attempt to carry out an evaluation in a way that was apparently unusual. The norm, they affirm, is a kind of inspection performed by an outside expert with little local knowledge and less time to acquire it. The outsider is perceived as a threat by project developers, co-ordinators and teachers, and therefore they are unlikely to make use of whatever recommendations may be made. In order to promote utilisation of their evaluation, an attempt was made to involve project staff as participants in the data collection, analysis and reporting. This notion of collaborative evaluation is strongly advocated by Alderson and Scott, and they bring a number of persuasive arguments to bear.

It is widely agreed by now that an evaluation should above all aim to promote short-run utilisation. Thus, there is much to recommend collaboration: it seems a fair assumption that participants in an inquiry will learn more and take it more seriously than those upon whom it is imposed from without. It is an approach to evaluation that has many adherents and the pages of the evaluation journals reflect this interest. However, there are problems that emerge in the Alderson–Scott study, most of which are thoroughly discussed. Highlighting some of these problems, giving further attention to them here, may help other evaluators contemplate the issues involved.

First, the evaluators seem convinced that 'participatory' evaluation is the way to approach evaluations wherever possible. It could be argued that this is too rigid. Sometimes there is a clear need for straightforward empiricism. For example, when Lambert and Tucker first investigated the Canadian French immersion programs some 20 years ago, the policy-shaping community (parental pressure groups, the Ministry of Education, local politicians) wanted to know if the children were disadvantaged in their L1, their school subjects, and if they were far ahead of their peers in French. It is not hard to imagine in those early days of immersion that it must have seemed quite frightening to parents. The need was for test results as soon as possible. A formative, participatory study could hardly claim limited resources of time and money in such circumstances. The point is that it is not profitable to recommend one approach no matter what.

Second, it is hard to tell how much project participants really participated in the evaluation, in spite of the authors' candid attempts to convey the facts. Regarding the data analysis, it is stated that Alderson knew most about it, and held some sort of responsibility. Given this state of affairs, it is possible that teachers would only participate in a token fashion. As far as instrument construction is concerned, this was originally done by the teachers and the co-ordinators, but it was then checked and changed by Alderson and others. It may be that with the best of intentions, the control exercised in this checking phase ensured that the views of Alderson and the Project Co-ordination would be to the fore, although to the best of their knowledge, this was not the case. As for the drafting of the report, Alderson's 'role was to oversee, not to write'. So what did this overseeing consist of? How much did it influence the writing? The authors are aware that no evaluation can be wholly participatory or non-participatory, and it could be that some slippage in transmission between participation as conceived and participation as realised accounts for the acknowledgement by Celani *et al.* (1988) that some local teachers and co-ordinators may not have felt ownership of the study.

Third, Alderson and Scott mention that the 'ODA's perspective was presumably to determine whether the British taxpayer had received "value for money" over the years from the project, and specifically to decide whether to fund some continuation of the project'. ODA commissioned the evaluation, so they were clearly major stakeholders and their input to the design of the evaluation would be important. Funders, it may be safely assumed, have needs too. A fully negotiated evaluation charter would sensibly take account of these needs. In the event, there does not appear to have been any reprimand or praise from ODA, but this lack of reaction cannot always be counted on. The time to point out the vagueness of concepts like 'value for money', or even to determine that this really is the wish of the funders, is *before* the evaluation begins.

While the funders were perhaps drawn into negotiation less than was appropriate, the teachers could have no reason to feel neglected. Indeed, they were not observed because they did not want to be. Pre-evaluation negotiation might have drawn attention to the danger that the evaluation would thus be left with nothing but self-report data, and that this would leave everyone less well informed than they needed to be. Teachers, after all, were not the only stakeholders.

Fourth, there is the question of who should conduct evaluations: insiders or outsiders. Alderson and Scott are clear where they stand. On the inside. They are quite frank about this and properly declare their interests. Alderson was approached by the British Council at the suggestion of the project staff. Why Alderson? Because he was 'not unfamiliar with the project', because he was associated 'with the in-service education courses that contribute to the project', and because he was 'not unsympathetic to its aims, philosophy of innovation and methods'. Scott, too, 'cannot be described as disinterested'.

The insider–outsider issue is currently hot in the evaluation literature. The FBI (Sonnichsen 1987) do not want external evaluation and prefer their own people to fulfil this function; a women's study programme should only be evaluated by someone who is a committed feminist (Kirkup 1986). Insiders have the advantage of knowing how their organisations work, knowing the programme intimately, and knowing the staff who make the programme work. They are trusted. Their evaluations are likely to be used. For this reason, their popularity seems sure to increase. But it is worth pointing out that there is a high price to pay. One of the principal arguments in favour of an outside evaluation is that it might provide a *fresh* perspective. Where everyone is nodding agreement, it seems less likely that something new will be learnt, that assumptions will be questioned. A dissident might argue that by seeking an evaluation from known sympathisers, the EAP project in Brazil was more concerned with vindication than with discovery.

Another reason that outsiders are perhaps to be preferred is that they may be perceived by stakeholders as less biased than insiders. Though Alderson and Scott point out that there is no guarantee that outsiders are neutral, it is the perception that is important. Outsiders have greater credibility, if not necessarily to project members, then probably to parents, politicians, funding bodies, and other interest groups and observers: this in itself could promote the likelihood of use of findings.

But for justice to be done to this topic, far more space would need to be devoted to it. In the end, it would probably be agreed that the choice of an insider or an outsider or both would depend on the purpose of the proposed evaluation, and on the make-up of the stakeholding parties. Alderson and Scott at least put the issue into bold relief and evaluators may draw their own conclusions about the relative merits and demerits.

Evaluators may also contemplate how they would address different kinds of stakeholders: would they be more sensitive to teachers than to funders? They might consider whether participatory evaluation is appropriate to their circumstances and they might mull over the details of exactly what kind of participation will deliver the goods. For all of these issues, the Alderson/Scott chapter will serve as a point of reference. This is, needless to say, its purpose.

References

Kirkup, G. 1986. The feminist evaluator. In E. R. House (Ed.) *New directions in educational evaluation*: 68–84.
Sonnichsen, R. C. 1987. An internal evaluator responds to Ernest House's views on internal evaluation. *Evaluation Practice* 8: 34–6.

2 Evaluating a program inside and out[1,2]

Brian Lynch

Introduction

The following study was designed to investigate the two major approaches to program evaluation: quantitative, experimental (in the traditional sense of the term) evaluation and qualitative, naturalistic evaluation. The data came from the University of Guadalajara (UdeG)/ University of California, Los Angeles (UCLA) Reading English for Science and Technology (REST) Project. This project was initiated in 1985 as a part of an agreement for academic exchange between the UdeG and UCLA. At present, UCLA assists in the recruitment of teachers from the United States, but the project is managed entirely by UdeG personnel. There are plans to use the model curriculum developed by the REST Project elsewhere in the UdeG.

The data from the first year of the REST Project will be used to investigate and make recommendations concerning the methodology of program evaluation rather than to evaluate the REST Project *per se*. No ultimate judgments of the REST Project will be presented here. Instead, the focus and conclusions of this study will be on the use of quantitative and qualitative data and their associated methods of analysis in the evaluation of language teaching programs in general.

Several methods were identified for each of the two general approaches being investigated in this study. The basic research design for the quantitative approach used in this study is the nonequivalent control group (NECG) design. This was chosen because of the nature of the

1 This article represents a revised version of the following papers: 'Evaluating a Program Inside and Out', paper presented at the 20th Annual TESOL Convention, Anaheim, California, March 4, 1986; 'Using Qualitative Data in Program Evaluation', paper presented at the 13th National Convention of MEXTESOL, Toluca, Mexico, October 17, 1986; 'Evaluating a Program with Qualitative Data', paper presented at the 21st Annual TESOL Convention, Miami Beach, Florida, April 22, 1987.
2 The author wishes to give special thanks to Elizabeth Borkowski, Juan Carlos Gallego, Margarita Matte, Suzanne McMeans, Carlos Oceguera, and Alfredo Urzúa of the UdeG/ UCLA REST Project for their help with the data collection; to Dr Grant Henning and Dr Harold Levine of UCLA for their guidance in the research design and data analysis for this study; and to Dr Leigh Burstein, Dr Russell Campbell, and Dr Evelyn Hatch for their comments on earlier drafts of this article.

REST setting (primarily the inability to randomly select and assign to program and nonprogram conditions) and because it seems to be the most feasible design for the majority of educational program settings. Four basic techniques for analysing quantitative data (in this case, test scores) will be presented: analysis of covariance (ANCOVA), standardized change-score analysis, effect size analysis, and the Chi-Square test. The strengths and weaknesses of each will be discussed and the · results compared across the analyses.

The qualitative approach will be investigated using a combination of data gathering and analysis strategies that borrow features from three basic models: the illumination model, the transactional model, and the decision-making model. In the analysis of the qualitative data (in this case, interview transcripts, observation notes, journal entries and correspondence), various types of displays, or matrices, will be used to reduce and interpret the data.

Ultimately, this study will argue for the use of both the quantitative and qualitative approaches to program evaluation. An attempt will be made to show clearly the information that each approach has to offer program evaluators and, furthermore, how one approach can inform or extend the information provided by the other. Rather than a choice between the so-called objective evidence of quantitative evaluation and the so-called impressionistic evidence of qualitative evaluation, this study presents evidence in favor of a balanced approach which looks both inside the program, at the process, and out, at the product (cf. Long 1984).

Methods and procedures

Subjects and setting

The subjects for this study are 116 students, four teacher/researchers (T/Rs), three T/R assistants, two program coordinators (one of whom is the evaluator/author of this study) and several university professors and administrators associated with the UdeG/UCLA REST Project. The data will come from the first year of that project: August, 1985 to June, 1986.

The students were in their third year at the Chemical Sciences Faculty of the UdeG, with an academic major in Chemical Engineering. They ranged in age from 19 to 23 with an average age of 21. There were 86 males and 30 females.

The rationale for the REST Project came from extended negotiations between academic representatives of the UdeG's Center for Foreign Language Research and Development (CIDLE) and UCLA's TESL/ Applied Linguistics department in 1984. Following those negotiations, it was decided that the most important need for English as a foreign language at the university level in Mexico was the ability to read EST. The REST staff began to develop a curriculum to meet that need in June of 1985. The staff decided to focus on reading skills and strategies as the core of the curriculum.

Given this background information, the REST staff felt that a curriculum which was focused on reading skills would have a better chance of success than the traditional, four-skills course. Perhaps part of a reluctance to such a focus had been the unsatisfactory nature of its presentation in the classroom. In Mexico, reading instruction had, in the past, focused on word-for-word translation, which made the reading activity a slow, tedious, and ultimately unproductive one. Students were seldom taught how to obtain useful information from a reading, nor had they been presented with relevant, authentic reading texts. In order to counteract these past problems with reading instruction, the design of the REST curriculum began with a concern for motivating students with relevant, authentic reading materials as well as a concern for applying current reading theory to foreign language instruction.

The following represents an outline of the *modules* that was developed for the first year of the REST curriculum:

I   Introduction
    A Rationale for reading skills course
    B Organization for the course
II   Grammar review
III Previewing skills
    A Text survey – to form a quick, general idea of what the text is about (avoiding word-by-word reading)
      1 using the title, subtitles, pictures, diagrams, and physical layout of the text
      2 using cognates, repeated words, numbers, names, and dates
      3 prediction and hypothesis formation – using prior/background knowledge
IV   Text sampling – skimming for main ideas
    A Skimming for the main idea of the text
    B Skimming for the main idea of each paragraph
V   Scanning for specific information
VI   Text structure
    A Organizational layout (overall text)
    B Paragraph organization
    C Rhetorical functions and structures (definition, classification, process, cause and effect, etc.)

VII Comprehensive reading
    A Interactive reading (author–reader)
    B Inferencing
    C Identifying the author's point of view, tone, etc.
    D Critical reading

Originally, the REST curriculum was to be given to all Chemical Engineering and Pharmacobiology students as a required part of their Chemical Sciences course load. Later, the REST curriculum was changed to the status of an elective for Chemical Engineering students only – the status being changed by the Chemical Sciences administration and the REST staff electing to deal with only one academic major at the beginning of the Project (given the number of teacher/researchers available).

Thus, the students volunteered for the course, but were then committed to it for two years. They were, for the most part, highly motivated to learn English. However, they were apparently informed at the time they enrolled that the course was going to be a traditional EFL course with instruction in all of the 'four skills' (reading, writing, listening, speaking). This was not discovered by the REST staff until the first week of classes, when interviews were conducted with all students. At this point, a special lesson was prepared to explain the rationale for teaching reading only and the mismatch between student expectations and the REST curriculum became a central evaluation issue.

The project's setting was one of the Faculties of the UdeG, which is a 'state' university that is essentially free for all students. While this free or low cost enrollment encourages overcrowded classrooms, the student population has thinned out somewhat by the third year due to the rigors of university study. The Chemical Sciences Faculty, like the rest of the university, continues to have a 'space problem', with large class sizes and scheduling that includes evening classes for the regularly enrolled university students. As a result, it was difficult to find classrooms for the REST Project and to match the availability of those classrooms with the course schedules of our students. The outcome for this difficulty was that there were four classes – two at the hour of 1–2 and two at the following hour of 2–3 at the beginning of instruction, September, 1985. There were 40 and 41 students during the first hour, while only 17 and 18 per class during the second hour. At the beginning of our second 'term', five months after the start of classes in February, 1986, an additional classroom became free during the first hour and the two original classes were each reduced by one third in size (to 28 and 29, with 24 in the new class).

For the first term (five months) each class was 'team taught', a new teaching experience for everyone involved. The primary reason for this was that the students were sufficiently low in their level of English proficiency that instruction in Spanish was considered necessary for anywhere from 50 to 90 per cent of the time at the beginning of the program. It was therefore decided to have each team be made up of one native Spanish-speaker and one native English-speaker since neither of the two native English-speakers felt comfortable with teaching in Spanish.

During the second term, the addition of an extra class and the loss of the Mexican T/R required certain teaching assignment changes. For the most part, the classes were taught by single teachers. One UCLA T/R (native speaker of English) was aided by a T/R assistant and the other UCLA T/R – a native speaker of English – received only occasional assistance from native Spanish-speaking staff.

From September, 1985 to February, 1986 the REST T/Rs were able to cover the first five 'modules' (I to V, above) and part A of module VI. Based on the experience of the first term the staff decided to give the students more help with their basic language skills (grammar and vocabulary in context) in order to prepare them for module VII: comprehensive reading. Instruction focused on such grammatical points as passives, *-ed* and *-ing* forms and their functions, identifying the main verb and subordinate clauses, and logical connectors. These instructional points were incorporated into the reading of authentic chemical engineering texts that were being used in the students' other courses. The REST staff was guided in the selection and understanding of these materials by the Academic Coordinator (a chemical engineering professor employed part time by the project) and other members of the Chemical Engineering department. Work was also done on building subtechnical vocabulary of the type that occurred in the chemical engineering texts. In addition, the reading skills of previewing and skimming were recycled and part C of module VI, rhetorical functions, was taught. The REST staff decided to present the comprehensive reading module during the second year of the course.

Data collection

OVERVIEW

In order to investigate both the traditional, experimental or quantitative approach and the naturalistic or qualitative approach to program evaluation, both types of data were collected. The quantitative data were collected using a *quasi-experimental* (QE), *non-equivalent control group* (NECG) with pretest and posttest design (see Cook and Campbell 1979). The experimental or treatment group in this design consisted of the REST students (n=116) and the control group consisted of a group of volunteer students at the same faculty (Chemical Sciences) and in the same year (third) as the REST students but whose major was Pharmacobiology (n=61). The qualitative data were collected using a combination of models from the qualitative evaluation literature, limited to those which do not require an outside evaluator who is unfamiliar with the program.

THE QUANTITATIVE DATA

The major concern for quantitative data collection is the proper choice of a test or other instrument for measuring or quantifying the underlying construct or constructs that determine student achievement in the program. Many researchers feel that *standardized tests* (generally referring to published, *norm-referenced* (NRM) tests) are totally inappropriate for the evaluation of specific educational programs due to their insensitivity to the instruction and learning which has occurred (see Beretta 1986). The need for tests that are 'sensitive to instruction' has been the rallying cry of educators in favor of *criterion-referenced measurement* (CRM) and *domain-referenced measurement* (DRM) for some time (Hively *et al.* 1973; Popham 1978), particularly in the context of language for specific purposes programs (Bachman 1981).

There are, however, convincing arguments for considering the use of NRM tests in program evaluation, especially when used in conjunction with *teacher-made* tests (Sax 1974). NRM tests, for the purposes of evaluation, allow for references beyond the specific program or programs being evaluated or compared. Discovering that the experimental program group performs better than the 'traditional' program group will not necessarily mean that the experimental program was effective. Both programs may be ineffective, with the experimental one being statistically better than the traditional. Being able to reference the test scores to the external norms would yield more information regarding the effect of the program by allowing for comparisons with other, proven programs. The groups and programs should, of course, be comparable, and the test should be relevant, in general, to the curriculum or program objectives. Another important advantage of NRM tests is that they tend to be more *reliable*, in the classical test theory sense of the term, than teacher-made or CRM tests. This factor is important when considering the negative effects that unreliable test instruments have on the internal, statistical conclusion validity of experimental and quasi-experimental (QE) research designs for program evaluation.

In order to carefully address these measurement issues in the context of the REST Project evaluation, both NRM and CRM tests were used to gather the quantitative data. The *English as a Second Language Placement Exam (ESLPE), Form A, 1985* was selected as the NRM test for the evaluation. A fill-in-the-blank cloze test with an every seventh word deletion pattern was developed as an alternative NRM test. A multiple-choice cloze test with a rational deletion pattern was developed to serve as a CRM test (see Appendix p. 350 for test instruments).

The ESLPE, forms of which are currently in use at UCLA, was chosen as the NRM test for the quantitative data collection primarily because it was the only reliable and valid instrument available to the Project at this time. The form which was used by the Project had been developed over the 1984–1985 UCLA academic year using the Rasch one-parameter logistic model. While this test primarily measures general ESL proficiency, it was developed within the context of English for academic purposes, to reflect the UCLA ESL curriculum. Since the REST Project's reading skills approach is similar to the objectives of the UCLA curriculum, it was felt that meaningful comparisons concerning student progress could be attempted. These comparisons would be aided by the fact that the UCLA audience and the REST staff were familiar with the types of students and their proficiency levels at the various points along the placement continuum described by the ESLPE.

The test is composed of five subparts – Listening (20 items), Reading (18 items), Grammar (20 items), Vocabulary (20 items), and Writing Error Detection (20 items). Due to a problem with the listening audio-tape during the September, 1985 administration, only ten items (one passage) from the Listening subtest were used in this analysis, resulting in 88 total items. In previous administrations at UCLA, internal consistency reliability for the test measurements was estimated at .95 to .96 using the Kuder–Richardson 20 formula. Evidence for the validity of the test comes from correlational studies with the Test of English as a Foreign Language (TOEFL) as the criterion measure (Chen 1986) and from factor analyses which indicated that the subparts are measuring the same underlying construct (Davidson 1985; Lynch 1985).

In addition, a fill-in-the-blank cloze test was developed to gather quantitative data for the program evaluation. While a cloze test may seem more closely related to reading ability than a battery of subtests like the ESLPE, some would still classify the test as a 'general proficiency' measure, lacking in *authenticity* and face validity (e.g. Spolsky 1985:188). The fact that fill-in-the-blank cloze tests also require language *production* means that they can *not* be considered as measures of reading independent from other skills such as writing. However, as an alternative NRM test, it was felt that an instrument like the cloze would be useful to the Project. The fill-in-the-blank cloze test was constructed using a pseudo-random deletion pattern of every seventh word, resulting in 30 deletions/test items. The text was titled 'Planet X', an article on astronomy taken from *Omni* magazine. After an item analysis of the February, 1986 data, some of the deletions were changed and the resulting test was given in May, 1986.

In an effort to develop a reliable test that would eliminate the need for production and would serve as a CRM test by more closely reflecting the elements of reading taught in the REST course, a *multiple-choice* (MC) cloze test with a rational deletion pattern was developed. The words deleted were logical connectors, pronouns and demonstratives involving inter-sentential reference, main nouns and verbs. The nouns and verbs were chosen to reflect either subtechnical vocabulary taught in the course or words that could be guessed through context. The alternatives were selected from Spanish cognates or words otherwise familiar to the REST students. The original version of the MC cloze (given in February, 1986) gave the four alternatives in Spanish for every other blank. There were two forms: one with alternatives in Spanish for the odd-numbered blanks and the other with alternatives in Spanish for the even-numbered blanks. This version was revised for the May test administration to have all MC alternatives in English.

The ESLPE (UCLA, Form A, 1985) and the fill-in-the-blank cloze were given to the REST students (n=111) in September of 1985, before the REST Course began. The ESLPE was also given to the control group in September, 1985. The ESLPE was administered a second time, after four months of instruction, to both the REST group (n=103) and the control group (n=54) in February, 1986. It was administered again, in May, 1986 to the REST students only (n=101).

The fill-in-the-blank cloze test was administered to the REST Students for the second time in February, 1986 (n=108), and again in a revised form in May, 1986 (n=95). As noted above, the MC cloze was administered to the REST students in February, 1986 (n=107) and in a revised form in May, 1986 (n=105). The control group received the fill-in-the-blank cloze test and the MC cloze test only in May, 1986 (n=40).

The control group received only the ESLPE in September and February due to the volunteer nature of their participation in this research. It was felt that they could only be asked to take one test during each administration, partly because of the difficulty in scheduling time and classrooms. When, in May, the cloze tests had been developed to the point that they were demonstrating acceptable reliability with the REST students, the ESLPE was dropped in favor of the two cloze tests. This meant, however, that only the ESLPE data could be used in analyses that required the same pretest and posttest for both the Treatment and Control Groups (see Data Analysis section).

TABLE I TEST ADMINISTRATIONS, REST AND CONTROL GROUP

	September 1985	February 1986	May 1986
ESLPE	REST (n = 111) Control (n = 61)	REST (n = 103) Control (n = 54)	REST (n = 101)
Fill-in Cloze *revised version	REST (n = 111)	REST (n = 108)	*REST (n = 95) *Control (n = 40)
MC Cloze *revised version		REST (n = 107)	*REST (n = 105) *Control (n = 40)

THE QUALITATIVE DATA

The issue of measurement is fundamentally different in qualitative research and evaluation and in the quantitative approach. Rather than developing test instruments in order to quantify the variables or constructs being studied, qualitative research tends to rely on people as the instruments of inquiry. The trained observer replaces the pencil-and-paper test as the primary measurement tool. This type of measurement results in problems which tend to threaten the credibility of qualitative research. The problems are primarily related to the concept of *reliability*, while one of the major strengths of qualitative research is its *validity* (LeCompte and Goetz 1982). Several researchers have offered suggestions for guarding against threats to reliability and for answering the criticisms of subjectivity in qualitative research (Patton 1980; Miles and Huberman 1984).

Drawing upon these recommendations for the gathering of qualitative data, the REST Project evaluation made use of journal entries, daily logs, observations, meeting notes, questionnaires, and interviews. These were organized into two basic *files*: the *Treatment File* and the *Administrative File*, each of which consisted of several subfiles.

The Treatment File   All of the Teacher/Researchers (T/Rs) and Teacher/Researcher Assistants working on the REST Project were required to keep a daily journal describing what happened in their classroom(s). A format was developed over the first months of the Project which each T/R fills out and turns in each day (see Figure 1). In addition to allowing the REST staff to keep track of the curriculum as it was developing – the 'module', the materials used, the type of activities and exercises – this source of data described the process of curriculum implementation and offered the T/Rs' reactions to, and characterizations of, the program.

NAME: DATE: 1-24-86

Curriculum Module/Objectives	LESSON EVENTS		Material/Media
	Teacher Presentations	Student Participation	
Text Structure	CLASS I. T1 shows Ss text only from p.51 & has them read it, looking for main ideas & the type of text (classif.)	Ss decide it's classif.	RAM, PP. 51–52
understand par. of function & physical description; relationship between text & diagram	T1 then asks Ss what words in text indicate physical desc. or desc. of function.	Some Ss come up to OHP to fill-in the blanks, giving the pen to a new person to answer.	OHP
	T1 explains unknown words & then goes over the exercise at bottom of pg. T2 has Ss read paragraph on p.52 & then has Ss answer chart from that page.	Ss say which part of the eye has given function.	
	(For Class IV, over)		SPAN/ENGL % 13:00–14:00 SPAN = 80 ENGL = 20 14:00 –15:00 50/50

COMMENTS/OBSERVATIONS
Today, like yesterday, was strange because we did completely different things in the 2 classes. We decided to do the exercise from Class IV yesterday today because they were the ones who had originally asked to see the examples. They weren't pleased when we told them that the (over)

Figure 1: Teacher/Researcher Journal

DATE: March 19, 1986   OBSERVER: Brian
TIME: 2:00-3:00   NO. OF STUDENTS: 14
TEACHER: CLASSROOM: Aula 20

CONTENT/LESSON EVENTS

2:13 - Text from students' math class is presented on OHP; students were assigned the test as homework; T. presents 'my outline', warning students that theirs may be different because of their familiarity with the content.*

The objective of the lesson seems to be to outline the structure of the text: introduction, main ideas/points, supporting info; and to locate connectors and determine their function.

After presenting her outline of the text, T. asks students for theirs (all of this has been presented in English, so far, with students responding in Spanish); one student comments on one part of the text (I don't quite hear or follow what he is saying), but it seems to wind up that he agrees with T's outline/analysis; another student also volunteers comment (in Spanish) on this part of the text: at times there seem to be differences of interpretation of the text between some of the students.

2:32 - T. goes through the text pointing out connectors (practice for tomorrow's quiz): *so that, however, since, thus, and, however, similarly, or, when, whereas, hence.* These are explained/comprehension checked primarily by translating them into their Spanish equivalents, but also by T. mentioning that certain connectors signal certain functions, e.g., a conclusion, a relation to a preceding idea, a contradiction.

T. points out that in this text, there is often a series of math equations joined only by connectors - important to understand their meaning.
2:45 - T. explains tomorrow's quiz.
2:53 - Class ends.

COMMENTS/OBSERVATIONS

* good use of OHP - the text structure is clearly marked in different colors - excellent way to discuss text.

I would have been curious to know how many of them felt they could understand the text (and to what degree) without reading the English. Along these lines, it was interesting that some admitted the text would have been difficult even if it were written in Spanish. Perhaps there could be a HW assignment where they write down or mark the parts of the text where their comprehension breaks down and why (language or concept or both?). The problem is, of course, that many students seem to habitually fail to do the HW. I think we need to discuss/explore ways of getting them to take more responsibility for doing their HW (electric-shock comes to mind), so that

Figure 2:   Observation form

Figure 2 (cont.)

there can be more participation in class, e.g., have individual students come to OHP (have several unmarked text transparencies available) and explain their 'outline' of the text's structure.

A question I had about the example phrasal verbs you showed them for the quiz: all of the sentences/contexts seemed to be non-science – was this by design? Were phrasal verbs chosen because they are important for scientific discourse ? I guess these are naive questions, but the reason I'm trying to observe more often when I have the time is to try and get a better sense of where we're at. I realize it would be more helpful to be giving you answers (instead of more questions) but first I need to become clearer about what's going on 'in the trenches'.

I liked the way you brought information from your previous class (student comments on the meaning of certain equations and their interpretation of the resulting organization of the text) into this discussion, and I thought you did a very clear presentation of your text structure outline. The presentation of the connectors was excellent and should be very helpful to the students.

REACTIONS FROM T/Rs

Brian – This class was a bit unusual in that I did most of the talking . . . this was in great part due to the fact that most of the students had not done their homework, which is a constant problem. I don't know how we can resolve the problem . . . I've already told them that participation counts a lot, but most of them don't really care.

About the phrasal verbs . . . this was an aside. A couple of students had asked me about them and I decided to present something. P.M.'s book has no p.v.s, so I took what I could find in Azar. My idea was to present the concept so that when we encounter p.v.s in one of our texts, I can address it directly. (for example: 2 days ago, in a Heat Transfer text, we saw 'setting up'). This is something that's been done only in this class.

DAILY LOG: REST PROJECT

Monday, April 7 1986   Brian

EVENTS	BRIEF DESCRIP.	EX. DES.	SUBJ. IMPRESSIONS
1. Meeting w/ Carlos & Alfredo	Discussed lesson plan for today.	NO	We need to find a more comfortable way of helping them with their planning; seemed awkward; hard to tell how much guidance or in class help they want.
2. Meeting w/ Alvarez	See Meeting Subfile.	YES	Quick and successful except for class times not being arranged – vacations slowed everything up.
3. Work on Treatment File	Trying to get a description of what's been done second term.	NO	Very interesting to go through the journals – lots of info, but how to organize? Also time consuming.
4. Trip to CIDLE	Picked up checks; Turned in AF letter to PH.	NO	New office design seems quieter; good relations with most of staff, still.
5. Trip to USIS	Met J. Roney informally, set up formal appt. 4/15; got Fulbr. travel info from Iceland.	NO	

Overall comments and observations
Everyone seemed in good spirits following the two-week vacation; a
little difficult to get back in the swing of things however. I felt like
I had a full and productive day. The new USIS director seems nice
enough; a little distracted at this time as he is still settling in.
Rumor today from several sources that the Universidad has no money –
IA said that the work on the new classroom building has been postponed.

Figure 3:   Administrative Daily Log

This format also served as a communication link between the T/Rs and the Project coordinators.

The *T/R Journal Subfile*, then, was kept in chronological sequence in a three-ring binder, which also contained classroom observations conducted by the REST coordinators, the *Observation Subfile*. The format for the observations (see Figure 2, pp. 71–2) was also the result of a trial-and-error development process over the course of the first months of the project. It gave another description of the implementation of the program at the classroom level, from a non-participant observer's point of view, as well as allowing for a 'dialogue' between the observer and teacher (the 'Reactions from T/R to Observation Comments' section) concerning the class and lesson. The observer normally took extensive notes and then wrote up the observation using the format at a later time.

The Administrative File   The REST Project coordinators also kept daily journals. In the case of the UCLA coordinator, the journal was kept in a *Daily Log* format which is a subfile of the Administrative File (see Figure 3). This subfile created a relatively thorough listing of the major events in the life of the Project, as well as subjective comments and general observations concerning 'how things are going'. A key feature of this format is the cross-referencing to other subfiles and data sources.

The other major section of the Administrative File is the *Meetings Subfile*. This subfile contains notes from all Project related meetings taken by the coordinators. The notes were typed up from handwritten 'field notes' taken during the course of each meeting.

Two related sources of data are *interviews* and *questionnaires*. For the evaluation of the REST Project, these were kept as separate 'subfiles', technically under the Administrative File.

Interviews were conducted at two different times during the year with the students and once at the end of the year with the T/Rs. In the case of the students, the interviews were *not* recorded because the coordinators were worried about intimidating students any more than they already seemed to be. The interviews were conducted in Spanish and the data come from extensive notes taken by the coordinators. The student interviews were unstructured in the sense that the coordinators asked very general questions for the most part (e.g. 'How do you like the course so far?') and tried to get the students to tell us whatever they had to say about the program in their own words. The students were representatives from each class, chosen by the students and it was the impression of the T/Rs and the coordinators that there was a reasonably good mix of personalities and student types (e.g. 'leaders' and 'followers'). During the second set of student interviews the T/Rs selected five to six students from each of their classes to represent the range of EFL proficiency and REST class motivation and attitude (i.e. they included good students and weak students, students with positive attitudes and others with negative attitudes towards the REST course). The guideline list of topics for the interviews was based on issues that had arisen in the T/R journals, class observations, and staff meetings since the time of the first interviews.

The interviews with the T/Rs were tape-recorded in addition to notes being taken. Before the interviews, at their request, the T/Rs were given a list of topics to be covered. This list served as a guide, but was not followed in any particular order and questions that were not part of the topic list did arise during the course of the interviews. For the most part, the T/Rs spoke naturally and spontaneously about the Project, although they had obviously given the issues involved some thought.

Questionnaires are not always considered to be sources of *qualitative* data. Especially when the questions are to be answered on some sort of a rank-ordered scale, the researcher is obviously forcing the data into pre-existing categories. However, when the questions are general and open-ended enough, the resuiting data begin to resemble what people actually say in response to such questions during interviews. For the purposes of the qualitative analysis of the REST Project, only four questions from the questionnaire were used: 'What is your personal understanding of the objectives of the REST Project?', 'What do you think the strengths of the REST Project are/were?' 'What do you think the weaknesses of the REST Project are/were?' and 'Do you have any suggestions for the improvement of the Project?' These questionnaires were completed by the REST staff at the beginning (August 1985) and the end (June 1986) of the first year of the project.

The issues of validity and reliability were primarily addressed through the use of multiple data sources: the T/R journals, administrative daily logs, classroom observations which included responses from the T/R being observed, interviews and meeting notes. In addition, the journal format was changed based on suggestions from the T/Rs in order to encourage more and better information, and the interview formats were kept as open-ended as possible to encourage the informants to express their perceptions of the program in their own words. Finally, with its fairly detailed and explicit system of data collection, the replicability of the present study is enhanced.

As a related notion, *reactivity*, or the effect of the evaluator/observer on the research setting and vice versa, must be considered as a genuine threat to the validity and reliability of the study. In order to minimize the effects of this threat, the researcher held regular individual talks with all staff members. In these talks, the researcher was able to check his impressions of the data with several different points of view. It seems likely, however, that reactivity is a greater problem with respect to the student interview data. To guard against this threat the coordinators emphasized the anonymous nature of the interview data, assuring the students that the T/Rs would only receive general summaries of student opinion and reactions to the program.

Data analysis

OVERVIEW

All tests were scored and analysed using the SPSSPC+ statistical package on a COMPAQ PLUS personal computer. Four different quantitative analyses were carried out: analysis of covariance (ANCOVA), standardized change-score analysis, effect size analysis and the Chi-square test.

The qualitative data were 'reduced' through a series of steps that included the development of a thematic framework, coding of the data, and the entering of selected data into displays (see Miles and Huberman 1984). These displays are in the form of matrices that present the qualitative data in a spatial format that is compressed and systematic, making it easier to examine the data for patterns and relationships. This was an iterative process, working from the data to the display and back to data, etc. The displays used in the evaluation of the REST Project Year 1 were: effects matrix, and site dynamics matrix. These displays were then further reduced through various techniques of interpretation, to be discussed in the Results section.

THE QUANTITATIVE DATA

In the case of the analysis of covariance, the ESLPE total score and ESLPE reading subtest score from the February administration were used as the posttest/dependent variable and the September pretest scores were used as the covariate (to adjust for possible pre-existing differences between the REST group and control group). In addition, the fill-in cloze and the MC cloze (the May administration) were used as posttests/dependent variables and the ESLPE September pretest as covariate.

The standardized change score analysis is an essentially correlational technique for estimating the effect of programs being evaluated with a QE design (Kenney 1975). If the treatment is having zero effect on the subjects in a group (experimental or control), then the relationship between group membership and performance on the tests should not change significantly from pretest to posttest. As with the ANCOVA analysis, the pretest and posttest used in the REST Project evaluation were the September and February administrations of the ESLPE. The fill-in-the-blank cloze and the multiple-choice cloze could not be used in this analysis because pretest and posttest data did not exist for the control group.

The effect size analysis is another approach involving change, or gain, score analysis (see Stallings, Needels and Staybrook 1979). This approach calculates an *effect size* based on a comparison of the means and standard deviations for gain scores between the treatment and control groups. The calculation is as follows:

effect size $= X_T - X_C/s_C$
where: X_T=Treatment group gain score mean;
        X_C=Control group gain score mean;
        s_C =gain score standard deviation, Control group

In this analysis, which is similar to the calculation of z-scores, an effect size of .5 standard deviation units is considered moderate and an effect size of 1.0 is considered good. The ESLPE was used as the dependent measure for this analysis, since it was the only test which had pretest and posttest results for both the treatment and control groups.

The Chi-square test can be used to test for the effect of a program when the requirements for parametric statistical tests cannot be met. This involves a two-by-two Chi-square table in which the dependence between treatment (experimental group, control group) and gain (positive change-score, negative or zero change-score, on the dependent or outcome variable) is tested. If a dependence exists, this is an indication that the treatment has had an effect (Henning 1987). The data for the Chi-square test are entered as frequencies: how many subjects in the experimental group had a positive change-score, etc. In the REST Project evaluation, the two variables being tested for dependence were experimental group membership (REST versus Control) and change in EFL ability (positive change-score on the ESLPE from September to February, and negative or zero change-score on the ESLPE from September to February). Change-scores on both the ESLPE total score, the ESLPE Reading subtest, and the ESLPE Reading and Vocabulary subtests (composite score) were examined in this analysis.

THE QUALITATIVE DATA

The qualitative data for the REST Project evaluation were analysed following a methodology presented in Miles and Huberman (1984). The first step is the development of a *thematic or conceptual framework*. This is, essentially, a list of the major dimensions, or variables, to be studied. The researcher goes through the data in an effort to induce certain recurring themes and concepts. The conceptual framework which was developed for the REST Project evaluation focused on the following:
1 Program goals
2 Program processes
3 Events
4 Setting
5 Participants
6 Outcomes

Within this framework, more specific themes, or issues begin to emerge as the data are examined and the researcher begins to *code* the data – either in the margins of the transcripts and notes or on a separate sheet of paper with the extracted quotes or references from the original data source. For the REST Project evaluation, examples of the more specific themes/issues were:

1 Explicit grammar instruction versus reading skills
2 The use of English versus Spanish for instruction
3 Team teaching

As with every stage of qualitative data collection and analysis, the coding of the data is an *iterative* process, which is to say that it requires a continuous revision of both the codes and the thematic framework as the researcher works back and forth between the data and the list of themes. Some examples of the codes used in the REST Project evaluation are:

1 CLASSRM PROC (classroom process) – this code would sometimes be associated with sub-codes, such as:
1a GRAM/READ (the use of explicit grammar instruction versus reading skills)
1b AUTH MAT'S (the use of authentic materials)
2 S ATT/MOT (student attitude and motivation) – this code was sometimes combined with another.

The iterative nature of the process continues as the researcher moves on to the next stage of data reduction: *display* construction. *Displays* are charts and matrices which rearrange the data into ordered lists and categories of a single visual unit (this means getting it onto *one page*, regardless of how large that page needs to be).

The *Effects Matrix* is used to characterize the various outcomes and changes associated with the program. This matrix can be sorted in a number of different ways: focusing on different parts of one particular outcome such as organizational change within a school or program; sorting the outcomes or changes by degree of directness such as primary changes intended by the program versus secondary or 'spinoff' changes that were not anticipated.

The Effects Matrix for the REST Project evaluation focused on ultimate, end-of-year outcomes of the program implementation, categorizing these effects into three types/columns in the matrix: *Objectives/Goals* (what was accomplished), *Process/Methods* (how was it accomplished), and *Relations/Climate* (how did the program partici-pants, T/Rs and Students, interrelate; what was the social climate like?). Furthermore, the matrix was sorted into rows which represented these outcomes from various points of view within the Project: the *UdeG Coordinator*, the *UdeG T/R Assist's*, the *UCLA T/Rs*, and the *Students* (further differentiated by their English class 'level' and Chemical Sciences 'grupo'). The *decision-rule* for entering data into the matrix was to select any outcome mentioned by at least one person. If the outcome was positive, it was preceded by a plus sign (+) and if more than one person mentioned the outcome it was preceded by two pluses (++). A negative outcome was noted with a minus sign (−) or two minuses (−−) if mentioned by more than one person. An outcome that was mentioned by one or more persons but contradicted by another or others receives a question mark (?) (see the Results section for an example display).

The final display used in the REST Project evaluation is the *Site Dynamics Matrix*. This matrix attempts to address the question that follows from the Effects Matrix: '*Why* did these outcomes occur?' It does this by displaying the links between program outcomes or effects with the processes or aspects of the program that lead to those effects. First, events or situations that seem to set other things in motion for the program are identified. Next, the underlying theme or themes are searched for. Finally, the process of responding to these driving events or situations is described.

The focus decided upon for this matrix was the events or situations in the data that could be depicted as *dilemmas* or *problems* since these types of events seemed to be key to the dynamics of the first year of the Project. The dilemmas/problems that were chosen for the matrix were those that seemed to have the greatest impact on the project, based on the perceptions of the researcher and their frequency of mention in the data. An attempt was also made to clarify the nature of the dilemma/problems by describing their *underlying theme(s)* or *issue(s)*. At times the underlying theme is described as an interaction with other dilemmas in the matrix. For each dilemma/problem, the researcher attempted to identify the initial coping strategy ('*how coped with*') and the ultimate outcome ('*resolution/change*'). This categorization results in a great deal of overlap in the matrix. As previously mentioned, one dilemma/problem can become the underlying theme for another dilemma/problem, and certain coping strategies are used for more than one dilemma. However, these overlaps can be instructive when proceeding to the next phase of data analysis: interpreting the matrix. This phase (and the example display) will be presented in the Results section.

Results

THE QUANTITATIVE DATA

The ESLPE results for both the REST group and the control group are summarized in Tables 2–4. It should be noted that the control group was a 'control' in the classical sense of *no* treatment. That is, they received *no* instruction in English. In essence, this amounts to comparing the REST curriculum (as a treatment) to the absence of a treatment. The REST group appears to be better than the control group from the start (i.e. in September). These differences were found to be *not significant* for the Total test (t=1.74, α=.05, 170), but *significant* for the Reading subtest (t=2.68[*], α=.05, 170).

TABLE 2 ESLPE DESCRIPTIVE STATISTICS

| | September 1985 | | February 1986 | | May 1986 |
	REST	(Control)	REST	(Control)	REST
Mean	32.89	30.22	41.73	33.85	43.86
s	10.26	8.16	8.97	8.40	8.39
n	111	61	103	54	101
k	88	88	88	88	88
K-R21	.814	.710	.736	.713	.696

TABLE 3 ESLPE READING SUBTEST DESCRIPTIVE STATISTICS

| | September 1985 | | February 1986 | | May 1986 |
	REST	(Control)	REST	(Control)	REST
Mean	8.68	7.39	11.59	8.59	12.29
s	2.91	3.16	2.62	2.85	2.52
n	111	61	103	54	101
k	18	18	18	18	18
K-R21	.497	.597	.422	.474	.409

TABLE 4 'PLANET X' CLOZE TEST RESULTS

| | September 1985 | February 1986 | [*]May 1986 | |
	REST	REST	REST	(Control)
Mean	4.01	5.53	8.14	2.75
s	3.97	4.78	5.77	2.64
n	107	107	95	40
k	30	30	30	30
K-R21	.81	.83	.85	.66

(s=standard deviation; n=number of students; k=number of test items; K-R21=reliability estimate; [*]May 1986=revised test)

TABLE 5 MULTIPLE-CHOICE CLOZE TEST RESULTS

	February 1986 REST	*May 1986* REST	(Control)
Mean	13.42	15.12	9.73
s	3.82	4.62	3.25
n	107	104	40
k	25	25	25
K-R21	.60	.75	.46

(s=standard deviation; n=number of students; k=number of test items; K-R21=reliability estimate; *February, 1986=1/2 Spanish items; *May, 1986=all English items)

ANCOVA The results of the ANCOVA showed that the REST group performed significantly better than the control group on the ESLPE posttest, while controlling for differences in pre-program ability as measured by the ESLPE pretest. This was true when looking at both total test scores and reading subtest scores (see Table 6).

TABLE 6 ANALYSIS OF COVARIANCE — ESLPE TOTAL (FEBRUARY, 1986) BY TREATMENT GROUP

Source of Variation	Sum of Squares	DF	Mean Square	F	Signif.[a]
Covariate –					
ESLPE Pretest	8733.896	1	8733.896	311.848	.000
(September, 1985)					
Main Effects –					
Treatment	1062.974	1	1062.974	37.954	.000
Explained	9796.870	2	4898.435	174.901	0.0
Residual	4173.025	149	28.007		
Total	13969.895	151	92.516		

[a]The *alpha level* for all statistical tests performed on the REST data was set at .05. The actual probability values, which are all considerably less than .05, are reported in the tables.

ANCOVA was also performed using the fill-in-the-blank cloze and the multiple-choice cloze tests as the dependent measures and the ESLPE pretest as the covariate. Again, after adjusting for pre-existing differences in ESL ability, the REST group's performance was significantly better than that of the control group (see Tables 7 and 8).

TABLE 7 ANALYSIS OF COVARIANCE – 'PLANET X' CLOZE
(MAY, 1986) BY TREATMENT GROUP

Source of Variation	Sum of Squares	DF	Mean Square	F	Signif.[a]
Covariate –					
ESLPE Pretest	2068.127	1	2068.127	187.849	.000
(September, 1985)					
Main Effects –					
Treatment	456.717	1	456.717	41.484	.000
Explained	2524.844	2	1262.422	114.667	0.0
Residual	1332.148	121	11.009		
Total	3856.992	123	31.358		

TABLE 8 ANALYSIS OF COVARIANCE – MC CLOZE
(MAY, 1986) BY TREATMENT GROUP

Source of Variation	Sum of Squares	DF	Mean Square	F	Signif.[a]
Covariate –					
ESLPE Pretest	1223.029	1	1223.029	111.592	.000
(September, 1985)					
Main Effects –					
Treatment	631.537	1	631.537	57.623	.000
Explained	1854.566	2	927.283	84.6070	.0
Residual	1490.542	136	10.960		
Total	3345.108	138	24.240		

Standardized change-score analysis   Like the ANCOVA, the results of the standardized change-score analysis revealed that the REST program had a significant effect on the students. The null hypothesis of no treatment effect (that the correlation of pretest and treatment group was equal to the correlation of posttest and treatment group) was rejected (see Table 9).

TABLE 9 STANDARDIZED CHANGE-SCORE ANALYSIS

Null Hypothesis: $^rX_2T = {}^rX_1T$ (X_2 = Posttest; X_1 = Pretest; T = Treatment)

| For Total ESLPE: | $^rX_2T = .3897$ | Hotelling's t-statistic = 5.17* |
| | $^rX_1T = .1478$ | (for difference between correlation coefficients) |

| For ESLPE Reading Subtest: | $^rX_2T = .4566$ | |
| | $^rX_1T = .2104$ | Hotelling's t = 3.40* |

* = significant at $\alpha = .05$

Effect size analysis The results from the effect size analysis differed somewhat from those of the ANCOVA and standardized change-score analyses. Here, while the *effect size* for the REST program using total ESLPE as the dependent measure was considered 'good', the *effect size* using the reading subtest as dependent measure was only 'moderate' (see Table 10).

TABLE 10 EFFECT SIZE ANALYSIS

Effect Size $= \bar{X}_T - \bar{X}_c / s_c$
(T = Treatment; C = Control; s = standard deviation; X = group mean on *Change-Scores*)

| ESLPE Total | (change score) : | Effect Size = .92 std. dev. units |
| ESLPE Reading | „   „   : | Effect Size = .54 std. dev. units |

Chi-square analysis The results of the Chi-square analysis were similar to those of the effect size analysis. While there was a dependence shown to exist between treatment group and gain versus no gain on the total ESLPE (see Table 11), the treatment group variable was shown to be independent of gain on the reading subtest (see Table 12).

TABLE 11 CHI-SQUARE ANALYSIS — TREATMENT VS. TOTAL
ESLPE GAIN

		NO GAIN	GAIN	Row Total
	CONTROL	16	37	53
	REST	8	91	99
Column Total		24	128	152

Chi-Square = 11.08077*, Significance = .0009
*using the Yates Correction factor for degrees of freedom equal to 1; all
cells with expected frequencies greater than or equal to five

TABLE 12 CHI-SQUARE ANALYSIS — TREATMENT VS.
READING GAIN

		NO GAIN	GAIN	Row Total
	CONTROL	48	5	53
	REST	88	11	99
Column Total		136	16	152

Chi-Square = .00191*, Significance = .9651
*using the Yates Correction factor for degrees of freedom equal to 1; all
cells with expected frequencies greater than or equal to five

THE QUALITATIVE DATA

The results of the qualitative data analysis are, properly, the displays
which were discussed in the Data Analysis section. However, they do not
come with preordained means for interpretation as the quantitative
analyses do. Thus, in addition to presenting the displays, the Qualitative
Data Results section will also present the techniques for interpreting
certain matrices which essentially involve a further reduction of the data.

First Year Outcomes of the UdeG/UCLA REST Project

AS SEEN BY	OBJECTIVES/GOALS	PROCESS/METHODS	RELATIONS/CLIMATE
UdeG Coord	+ A curriculum framework to improve Ss ability to read EST. − Ss did not 'master' anything just introduced to. − did *not* convince Ss that they don't need to read word-by-word.	+ Use grammar in context as a *strategy* for reading. + Use read. strat's, e.g., preview, prediction, skim, scan. + Teach functions of log. connectors; rhetorical modes. + Use authentic Chem. E. texts, but *not* exclusively.	+ (Coord) overall positive to Proj. + T/Rs hard workers − Cultural misunderstandings: T/Rs 'took it personally'. − Ss more demanding than most & 'a few bad apples'. − T/Rs 'frustrated' − T/Rs did *not* get along well as a group.
UdeG T/B Asst's	+ Interesting curric.; helpful to Ss.	+ Well supported mat'ls; prep'd well by UCLA T/Rs. − (REST) Too dependent on other Univ. Dept's − Problems w/classrms and schedules. − tedious classes; too much time spent on some points; excessive repetition. − need to allow more talking & listening in English & expand grammar module.	+ Good attitude – all T/Rs. − lack of communication: T/R Assts − lack of understanding (UCLA T/Rs) of Mex. S behavior.
UCLA T/Rs	++ S confidence to 'attack' Engl. texts + signif. improv't in gen. ESL prof., reading & grades in REST + Ss Chem. E. profs now expect them to read texts in Engl., w/o translations, and do 'practicas' based on readings. + basic elements of a curriculum. + Lots of ideas and info. for a thesis. − − Not enough time for research. − − Ss will *not* be 'prof. readers' of EST in 2 years. − 'we didn't do enough for them'. − not able to give real training to Mexican T/Rs.	+ Using *texts* as basis for grammar discuss. ++ Give Ss more basic linguistic skills. + Began to use more '4-skills' type activit's for reading. − Lack of mat'ls. − Lack of focus & organization. − Relied too much on theory; didn't know how to implement it. − 'A clump of strat's': did them w/ every text. − T/Rs hindered by need to all do same mat'l same way, same rate.	++ UCLA support. ++ Some staff members dedicated. − − Lack of UdeG admin. support. − − S resentment of Project & T/Rs. − REST staff 'not taken seriously or taken advantage of' ? Lack of cooperation between T/Rs (1 'yes', 2 'no'). − − Frustration.
Ss Group B/Begin	+ Were able to use some Chem. E. texts (sugg'std by C.E. prof's) in their 'practicas' – helped them. + Now we can use the *strategies* taught. + Overall, course help us 'bastante'	+ Use of the OHP. − Need a different system for understanding grammar. − At times, too much mat'l too fast: no time to take notes. + Read. strat's do help us w/ reading.	
Ss Group B/Adv	+ Used texts (Engl.) in our 'practicas'.	+ Use of OHP. − Read. *strat's* approach doesn't work: 'we *look* at articles but don't *read* them'. − Need a review of grammar. − Need more participation on part of Ss.	− At times, we feel a little bored.
Ss Group A/C Int.	+ Now we know how to form/write a sentence in Engl. − Nothing well-defined in the development of the course. − Very little covered first 1/2 year.	+ More grammar & vocab. (since Feb.). − 'going in circles': same basic activities. − Reading strat's 'a waste of time': already known. − 'Timed' factor on tests unfair.	− 'boring' − Lack of attend.: because not what expected/wanted: i.e., '4-skills' & bad schedule for Engl. class.
Ss Group A/C Begin	+ Did learn something, *not* a waste of time. − Didn't learn as much as possible/hoped. − Didn't know where curric. was heading.	− Too much grammar: don't understand how log. connect's help us to read. − Lack of *dynamism* in class activities: always T to S. − Not enough 'pressure' from Ts.	− Lack of motivation. − Lack of attend.: due to lack of interest and to bad schedule for Engl. class.

Figure 4:   Effects Matrix

Effects Matrix   In the interpretation of the Effects Matrix (see Figure 4) one technique is a simple counting of plus and minus signs in the matrix. As an example, even a quick visual scan of the REST matrix reveals certain trends: there are many more 'negative' outcomes under *process/ methods* than there are under *objectives/goals*. This suggests that while certain claims can be made for the program in defining or reaching positive goals, the ultimate outcomes for the ways in which those goals were approached need some reappraisal.

Another approach to interpreting the matrix is to scan for more specific difference patterns. For example, in the REST matrix the UdeG Coordinator notes many more positive outcomes than do the T/Rs with regard to *process/method*. Conversely, the Coordinator has fewer positive outcomes to note in terms of *objectives/goals* than the T/Rs. Another example is that the Students and the T/Rs seem to agree on essentially negative outcomes for *process/method*, however they disagree on what those negative outcomes were. While the UCLA T/Rs and one group of students (A/C Int.) seem to feel that a positive outcome was the use of more grammar instruction ('basic linguistic skills'), most of the students seem to feel that it was either the wrong 'system' (Group B/Begin.), not enough (Group B/ADV.) or 'too much' (Group A/C Begin.).

There also seems to be a difference pattern between the last two groups of students on the matrix (A/C) and the T/Rs concerning the *objectives/ goals*. The T/Rs (and Coordinator) seem to be in agreement that a curriculum 'framework,' or 'basic elements' which is 'interesting' has been put in place. The only student groups to comment directly on this point felt there was 'nothing well-defined', or that they 'didn't know where the curriculum was heading'.

A final difference pattern exists between the Group B/Begin. students and the other students. They directly mention that they now use the reading strategies taught and that they were effective for teaching reading. The other students either explicitly disagree with this or do not comment. More data on the differences between the student groups may be necessary to account for this pattern.

The Effects Matrix can also be interpreted by scanning for similarity patterns. One example in the REST matrix is the ability to use authentic English texts in their Chemical Engineering courses, which is seen as an important outcome by both the teachers and the students. This is all the more important an outcome since it was a part of the original objectives for REST.

Another example of a similarity pattern is that both the T/Rs and the students seem to agree that there was a certain 'lack of focus and organization' in the process/method of the REST course. Another similarity pattern is the perception that there was a 'lack of motivation' on the part of the students. While the reference to this lack of motivation and attendance does not appear as an 'ultimate outcome' for the T/Rs, it is heavily and continually referenced throughout their journals. Furthermore, from the UCLA Teacher's point of view, it seems to result in a feeling of 'resentment' on the part of the students. The UdeG staff members, T/R Assistants and Coordinator, characterize the outcome as a 'lack of understanding' with cultural differences as the cause.

A final similarity appears within the REST staff outcomes concerning *relations/climate*. Both the Coordinator and the T/Rs mention a lack of 'getting along' between the T/Rs. This issue is somewhat clouded by the fact that one of the three T/Rs felt that the ultimate outcome was one of cooperation and good working relations. The other two disagreed, as did the Coordinator. This outcome is the only one in the matrix listed with a '?'. A situation like this should send the researcher back into the data to attempt an interpretation. Going through the journal entries, one finds many references to arguments and major disagreements between the T/Rs. In fact, the original Mexican T/R left the Project partly as a result of this situation. After reviewing the relevant data in the journals and other sources such as the Daily Log and Meeting notes, it seems clear that there were major personality problems on the Project which adversely affected its development. It is interesting to note that the T/R who mentioned the social relations and climate as being positive tends to either refrain from mentioning particular incidents of group disagreement or to contradict the perceptions of the other participants.

Site Dynamics Matrix   By the time the Site Dynamics Matrix (see Figure 5, p. 89) has been filled in, a great deal of analysis and interpretation has already occurred. In order to determine the flow of entries across the rows of the matrix, the researcher must come to some understanding of the dynamics involved. This happens as a logical course of the movement back and forth between the data and the matrix that the construction requires. When the matrix is complete, the researcher can then look down the column of *resolution/changes* to see what type of outcomes seem to predominate. Using the REST Site Dynamics Matrix as an example, the interpretation would be that the changes seem to be predominantly in terms of procedures – splitting classes into levels, team teaching, grading policies – especially when considering the *how coped with* column as well.

Another way of interpreting the matrix is to scan for repeating and overlapping elements. For example, one repeated element in the REST matrix is that of *team teaching*. It seems to have been used as a coping strategy and resolution outcome in several instances. This suggests that it should be more closely studied as a critical event or key process in the development of the first year. It might be useful to plot references to this theme over time, from various points of view, and to try and link those references with other processes or events in the program.

A further example of a repeated element in the matrix is the word/concept of *lack* – 'lack of support', 'lack of classrooms', 'lack of attendance', 'lack of EFL proficiency'. At first this may seem an obvious fact of life for any educational project. However, a pattern begins to emerge here which is very important for this particular evaluation. The pattern is related to the first dilemma listed in the matrix: 'The REST curriculum was not what the students had expected.' When the original group of Chemical Engineering students signed up for the course, they were told by their faculty administration that it would be a 'four-skills English course'. There is no reasonable explanation for why this happened. The important thing, however, is that there was a mismatch between expectations and reality. Similarly, the various perceptions of 'lack' can be seen as this same mismatch. Most, if not all, the REST staff was expecting students with intermediate level proficiency in EFL, enough classrooms to have small class sizes, and unconditional support from the UdeG. The reality was that the students had, for the most part, forgotten any English they might have learned in high school and that the economic crisis in Mexico had made it difficult for the university to provide the kind of support for the Project which was originally intended.

Discussion

THE QUANTITATIVE DATA

There was, apparently, a positive effect on the part of the program, although it has already been pointed out that this may be saying nothing other than the program is better than no program at all. However, the significance of the performance of REST students in comparison to the control group, as indicated by the ANCOVA and the standardized change-score analysis is useful information to have. The effect size and Chi-square analyses support this interpretation of a strong program effect when considering general ESL proficiency.

However, when considering ESL reading proficiency, as measured by the ESLPE reading subtest, the effect size and Chi-square analyses contradict, to a certain degree, the results of ANCOVA and standardized change-score analysis. These analyses indicate that the improvement of the REST students in relation to the control group was either non-significant (Chi-square) or moderate (effect size). This may be entirely due to the unreliability of these sets of measurements (K-R 21 = .50 in September and .42 in February). Another possible explanation is that the REST students have not improved significantly in their ability to answer detailed questions concerning a short academic English passage (which is

The First Year of Curriculum Development for the REST Project.

DILEMMA/PROBLEM	UNDERLYING THEME(S)	HOW COPED WITH	RESOLUTION/ CHANGE
REST Curriculum not what Ss expected/wanted.	'Reading strategies approach' vs. traditional '4-skills';	Tried to 'win Ss over' to new appro; gradually moved to more grammar & vocab. while constantly recycling reading strategies (at times a feeling of not knowing how to put theory into practice).	Curriculum change: Focus on 'grammar in context', 1st year (decision that Ss need a minimum level of English before taking advantage of reading strats).
REST Ss' EFL proficiency level; a wide range & many 'false beginners'.	Need for grammar before read strategies; relationship of linguistic knowledge to reading.	Divided classes into 2 levels of prof.; eventually levels (1st hour classes); TEAM TEACHING; use of Spanish in class.	Rethink curriculum in terms of 2 levels of prof.
Lack of classrooms = class sizes too large.	Combined with 'prof. level' dilemma, above.	Pleaded for extra classrooms; tried to use group work and TEAM TEACHING to deal with size problems.	Given 1 extra room (Feb. '86): formed 3rd/'Int.' level (1st hr.); split one 'Team' to cover new class.
Lack of EFL prof. for most Ss makes use of Engl. for teaching reading strat's ineff.; 2/3 of UCLA Ts are not capable of 'teaching in Spanish'.	Combines with innovative, reading strats approach vs. grammar and relationship of ling. know. to reading; use of Engl. vs. Span. in the classrm.	TEAM TEACHING (1 Nat. Span. Speaker in each class); Use of more Span. than Engl. to start with; move to use more and more English.	UCLA Ts (non-nat. Span. speakers) became more confident of ability to use Span. in classrm. (by end of year); Ss became more confident about understanding Engl. in classrm.
Lack of S attendance.	S motivation & attitude; cultural differ's btwn UCLA T/Rs and Ss.	Allow/ask Ss to change 'levels'; individual 'talks' w/ Ss; formal roll call; referral of Ss not attending to Academic Adv.; 'talks' with Ss and REST coord's.	Creation of a grading policy that includes a 40% attend. & participation factor.
Bad relations between T/Rs and Ss; disc. problems in class	Interacts w/ attend. prob. & S mot/att. & mismatch btwn. REST & S expectations; cultural diff's.	Seating Chart (1 class) separate 'problem Ss'; referral of Ss to Academic Ad; individual 'talks' T to S; 'talks' betwn. REST Coord's and Ss.	Grading policy (see above); some Ss petition to leave program; no real solution.
Lack of cooperation betwn T/Rs; tension; arguments.	Group planning vs. indiv. plan; 'competition' betwn. teams & individuals.	Various group planning schemes. Individuals 'withdraw' from group; ignore/deny prob; individual 'talks' with REST coords.	Change TEAM TEACH. by splitting one 'team' into 2 individual Ts/class (relates to 3rd classrm avail); Mexican T/R leaves Project; no real resolution.
Cramped work/office space; lack of equip. & materials.	Lack of support from UdeG.	Reliance on extra help from UCLA; personal expend's; waiting for new work/office bldg.	No real solution; (new work/office bldg. still under construction); increased depend. on UCLA and indep. from UdeG.

Figure 5: Dynamics Matrix

what the ESLPE subtest seems to measure). These results are perhaps not so surprising: while the REST curriculum did work with academic reading texts, it did not deal with this type of reading. However, the REST curriculum does not deal with general ESL proficiency (including listening) either, and yet all forms of analysis indicate that the REST students outgained the control group on their general English proficiency, even when controlling for differences in pretest ability.

Another major problem with the quantitative approach in this study was the control group. These students were volunteers, who had no motivation for scoring well on the exam other than pride. Of course, this may have been true for the REST students, as well, since they knew they were not being 'graded' on their ESLPE performance. The control group was told, however, that by agreeing to take the exam they would be given preference for English classes to be given next year by members of the REST staff. As it turned out, even though one might have expected the volunteers to be those students who were confident in their English language ability, these students were not better than the REST group, and in fact were significantly lower (see Results section, Descriptive Statistics) in their reading subtest scores. The ANCOVA, of course, corrected for any pre-existing differences in ESL proficiency, but Campbell and Erlebacher (1970) feel that there will be an underestimation of the treatment effect (when the experimental group can be considered the less advantaged because the advantaged group is presumably growing at a faster rate – the *fan spread hypothesis*). In the case of the present study, the experimental group is the advantaged group, which would result in an overestimation of the treatment, presumably. However, Kenney (1975) claims that standardized change-score analysis takes care of this problem. In light of this, it is interesting to note that the ANCOVA and standardized change-score results agree.

In addition to the pre-existing differences between the groups, it should be noted that the control group received no English instruction whatsoever, not even traditional EFL classes. Thus, as a comparison group, they reduce the question of treatment effect to 'is the REST curriculum better than nothing?' A better comparison, perhaps, would be with a control group which is receiving some type of English instruction – a 'four skills' course at one of the private language institutes in Guadalajara, for example. If such a class, with similar background characteristics, could be identified, stronger statements concerning the success of the REST program could be made.

More important than the issue of the control group, perhaps, is the need for a better outcome measure to evaluate the REST program. What is needed is a measure of academic reading skills for EST such as the REST curriculum is focused on. Following Bachman (1981), it is hoped that the criterion-related measurement (CRM) achievement tests being developed by the staff can serve as such a measure in the future. As a beginning step in this direction, the results of ANCOVA using the multiple-choice cloze test (developed to reflect aspects of the REST curriculum) are encouraging. While the lack of pretest data precluded the possibility of using the gain score and Chi-square analyses, ANCOVA with the MC cloze as dependent variable and ESLPE pretest as the covariate results in an interpretation similar to that using the ESLPE as outcome measure: the REST students appear to be outperforming the control group. In the case of the MC cloze test, the ability being measured is more closely related to reading FST than in the case of the ESLPE. It should also be noted that the fill-in-the-blank cloze test (a 'popular science' text) agreed with the ESLPE and MC cloze results.

An added benefit of using the NRM/type ESLPE as a dependent measure was that it allowed for comparisons beyond the REST setting to the UCLA setting. Rough equivalencies were formed based on the ESLPE scores of the REST students and the cut-scores for the various levels of the ESL Service Courses at UCLA. While these were admittedly rough approximations using percentages and do not form part of the quantitative analysis presented here, they were useful to the REST Project in terms of making general comparisons with an established English for Academic Purposes curriculum that would have not been possible with CRM tests alone.

THE QUALITATIVE DATA

In the Results section, various interpretations of the data displays were made. Some of these were expressed as tentative conclusions. For example, the reading strategies approach seems to have been negatively received, for the most part, by the students. The teachers appear to have changed their emphasis on these strategies to a greater focus on basic language skills as a result of the low EFL proficiency level of most students and their reaction to the strategies approach. There seemed to be fairly negative relations between the students and the teachers and problems of cooperation amongst the teachers. The outcomes which were seen as resolutions or changes in relation to various dilemmas or problems for the Project seem to have been predominantly procedural. Team teaching, in particular, was used as a coping strategy several times. This was in response to the need for teaching in Spanish and to cope with the large class sizes. It should be pointed out that the lack of cooperation amongst the teachers was primarily across teams, although there were also problems within teams at times. All in all, this was a problematic coping strategy that was ultimately dropped in order to create more classes and free up time for research.

Other tentative conclusions that can be drawn from the interpretation of the displays include the observation that the REST curriculum does *not* appear to have resulted in 'proficient readers of EST', nor does it appear to be capable of doing so at the end of two years. The REST curriculum *does* appear to have introduced its students to reading strategies and basic grammar and vocabulary skills necessary for efficient reading of EST texts. The teachers felt that the students were given a sense of confidence in their ability to 'approach' texts in English. The students, for the most part, felt that they did learn something, but it was not as much as they had hoped to.

In addition, certain conclusions regarding explanations for the various outcomes and changes began to emerge, especially from the Site Dynamics Matrix. The mismatch between expectations and reality appeared to be an explanation for many of the perceived dilemmas of the Project. One instance of that mismatch – the belief that there would be sufficient office space and the reality of extremely cramped working conditions – is a possible explanation for the negative T/R relations outcome.

One major flaw in the REST evaluation was that no qualitative data were gathered on the control group. There are data concerning their age, sex, and amount of previous study in English, but there is nothing comparable to the qualitative data collected for the REST students concerning their attitude towards the REST Project and its effect and purpose at the UdeG. This is a lack of information that can be justified given the voluntary nature of the control group involvement and the lack of contact between the REST staff and these students, but it cannot be overlooked as a lack of important data.

At this point, no ultimate evaluation of the REST Project is intended. The purpose of this study is to present quantitative and qualitative evaluation methods, using REST for examples only. The conclusions to be drawn, then, are in terms of the methodology, not the Project. Towards this end, an observation concerning the drawing and verifying of conclusions using qualitative data is in order.

Conclusions concerning explanations tend toward statements about causal relationships: it is tempting to say, for example, that the cramped work space caused the negative relations between teachers. It is similarly tempting to say that the students' negative attitude toward the reading strategies approach caused the lack of attendance. This, in turn, could be seen as causing the bad relations between student and teacher. As Miles and Huberman (1984:226) point out, 'any causal statement made about a social situation should immediately be reversed, to see whether it looks truer that way.' In the previous example, we would take the causal statement, 'The students are not attending regularly because they hate the reading strategies approach, and, as a consequence, hate the teacher' and reverse it: 'The students hate the approach/teacher because they do not attend class regularly.' This presupposes that they are not attending regularly for some other reason. In the case of REST, this turned out to be a plausible explanation: there were many reasons for the lack of attendance that had nothing to do with their attitude toward the teacher or approach (courses which the administration had not told us about, that certain students were 'repeating', and that were scheduled at the same time as the REST course; and a generally inconvenient schedule for REST).

Conclusion

Program evaluation will probably always require a traditional, quantitative component, and there seems to be nothing wrong with this. Especially for summative evaluation, and even for aspects of formative evaluation, the clarity and rigor of an appropriate experimental (or quasi-experimental) design can give a useful picture of the extent to which the program has or has not reached its goals. This kind of information will most likely always be asked for by administrators and funding agencies. Because of this, it is important to make proper use of the quantitative methods at our disposal, and this means a careful selection of research design and statistical analysis techniques, paying attention to the underlying assumptions of the particular models being used. While these assumptions are not always tenable, they should be presented and discussed along with the analysis. In addition, given the results of this study, it would seem wise to always use a variety of analyses, rather than trusting any one particular statistical test.

   The conclusions to be drawn from the experience of using qualitative data in the evaluation of the REST Project are generally positive. The central problem with qualitative data should be obvious to everyone: it is incredibly time-consuming to collect and analyze. On the REST Project, the keeping of the T/R Journals and the Daily Log alone represented close to 50 hours of work per person over the first year of the Project. Adding the time taken for observations, meetings, and interviews the total amount of time spent is clearly in the hundreds of hours. A major recommendation, then, is to always have an explicit purpose in mind for any data that are collected. If other people are going to be asked to collect the data, it is important that they understand the purpose behind their collection. The experience from the REST Project suggests that if the data are kept in a system of files and subfiles, the researcher will be forced to become clearer about the purposes for the data and that this, in turn, will help when it comes time to analyze the data.

   The fact that there were so many data collected in the REST evaluation is a direct result of there being so many *sources* and different viewpoints represented. This, as a positive aspect of doing qualitative research, should be encouraged. The evaluation would have been improved further if an 'outsider' – someone not familiar with the UdeG or REST – had been able to spend some time with the Project to observe and interview the participants. These data would provide useful reliability checks against conclusions drawn by the in-house evaluation and perhaps add new conclusions. In addition, the conclusions reached by both types of evaluators could be given, along with the data displays, to the 'informants' (students and teachers) and their feedback used as a further refinement in the analysis.

Another problem with qualitative research is that it can be very frustrating. Many of the researchers who use the qualitative approach compare it to investigative journalism. For the researcher who enjoys searching for clues, playing the detective, and drawing together various sources of information into a coherent whole, qualitative research will be a pleasant and successful experience. For those researchers not so inclined, the data collection techniques and formats and the methods of analysis presented here, along with the references cited, should at least make the task more approachable. Furthermore, as more program evaluators and administrators in our field begin to use qualitative research techniques, it should be possible to discover new and better ways of adapting the methodology to the specific problems of language teaching programs.

The approach that would seem to offer the most to program evaluation, in any field, is a combination of quantitative and qualitative data. In many cases quantitative data can be used to clear up ambiguities in the qualitative data: 'The students say they haven't learned anything; the teachers think that they have.' Here, the *linking* of qualitative and quantitative data can be very useful and illuminating (e.g. Fielding and Fielding 1986). Student performance on various types of tests can be linked with specific perceptions (both student and teacher) of the program curriculum and methodology. For example, how do the students perform on tests of the skills they think are important versus the skills the teachers think are important?

While quantitative evidence in program evaluation may continue to be preferred over the supposedly subjective and impressionistic nature of qualitative evidence, it is not enough to simply show that a program was successful on some outcome measure. It must also be possible to make some judgments of *what*, in particular, it was that made the program successful. As Long (1984) has similarly argued, without this process-oriented approach to evaluation – the 'inside' view – an analysis of student performance – what comes 'out' of the program – will be ambiguous, at best.

References

Bachman, L. 1981. Formative evaluation in Specific Purpose program development. In R. Mackay and J. D. Palmer (Eds.) *Languages for specific purposes*, pp. 106–16. Rowley, MA: Newbury House.

Beretta, A. 1986. Program-fair language teaching evaluation. *TESOL Quarterly* 20(3):431–45.

Campbell, D. T. and A. E. Erlebacher. 1970. How regression artifacts in quasi-experimental evaluations can mistakenly make compensatory education look harmful. In J. Hellmuth (Ed.) *Compensatory education: a national debate*. New York, NY· Bruner/Mazel.

Chen, Z. 1986. Predicting Test of English as a Foreign Language scores from English as a Second Language Placement Test scores: total and subscale scores. Unpublished M.A. Thesis, University of California, Los Angeles.

Cook, T. D. and D. T. Campbell. 1979. *Quasi-Experimentation: Design and analysis issues for field settings*. Boston, MA: Houghton Mifflin Company.

Davidson, F. 1985. The factor structure of the Fall 1984 ESLPE. Unpublished paper, University of California, Los Angeles.

Elashoff, J. D. 1969. Analysis of covariance: a delicate instrument. *American Educational Research Journal*, 6:383–401.

Fielding, N. G. and J. L. Fielding. 1986. *Linking Data*. Beverly Hills, CA: Sage.

Henning, G. 1987. *A guide to language testing: development, evaluation, and research*. Rowley, MA: Newbury House/Harper and Row.

Hively, W., G. Maxwell, G. Rabehl, D. Sension and S. Lundin. 1973. *Domain-referenced curriculum evaluation: a technical handbook and a case study from the Minnemast Project*, CSE Monograph Series in Evaluation, No. 1. Los Angeles, CA: Center for the Study of Evaluation, UCLA Graduate School of Education, University of California, Los Angeles.

Kenney, D. A. 1975. A quasi-experimental approach to assessing treatment effects in the nonequivalent control group design. *Psychological Bulletin* 82(3):229–34.

LeCompte, M. D. and J. P. Goetz. 1982. Problems of reliability and validity in ethnographic research. *Review of Educational Research* 52(1):31–60.

Levine, H. G. 1985. Principles of data storage and retrieval for use in qualitative evaluations. *Educational Evaluation and Policy Analysis* 7(2):169–86.

Long, M. H. 1984. Process and product in ESL program evaluation. *TESOL Quarterly* 18(3):409–25.

Lynch, B. 1985. The factor structure of the Winter 1985 ESLPE. Unpublished research study, University of California, Los Angeles.

Miles, M. B. and A. M. Huberman. 1984. *Qualitative Data Analysis: a sourcebook of new methods*. Beverly Hills, CA: Sage.

Parlett, M. and D. Hamilton. Evaluation as illumination: a new approach to the study of innovatory programs. 1976. In G. V. Glass (Ed.) *Evaluation studies review annual, vol. 1*. Beverly Hills, CA: Sage.

Patton, M. Q. 1980. *Qualitative Evaluation Methods*. Beverly Hills, CA: Sage.

Popham, W. J. 1978. *Criterion-referenced measurement*. Englewood Cliffs, NJ: Prentice-Hall.

Sax, G. 1974. The use of standardized tests in evaluation. In W. J. Popham (Ed.) *Evaluation in education: current applications*, pp. 243–308. Berkeley, CA: McCutchen Publishing Corporation.

Spolsky, B. 1985. What does it mean to know how to use a language? An essay on the theoretical basis of language testing. *Language Testing* 2: 180–92.

Stallings, J., M. Needels and N. Staybrook. 1979. How to change the process of teaching basic reading skills. Report (May '79) for SRI International. Menlo Park, CA: SRI.

Editors' postscript to Lynch

The evaluation described in Lynch's full account of the REST Project is interesting for a variety of reasons: the very fullness of the description makes it possible to gain an understanding of the methodology and results that is normally only possible from book-length accounts; the use of both qualitative and quantitative approaches to evaluation enables an examination of the relative merits of each approach; the problems encountered by the study are germane to anybody trying to evaluate similar programmes elsewhere in the real world; and the results of the evaluation as reported here are themselves of interest to many curriculum developers in similar settings, since this is one of the first thorough attempts to evaluate an EST programme in a university setting.

Lynch demonstrates in detail the use of the various methodological approaches in practice and shows the kinds of information about a programme that they can generate. The summary of his experience will hopefully be of value to others. Various methodological issues are raised by this account. It is clear that qualitative approaches are extremely time consuming, both in the data-gathering phase, and at the stage of analysis. In many situations the demands made by such methods may simply outstrip the resources available. It is a fairly common experience that people are willing to invest time and effort into keeping detailed journals and logs, observation reports and so on, but that the time is very often simply not available for the extended process of categorisation and iteration that Lynch describes. It may be that the process of completing such documents is itself influential, or formative. It may also be that having such records available means that future course designers or curriculum planners can consult them when they have a need.

Nevertheless, the danger exists that mountains of data will accumulate which evaluators will be unable to process, or, an additional problem, will feel ill-equipped to process. The analysis of qualitative data requires considerable interpretive skills which many people involved in evaluation do not necessarily feel they possess. Even if they are prepared to develop such skills experientially – the deep-end approach – a doubt often lingers about the validity of their account: are they interpreting the data 'correctly'? Would other interpreters arrive at different accounts? Lynch makes clear that different people may well have different interpretations of events, yet it appears that the summaries and conclusions to the chapter are his own, not those of other evaluators.

Lynch raises in this context an issue that is taken up in Alderson and Scott's chapter: the possible role of an outside evaluator, who might provide an 'unbiased', or at least different, perspective and interpretation. Lynch believes such an outsider could have made a valuable contribution, but he does not mention the suspicions, hostility, obstructions and evasions that outsiders might meet.

Of course, it is in order to achieve a degree of replicability that Lynch went to great lengths to devise such means of categorising, summarising and displaying the data. The reader must, however, have a lingering doubt as to whether such elaborate procedures offer significant advantages over the more usual subjective reading of accounts and reports, and highlighting 'main' or 'salient' points to be included in a report. In such a case, the original documents rather than the transformed matrices form the data that are available for replication or reinterpretation.

Despite the wealth of information available, it is unclear whether data exist which would enable one adequately to characterise what actually happened in classrooms during the Project: how different were they from normal classes? How different was one class from the next? What were the effects of motivation, mismatched expectations, class size, teacher competence, and so on? In other words, how can the apparent outcomes of the quantitative approach be related to what happened in class, in an explanatory manner? As Lynch points out, no qualitative data were gathered – or were indeed gatherable – on the control group, so these questions could probably not be answered in principle with the design employed. Yet it is frequently claimed that evaluations should not only describe what the effect of a particular course of action was, but how that effect was achieved. This is, of course, not to criticise this evaluation, but rather to hint at the enormity of the burden facing evaluators if they are expected to explain programme effects – an expectation they themselves all too often give rise to.

The quantitative approach to evaluation exemplified in this chapter is not without problems, as Lynch admits. The most obvious one is that of the suitability of the tests to the project's aims and content. Although Lynch justifies the use of standardised instruments like the UCLA's ESLPE on the grounds that they enable comparisons with other populations, and other norms, it is not at all clear why one would wish to do such a thing. In the case of the REST project, it is claimed that the students' performance can be compared with the population of students taking the ESLPE at UCLA. What would such a comparison tell us: that Mexican students were weaker or stronger than such a population? Yet what use could a curriculum planner have for this information: surely the circumstances of the REST project and language teaching at UCLA are so different, the aims and activities of the students so disparate, their background, language learning history, motivation and so on likely to be so varied as to make any comparative data uninterpretable. What use would anybody wish to make of such comparisons? And if one cannot find a use for the data being gathered, should one continue to gather them?

Of course, the opposite problem was experienced with the cloze tests, which were intended to reflect project aims and content, yet which Lynch admits are not clearly designed to do so in an adequate manner. Can one really believe that a cloze test can reflect the REST syllabus as detailed in Table 1?

One advantage that accrues from using tests that do not relate directly to the project's aims is that experienced by this evaluation; unexpected outcomes are more likely to be detected. Indeed, this is one of the more interesting results with respect to programme content that emerged, and that may not have emerged if the ESLPE had not been used: the students appear to improve more in the area of general language proficiency – possibly even in skills like listening – than in the specific skill of reading that was the focus of the course. Of course, this conclusion must be tempered by an awareness of the limitations of the tests, but if the result could be replicated elsewhere, it would suggest that specific purpose courses might be more generally beneficial than intended. A controversy has existed for years in specific purpose teaching over whether students' specific needs are best met by specific programmes or by general ones. This study provides some evidence that specific purpose programmes may be less limited in their effects than is sometimes asserted. The contribution of evidence from an evaluation study to such a debate is a welcome development!

Despite the care taken in the design of the study, Lynch makes it clear that a quasi-experimental – control type of design is very difficult to realise in practice. The problems associated with the use of ANCOVA to control for pre-existing differences between control and experimental groups pale into insignificance compared with the problems of interpreting differences between experimental and control groups over time, when the control group has had no treatment, and when the tests used in the pre- post- design have varied. Lynch admits the problem, but offers no solution – of course, one may not be available in the real world, as contrasted with the unreal world of the laboratory experiment. At least it is clear that very careful attention needs to be paid to the detail of the design, the practicality of plans for administration of instruments and the gathering of data, long before any programme can be evaluated. This is a theme touched upon in Chapter 1, to which we shall return in the final chapter.

One final comment: however careful the design of the study, however many controls and however well designed the data collection devices and procedures, the real world can still conspire to thwart the evaluator. One of Lynch's findings – which indeed may not have surfaced if only quantitative approaches had been employed – was that the students' expectations of the course were very different from the intentions of the programme developers. He supposes that this is because of an administrative error: students were told the course would be about one thing, but in reality it had different aims and content. In the best of all possible worlds, things will still go wrong.

Nevertheless, Lynch's study documents the value of using a combination of qualitative and quantitative approaches to evaluation in order to get a better, fuller understanding of what happens on an innovative programme, even when the unexpected and undesired occurs!

3 The 'independent' evaluation of bilingual primary education: a narrative account

Rosamond Mitchell

Introduction

The Western Isles of North-West Scotland (comprising the islands of Lewis, Harris, and the Uists) are today the main surviving stronghold of the Scottish Gaelic language, once spoken throughout much of Scotland. Out of a total Western Isles population of 29,492 people aged three or over, 80.0 per cent were reported in the last Census to be Gaelic-speaking (Government Statistical Service 1983), and the language is widely used throughout the islands. However there are now few if any islanders who are not also fluent in English, the dominant language of the media, of many official functions, and traditionally also of education. There is evidence of language shift in some parts of the islands, in the direction of English (see e.g. MacKinnon 1977), a trend which has gone much further in recently Gaelic-speaking parts of the mainland and the Inner Hebrides.

By comparison with the other surviving Celtic languages of the British Isles, Scottish Gaelic has a much less well developed language maintenance/revival movement. Local varieties of English have been the focus of language loyalty in the Lowlands of Scotland, so that Scottish Gaelic has not acquired the symbolic status of 'national language' accorded to Welsh or to Irish Gaelic. None the less, when the contemporary local government structure was established in Scotland in the early 1970s, there was sufficient concern for the status and future of the language for the newly-formed 'Western Isles Islands Council' to adopt a Gaelic title ('Comhairle nan Eilean'), and to commit itself to the promotion of Gaelic in various aspects of official life, through the adoption of an official bilingual policy.

Most strikingly, the Comhairle committed itself to strengthening the position of Gaelic in island schools, by means of a Bilingual Education Project (BEP) first established in 20 primary schools in 1975. The Project was planned as a research and development project, and as such was partially funded for six years by the Research and Intelligence Unit of the Scottish Education Department (SED). (At the time, this was the only central government source from which individual local authorities could obtain funding for initiatives of this type.) In 1978 a further fourteen schools joined the Project, and in 1981 bilingual teaching became official policy in all Western Isles primary schools. By this time the staff of the Project had expanded to four, with a Director and Field Worker based in Stornoway concerned with schools in Lewis and Harris, and two Field Workers based in North Uist with responsibility for the southern islands. In 1981 also, the Comhairle took over full financial responsibility for the primary initiative, hoping to maintain the existing level of activity, and giving a permanent advisory and curriculum development role to the former Project staff. Meanwhile, an extension into secondary schooling was envisaged, and in 1980 an application was made to the Scottish Education Department for financial support for this further initiative.

In 1981, however, the application was turned down, on the grounds that the success of the primary level initiative had not been clearly established. Instead, the SED offered to fund an independent evaluation of the primary school work, and it was made clear that requests to fund a secondary level initiative would not be favourably considered, unless this offer was accepted.

The SED's proposal for an independent evaluation caused considerable resentment within the Western Isles. Thus for example, it was strongly argued that the 1978 and 1981 Reports produced by Bilingual Education Project staff (and subsequently published as Murray and Morrison 1984), which contained substantial accounts of classroom work of a qualitative, case study nature, provided adequate evidence of the Project's success. However, after some internal controversy, the local authority eventually decided to agree in principle to an SED-funded external evaluation.

In the spring of 1983, two members of the Department of Education of the University of Stirling, Donald McIntyre and the present author, were invited by the SED to prepare proposals for the independent, retrospective evaluation, on the basis of an outline agreement between the SED and Comhairle nan Eilean. During the summer of 1983 an agreed plan was negotiated with both parties. After some delay due to initial difficulties in recruiting suitably qualified islands-based staff, fieldwork for the independent evaluation study began at Easter 1984, and continued until Christmas 1985. Data analysis and report writing took longer than envisaged; the Final Report of the evaluation project was eventually submitted to the SED early in 1987 (Mitchell *et al.* 1987).

The evaluation project described in this chapter thus had a long and acrimonious gestation period, and can itself be viewed as one expression of a politically sensitive, continuously negotiated relationship between Scotland's educational centre (the SED) and a culturally significant yet peripheral community. In following sections of this chapter, the consequences of such origins for the nature of the evaluation enterprise are explored. First, the overall character of the original BEP is briefly outlined, and implications for the design of an appropriate evaluation strategy are considered. Next, an account is given of the development of the design for the evaluation, involving an interplay between academic, political and practical considerations. This is followed by a description of our experience in implementing the planned evaluation strategy, and a limited account of external perceptions of the evaluation. In conclusion, the place of evaluation grounded in empirical research in the formation of language education policy is briefly considered.

The 1975–81 bilingual education project

The original, essentially developmental intentions of the 1975–81 Project were summarised as follows:

> The production of teaching materials and of aids to teachers to facilitate the development of a Gaelic-English bilingual curriculum in a sample of primary schools where the children are mainly from Gaelic-speaking homes.

> (SED 1976)

A full account of the Project from the perspective of its two successive Directors, John Murray and Catherine Morrison, is given in their book *Bilingual Education in the Western Isles, Scotland* (Murray and Morrison 1984). The authors make it clear that the Project was intended to have a far-reaching impact on the primary curriculum in bilingual communities:

> The project was from the beginning concerned with the primary school curriculum and with curricular change, with the language development of children in primary school. The work done through Gaelic would have to enrich the primary school curriculum as a whole.

> (Murray and Morrison 1984:8)

Similarly, Finlay MacLeod (ex-Depute Director of Education with Comhairle nan Eilean) writes in his introduction to the book:

> The lay person could be excused for thinking that this project seemed to be concerned more with education than with Gaelic – as if the two could be separated in this way. A major problem facing the project was that, in the past, Gaelic in education was embedded in a medium-orientated didactic mode which relied largely on reading by rotation. What this project enabled teachers to do was to create a range of experiential situations where each child's ever-extending repertoire of Gaelic linguistic skills was being utilised by him so as to realise these situations. The pedagogic shift was fundamental.

> (Murray and Morrison 1984:x–xi)

Thus the Project could be seen as having two main, interlinked sets of objectives. On the one hand, implicit in all its work was a commitment to the maintenance of Gaelic as a community language, in a context of perceived potential language shift. In addition, the Project was clearly concerned with the implementation in Western Isles schools of the general principles of the 1965 Primary Memorandum (the principal official document articulating the idea of the child-centred, experiential curriculum for the Scottish primary school: SED 1965), appropriately adapted to local circumstances. These two sets of objectives were fused in the adopted model of the bilingual curriculum. It made sense in general educational terms, for the individual child to explore his/her local environment actively, through the medium of the language most closely associated with it; and in turn, it was hoped that children's proficiency in Gaelic would be consolidated and extended through this expanded use of the language, alongside English.

Corresponding to these two broad purposes were two distinct kinds of outcome intended by the Project. One set had to do with children's bilingual proficiency and attitudes towards culture and community:

> ...the aim of the project was to produce Gaelic/English bilinguals with a mastery of the skills of understanding, speaking, reading and writing in both languages together with the appreciation of the nuances, emotional overtones and cultural dimensions of the two languages.

(Murray and Morrison, 1984:16)

> It was also hoped the Project would 'help to instil in the pupils a much-needed sense of identity and confidence in themselves as people, and would help to foster in them an interest in and a sympathy with the affairs of their own locality'.

(Murray and Morrison 1984:91)

The other set of intended outcomes concerned the quality of learning experiences provided for bilingual children in the classroom. Here, a set of general principles was articulated, to do with curriculum integration around themes/projects, the promotion of learning through discussion and through direct, practical experience of the local environment, the development of pupils' research and reporting skills using a variety of media, and the use of both Gaelic and English as languages of instruction. The curriculum areas of Gaelic Language Arts and Environmental Studies received particular attention, and a series of detailed recommendations were made regarding teaching methods for these areas. In addition, a variety of Gaelic reading materials was produced, as well as videos and other audiovisual materials.

In order to attain these diverse process and product goals, the BEP team relied principally on extended liaison with class teachers. (As a result of previously well-established recruitment policy favouring the appointment of bilingual staff in Gaelic-speaking areas, the team could assume bilingual competence on the part of the teachers in all 34 Project schools. Clearly this was a critical enabling factor for the particular innovation strategy adopted by the BEP.) Contact with teachers was sustained partly through teachers' meetings and working groups, and partly through visits to individual teachers in their classrooms. Project work in particular was often collectively discussed and evaluated, and teachers were also closely involved in the work of Gaelic materials development.

In addition to working with teachers, the Project team originally envisaged the close involvement of parents and community members with bilingual work in schools. However this dimension of the Project's work was never fully developed.

Planning an appropriate evaluation strategy

After accepting the invitation of the SED to develop a proposal for the independent, retrospective evaluation of the 1975–81 Project, the two prospective Directors of the evaluation project visited the Western Isles for several days in the summer of 1983 at the invitation of the Education Department of Comhairle nan Eilean. This visit involved meetings with the bilingual advisory staff of the Department (i.e. with the former BEP team, all still at that time in post), as well as with other Education Department officials and with local councillors, past and present; in addition some brief school visits were made. This politically sensitive trip had an important familiarisation purpose for the Stirling University researchers, and provided their major opportunity for face-to-face discussions with those responsible for the creation of the original BEP. In addition, a range of documentation concerning the original project was collected, including the BEP Directors' first and second phase Reports (subsequently published as Murray and Morrison 1984).

Following on this visit, the university researchers set about developing their initial proposals for the evaluation study. These proposals took account of a number of principles, as well as of a range of constraints to do with timing and resources:

1 It was accepted that the concerns of the evaluation study should reflect those of the original BEP as far as possible. That is, the evaluators would concentrate on investigating to what extent the innovations proposed by the BEP were actually operative in the schools, ten years on, and to what extent the hoped-for outcomes (in terms of pupils' bilingual proficiency and attitudes) were being achieved. More

specifically, it was felt appropriate that an investigation of classroom processes would form the most substantial element of the evaluation (reflecting the BEP's concern with developing a distinctive pattern of classroom experience).

2 For practical reasons, the need to strike a balance between breadth and depth of data collection was recognised. While limited data could be collected in all schools, it was necessary to select a smaller sample for extended classroom observation and pupil assessments. It was felt that most could be learned about the feasibility of the BEP curriculum proposals in environments where these had been taken most seriously. Consequently it was proposed that classroom observation etc. should be conducted mainly in those schools which appeared on the basis of preliminary survey work to have been most 'committed' to the BEP (rather than in a randomly selected sample).

3 It was recognised that (in the light of SED dissatisfaction with the qualitative, case study evidence presented in earlier reports) systematic, quantitative methods would have to be adopted for the observation of bilingual teaching and learning.

(Murray and Morrison 1984 present 15 teacher-authored case studies of teaching/learning activities in BEP schools. These accounts of curriculum innovation naturally concentrate on success; little information is provided on the degree of continuity with the pre-BEP curriculum, or on problems and constraints encountered. Besides, the accounts are written from a teacher perspective; evidence on pupil attitudes, involvement and achievement is indirect. To document the range and depth of BEP influence across the full curriculum, on a basis which would allow direct comparisons between classrooms, and also to investigate pupil achievements more directly, other methods were needed.)

4 It was also recognised, however, that the timing of the evaluation project ruled out the adoption of research designs which would permit the establishment of unambiguous causal links between the innovation strategy of the 1975–81 BEP and the school curriculum of the mid 1980s. There was no satisfactory way of collecting detailed information regarding the nature of the primary curriculum in Western Isles schools prior to the establishment of the BEP; nor was it possible to determine retrospectively what other national or local factors may have been influencing the development of the curriculum after 1975, in addition to the direct influence of the new Project. Furthermore, the use of any formal control group design was ruled out, if only by the fact that since 1981, all Western Isles schools had been officially involved in the bilingual education scheme. In these circumstances the evaluation could be expected to make only cautious and conservative suggestions regarding causal relationships.

5 The timing of the evaluation also made it inevitable that the focus of the work would lie in the schools; the curriculum development strategy adopted by the BEP team between 1975 and 1981 was clearly not accessible to investigation. A decision was also taken to omit any further study of their materials development work from the evaluation proposals. The rich bank of Gaelic materials produced had been widely available for some time, and their quality was not in question from any quarter.

6 It was however felt desirable to make one exception to the school focus of the evaluation study: in the light of the BEP's original aspirations to involve parents and community members more fully in the bilingual curriculum, it was felt that a limited exploration of parental attitudes and involvement should be carried out.

7 It was accepted that a Stirling-directed evaluation was feasible only if at least one suitably qualified, bilingual field worker could be recruited to the evaluation team.

From these starting points, a detailed proposal for the evaluation study was worked out. It was envisaged that the evaluation would take two years to complete, and that a full time, islands-based bilingual field worker would be employed, as well as a bilingual secretary based at Stirling. One of the two Stirling-based Directors (a contract researcher) would be employed on the evaluation project on a part-time basis; the other (a tenured lecturer) would contribute personal research time.

The full proposal envisaged a number of distinct phases:

1 A preliminary interview survey with the head teachers of all schools involved in the 1975–81 BEP, at any time (there were 33 surviving schools). In a semi-structured interview format, it was proposed to ask these teachers about the history of their schools' involvement with BEP, their attitudes towards BEP policies, and the present extent of implementation of these policies in their school.

2 On the basis of the preliminary survey, it was proposed to select a sample of ten schools for further investigation. The main criterion involved in selecting these schools would be their reported level of commitment to the policies of the BEP; in accordance with the principles outlined earlier, eight schools judged to have a high level of uptake of BEP ideas would be selected, as well as two 'low uptake' schools. While this was the main criterion, care would also be taken to select as balanced a sample as possible in terms of size of school, geographical distribution, and proportion of children from Gaelic-speaking homes.

3 Within each school two classrooms would be selected for detailed study (as most schools had only one or two teachers, this sample would include most classes in the ten schools). A range of techniques (teacher interviews, structured and unstructured observation of class

teacher and pupils) would be used to develop a full picture of aspects of classroom life judged relevant to BEP policies. As far as possible, existing research procedures (such as systematic observation instruments) would be used, but where necessary new procedures would be designed.

4 In response to the stated outcome goals of the BEP, it was proposed that pupils' spoken and written proficiency in both Gaelic and English should be assessed, at two different age levels (midway through primary schooling and towards its end). It was also proposed to explore their perceptions of themselves in relation to Gaelic language and culture, and to their island background, as well as their more direct perceptions of the BEP itself, and their attitudes towards it.

5 Lastly, it was proposed that a limited sample of parents should be interviewed, regarding their knowledge of the BEP and possible involvement with it, as well as their attitudes towards it.

This initial proposal was discussed at some length with officials of both the SED and the Education Department of Comhairle nan Eilean. In these discussions, on the SED side, the failure to adopt a control group design was queried, but the researchers' arguments on this point were ultimately accepted. On the Western Isles side, the proposal to investigate pupil attitudes towards island life, language and culture was strongly deprecated by the bilingual staff of the Education Department, on the grounds that any positive impact on attitudes was a long-term matter, which a short-term investigation could fail to detect. Ultimately this proposal was dropped from the evaluation design, along with the proposed investigation of pupil attitudes towards the BEP itself. Otherwise, however, apart from some other minor revisions, the evaluation proposals were accepted by both official bodies in the late summer of 1983. At this stage also a small Advisory Group was established, comprising the Director of Education of Comhairle nan Eilean and two representatives of the SED Research and Intelligence Unit, to whom it was agreed the evaluation team would regularly report.

Implementing the evaluation design

In the autumn of 1983, attempts were made to recruit the necessary bilingual staff for the evaluation project fieldwork. Firstly, an islands-based field worker was required, with the personality, qualifications and experience necessary to undertake the main responsibility for the collection of data in schools. Such a person would ideally have experience both of primary teaching and of research, as well as being fluent in both Gaelic and English, and capable of being accepted in schools in a politically sensitive role. Given the small size of the Gaelic-speaking community, the potential pool of suitably qualified people was necessarily small. At the first attempt, while several applicants were interviewed, it did not prove possible to make an appointment to the field worker post. However, it was agreed that the post should be readvertised, at the cost of some further delay, and that the option of making two part-time appointments should be considered. This turned out to be a practicable solution, and in the spring of 1984 two part-time Research Fellows were appointed on two-year contracts, each with responsibility for evaluation fieldwork in her own geographical area. Office accommodation was provided for them by the Comhairle in their home locations; and at the same time, a part-time bilingual secretary was fortunately recruited at Stirling.

Both field workers were native speakers of Gaelic; one was a psychology graduate with extensive research experience, and currently completing a doctorate in the sociology of language. The other was a graduate in Gaelic with teaching qualifications and experience at both primary and secondary level. Thus between them they possessed an ideal range of knowledge and experience, complementary to that of the Stirling researchers. Their availability was critical for the conduct of the evaluation study.

While engaged in this lengthy search for suitable staff, the Stirling researchers continued with the development of more detailed plans for the evaluation. In particular, a detailed analysis was carried out of the final reports of the original BEP (as published in Murray and Morrison 1984), in order to develop a series of specified research questions deriving from the objectives of the project, which could appropriately be asked about classroom life in Western Isles primary schools. Preliminary work was also undertaken regarding the selection and design of systematic observation instruments and interview schedules.

By Easter 1984, the evaluation team was in a position to begin its fieldwork. During the summer term of 1984, therefore, the 33 original BEP schools still surviving were visited, and the preliminary survey of head teacher opinion was carried out. In view of the long public controversy which had surrounded the establishment of the evaluation, and in view of the recent resignations from the Education Department of two bilingual advisory staff (former BEP team members), the research team members had been uncertain as to how they would be received when making their first substantial face-to-face contacts in schools. In the event they were received courteously and co-operatively, and the programme of visits was conducted without any serious hitch.

Two members of the evaluation team were involved in each of these preliminary visits (one of the Stirling-based Directors, plus one of the locally based field workers), and each member led a proportion of the semi-structured interviews. (The outline interview schedule is given as Appendix 1 in this chapter.) As well as its primary familiarisation and data-gathering purpose, this series of joint visits was helpful in consolidating the evaluation team itself, and provided a useful opportunity for the development of team members' interviewing techniques. Teachers were usually asked whether they preferred to be interviewed in English or in Gaelic (except when the sole member of the research team with no Gaelic was involved); in the event about half of the interviews were conducted in Gaelic. The team had hoped to audiorecord these interviews, and this proved possible in the majority of cases, though a substantial minority of teachers asked for written notes to be taken instead.

The autumn of 1984 was a period of intensive preparation for the main phase of classroom-based research. First, on the basis of a systematic analysis of the head teacher interviews, ten schools were identified as a potential main sample, according to the previously determined criteria (eight 'high uptake', and two 'low uptake', with an appropriate balance regarding size, location, and extent of Gaelic use in the local catchment area). Two of the schools identified had only one teacher, so that between them these schools would provide a total of eighteen classrooms for the study. All ten schools were written to and invited to co-operate in the main classroom study; all agreed. (The evaluation team had assured the schools that in any publication arising from the project, their anonymity would be preserved, and made no public statement regarding the selection of schools. However, during the autumn, to their considerable embarrassment, the names of the ten chosen schools were published in a local newspaper. Despite this breach of confidentiality, all ten schools maintained their co-operative attitude and went on to participate fully in the classroom study.)

Meanwhile, the development and trialling of the instruments to be used in the classroom-based work continued. It was decided that two separate systematic observation instruments were needed, one teacher-focused, one pupil-focused.

The teacher-focused instrument chosen was a slightly modified version of the Teacher Record originally developed by Boydell (1974), and extensively used in the large-scale ORACLE Project based at Leicester University, and concerned with the extent to which child-centred methods had been adopted in English primary schools (Galton *et al.* 1980). The Teacher Record is a sign system in which the topic and quality of teacher utterances (questions and statements) are documented. It was considered that the instrument would yield evidence both on the extent to which teacher–pupil interaction reflected a child-centred style of instruction, and on the range of purposes for which the teachers used the two languages, English and Gaelic. (A summary of the teacher observation instrument is included as Appendix 2 in this chapter.)

It was felt necessary to devise an original instrument for pupil observation, in order to answer a range of research questions regarding the content of the curriculum, the activities in which pupils were engaged, and the linguistic medium through which they worked. (Further details of the instrument are given in Appendix 3 in this chapter.) It was recognised that the individualised nature of much primary school work necessitated the observation of individual pupils rather than of groups/whole classes. A sampling procedure was therefore proposed, whereby eight members of each class would be selected for individual observation during a fixed proportion of the school day. (Account was to be taken of pupils' age, sex, and bilingual proficiency as reported by their teacher, in selecting a balanced sample within each classroom; the school day would also be systematically sampled, with a balance between morning and afternoon observations.)

The development of these instruments, and the training of the field workers in their use, took place partly at Stirling and partly in the Western Isles. The instruments were piloted in two Western Isles schools not included in the main sample, and further training was carried out in small rural primary schools in the Stirling area. In addition, two interview schedules (pre- and post-observation) were developed for use with teachers, primarily to document aspects of classroom life not observable within the space of a few days' visit. The field workers' schedule of work in the main study schools also included periods of unstructured observation, to document aspects of school life such as pupils' language use outside the classroom setting, or Environmental Studies field trips.

In January 1985, the field worker responsible for the northern group of schools began her series of main study visits. Despite some difficulties caused by teacher illness and bad weather, she succeeded in keeping up with her demanding schedule, and it became clear that the ambitious programme of observation/interview procedures was manageable – just!

During the spring of 1985, while the first group of main study visits were being carried out, the Stirling-based researchers were engaged in developing the data-gathering techniques required for the investigation of children's proficiency in Gaelic and in English, and for the exploration of parents' opinions.

At this point one substantial modification to the general plans for the evaluation was considered. Given the strong commitment of the original BEP to the development of reading materials for Gaelic, it was suggested by the Advisory Group that the team might undertake an investigation of children's reading skills, in addition to their speaking and writing. After consideration, however, (including the evaluation and rejection of some commercially available reading tests) it was recognised that the work required to develop appropriate bilingual reading assessment materials was too great for the resources of the evaluation team, already stretched to their limit.

The team thus concentrated on developing procedures for the assessment of speaking and writing in both Gaelic and English. For this they drew heavily on the language work of the Assessment of Performance Unit, based at the National Foundation for Educational Research in England (e.g. Gorman *et al.* 1981, 1984). It was decided that all Primary 4 and Primary 7 pupils in the main study schools should be involved in the language assessment. For the assessment of speaking, three main tasks were developed in parallel English and Gaelic versions (talking about self, talking about school work, and retelling a story). These tasks were to be administered by the bilingual field worker on an individual basis (paired procedures were initially proposed, but abandoned at the piloting stage). All pupils were to be allocated randomly to either the English or the Gaelic version of each task; however to avoid undue stress to pupils with little or no Gaelic, a simple 'Gaelic Screening Test' was also devised, for administration to all pupils early on in the testing process. Pupils performing poorly on this task would not be asked to complete the Gaelic medium tasks they had been allocated. All the speaking tasks were to be audiorecorded for subsequent assessment using rating scales on a variety of dimensions judged relevant to communicative proficiency.

For the assessment of writing, separate tasks were developed for use with P4 and P7 pupils. The P4 pupils were to be asked to write a simple narrative on the basis of a series of four pictures, in either English or Gaelic (with random assignment of pupils to either language). Two tasks were devised for the P7 pupils: a story-writing task, and a non-fictional reporting task relating to current school work. Again, pupils were to be randomly assigned to do one task in English and the other in Gaelic.

These procedures were piloted in two northern schools at Easter 1985. With minor modifications they appeared to work well (notably, the business of audiorecording appeared perfectly acceptable to the pupils); and during the summer term of 1985, the northern field worker re-visited her sample of main study schools, in order to carry out the language assessment work. Again, by the end of the school year this intensive programme was successfully completed.

The last element of the fieldwork, the parent interviews, was also begun at this time. It had been accepted that this could form only a minor element in the evaluation study, given the clear school focus of the original BEP and the limited resources of the evaluation team. However, a semi-structured interview schedule was devised, for administration to a small sample of parents of children attending four main sample schools (two 'high uptake', two 'low uptake'). Two of these schools lay in the northern region, and the northern field worker made contact with the parent sample through the schools, while re-visiting them for the purpose of the language assessment work. All parents contacted agreed to be interviewed, some in Gaelic, some in English, though most preferred not to be audiorecorded.

In the autumn of 1985 the fieldwork in the northern schools was complete, and the focus switched to the southern schools. The southern field worker had been abroad for some months, and it was envisaged that on her return, the two field workers would conduct some joint observations in a non-main sample school, as a training exercise, and in order to collect data regarding the reliability of the structured observation instruments. Unfortunately, due to the sudden illness of the northern field worker, this did not prove possible, and the southern field worker had to embark on her tight schedule of school visits without the support of a preliminary induction phase. The task of the southern field worker was also necessarily more complex, as she was aiming to conduct the complete range of procedures (language assessment work and parent interviews, in addition to classroom observation procedures) in the course of a single visit to each locality. However, in the event, the programme again proved manageable (just), and considerable travel difficulties were overcome, so that the second field worker completed her data collection on schedule, by Christmas 1985. It also proved possible for the two field workers to conduct a small-scale reliability study regarding the use of the classroom observation instruments retrospectively, after the collection of all the main study data. This reliability study involved an additional, joint classroom observation session lasting two days, with independent coding of the same observed events using the teacher and pupil instruments in turn. The late stage at which this could be done was naturally a source of anxiety for the evaluation team; had the instruments turned out not to be reliable, it was obviously too late for any remedial action to be taken. However in the event acceptable levels of observer agreement were recorded.

Analysing and reporting on the evaluation data

Due in the main to the professional commitment of the two field workers, and their capacity to win co-operation in the schools, the ambitious plans for data collection had been fulfilled in virtually every respect. There was thus a very large volume of material to be analysed – and there remained three months in which to complete the work. In this respect, the original planning must with hindsight be viewed as somewhat unrealistic, even had no accidents occurred to delay the process of analysis and report writing. In the event, these activities took a further year to complete.

The professional circumstances of both the Directors of the evaluation project changed during 1985. Rosamond Mitchell was appointed to a lecturership at Edinburgh University in January. In October, Donald McIntyre took up a Readership at Oxford University. Both retained the role of Director, but the chains of communication between members of the evaluation team became more complicated (notably, the bilingual secretary was the only team member now based at Stirling University, which remained the grant-holding institution). Mitchell's move released some project funds, which were used to extend the periods of employment of the two islands-based field workers. Even so, it became clear that adequate time had not been allowed for data analysis and writing up.

From autumn 1985, the northern field worker was engaged in the primary analysis of her own classroom observational data, and in the analysis of the entire corpus of pupil language data. (The procedures for the latter were developed in early 1986 and trialled at Stirling.) From Christmas 1985, the southern field worker undertook the primary analysis of the remaining observational data; she had also previously analysed and written up the interview material from the head teachers' survey. Thus by the end of March 1986, the notional end of the evaluation, the bulk of the data analysis had been carried out but little of the Final Report had been drafted. This work remained to be undertaken by the two Directors, with the additional voluntary commitment by one of the field workers to produce a Gaelic version of the text.

In the event, the drafting and re-drafting of the Final Report occupied the remainder of 1986. The absence of one Director on maternity leave during the summer of 1986, as well as her further job move from Edinburgh to Southampton University, plus illness of the other, slowed down the process. Additional meetings were held during this time of both the evaluation team and its Advisory Group to consider and revise the draft; eventually, the Final Report was submitted to the Scottish Education Department early in 1987. The Department privately considered its reaction to the Report for some weeks, but requested no changes; the document was publicly released in April 1987.

The evaluation findings

The findings of the evaluation project were complex, and can only briefly be summarised here. (For fuller details, see Mitchell *et al.* 1987, and Mitchell 1987a, 1987b.) The head teachers in all schools were well-informed about the aims of the BEP, and generally supportive of them, though reported levels of implementation varied considerably. (This contrasted with the limited number of parents interviewed, who had little detailed information about the working of schools' bilingual policy, or involvement in the school curriculum, though schools' perceived efforts to maintain Gaelic were generally appreciated.)

In the ten main study schools, the overall curriculum structure conformed well with BEP intentions. 'Environmental Studies' (ES) with a local orientation was well established, in the form of theme/project work, with a wide range of practical activities. Gaelic Language Arts (GLA) teaching was largely integrated with Environmental Studies work, and had a strong oral bias (though traditional practices for the teaching of Gaelic literacy also persisted). As far as general methodology was concerned, the occurrence of discussion and of practical activities was positively linked with both ES and GLA, the curriculum areas particularly targeted by BEP. However interaction between teachers and pupils remained dominated by factual and organisational matters, with discussion of problems and ideas remaining relatively unusual. (This finding is in line with other recent studies of primary schooling, e.g. Galton *et al.* 1980; it seems generally true that the full implementation of a 'child-centred' ideology remains in this respect an aspiration.)

As far as language use was concerned, all teachers were bilingual, and Gaelic and English were both in widespread use as languages of instruction, across the whole curriculum in most schools. However, there were wide variations between classrooms; the main factor influencing the use of Gaelic as a medium of instruction seemed to be the proportion of pupils in a class judged by their teacher to be already fluent in the language. Where such pupils predominated Gaelic was the commonest language of whole-class instruction; fluent bilinguals were addressed individually by their teacher in either language. Pupils perceived as non-fluent were however individually addressed almost exclusively in English; where they predominated, Gaelic was little used for whole-class work. Thus where bilingual pupils were numerous their school language experience was much as intended by the BEP. Where they were in a minority, however, their opportunities to work bilingually were restricted, and opportunities for English-speaking children to develop fluency in spoken Gaelic were also more limited than the Project had hoped.

The language assessments provided rich information on the current state of children's bilingual competence. All the children possessed effective oral communication skills in English, appropriate to their age level, whatever the first language of their home. Gaelic was also spoken, with varying degrees of fluency, by most of the children; for the older age group assessed (those in Primary 7, the final year of primary schooling), differences between oral performance in Gaelic and English were relatively small. However children equally fluent in both languages were less likely to be found among the younger group (those in Primary 4); here, oral Gaelic competence was much less securely established.

As far as writing was concerned, the overall picture was one of steady positive development in both languages. At each stage (Primary 4 and Primary 7), higher levels of performance were being achieved in English (not surprisingly, as other evidence indicated clearly that greater attention was being paid throughout primary schooling to English literacy skills). In particular, Gaelic spelling and morphology were generally weak. However a large majority of pupils, including many non-fluent Gaelic speakers, had achieved at least some mastery of writing skill in Gaelic by Primary 7, alongside a good mastery of English writing. As far as English was concerned, the findings were broadly in line with those of other studies of monolingual English pupils of similar age (e.g. Gorman *et al*. 1984).

Overall, therefore, the evaluation study could conclude that much of what was happening in the primary schools studied was in line with BEP recommendations and principles. This turned out to be true almost equally for supposedly 'low uptake' schools, as for the others; except for a tendency to use Gaelic somewhat less frequently as the medium of instruction, the observed practices of these schools differed little from those identified as 'high uptake'. Thus it seemed likely that the observed levels of practical commitment to BEP principles were general to all schools within the scheme, and not peculiar to the 'high uptake' schools on which the evaluation had deliberately focused itself.

It could also be concluded that participation in the Project had in no way been detrimental to pupils' English language development, whatever their home language background. Monoglot English pupils had not been marginalised in any detectable way; indeed their power as a group to influence the classroom language environment was underlined by the evaluation evidence. None the less, good opportunities were being provided to consolidate and extend the Gaelic skills of bilingual children, and monolinguals were developing some Gaelic skills (mainly writing). Thus on a variety of process and product indicators, the evaluation study could provide reassurance regarding the overall quality of education being provided within the framework of the BEP.

Public perceptions of the evaluation project

From its inception the evaluation project attracted media attention. The disagreements between the SED and Comhairle nan Eilean concerning the request for funding of bilingual work at secondary school level, and the proposal in principle that an evaluation of the primary school work be carried out, had already been matters for debate in the local media and the national Gaelic and educational press.

Once it became known in 1983 that Stirling University researchers had been invited to direct the evaluation study, their qualifications for the work came under media scrutiny, with their 'outsider' status and perceived lack of fluency in Gaelic being consistent sources of criticism.

Two commentators in particular maintained a consistent interest in the progress of the evaluation, though neither communicated directly with the Stirling researchers: Neil Munro, a journalist with the *Times Educational Supplement Scotland* (TESS) and Finlay MacLeod, ex-Depute Director of Education for Comhairle nan Eilean, and now a freelance writer and journalist.

Munro commented in August 1983 on the slow start of the evaluation study, attributing this to difficulties in negotiating the research remit:

> Almost a year after the Western Isles Council reluctantly agreed to a Scottish Education Department investigation of its 8-year-old bilingual project in primary schools, research has still to start ...
>
> The report to the [Western Isles] council's bilingual subcommittee at the end of this month is likely to insist that a Gaelic-speaking fieldworker with a background in primary teaching and research be appointed to the research team. The SED is unlikely to refuse ...
>
> Islanders fear ... that the SED will impose impossible conditions on the researchers, such as attempting to find out if the project has improved the self-esteem of Gaelic speakers and has improved the use of the language, and bilingualism will be judged a failure. As one put it: 'That would be like asking whether learning English turned you into a good citizen: it's absurd and it would only become obvious in 20 years anyway.'
>
> (*TESS*) no 875, 12 August 1983)

This commentary on the negotiations shows some distortion (the necessity for a bilingual field worker was never questioned in any internal discussions regarding the evaluation proposals), but also illustrates the pressures which led to the abandonment of the proposal to investigate children's attitudes.

MacLeod, a prime mover in the establishment of the original BEP, remained consistently opposed to the principle of an external evaluation. In his regular Gaelic column in the widely-read *West Highland Free Press*, he returned several times to the issue. Most strikingly, in May 1984 (that is, as the evaluation team was embarking on its first piece of fieldwork, the interview survey with head teachers), MacLeod published an exceptionally fierce attack:

> ... And the SED representatives have arrived. The parasites, as they have said themselves [sic]. Living off other people's work. The Stirling Adventurers. Sending a pleasant, innocent local woman ahead of themselves, to smooth the path. A tape recorder up under the coat. Evaluators, ha ha. So objective, ho ho. Funny, did you say? O, man alive ...
>
> (*WHFP* 18 May 1984: translation, RM).

This attack on the professional integrity of the researchers (isolated though it was), together with the previously mentioned 'leak' of the names of the schools involved in the main study, were seen by the evaluation team as potentially the most serious media interventions, for their possible effects on co-operation in the schools. Concern was also felt in the autumn of 1985, when comments made by an ex-SED official, now retired, criticising the rejection by the evaluation team of a control group design, were also reported in the educational press. In the event, however, school co-operation appeared substantially unaffected, though teachers were clearly very aware throughout of the sensitive nature of the evaluation, and nervous of its possible political consequences.

Intermittent media comment on the project continued throughout the rest of the period of the evaluation, though the general financial difficulties of the education service in the Western Isles, with a consequent failure to fill the vacant bilingual advisory posts until 1986, as well as threats of widespread rural school closures, generally loomed much larger as issues of concern.

Inevitably questions were also asked in the media regarding the delays in producing the Final Report. On its eventual appearance, the Report received considerable coverage in the national, educational and local media. These concentrated almost entirely on the substantive findings of the Report. These findings were complex, and though they were generally accurately reported, different emphases appeared in different accounts, as can be seen from a selection of the headlines used in the general press, for articles generally concentrating on the Gaelic dimension:

> It's Top Marks for Bilingual Teaching
> (*Aberdeen Press & Journal* 1 May 1987)
>
> 'Substantial Success' Verdict on Bilingual Education
> (*Stornoway Gazette* 9 May 1987)
>
> Schools Gaelic Lagging
> (*Scotsman* 1 May 1987)

In the *Times Educational Supplement Scotland*, Munro published a clear and balanced summary of the findings of the report (and the only one to include an account of the evaluation findings regarding general curriculum matters), though under the somewhat one-sided headline 'Bilingual Success Confirmed' (*TESS* 1 May 1987). This report discussed prospects for the future, and reported the controversy regarding the evaluation as past history:

> ... There are echoes of the dispute in the report, which refers to doubts held by some of the value of an 'independent and retrospective investigation'. But the research team ... say they received the fullest local cooperation.

MacLeod reviewed the Report for the *West Highland Free Press* (in English), and was the only reporter to comment at all on the methodology of the evaluation, in a generally accurate account. While maintaining his view that an independent evaluation was superfluous, arguing that the report was hard to read and that its findings provided no new information, the professional integrity of the researchers was no longer questioned:

> The main approach of this study was to apply existing educational research instruments to the situation in the Western Isles ... All this is done in a competent but limited way, and the findings are unremarkable on the whole. Not only are the findings positive for bilingual education, but the report is generous in its account of what was being attempted and why it was undertaken in the first place ...
>
> ... But I do wish it could have been a little more interesting, or written in a form which didn't encourage one to go for yet another cup of coffee. [!]

> (*WHFP* 8 May 1987)

Thus it seemed overall that the generally positive findings of the evaluation study regarding current practice in Western Isles schools had defused much of the earlier media suspicion regarding the personnel and methods of the project. Had the findings been less positive, of course, the story might have been different.

Reflections on the evaluation strategy

In retrospect, how effective was the Stirling evaluation design? This question may be addressed in a narrow technical sense: did the data-gathering procedures work as expected, and how might they have been improved? was it possible to complete the programme envisaged? etc.; and in a broader sense: did the funding agency get good value for its money? were the right audiences addressed in dissemination? and ultimately, was an effective contribution made to the debate on the future of bilingual education? Attempts will be made to address the issue in both senses, in this and the final section of this chapter.

In the first, technical sense, the plans devised by the Stirling evaluation team worked out well on the whole. The wide range of data-collection procedures all proved feasible, and each contributed something worthwhile to the overall findings of the evaluation. The initial interviews effectively documented the degree of familiarity with BEP principles, and levels of support for them across the entire population of head teachers concerned; they also functioned as an essential induction for the

·evaluation team. However, these interviews were also used to identify an appropriate sample of schools for the main study, with somewhat unexpected results. On the basis of the interviews schools were categorised on a continuum from 'high' to 'low', regarding their apparent levels of commitment to BEP policies. As outlined earlier, the sample of schools selected for observation was drawn from the extremes of this continuum with a bias towards the 'high' end. However, in the event classroom practices in both 'high uptake' and 'low uptake' schools turned out to be very similar in most respects (and to be very substantially in line with BEP principles). On balance, the evaluators concluded that some head teachers had 'undersold' their schools' BEP commitment to some degree, in the initial interviews; there was certainly no evidence at all of 'overselling', even among the 'high uptake' group. Thus ultimately the inclusion of the 'low uptake' schools in the sample for classroom observation proved valuable mainly as an indication of the likely existence of positive levels of activity in the entire population of schools, rather than as a source of sharply contrasting examples of school practice.

The mainly quantitative classroom observation procedures yielded a well-founded description of the overall distribution of curriculum time, and of the pattern of activities being undertaken in different curriculum areas. For an evaluation project seeking to document the influence of a particular set of curriculum proposals this was invaluable. Evidence was lacking of the state of affairs obtaining in Western Isles schools before the start of the evaluation project; there was also the possibility that even if current classroom practice was by the early 1980s substantially in line with BEP policies, much ·of this could have been due to the nationwide promotion of 'child-centred' models of primary education, by teacher trainers, advisers etc., rather than to any specific BEP influence. However, the classroom observation procedures were sufficiently broad in focus to document significant differences in practice between curriculum areas which had been the focus of BEP attention and the rest, which allowed us to conclude that BEP influence had been considerable. (Most striking were the observed differences between the mainly oral-focused Gaelic Language Arts, and the literacy-focused English Language Arts.)

The systematic procedures used had significant limitations however. Most obviously, they were not an effective means of judging the quality of classroom experience: for example, to record that a group of pupils are working for 20 minutes on a practical activity involving Gaelic Language Arts and Environmental Studies says nothing very precise about the educational value of the task. The ORACLE-style Teacher Record did address the quality of classroom interaction (categorising teacher utterances for topic and cognitive level), but in a very limited way. While conclusions could be drawn about broad trends in teacher talk, reasons

E

underlying for example the high incidence of narrow factual questions could not meaningfully be explored.

Regarding classroom language use patterns, the time sampling instruments again provided good data on the broad relationships obtaining between medium of instruction, curriculum area and teaching/learning activity. However, they provided relatively crude evidence on more detailed issues such as Gaelic/English codeswitching. The evidence was sufficient to identify the unexpected power of monolingual English-speaking pupils over their immediate linguistic environment, from which Gaelic was excluded to a substantial extent. But the precise mechanisms triggering language choice could not be explored in depth. (The researchers' main regret here was that classroom audiorecording was ruled out, as too intrusive a device in an evaluation context.)

The language assessment procedures also proved workable, with children co-operating readily in the range of spoken and written tasks, and generally willing (even eager) to be audiorecorded. Obviously the data produced reflect to some extent the 'special' assessment situation in which they were collected, and their generalisability to other contexts must be treated with caution; it may well be that pupils achieve more highly in writing, for example, in normal classroom contexts where writing itself may be supported by more extended discussion and redrafting. None the less the benefits of eliciting comparable data from the whole cohort of P4 and P7 children far outweighed the disadvantages, in this evaluation context. The children's universally effective performance on the English language tasks could allay fears that children's English language development might be suffering; and the expectation that everyone would attempt at least some Gaelic tasks allowed even the semi-proficient to show some of their Gaelic skills, which might have remained hidden if less formalised assessment procedures had been used.

One of the most difficult undertakings from an evaluation perspective, however, was the attempt to tease out the relationship obtaining between children's current language proficiency and their bilingual school experience. Even when true experimental research designs can be used, establishing process–product relationships of this kind is problematic; under the very different circumstances of the BEP evaluation, fairly tentative suggestions of an interpretative kind were the best that could be offered. However, clues could be sought from a number of different comparisons: between the teachers' independent ratings of children's bilingual proficiency and the assessment data, between the performances of the younger and older children, and between the performances in speech and writing. Explanations of levels of performance might also be sought in evidence other than that deriving from the classroom itself; thus the teachers very generally reported an unstable situation of language shift away from Gaelic, among young children in the playground and in the home, as a phenomenon which had very much developed during the lifetime of the BEP. Obviously this was a potentially strong non-classroom influence on levels of Gaelic proficiency.

As far as the spoken language was concerned, the teachers' ratings of global Gaelic proficiency correlated very strongly with scores on the evaluators' Gaelic Screening Test. The older children also did very substantially better on all Gaelic tests than the younger; this discrepancy was greater for Gaelic than for English. There was some evidence that the older children's better spoken Gaelic derived from longer experience of bilingual education (notably in their greater mastery of technical/ academic vocabulary). However the discrepancy overall appeared too great to be accounted for in this way; it seemed more likely that the gap mainly reflected the language shift in the community, for which the experience of bilingual education was compensating only in part. (It will be remembered also that teachers were observed to speak little Gaelic to pupils they perceived as non-fluent in the language, and thus were providing limited opportunities for this group to become fluent. Paradox- ically of course, it is for this group that school Gaelic use might have been expected to produce the most dramatic effects, since their community exposure to the language was more limited. The pupils perceived as already fluent by their teachers were much more regularly addressed in Gaelic; but for this group, school Gaelic use was only one among many encounters with the language in home and community, and its impact on spoken language proficiency was impossible to trace in detail in a study like this.)

The picture was somewhat different regarding written Gaelic however. Here the correlations between achievement on our writing tasks and teachers' ratings of overall fluency were much weaker; most pupils were developing some Gaelic literacy skill at least, including those who were not orally fluent and did not encounter Gaelic in the home. There was little evidence of Gaelic writing by the children outside the classroom context; thus development of this dimension could be attributed much more clearly to the influence of the school.

The parent interviews were limited in number (26 parents in all, with children currently attending four of the main sample schools). However, they produced a consistent picture of general goodwill towards the schools, and support for the general educational policies being followed; in most respects these were contrasted favourably with the parents' own experience. In particular, the parents were supportive of the schools' strengthened commitment to Gaelic. These interviews thus contributed substantially to the 'reassurance' function of the evaluation, regarding the acceptability of the BEP in the wider community. However the interviews also showed clearly the very limited knowledge parents possessed regarding particular details of the BEP (in striking contrast to all the teachers interviewed). Thus it was apparent that the early ambitions of the Project to involve parents systematically in school life had not been fulfilled in any sustained way.

Overall then, virtually every aspect of the evaluation design proved practicable, and made some distinctive contribution to the overall findings. Clearly, it was not the 'ideal' design; it was retrospective not concurrent, some important issues concerning the quality of classroom interaction were addressed fairly crudely, and the attitudes of one key group of participants (the pupils themselves) could be inferred only indirectly. But was it none the less an appropriate evaluation design for the circumstances?

One important question here inevitably concerns cost effectiveness. The evaluation was lengthy and expensive, disproportionately so, it could be argued, in relation to the scale of the BEP itself. To what extent could a slimmed down operation have answered the questions addressed in an effective way?

The interviews exploring knowledge of, and attitudes towards, the BEP (with head teachers, class teachers and parents) would seem the irreducible minimum for any independent evaluation study. Numbers of interviews conducted might have been reduced somewhat (e.g. a sample of head teachers, rather than the total population, might have been interviewed); but there would have been negative consequences at least for the face validity of the data collected, if no more.

If questions regarding classroom processes were to be addressed at all seriously, some element of classroom observation was essential, given the known limitations of self-report in this respect. Due to the need for adequate sampling of different times of day etc., the duration of each school visit could not have been reduced; had the overall number of such visits been reduced, however, most evaluation questions on 'process' issues could still have been answered, though inevitably much more tentatively.

If direct assessment of pupils' language skills was to be undertaken at all, however, little reduction could have been made in either the numbers of pupils or the range of tasks without serious diminution of the usefulness of the results.

The original evaluation plan still appears defensible, therefore, apart perhaps from questions of scale, if answers were really wanted to questions about attitudes towards the BEP, the classroom experiences it stimulated, and language achievements of children within the programme. But ultimately, effective evaluation studies must be useful not only retrospectively, in making judgements on what has happened, but also prospectively, contributing to the development of new policies for the future. The final section of this chapter considers the problematic relationship of the evaluation study with the further development of bilingual education.

The evaluation project and bilingual education policy

As we have seen, the evaluation project described here was originally proposed at least partly to inform SED decision making regarding the provision of support from its general research budget for a local policy initiative (the extension of bilingual teaching into Western Isles secondary schools). However, the amount of time involved in setting up the evaluation project was such that even by the time the team was gathering its data, conditions and policy issues had substantially changed from those obtaining in 1981.

First, before the evaluation project had ended, the SED itself took a policy decision regarding the funding of Gaelic-related work in schools. The decision, first implemented in the 1986–7 financial year, was to provide regular earmarked funds for which local authorities could directly apply, 'for new projects which will allow for developments in the teaching of the Gaelic language and teaching of other subjects through the medium of Gaelic'. In the first year of the scheme, funds totalling £250,000 were provided. That is, Gaelic-related projects would no longer have to compete with other interests for funding from the general SED research budget; and (at least by implication) this funding could be available for work in secondary schools.

Second, within the Western Isles themselves, circumstances were also changing. Local authority financial difficulties had led to financial cutbacks, actual and threatened, in the education service in the islands, which were a major focus of debate in the mid 1980s. The vacant posts in the bilingual advisory service remained unfilled throughout the period of the evaluation, which meant that no development in policy could take place at primary level. (In 1986, one replacement appointment was made, but the Stornoway-based post now involves a general primary advisory remit in addition to the specifically bilingual work.) The authority was itself providing limited support for bilingual teaching at secondary level, but teachers' national industrial action regarding pay and conditions was an important constraint on all curriculum development work at this level. At various times, the authority also considered proposals for closure of a proportion of its small rural primary schools, as a partial solution to its financial difficulties. Meanwhile in the southern islands, construction of a new, central secondary school facility was expected to have radical knock-on consequences for the organisation of primary schooling. Clearly, permanent changes in advisory staffing levels, and substantial reorganisations of the small rural primary schools which have been disproportionately significant in the bilingual work, have potential implications for the future evolution of bilingual policy, quite independently of any evaluation findings.

In these difficult economic circumstances, some faltering of commitment to bilingualism within Comhairle nan Eilean itself was thus apparent in the mid 1980s. However, thinking within the wider Gaelic-speaking community was continuing to evolve, regarding what constituted appropriate educational provision. Alarmed at the continuing advance of English among children in Gaelic-speaking areas, educationalists with a commitment to language maintenance have argued increasingly that schooling must become entirely Gaelic-medium (rather than bilingual), if the language shift is to be stemmed. This feeling is evident in the development of the Gaelic playgroups movement, and also in demands in a number of localities for Gaelic-medium primary schooling. This demand has surfaced in the Western Isles, as elsewhere, and Comhairle nan Eilean has itself responded with a Gaelic-medium stream in at least one of its schools, though remaining officially committed to a general bilingual policy.

Thus when the evaluation team eventually reported, the general educational climate as well as the specific terms of the debate on Gaelic education had altered. The Final Report concludes by listing a number of issues which the evaluators felt must be faced if bilingual schooling was to survive and develop (for example, how to involve parents more fully; how to integrate monolingual English-speaking children into Gaelic-medium work; how to ensure a continuing supply of bilingual teachers). How directly (if at all) these will be addressed by policy makers within and beyond Comhairle nan Eilean, in the changing circumstances of the later 1980s, remains as yet unclear.

As a policy-making instrument, therefore, it must be concluded that this evaluation project (like many others?) was relatively inefficient. In undertaking the project, however, the evaluators themselves expected not so much to solve one specific policy question, as to provide substantial and detailed accounts of the workings of bilingual education, and of the contextual parameters which appeared to constrain or to promote it, which could form a more general background to policy making by others. In these terms, the goals of the project were very largely fulfilled. But the 'usefulness' of research-based evaluation on this lengthy and expensive model depends not so much on the researchers who conduct it, but on the existence in the wider society of relatively stable commitments to the longer-term development of policy. In times of relative financial and political insecurity, such commitments cannot be assumed.

Appendix 1:   Interview Schedule, Primary Head Teacher Survey (English Version)

A.   PRESENT SITUATION IN SCHOOL

1.   The main purpose of the interview is to talk about the bilingual education policy of the Comhairle. But could you begin by telling us something about your school?

   1.1   Could you tell us something about the ORGANISATION of the school?
   How many teachers? How many pupils? How are classes / age levels grouped? Any specialist visiting teachers?

   1.2   Could you tell us something about the CURRICULUM overall?
   Do you have a *curriculum policy* and if so, what form does it take?
   To what extent is there a *formal timetable*, and how does it work?
   What is the range of *subjects / curriculum areas*? and roughly how much time is devoted to each?
   To what extent are *projects / themes / centres of interest* used? Could you exemplify?
   (GIVE SPECIAL ATTENTION TO THIS PROMPT)
   How does the curriculum vary *between classrooms*/age levels?

   1.3   Could you say something about TEACHING METHODS?
   To what extent, and for what purpose, do you use *individual / group / whole class work*?
   To what extent do you use *practical / experimental / 'activity' work* in the various parts of the curriculum?
   Is there much variation between *classrooms / age groups*?

   1.4   Could you say something about LANGUAGE USAGE in the school?
   What is the balance of use of English and Gaelic as *medium of instruction*?
   Are *particular curriculum areas* associated with either language?
   Do particular individuals (Ts and/or Ps) have language use preferences?
   What is the pattern of English and Gaelic use in *informal communication* in the school?
   (P – P, T – P, T – T)
   Is there much variation between *classrooms/age groups*?

B.   TEACHERS' ASPIRATIONS

2.   To what extent are you satisfied / dissatisfied with the pattern of teaching and learning you have described?

3.   Do you have any ideas and/or plans for changes you would like to make in the running of the school?

3.1 As far as ORGANISATION is concerned?
(USE THESE PROMPTS ONLY IF SOME POSITIVE
RESPONSE TO CORE QUESTION.)

3.2 As far as CURRICULUM is concerned?

3.3 As far as TEACHING METHODS are concerned?

3.4 As far as LANGUAGE USE PATTERNS are concerned?

3.5 As far as PUPIL OUTCOMES are concerned?

C.   THE BILINGUAL EDUCATION PROJECT AND POLICY

(C1:   The teachers' interpretation of the BE Project/Policy)

4.   Could you tell us about the history of this school's involvement with
        the 1975–81 Bilingual Education Project?

4.1 What was the extent and nature of contacts between your
        school and the project team during 1975–81?
        Visits by team members? Documentation? Teaching materials?
        Inservice meetings/contacts with other Project schools?
        How useful did you find each of these?

5.   What in your opinion were the main things that the 1975–81 Project
        was trying to achieve?

6.   Did the Project have objectives in relation to CURRICULUM? If so,
        what were they?

6.1 Were you aware of any differences or tensions between the
        Project's objectives in relation to curriculum and your own
        ideas?

6.2 Were the tensions resolved, and if so, in what ways?

6.3 To what extent are these curriculum objectives as you have
        described them being fulfilled in your school?

7.   Did the Project have objectives in relation to TEACHING
        METHODS? If so, what were they?

7.1 Were you aware of any differences or tensions between the
        Project's objectives in relation to teaching methods and your
        own ideas?

7.2 Were these tensions resolved and if so in what way?

7.3 To what extent are these Teaching Methods objectives as you
        have described them being fulfilled in your school?

8.   Did the Project have objectives in relation to LANGUAGE USE
        PATTERNS in the school? If so, what were they?

8.1 Were you aware of any differences or tensions between the
        Project's objectives in relation to language use patterns and
        your own ideas?

8.2   Were these tensions resolved, and if so, in what way?

8.3   To what extent are these language use patterns objectives as you have described them being fulfilled in your school?

9.   Did the Project have objectives in relation to PUPIL OUTCOMES (Attainments)? If so, what were they?

9.1   Were you aware of any differences or tensions between the Project's objectives in relation to pupil attainments and your own ideas?

9.2   Were these tensions resolved, and if so, in what way?

9.3   To what extent are these pupil attainments objectives as you have described them being fulfilled in your school?

10.   Did the Project have objectives in relation to PUPIL OUTCOMES (Attitudes)? If so, what were they?

10.1   Were you aware of any differences or tensions between the Project's objectives in relation to pupil attitudes and your own ideas?

10.2   Were these tensions resolved, and if so, in what way?

10.3   To what extent are these pupil attitudes objectives as you have described them being fulfilled in your school?

(C2: Researchers' interpretation of BE Project)

(Note: Questions 11–20 should be asked only if individual topics have not already been raised by the teacher in response to questions 5–10)

C2 a)   CURRICULUM

11.   We identified ENVIRONMENTAL STUDIES as a major curriculum area of concern for the Project. Do you have any additional comments on this issue?

11.1   What were the Project's aims for the *contents and methods* of Environmental Studies?

11.2   To what extent was the focus on *local* Environmental Studies?

11.3   What was the intended *medium of instruction* for E.S.?

11.4   What were the hoped-for *pupil outcomes* in E.S.? (attitudes and attainments)

11.5   How far are you in sympathy with these Environmental Studies aims?

11.6   What are your present practices in relation to this area of concern? To what extent do you see your practices as realising the Project's aims?

12.   We identified GAELIC LANGUAGE SKILLS DEVELOPMENT as another major area of concern. Do you have any additional comments on this issue?

12.1   What methods did the Project advocate, for the development of pupils' Gaelic language skills?

12.2   How did they suggest pupils' *oral skills* in Gaelic should be developed? (Speaking and Listening)

12.3   How and when did they suggest *Gaelic literacy* should be developed? (Reading and Writing)

12.4   What about the 'Breakthrough'? How and when was it meant to be used?

12.5   What was the intended *medium of instruction*?

12.6   What were the hoped-for *pupil outcomes* in Gaelic language skills? (attitudes and attainments)

12.7   How far are you in sympathy with the Project's aims in this area?

12.8   What are your present practices in relation to this area of concern? To what extent do you see your practices as realising the Project's aims?

C2 b)   METHODOLOGY

13.   We identified the use of CHILD CENTRED, DISCOVERY METHODS as an aim of the Project. Any additional comments?

13.1   To what extent are you in sympathy with this objective? (For which curriculum areas? With which age groups?)

13.2   What are your present practices in relation to this area of concern? To what extent do you see your practices as realising the Project's aims?

14.   We identified PROJECT CENTRED WORK as another methodological aim. Any additional comments?

14.1   To what extent are you in sympathy with this aim?

14.2   What are your present practices in relation to this area of concern? To what extent do you see your practices as realising the Project's aims?

15.   We identified the use of DISCUSSION AND ORAL ACTIVITIES as another methodological aim. Any additional comments?

15.1   To what extent are you in sympathy with this aim?

15.2   What are your present practices in relation to this area of concern? To what extent do you see your practices as realising the Project's aims?

C2 c)   LANGUAGE USE PATTERNS

16.   We identified USE OF BOTH LANGUAGES as media of instruction as an aim of the project. Any additional comments?

16.1 To what extent are you in sympathy with this aim?
For which pupils? In which curriculum areas? Using which methods of instruction?

16.2 What are your present practices in relation to this area of concern? To what extent do you see your practices as realising the Project's aims?
With which pupils? In which curriculum areas? With which methods?

C2 d) OUTCOMES

17. We identified EQUAL DEVELOPMENT OF BOTH LANGUAGES IN ALL SKILLS as an outcome goal of the Project, for children from Gaelic-speaking backgrounds. Any additional comments?

17.1 To what extent are you in sympathy with this objective?

17.2 To what extent is this outcome being achieved in your school?

18. We considered the DEVELOPMENT OF A POSITIVE SENSE OF (LOCAL) IDENTITY to be another outcome goal of the Project for these children. Any additional comments?

18.1 To what extent are you in sympathy with this objective?

18.2 To what extent is this being achieved in your school?

19. We aren't clear about the Project's goals for children from non-Gaelic speaking backgrounds. Can you tell

19.1 What were the Projects's goals (if any) for these children's *language development*?

19.2 What were the goals (if any) for these children's *attitudinal development*?

19.3 To what extent are you in sympathy with these objectives and what are your own practices in relation to children from non-Gaelic speaking backgrounds?

20. In 1981 the Bilingual Project became a permanent part of the scene, and the Bilingual Unit. Did you perceive any changes as a consequence?

20.1 Any changes in relation to bilingual POLICY and OBJECTIVES?

20.2 Any changes in relation to CONTACTS WITH SCHOOLS? (Levels of support? Visits from team members? Documentation? Teaching materials? Inservice meetings/contacts with other schools?)

20.3 Have there been any significant consequences for the PATTERN OF BILINGUAL EDUCATION in the school?

D.   INFLUENCES ON DEVELOPMENT OF BILINGUAL
       EDUCATION

21.   We have disussed the objectives of the Bilingual Project, and you have
       described the pattern of bilingual education in your school. What
       have been the major influences in your opinion, which have brought
       the present situation about?

    21.1   How far is the present pattern due to the *influence of the
               1975–81 BE Project*? (Would something like the present
               pattern have come about anyhow?)

    21.2   What has been the influence of *other developments in
               educational thinking*? (e.g. the 1965 Primary Memorandum;
               the COPE policy on Environmental Studies)

    21.3   What has been the influence of *secondary school requirements*?

    21.4   What has been the influence of the *general bilingual policy* of
               Comhairle nan Eilean?

    21.5   What has been the influence of *parents* in the development of
               the present pattern of bilingual education?

    21.6   What are parents' *present attitudes* towards bilingual
               education?

22.   Do you view the present pattern of bilingual education in your school
       as stable, or evolving?

    22.1   What factors do you expect to influence the future
               development of bilingual education? (positively or negatively)
               Any factors previously mentioned?
               Any other factors? (e.g. the survival of small schools)

23.   What level and type of external support do you feel schools will need
       for bilingual education in the future?

24.   Is there anything you would like to add to what you have said?

Appendix 2: Teacher Observation Instrument

The evaluation project was concerned with what teachers did, and especially
with how they interacted with pupils. There was therefore a need for an
observation instrument, focusing on teacher–pupil interaction and especially on
two general aspects of such interaction. First, we wanted to know about the
language used by teachers in interacting with pupils, and how that language
varied according to different aspects of the context, such as the curriculum area,
the size of the audience, and the language background of the audience. Second,
we were interested in the educational nature of the interactions: to what extent
were teachers asking questions, stating facts, or giving directions? how open-
ended were the questions, i.e. were there always definite right answers or were
pupils being encouraged to think in their own independent ways? and what was

the intellectual level of the interaction, was it concerned with facts and routine practice or was it concerned with ideas and problems?

In this second interest, we were reflecting the Project's general concern with 'progressive' teaching. Some of its more particular concerns were reflected in such research questions as 'To what extent is discussion used as a teaching/ learning method?' and 'Are pupils analysing, interpreting and drawing conclusions from factual input?' In attempting to promote such emphases (as in much else), the Project was fostering ideas which had become established as orthodox in Scottish education with the publication in 1965 of the Primary Memorandum. In seeking to investigate how far these ideas had been implemented in practice, we felt able to draw upon work which had already been done in England with the purpose of finding how far the very similar ideas of the Plowden Report had been implemented in primary schools. Galton, Simon and Croll (1980) had developed two instruments, a Pupil Record and a Teacher Record, devoting considerably more time than we had available to the construction, testing and refining of these procedures. We considered that their Teacher Record came very close to what we needed for our teacher–pupil interaction observation instrument, and so we adapted this to meet our needs.

The Teacher Record is described very fully on pp. 52–104 of a *Manual for Observers* (Boydell and Jasman), and it will be described only very summarily here. The observer wears an earpiece through which a signal is received at regular intervals – we used an interval of 30 seconds – and on hearing that signal, she records the kind of interaction, if any, that the teacher is engaged in at that moment. A major distinction is made between Silence and Verbal Interaction; if Verbal Interaction is going on, the current or next teacher utterance is identified as a Statement or a Question, and one of several types of statement or question is coded: if there is Silence, a further distinction is made between Silent Interaction and No Interaction, and one of several types of either of these is identified. In addition, Pupil Audience is coded (Whole Class, Group or Individual) for each interaction, as is Curriculum Area.

Only slight amendments were made in our adaptation of this system. The only modification we made to the categorisation of utterances was that we considered it important for our purposes to differentiate 'social' utterances, dealing with personal or out-of-school affairs which were not the focus of any teaching or learning activities, from 'routine' utterances. A very important addition to the system, however, was that each utterance was coded in terms of the language used: Gaelic, English, or Mixed. In addition, each coding of Audience was annotated in terms of the Class Standard of the audience (e.g. Primary 1; Primary 1/2/3; Unknown) and in terms of their Gaelic Proficiency ('Fluent in Gaelic'; 'Understands Gaelic but not a Fluent Speaker'; 'Little or No Gaelic').

The coding sheet for teacher observation is reproduced on the next page.

Appendix 3: Pupil Observation Instrument

The basic unit of observation in this procedure is what we call a 'learning segment'. This is defined as a classroom teaching/learning activity, planned and/or authorised by the teacher, in which one or more pupils are meant to be working in a particular way, at a specified location, on a particular curriculum

STIRLING BILINGUAL EDUCATION RESEARCH PROJECT
CODING SHEET 2
(TEACHER OBSERVATION)

School:..............   Teacher:..............   Observer:..............

Date:..............   Time: AM1/   AM2/   PM1/   PM2   Observation no:.......No. pupils:......

QUESTIONS

Task   1 2 3 4 5 6 7 8 9 10 11 12 13 14 15 16 17 18 19 20
Q1 recalling facts
Q2 offering ideas, solutions (closed)
Q3 offering ideas, solutions (open)
Task supervision   1 2 3 4 5 6 7 8 9 10 11 12 13 14 15 16 17 18 19 20
Q4 referring to task supervision
Routine   1 2 3 4 5 6 7 8 9 10 11 12 13 14 15 16 17 18 19 20
Q5 referring to routine matter
Social   1 2 3 4 5 6 7 8 9 10 11 12 13 14 15 16 17 18 19 20
Q6 referring to social matter

STATEMENTS

Task   1 2 3 4 5 6 7 8 9 10 11 12 13 14 15 16 17 18 19 20
S1 of facts
S2 of ideas, problems
Task supervision   1 2 3 4 5 6 7 8 9 10 11 12 13 14 15 16 17 18 19 20
S3 telling child what to do
S4 praising work or effort
S5 feedback on work or effort
Routine   1 2 3 4 5 6 7 8 9 10 11 12 13 14 15 16 17 18 19 20
S6 providing routine info, directions
S7 providing routine feedback
S8 of critical control
Social   1 2 3 4 5 6 7 8 9 10 11 12 13 14 15 16 17 18 19 20
S9 of social matters

SILENCE

Silent interaction   1 2 3 4 5 6 7 8 9 10 11 12 13 14 15 16 17 18 19 20
    Gesturing
    showing
    marking
    waiting
    story
    reading
    not observed
    not coded
No interaction   1 2 3 4 5 6 7 8 9 10 11 12 13 14 15 16 17 18 19 20
    adult interaction
    visiting pupil
    not interacting
    out of room

AUDIENCE   1 2 3 4 5 6 7 8 9 10 11 12 13 14 15 16 17 18 19 20
    whole class
    group
    individual
                                                1 2 3 4 5 6 7 8 9 10 11 12 13 14 15 16 17 18 19 20
    CLASS STANDARD
    LANGUAGE BACKGROUND
    CURRICULUM AREA

NOTES:

area. The observer aims, then, to break up the stream of organised academic activity into a sequence of segments, each of which has to be coded on a number of dimensions, such as 'curriculum area', and 'pupil activity'.

We originally borrowed the idea of segment from the American researcher Gump (1967), and have developed it through several observation systems that we have used in investigating secondary school science and foreign language teaching (e.g. Mitchell *et al.* 1981; Parkinson *et al.* 1982). For the present study, we had to change our procedures again, especially in one fundamental respect. In all our previous studies, the focus of study had been the teacher's interaction with the entire class. This was possible because undifferentiated whole class teaching was the norm; even when pupils were in small groups, all groups normally had the same task. In Western Isles primary schools, however, differentiation among pupils in the tasks they are set is almost inevitable, given that teachers not only have mixed ability classes, but also classes with several age-groups, and often in addition wide variations in bilingual competence. In such settings, even small instructional groups are frequently broken up, so that it was only by tracking individual pupils that a coherent record could be kept of the patterns of learning activities. Our procedure was therefore to observe specific target pupils.

The minimum length of a segment was a minute, activities lasting for shorter periods being ignored. All timetabled time during a given period of observation was coded, and the first coding decision to be made was whether or not the target pupil had been assigned, and was (more or less) engaged on, a substantive task. If not, the Activity dimension was coded either Routine Activity (for activities such as tidying up or queueing) or No Activity, and no Curriculum Area coding was made. Otherwise, each segment of a pupil's activities was coded on all of the following dimensions. Three of these dimensions were critical for deciding when one segment was ending and another beginning: any change from one category to another on the Curriculum Area dimension, or on the Pupil Activity dimension, or on the Organisational Pattern dimension, meant that there was a change to a new segment.

Curriculum Area: the broad curriculum area(s) in which the target pupil is working (e.g. Mathematics, Environmental Studies (history focus)/Art and Craft; Gaelic Language Arts/Music). There were twelve basic categories, and any double coding was in principle possible. All codings were in addition annotated both to indicate any relationship of the curriculum content to current themes or projects, and also to indicate the degree of personal/local orientation of the curriculum content.

Pupil Activity: the general pattern of learning activity being engaged in by the target pupil (e.g. Interactive Speaking; Reading Fiction; Writing Practice; Computation; Creative Activity (movement)). There were 24 categories on this dimension; only certain double codings were allowed.

Organisational Pattern: the organisational grouping in which the target pupil was working (e.g. whole class; co-operative group; individual, same task). There were five categories on this dimension. All codings were in addition annotated to show the degree of choice exercised by the target pupil, alone or with his/her co-operating group, in determining what task would be undertaken.

Teacher Mode of Involvement: the ongoing activities of the teacher, whether directly involved in the observed segment or not (e.g. fully involved with the target pupil, instructional contact; intermittently involved with the target pupil, checking work; involved elsewhere). There were eight categories on this dimension.

Medium of Learning: broad indications as to the use of Gaelic and English as media of learning (e.g. mixed English and Gaelic; mainly English medium). There were three categories on this dimension.

Equipment and Materials in Use: a list was made, for each observed segment, of all equipment and materials in use by, or being produced by, the target pupil or his/her group (e.g. books, photographs, camera, natural specimens).

Time: for each segment, the beginning time and ending time were each recorded to the nearest minute.

It was considered that, using this instrument, we could build up a useful general picture of how pupils spent their time in these Western Isles primary school classrooms. More particularly, the instrument should enable us to obtain answers to many of the research questions formulated, such as:

'To what extent is Gaelic Language Arts teaching integrated with other curriculum areas, especially Environmental Studies?'

'To what extent is pupils' practical, first hand experience and exploration of the environment used as a stimulus for oral expression?'

'What is the range of types of writing which pupils undertake in Gaelic?'

'Are practical and reference skills systematically being taught?'

'What means are pupils generally using to describe, and to record, their experiences in the various curriculum areas?'

'Does the extent to which Gaelic is used vary with pupil age?'

'Does the extent to which Gaelic is used vary with class organisational patterns?'

A summary list of the categories used for the pupil observation procedure, and the coding sheet, are reproduced as the last part of this Appendix.

STIRLING BE RESEARCH PROJECT
SYSTEMATIC OBSERVATION 1: PUPIL OBSERVATION

SUMMARY OF CATEGORIES

Dimension 1:

Curriculum area

1.1 Gaelic language arts
1.2 English language arts
1.3 Environmental studies
    (history focus)
1.4 Environmental studies
    (geog/soc. studies focus)
1.5 Environmental studies
    (science/health focus)
1.6 Environmental studies
    (other focus)
1.7 Mathematics
1.8 Art and Craft
1.9 Music
1.10 Physical education
1.11 Religious education
1.12 Other

ANNOTATIONS:
{ EST Environmental Studies Theme
  OT Other theme
  NT No theme }

{ PO Personal orientation
  LO Local orientation
  NO Neither personal nor local orientation }

Dimension 2:

Pupil activity

a) Language-based

2.1 Oral practice
2.2 Listening to factual/informational input
2.3 Listening to fictional/imaginative input
2.4 Interactive speaking
2.5 Extended speaking
2.6 Reading practice
2.7 Functional reading
2.8 Reading fiction
2.9 Book-based research
2.10 Writing practice
2.11 Functional writing
2.12 Creative writing
2.13 Other language-based

b) Practical

2.14 Computation
2.15 Practical and applied maths
2.16 Observing and recording
2.17 Practical reporting
2.18 Creative activity (movement)
2.19 Creative activity (music)
2.20 Creative activity (art and craft)
2.21 Other practical

Dimension 3:

Teacher mode of involvement

3.1 Fully involved (instructional contact)
3.2 Fully involved (supervisory/managerial)
3.3 Intermittently involved (supervisory/managerial)
3.4 Intermittently involved (instructional)
3.5 Involved elsewhere
3.6 Not involved

Dimension 4:

Organisational pattern

4.1 Whole class
4.2 Cooperative, group
4.3 Cooperative, pair
4.4 Individual, same task
4.5 Individual, different task

ANNOTATIONS:
{ TAT Teacher assigns task
  PST Pupil selects tasks
  PIT Pupil initiates task }

Dimension 5:

Medium of learning

5.1 Gaelic sole medium
5.2 Mainly Gaelic medium
5.3 Mixed Gaelic and English medium
5.4 Mainly English medium
5.5 English sole medium

Dimension 6:

Equipment and materials in use
(No predetermined categories)

STIRLING BE RESEARCH PROJECT

Classroom observation 1: Pupil observation coding sheet

School: .... Teacher: .... Coder: ....

Date: .... Time block: ..... Target pupil: ....

Seg no.	Time	Curriculum area			Pupil activity		T mode	Orgn		M of I	Equipment, materials	Notes
			T.	O.	Lang.	Practical			C.			

References

Boydell, D. 1974. Teacher-pupil contact in junior classrooms. *British Journal of Educational Psychology* 44:313–18.

Boydell, D. and A. Jasman. 1983. *The Pupil and the Teacher Record: a manual for observers*. ORACLE Project, School of Education, University of Leicester.

Galton, M., B. Simon and P. Croll. 1980. *Inside the primary classroom*. London: Routledge and Kegan Paul.

Gorman, T. P., J. White, L. Orchard, and A. Tate. 1981. *Language performance in schools: Primary Survey Report No. 1*. London: Department of Education and Science.

Gorman, T. P., J. White, M. Hargreaves, M. MacLure and A. Tate. 1984. *Language performance in schools: 1982 Primary Survey Report*. London: Department of Education and Science.

Government Statistical Service. 1983. *Census 1981 Scotland: Gaelic Report*. Edinburgh: HMSO.

Gump, P. V. 1967. *The classroom behavior setting: Its nature and relation to student behavior*. Final Report, Project no 2453, US Department of Health, Education and Welfare.

MacKinnon, K. 1977. *Language, education and social processes in a Gaelic community*. London: Routledge and Kegan Paul.

Mitchell, R. 1987a. Assessing the language skills of bilingual primary pupils. *Spotlights* 6. Edinburgh: Scottish Council for Research in Education, 4 pp.

Mitchell, R. 1987b. Implementing a child-centred approach to primary schooling in a bilingual setting. *Spotlights* 7. Edinburgh: Scottish Council for Research in Education, 6 pp.

Mitchell, R., B. Parkinson and R. Johnstone. 1981. *The foreign language classroom; an observational study*. Stirling Educational Monographs no 9. Department of Education, University of Stirling.

Mitchell, R., D. McIntyre, M. Macdonald and S. McLennan. 1987. *Report of an independent evaluation of the Western Isles' Bilingual Education Project*. Department of Education, University of Stirling, 197pp.

Murray, J. and C. Morrison. 1984. *Bilingual primary education in the Western Isles Scotland*. Stornoway: Acair.

Parkinson, B., D. McIntyre and R. Mitchell. 1982. *An independent evaluation of 'Tour de France'*. Stirling Educational Monographs no 11. Department of Education, University of Stirling.

Scottish Education Department. 1965. *Primary Education in Scotland*. Edinburgh: HMSO.

Scottish Education Department. 1976. *Educational Research 1976: A Register of Current Educational Research Projects*. Edinburgh: HMSO.

Editors' postscript to Mitchell

Mitchell's chapter is a clear and detailed account of the process of setting up and implementing a retrospective evaluation in a politically sensitive area, and should be very useful for those who may be involved in designing evaluations in politically stormy settings. The chapter presents a history of the basic political issues, takes us through the negotiations that led to the development of an evaluation proposal, and documents the anxiety of various stakeholding groups. Problems emerged with newspaper leaks, changing professional circumstances, sudden illness of key personnel, fierce press denunciation, unease on the part of non-experts about the research design, underestimating the time required for analysis and report writing, and a shifting political agenda: all of these issues are treated in an unvarnished manner along with deliberations on the kinds of impact the study could and could not have on policy. Particularly useful are Mitchell's reflections on the design and conduct of the evaluation, and her conclusion that, essentially, even with hindsight, she sees little reason to modify the evaluation.

The chapter raises a number of important issues, some of which are also raised by other chapters in this volume.

First, although the main sponsors were obviously convinced of the need for evaluation of the Bilingual Education Project, no studies had been planned that were acceptable to the Scottish Education Department. Therefore, this evaluation was retrospective, and no baseline data were available for the purpose of comparison with subsequent results. The retrospective nature of the study also meant that no control group comparisons were possible, again limiting the nature of the general-isations that could be made on the basis of the data gathered. And, importantly, it was therefore also virtually impossible to make connec-tions between the degree of language proficiencies attained, and the extent or nature of the bilingual schooling experience of the children. In other words, it was not possible to make statements about the causal links between methods and outcomes, or, as Mitchell has it, processes and products. This may be frustrating for the educational researcher, and even for the evaluator who would like her results to generalise beyond the immediate setting, but it is perhaps somewhat unrealistic in any case to expect an evaluation study, especially one as politically exposed as this, to investigate basic issues of the relationship between teaching and learning.

Second, the evaluation was supposedly independent of the project being evaluated: the SED expressly required an external evaluation. Thus the team was based at a university geographically remote from the Western Isles, with at least one non-Gaelic speaker, and the directors of the evaluation were academics rather than 'practising teachers'.

Related to this is the fact that the focus of the evaluation was a politically and emotionally sensitive issue: that of language maintenance and shift in a community that perceived itself as under threat. Small wonder that the SED's rejection of internal 'case study evaluations', their insistence that an evaluation of the project be carried out before further funding could be agreed, and the commissioning of an external and potentially unsympathetic team of evaluators should have created the atmosphere of suspicion and hostility that ensued. Indeed, although the circumstances of this particular project may appear to be somewhat extreme, it is frequently the case that evaluations and evaluators are regarded with distrust and suspicion by stakeholders: usually those on the inside of a project. The negative image that evaluation frequently has is an important factor to be taken into account when planning and implementing evaluations. This, of course, is one reason why the involvement of insiders in conducting evaluations is so important, where possible. It may also be the reason why evaluations are carried out less often than one might like: they represent a potential threat and disruption to established practices and thought patterns. In the case of the BEP, as it happened, the results of the evaluation were largely favourable to the Project. As Mitchell herself wonders, however: 'Had the findings been less positive, of course, the story might have been different.'

A further issue that the chapter touches upon is that of the professional integrity of the evaluators, and the role of sponsors in determining what an evaluation should cover and the methodology it should use. It is clear that the SED did not approve of 'qualitative, case study' approaches, which may have been justified in the particular case of the internal case studies mentioned in the chapter, which appear to have concentrated upon reciting the successes of the Project and not to have addressed other issues. One does wonder, however, how justified the SED was in calling for an evaluation that would be largely quantitative in nature, with little in the way of a case study approach possible. The role of the West Highland Council is also questionable in apparently vetoing any study of pupil attitudes. The reasons given – that positive attitudes take time to develop – seem specious, and surely preempt the issue inappropriately. Mitchell herself comments upon the lack of data in this area, which would clearly have been of value. Again, one wonders how justified the Council was to censor the evaluation in this way, and how qualified its members were to opine on such professional matters: one suspects they were afraid that the evaluation might reveal less positive attitudes than they would like. Again, the threatening nature of evaluation appears to lead to less than comprehensive studies. And finally, one wonders how well informed the commentators in the media were on matters of evaluation methodology. The nature of the sniping that is reported suggests that they were less qualified than one might have desired. However much one might disapprove of apparently uninformed judgements influencing the content and method of evaluations, the fact is, of course, that evaluations have to take place in the real world and submit to a range of less than desirable pressures. Compromise is the usual outcome of such pressures, however professionally frustrating that may be.

A fifth issue that emerges clearly from the Western Isles experience is that evaluations take longer to conduct and report on than one might expect. Problems of design, of staffing, of logistics and communication, of data collection and analysis, not to mention the range of normal problems of life, all conspire to ensure that things always take longer than expected, with the best will in the world. The chapter gives a good account of the need for time and resources to develop, trial and amend the special instruments that may be required by an evaluation study – although the newspaper correspondents seem to believe that an evaluation can be implemented as soon as the proposals have been accepted. The need for adequate time is especially true in the case of the writing of the final reports. People planning evaluations would do well to remember Mitchell's experience, and to allow at least twice as much time for the preparation of final reports as they think they could possibly need. After all, the final report is a crucial document which will communicate one's findings and recommendations to many audiences, and getting that right requires time.

Finally, Mitchell's paper reflects with feeling on the relationship between evaluation and policy making. The evaluation study was commissioned because it was thought to be an important input to financial and educational political decision making. Yet in the event decisions were made and policies formulated without waiting for the results. As it happened, this may not have been important in this particular case, since the evaluation was largely favourable towards the Project. But what if the findings had been resoundingly negative? Where would the policy makers and implementers have stood then? How acceptable would the evaluation have been, in a changed climate of educational innovation and financing? Mitchell's conclusions on this are sobering for evaluators convinced of the need for their profession: educationalists and politicians alike will continue to ignore the results of evaluation if it suits them and their changing circumstances, but an evaluation that is not used is an evaluation not needed, whatever the cost of not conducting an evaluation. Evaluators need to remind themselves that their recommendations must be capable of implementation, but they must also be aware that they are as likely to be ignored in a changing world as they are to be implemented. Trying to ensure that one's evaluation is as practical and acceptable as possible is important in evaluation, but in the end, such a goal may be beyond our control.

4 Issues in evaluating input-based language teaching programs

Adrian Palmer

Introduction

During the academic year 1985–6, an eight-month experimental course in first-year German was offered at the University of Utah. The experiment was designed to test the feasibility of using a radical implementation of Krashen's theory of second language acquisition. Steven Sternfeld directed the program, and Paul Kramer and Louise Lybbert Nygaard taught the experimental courses. These individuals, along with several graduate students in the Department of Linguistics, developed and administered the tests and questionnaires used to evaluate the courses. I assisted in the planning phase of the evaluation and worked with the two German instructors (Kramer and Nygaard) in developing and refining the instructional methodology. I was also involved in designing the attitude questionnaires. Kramer is responsible for the analysis of the German performance measures, which were scored by him and several other raters. Thus, this chapter should be considered a report on the program evaluation efforts of a fairly large team of individuals.

When we started thinking about how to evaluate the experimental German course, we had to consider the options, organize them, and select those in which we were interested. We would have found it useful to have on hand a document describing how someone else had dealt with the issues we were facing, and we might have saved considerable time and energy in developing a plan that worked for us. The general purpose of this chapter is to provide other researchers with this kind of a head start.

First, I will describe the program briefly. Then, following Alderson (1987) I will discuss options we considered when addressing six questions: 1) why evaluate, 2) when to evaluate, 3) whom to evaluate, 4) what to evaluate, 5) how to evaluate, and 6) for whom to evaluate. Finally, I will comment briefly on some of the findings.

Description of the program

Theory behind the program

KRASHEN'S GENERAL THEORY

Krashen (1982, 1985) hypothesizes that a language is acquired (picked up in such a way that it can be used effortlessly and without conscious thought) in only one way: a) by exposure to interesting, comprehensible input b) under non-threatening conditions. These are Krashen's first two hypotheses: the 'input hypothesis' and the 'affective filter hypothesis'. A third hypothesis, the 'production emerges hypothesis', is that c) speech emerges as the result of acquisition. Thus, according to Krashen's theory no production practice is needed for subconscious language acquisition, nor is any analysis or explanation of the target language.

In addition, Krashen's theory includes other hypotheses. For example, his full theory includes a hypothesis that conscious 'learning' (through analysis, practice, and explanation) is possible and is useful in certain ways; however, conscious learning is not thought to be useful in developing acquired competence, and consciously learned material is not thought to become 'acquired' as the result of practice.

VERSION OF THE THEORY TESTED

In the experimental program, we decided to test as 'pure' a version of Krashen's theory as possible. Therefore, we *only* provided interesting, comprehensible input. We deliberately avoided activities that would tend to produce conscious learning so that we might observe the effects of the subconscious acquisition process. We also avoided *requiring* the students to speak for three reasons: speaking might create stress, raise the affective filter, and block acquisition; speaking (according to Krashen's theory) is not required for speech to emerge; and early speaking might lead to acquisition of deviant forms through exposure to a large amount of imperfect German (Krashen 1985:46–7).

Methodology

TEACHING

J. Marvin Brown (director of the Thai Language Program at the A.U.A. Language Center in Bangkok, Thailand) and I developed the general teaching methodology used in the study. This is described in detail in a teachers' manual called *The Listening Approach: methods and materials for applying Krashen's Input Hypothesis* (Brown and Palmer 1988).

Probably the most distinctive characteristic of the Listening Approach is that there are two teachers. The teachers talk and interact primarily with each other but always try to make what they say both comprehensible and interesting to the students. The students just look, listen, and try to understand what is happening. They try to keep their attention on the meaning, not the language. And what is more, they are advised not to construct sentences consciously in order to speak but, instead, to wait until the language comes out by itself ('emerges' in Krashen's terms). In addition to receiving spoken input, the students are also exposed to written input. The teachers talk about written material which the students see on overhead transparencies and handouts, and the students also read interesting, simple, contextualized material on their own.

ACTIVITIES

The activities were selected from the large variety described in *The Listening Approach* and were sequenced entirely according to their potential interest value and ease of comprehension. That is, the teachers tried to use activities which would prove as interesting as possible yet still be comprehensible. They made no conscious attempt to sequence the activities according to notional, functional, or grammatical criteria. And there was no student textbook. A typical class included activities such as the following:
1 *discussion*: The weather (the previous night's heavy snowstorm).
2 *discussion*: A teacher's cold and possible remedies.
3 *discussion*: The geography of Germany.
4 *game*: The teachers read from sheets containing information about the students. The students guessed which student was being described.
5 *reading*: The teachers read a fairy tale aloud to the students from an overhead transparency and discussed it.

STUDENTS

The students were drawn from a population of regular university students enrolled in a first-year German course offered for credit at the University of Utah. The class consisted of two ordinary sections of German 101 combined into a single class. The students were not told that the method to be used was experimental until after they had signed up for the course. The control group consisted of students who had signed up for a different section of the same course.

CLASSES

Classes met five days a week for one hour a day. The entire program continued for three ten-week terms, for a total of about 150 hours of instruction.

TEACHERS

The two teachers, Paul Kramer and Louise Nygaard, graduate students in the University of Utah's Department of Foreign Languages and experienced in contemporary language teaching methodology, taught the classes.

Why evaluate?

One of the first questions we asked was why we were evaluating the program. We considered a number of possible reasons. One was to find out whether our program was feasible: could the teachers teach it and would the students put up with it? Another as noted above was to find out whether the program was productive. Would it produce the results one might expect of it given the claims of the theory of language acquisition upon which it was based? Another was to find out whether the program was appealing. Perhaps the program could be taught, but would it be enjoyed?

We decided to address all of these issues, but our primary reason for evaluating the program was to find out more about language acquisition theory. Therefore, our initial program design and any modifications we made to it during the year had to be consistent with the pure version of Krashen's theory we were interested in testing, so that we could be as clear as possible about which teaching processes were being tested (Beretta 1986a:296). As a result, we accepted the possibility that students would be resistant to some of the elements in the program, and we decided not to modify the program in ways that would make conclusions about the validity of the theory difficult to arrive at.

When to evaluate?

Our next question was when to evaluate. Should we evaluate the program periodically during the year (formative evaluation), or should we wait until the end (summative evaluation)? Our decision was based upon both practical and theoretical concerns.

On the practical side, we were busy keeping up with the instructional side of the operation (which included visiting classes, giving one another feedback, planning lessons, etc.), and we had little time to design and implement a systematic formative evaluation study. And on the theoretical side, we were strongly influenced by Krashen's affective filter hypothesis. According to this hypothesis, students acquire best under non-threatening conditions, and large scale, formative evaluation might be likely to raise the filter (Krashen 1982:30–2).

As a result, we decided to evaluate the program in two phases: a small-scale, somewhat informal formative evaluation of students' attitudes toward the program and a large-scale, formal, summative evaluation of the students' language abilities. We thought that the formative evaluation of attitudes would allow us to keep track of attitude changes as they occurred, which would help us adjust the input to keep it interesting and comprehensible. The summative evaluation of students' language ability would allow us to determine how well the students could perform at the end of the program.

Whom to evaluate?

I will break down this question into two main issues. The first is whether to evaluate the experimental group by itself or to compare the experimental group with a control group. After discussing this question, I will turn to the issue of whom to evaluate within the group(s): teachers, students, administrators, or some combination of the three.

Comparative or independent group evaluation

COMPARATIVE EVALUATION

When we first started to think about how to evaluate the program, what came to mind immediately was a methods comparison study using experimental and control groups. Such a study would provide us a means of comparing results of the input-based program with the results of traditional (eclectic) instruction, along the lines of the studies by Asher, Kusudo and de la Torre (1983); Burger (1989); Edwards *et al.* (1984); Hauptman, Wesche and Ready (1988); Lafayette and Buscaglia (1985); Lightbown (1989); and Sternfeld (1989).

While comparative studies are interesting, designing and interpreting them is difficult. Ideally, students should be assigned to the two groups at random, or if this is not possible, attempts should be made to control for self-selection. Also, teacher variables are difficult to control. The results of the Pennsylvania Study (Smith and Baranyi 1968) indicated that the teacher variable was more important than the method used. In addition, experimental programs are likely to be new, and one might expect that they would generate more excitement and enthusiasm than the traditional programs (the Hawthorn Effect). Finally, the goals of programs employing different language teaching methods are likely to be quite different, which would make finding criterion measures appropriate to both programs difficult (Beretta 1986b).

On the other hand, such studies do ask questions about alternatives, which many people find interesting. And while they carry along with them design problems (Kramer and Palmer 1990) and testing problems (Palmer 1990), when a number of such studies are carried out questions of interpretation which come up for one study may be answered by another study conducted under different conditions. For example, if one suspects that a negative outcome in one study might be the result of instructor variables (rather than the method used) but then finds similar negative outcomes in a study conducted with instructors known to be superior, one might be able to rule out the instructors as a confounding variable and begin to draw some general conclusions about the effect of the method itself.

INDEPENDENT EVALUATION

The other alternative would be to evaluate the experimental program on its own merits, which would involve stating the objectives of the program and collecting data to evaluate how well these objectives had been met. Such a study would avoid many of the problems described above, but it could not provide the kinds of comparative data which many people want.

SOLUTION

We decided to conduct both independent and comparative evaluations. To evaluate the experimental treatment on its own merits, we specified objectives for the experimental program, against which we could compare actual outcomes. To compare the relative effectiveness of the experimental method with something else, we created a control group of traditionally taught students and gave the same set of proficiency tests to each group.

People affected by program outcomes

Whether a program is or is not considered successful may depend upon whom we ask. We may decide that it succeeds if the students learn something and are happy with the learning experience. In this case, we would obtain measures or descriptions of student behavior. Or we might decide to evaluate the program in terms of teachers' attitudes. Are they pleased with their teaching and with their perceptions of what their students learned? Or we might evaluate a program's success in terms of administrators' attitudes. Or, as Rodgers (1986) suggests, we might even go outside of the educational setting altogether and evaluate the program in terms of the attitudes of people within the community.

We decided to obtain information from students, teachers, and administrators. The following is a discussion of the kinds of information we obtained from each population.

What to evaluate?

In attempting to make sense of the issue of what to evaluate, we first had to decide how to organize the options. We found Bloom's cognitive, behavioral, and affective domains (Krathwohl, Bloom and Masia, 1956) to be a useful framework.

Cognitive domain

The cognitive domain consists of knowledge about the language. In input-intensive acquisition based programs such as ours, there is little to evaluate within this domain. Such programs do not present grammar explicitly (cognitively). Nor do they expect the subconscious acquisition process to lead to cognitive control. Thus, we decided not to evaluate cognitive changes or knowledge, even though such outcomes would be expected for the control group.

Behavioral domain

To evaluate students' behavioral performance, we needed to start by determining what kinds of outcomes we could reasonably expect of students completing the program. The most specific statement we could find came from Krashen and Terrell (1983):

> After 100–150 hours of Natural Approach Spanish, you will be able to: 'Get around' in Spanish; you will be able to communicate with a monolingual native speaker of Spanish without difficulty; read most ordinary texts in Spanish with some use of a dictionary; [and] know enough Spanish to continue to improve on your own.
>
> After 100–150 hours of Natural Approach Spanish, you will not be able to: pass for a native speaker; use Spanish as easily as you use English; understand native speakers when they talk to each other (you will probably not be able to eavesdrop successfully), use Spanish on the telephone with great comfort, [or] participate easily in a conversation with several other native speakers on unfamiliar topics.
>
> (Krashen and Terrell 1983:74)

Krashen and Terrell also discuss the role of grammar in defining expected outcomes (pp. 71–2). While they indicate that beginning students may simply string together appropriate lexical items in some logical order, they do not expect that students will continue to use these simple stringing techniques. They believe that the language acquisition that takes place in the classroom will result in students acquiring grammatical competence. Thus, based upon Krashen and Terrell's guidelines, appropriate tests for the experimental group might assess the students' listening, speaking, and reading skills, as well as their subconscious control of grammar.

We did not have available a description of behavioral objectives for the control group, so we had rely on our experience as teachers and administrators to inform our selection of tests. We concluded that tests of listening, speaking, and reading skills, as well as subconscious control of grammar (already needed to evaluate the experimental group) would also be appropriate for the control group. In addition, we decided that one of the objectives for the control group would be developing writing skills.

Thus, our final selection of tests included measures of the four skills (listening, speaking, reading, and writing) and two elements (grammar and vocabulary).

Affective domain

In addition to evaluating behavioral outcomes, we also wanted to evaluate the attitudes of three populations (students, teachers, and administrators) toward the program. In deciding what attitudes to assess, we tried to balance the advice of others, lists of questions appearing in other research studies, and our own research interests in preparing our questionnaires.

STUDENTS

We divided our questions to the students into three types. The first type consisted of questions about fairly general aspects of their attitude toward the program. The process we used in preparing these questions included discussions with experts in program evaluation, discussions with people involved in the program, examination of other program evaluation studies, and examination of general issues in program evaluation (for example, Beretta 1986a and 1986b, Richards and Rodgers 1986 Chapter 11). We eventually elicited the students' opinions on the following topics:

1 reasons for studying German at the beginning of the program and at present: fun, curiosity, for use in future studies, for use in work, to satisfy a university requirement, to get a good grade, and importance of developing proficiency in the four skills and grammar
2 current satisfaction with their instruction in the areas of listening, speaking, reading, writing, and grammar
3 satisfaction with their instruction in the areas of listening, speaking, reading, writing, and grammar compared with their expectations when they began the experimental course
4 confidence that they could cope with listening, speaking, reading, and writing German in a German-speaking country

5 interest in being in contact with German culture and language outside of class
6 interest in electing sheltered subject matter (subject matter courses taught entirely in German to students who are non-native speakers of German)
7 interest in continuing to study German
8 importance of absence of pressure in class and receiving a good grade
9 satisfaction with the cost of the program in terms of time and money
10 appropriateness of the levels of spoken and written German to which they were exposed in class
11 what they would want more of, and less of, in class
12 how much fun they had in class
13 confidence in the method
14 whether or not they would recommend the class to their friends
15 level of participation
16 amount of structure (organization) they liked in a language class
17 amount of risk they enjoy in class
18 amount of interaction with classmates they enjoy
19 opinions of each instructor's control of language, ability to teach, and personality
20 satisfaction with the way the instructors interacted

The second type of question elicited students' opinions about specific learning activities: Did they like the activities and find them interesting? We asked many questions of this type because Krashen's theory of language acquisition states that affect is one of the two causal factors in language acquisition.

The third type of question elicited students' general attitudes toward whatever aspect of the program concerned them at the time. We used this kind of question to elicit feedback on issues we had perhaps not taken into consideration when developing the list of specific questions.

TEACHERS

We also assessed teachers' attitudes on a variety of issues. In deciding what questions to ask, we followed a procedure similar to that used in deciding what questions to ask of the students. In addition, where possible we tried to ask the teachers questions which were similar to those we asked the students so that we could determine the extent to which students' and teachers' impressions and attitudes differed. We eventually decided to obtain information on teachers' attitudes on the following topics:

1 satisfaction with the students' competence in the four skills and grammar; satisfaction relative to that in other courses they had taught
2 confidence in the students' ability to cope in German in four skills

3 satisfaction with the amount of German culture they were able to present in class
4 interest in the content of what they talked about in class
5 satisfaction with the amount of pressure placed on students
6 satisfaction with the grading policy
7 satisfaction with the amount of support they received from supervisors/staff, materials supplied, training program
8 satisfaction with the amount of class preparation time required
9 confidence in their ability to train others in method
10 importance of their experience in obtaining future employment
11 what they would want more of, or less of
12 amount of fun they had teaching the course
13 whether they would want to teach the same class again
14 whether they would want to study a language using the experimental method
15 what they liked most and least about teaching the experimental class

ADMINISTRATORS

Finally, we wanted to know how the department chairman felt about the program. In addition to questions about perceived effectiveness of instruction, we asked the chairman a number of questions about how the experimental program contributed to the Language Department's overall image and visibility. Where possible, we asked questions parallel to those that we asked of the students and teachers. The following are the topics we decided upon:

1 the importance of each of the following goals for the experimental first year German program:
   a) preparing the students to use German for fun as in travel, speaking with relatives and friends, reading for pleasure, etc.
   b) preparing the students to use German to study in a German-speaking country
   c) preparing the students to use German in their work or future work, including missionary activities, business, teaching, etc.
   d) helping the students satisfy a university requirement
   e) helping the students satisfy their curiosity or have an enjoyable experience
2 the importance of first year German students developing competence in each of the following areas: listening, speaking, reading, writing, and grammar
3 satisfaction (from whatever impressions he might have formed) with students' achievement in each of the following areas: listening, speaking, reading, writing, grammar

4 satisfaction (from whatever impressions he may have formed) with the method used to teach listening, speaking, reading, writing, grammar
5 confidence in the students' ability to cope with listening, speaking, reading, and writing in a German-speaking country
6 importance of students a) being exposed to German culture in the classroom, and b) being interested in the content of what is talked about in class
7 amount of pressure he thought students should feel in a first year language class
8 satisfaction with the amount of support the teachers received from their supervisors and from the course developer
9 satisfaction with the quantity of materials/ideas for teaching with which the teachers were supplied
10 satisfaction with the training program for the teachers
11 importance of the experimental German program teaching experience in helping the teachers obtain future employment
12 satisfaction with the cost of the experimental program in terms of teacher preparation time
13 satisfaction with the cost of the experimental program in terms of materials the students had to purchase
14 satisfaction with the cost of the experimental program in terms of the utilization of classroom space
15 satisfaction with the cost of administering the experimental program
16 satisfaction with the ability of the experimental German program to create university-wide visibility for the Department of Languages
17 satisfaction with the ability of the experimental German program to create visibility for the Language Department within the community
18 satisfaction with the ability of the experimental German program to contribute to the Language Department's reputation for professionalism and ability to innovate
19 satisfaction with the experimental German program's contribution to his ability to recruit new faculty
20 satisfaction with the experimental German program's ability to stimulate student and faculty research in language acquisition
21 satisfaction with the experimental German program's ability to stimulate student and faculty research in program development
22 satisfaction with the experimental German program's ability to generate increased interaction between Language Department personnel and personnel from other departments

F

How to test

Here I discuss the methods used to obtain the information given above. I first discuss the issue of method effect. Then I provide examples of the various instruments.

Method effect

Numerous research studies (Bachman and Palmer 1981, 1982, 1989; Brütsch 1979; Clifford 1981) indicate that we cannot get directly at language competence without the method used influencing the results. And while with a lot of effort the *relative* influence of method can be quantified for a small number of competing methods (Bachman and Palmer 1981, 1982, 1989), I know of no way to discover such a thing as 'the best' or 'the perfect' method.

Recently, Bachman (1990) has proposed a system for the componential analysis of test methods. However, since the study described in this chapter predated Bachman's system, our own thinking about method was less systematic than would be the case today. Basically, we attempted to select methods that would not be obviously disruptive. For example, in evaluating the students' ability to read German, we had them summarize a reading passage in English rather than German. This did not introduce their ability to write German as a factor contributing to the test results. On the other hand, we knew that perhaps the students' ability to summarize would influence the test results. We simply considered this the lesser of the two problems.

Practicality

Second, our decisions on how to test were influenced by practicality considerations. Because of constraints on time, money, and personnel, tests had to be easy to develop, administer, and score. And the rating procedures had to be quick and uncomplicated. The following examples or descriptions of different methods illustrate how we chose to balance method effect considerations with practicality issues.

SPECIFIC METHODS: OVERVIEW

The specific test methods for each skill/element are described below. Many of these tests were developed by Steven Sternfeld and Batya Elbaum (members of the Department of Languages faculty), with the assistance of graduate students in the Department of Languages and the Linguistics-TESOL Masters Degree program. I will first explain the 'standard' procedures used to rate most of the protocols. (I also describe a different 'special' rating procedure below under the description of the oral interview test.) Then I will describe the procedures used to obtain the performance samples to be rated.

A pool of raters (teachers in the German program) used the following 'standard' procedure to rate the students' performance on most of the tests. They were told to decide whether a student who could listen, speak, read, or write at the level demonstrated on the protocol being rated would be able to perform satisfactorily in the second year sheltered subject matter course (a content course taught in German specifically for non-native speakers of German). A rating of 'high' indicated that the student would definitely be able to perform satisfactorily. A rating of 'mid' indicated that the student would probably be able to perform satisfactorily. And a rating of 'low' indicated that the student would clearly not be able to perform satisfactorily. We have reason to believe, however, that the assigned ratings were more indicative of the raters' decisions about general language proficiency than ability to perform in sheltered subject matter courses, because some of the tests were measuring language abilities which would likely have little to do with performance in such courses. Moreover, since the raters had never taught such a course, they had no specific sheltered content course experience from which to make the ratings.

Practical considerations also dictated this global approach to most of the protocol rating. A more detailed rating procedure would have required both a training program for raters and a small group of raters with the time to participate in the training program and the actual rating sessions. Funding and time constraints made this impossible.

Two methods were used to evaluate the students' German language proficiency: traditional language tests and students' self-ratings.

LISTENING: LECTURE SUMMARY

A ten-minute videotaped lecture was prepared by a professor who is a native speaker of German. The lecture concerned some of the technicalities of East and West German politics. The German used was academic with complicated syntax. It was unsimplified and was at a much higher level than the students had been exposed to in class.

Students were allowed to take notes during the lecture. Following it, they were instructed to summarize the lecture as well as possible, in as much detail as possible. Protocols were rated using the standard procedure described above.

LISTENING: STUDENTS' SELF-RATINGS

The students were asked to write brief descriptions of their ability to understand spoken German. We grouped these descriptions into high, mid, and low categories, counted the numbers of students in each category, and provided examples of students' comments in each category.

SPEAKING: ORAL INTERVIEW

A native speaker of German who did not know the students interviewed each student for five to eight minutes, the length depending upon how proficient the students were. The interviewer went through a list of questions which included alternate questions so no two interviews were exactly the same. Questions were of the sort one might ask someone when trying to become acquainted. For example:

1 Where do you live?
2 Where do you work?
3 Have you studied other languages before?
4 Why are you studying German?

In the middle of the interview, the student was given some information to elicit by asking questions in German. For example:

1 Where does the interviewer come from?
2 What is the interviewer doing in America?
3 Where does the interviewer normally work?
4 What does the interviewer's family consist of?

Kramer scored these interviews using two criteria: sentence complexity and well-formedness, and control of inflectional morphology. He then added the two scores together and then converted these scores to ratings using a 'special' procedure different from the standard one described above. Kramer compared the students' performance on the oral interview with their performance on the remaining tests that had been rated using the standard procedure. He determined which students tended to fall consistently into the high, mid, and low categories on the other tests and used this information, together with the original rating criteria, to estimate high, mid, and low break points for the interview scores.

SPEAKING: STUDENTS' SELF-RATINGS

The students were asked to write brief descriptions of their ability to speak German. We grouped these descriptions into high, mid, and low categories, counted the numbers of students in each category, and provided examples of students' comments in each category.

READING: TRANSLATION

The students were given a humorous passage in German about a child who threw a rock through a window and then bragged about having answered the teacher's question (about who threw the rock through the window) correctly. They then wrote an English translation, which was rated using the standard procedure.

READING: SUMMARY

The students were given a written passage about a German satirist written in academic, unsimplified German, followed by a written summary of an interview with the satirist. The students were then given five minutes to write a summary of the passage in English, which was rated using the standard procedure.

READING: STUDENTS' SELF-RATINGS

The students were asked to write brief descriptions of their ability to write German. We grouped these descriptions into high, mid, and low categories, counted the numbers of students in each category, and provided examples of students' comments in each category.

WRITING: GUIDED COMPOSITION

The students were given a 70-word passage in German about the weather in Germany. They then wrote a passage in German about the weather in America. These compositions were rated using the standard procedure.

WRITING: DICTATION

A 65-word passage was dictated to the students. The content consisted of a brief comparison of the political differences between East and West Germany. The dictation was scored by marking one point off for each omitted word, extra word, and pair of permuted words. Words were considered correct if the spelling was phonetically appropriate. In addition, a half point was deducted for each error in inflectional morphology. The compositions were then rated using the special procedure described for the oral interview test.

WRITING: STUDENTS' SELF-RATINGS

The students were asked to write brief descriptions of their ability to write German. We grouped these descriptions into high, mid, and low categories, counted the numbers of students in each category, and provided examples of students' comments in each category.

GRAMMAR: RATIONAL CLOZE

The students were given a 118-word multiple-choice cloze test with rational deletions (developed by Paul Kramer). The passage, modified somewhat by Kramer, was taken from a German reader. The subject matter was a humorous story about a student who went into a restaurant and made a deal with the waiter that if the student could sing the waiter a song that pleased the waiter, the student would get his dinner free.

The first sentence was left intact. Twenty-five words were rationally deleted from the remainder of the passage to test grammar, discourse competency, and knowledge of the world. Deletions occurred at intervals ranging from four to eleven words. Four answer choices were provided for each deletion.

Kramer scored the cloze test using the exact word method. He then assigned ratings using the special procedure described for the oral interview test.

GRAMMAR: STUDENTS' SELF-RATINGS

The students were asked to write brief descriptions of their control of German grammar. We grouped these descriptions into high, mid, and low categories, counted the numbers of students in each category, and provided examples of students' comments in each category.

VOCABULARY: UNCONTEXTUALIZED TRANSLATIONS

The students were given a list of German words to translate into English. These were scored and then rated using the special procedure described for the oral interview test.

VOCABULARY: CONTEXTUALIZED TRANSLATIONS

The students were then given a reading passage containing the same vocabulary words used in the uncontextualized translation test. They then translated these words into English using the additional information they could obtain from the context. Kramer scored these translations and converted them to ratings using the special procedure described for the oral interview.

VOCABULARY: STUDENTS' SELF-RATINGS

The students were asked to write brief descriptions of their control of German vocabulary. We grouped these descriptions into high, mid, and low categories, counted the numbers of students in each category, and provided examples of students' comments in each category.

Affective domain

STUDENTS

Three methods were used to assess students' attitudes: activity rating slips, journals, and attitude questionnaire. First, the students were given an activity rating form to fill out at the end of each class. On this form, they rated two attributes of each of the day's activities: interest and comprehensibility. Ratings were done on a subjective scale of 0–100. The instructors used these ratings to decide how successful the activities were.

Second, the students kept journals in which they described their language learning experience. These journals were collected on a weekly basis, read by the instructors, and summarized at the end of the program by a graduate student in the Linguistics-TESOL M.A. Program.

Third, the students were given a questionnaire at the end of the first and third terms. Most of the questions asked the students to rate on a four-point scale their responses to questions of the sort described above in the section *What to evaluate?* In addition, the students responded to a few open-ended questions.

INSTRUCTORS

Three methods were used to assess the instructors' attitudes: ongoing conversations, a questionnaire, and a paper. I visited classes frequently and talked informally with the instructors afterwards. In these conversations we discussed how the class had gone, which activities seemed to work and which ones didn't, and how the students seemed to be reacting. On the basis of this information we decided how to modify the instruction appropriately.

Also the instructors wrote a paper at the end of the program describing their impressions of the experience.

Finally, the instructors completed a 44-item questionnaire at the end of the program. The questions covered demographic information and the instructors' attitudes toward various aspects of the program (see the section on *What to evaluate?* above). With the exception of two open-ended response questions, questions were of the multiple-choice variety.

ADMINISTRATION

The department chairman filled out a 44-item multiple choice attitude survey at the end of the program.

For whom to evaluate?

Possible audiences

As Rodgers (1986) has pointed out, a variety of people have an interest in the language teaching program evaluation reports. Students want to learn and have an enjoyable experience in the process and might want to know what they could expect of a specific program. Teachers want to know how effective instruction proves to be and how enjoyable the teaching experience is. Administrators are concerned with results and their effect on enrollments. Members of the community may be concerned with the effect of the students' language skills on how well they function in the community. Researchers are concerned with the results of applying language acquisition theory in the classroom. And program evaluators may be interested in the report as a guide to future evaluation studies.

Depending upon which audience the program evaluator is addressing, the kind of information obtained and the way it is presented would likely vary. For example, one would make fairly different assumptions about the interests and background knowledge of readers of *Language Learning* and members of a college curriculum review committee.

Options for reporting results

We found audience considerations to be important when deciding upon procedures for reporting on student performance, for we wanted readers to be able to form a concrete picture of what students completing the program could do. Therefore, in addition to providing quantitative data, Kramer (1989) reported both the numbers of protocols falling into the high, mid, and low categories and provided examples of typical protocols at each level. In addition Kramer provided a corrected version of each protocol, as well as a translation.

I followed a similar procedure useful in reporting the results of the attitude surveys (Palmer 1987). When students provided self-ratings of their ability to use German, I grouped their responses into high, mid, and low categories, reported the number of responses in each category, and supplied examples of these responses. And when students responded to open-ended questions about what they liked most and least about the program, I quoted typical responses.

A few comments on the findings

The purpose of the following comments is to give the reader some indications of the sorts of conclusions we reached about the general effectiveness of the program. (For a detailed account, see Kramer 1989.) I will summarize the findings in three areas: instructors' attitudes toward the program, students' attitudes toward the program, and students' performance on behavioral measures.

Practicality of the approach

The instructors felt that the radical implementation of Krashen's theory used was practical. They were able to provide three terms of interesting, comprehensible input. The two-teacher classroom was indeed feasible and generated a lot of useful interaction between the instructors, and the students seemed to be interested in this interaction. The drop-out rate for the course was no worse than for traditionally taught classes.

Student attitudes toward the program

Students' reactions to the method were very positive at the beginning of the program, when they appreciated the lack of pressure to produce the language and the absence of formal testing. As the program progressed, however, they began to worry about whether they would eventually be able to speak, and there is some indication that they would like to have been tested in order to know that they were indeed acquiring the language. Their comments indicated that a number of them would have liked some specific encouragement to speak and make mistakes in order to get used to this experience.

One conclusion that we could draw from this change in student attitudes is that it may be difficult to completely satisfy both of the conditions necessary for acquisition in Krashen's theory. Specifically, we may not be able to provide students like the ones in our program only with interesting, comprehensible input (and no output practice) while maintaining a low affective filter strength in a relatively long-term program.

This situation creates a problem for researchers interested in evaluating Krashen's theory. Specifically, in order to test the theory, we would like to provide all and only what the theory says is absolutely necessary for acquisition (comprehensible input with low filter strength). Yet to keep the filter strength low over a long period of time with students such as ours, we may have to provide output practice. Doing so, however, makes the interpretation of the results difficult, since if the students do acquire and if speech does emerge, we can no longer ascertain whether this would have happened without the output practice. It may be the case that to provide a good test of a radical implementation of Krashen's theory we will need to find a population of students who will not find the absence of output practice over a long period of time threatening. It will be interesting to discover whether such a population of students exists.

Student performance on behavioral measures

THE EXPERIMENTAL GROUP CONSIDERED BY ITSELF

Students' abilities to produce German ranged from slight to quite surprising (Kramer 1989). Students rated as low were functioning as one would expect of acquirers within the early stages of an expected interlanguage phase. For students rated as high, evidence of acquisition was much more apparent, with these students at times able to produce well-formed, contextually appropriate, complete sentences.

Also, actual levels of acquisition may have been higher than the overall performance of the students in this study indicate, since attitude measures became more negative over time. This may have raised the 'output filter', which is said to limit the performance of acquired competence (Krashen 1985).

COMPARISON BETWEEN EXPERIMENTAL AND CONTROL GROUPS

A MANOVA (Multiple Analysis of Variance) conducted by Kramer (1989) indicated that the control group students (who received traditional instruction) performed significantly better overall than the acquisition students. They also performed significantly better on four of the seven tests (oral interview, reading translation, writing summary, and vocabulary). The experimental students did not perform significantly better on any of the tests (Kramer 1989).

Discussion

Amount of data

We may have gotten somewhat out of balance with respect to quantity versus quality of data. In some cases we noticed that when we used several different methods to obtain the same data, we tended to reach the same conclusions. For example, with student attitude data we tended to reach the same conclusions from the questionnaires and journals. Also, since our primary research interest was the issue of the validity of Krashen's theory of second language acquisition, we found little immediate use for the information obtained from the department chairman.

Quality of the data

In future studies, I would probably spend more time on test development and use fewer methods. For example, if we were to use a scaled attitude survey again, I would research options for wording questions and scaling responses. (See Oskarsson 1978; Bachman and Palmer 1989.) Bachman and I found that questions about 'difficulty' in using language provided more useful information on the ability than did 'can-do' questions about what the students were able to do.

In addition, some of the data we obtained would have been of little value even if we had specific uses for it. For example, we asked the department chairman to rate various aspects of the program without providing him with enough information to make his task meaningful. We should have provided him with examples of student test performance and asked him to visit the class instead of having him rely on what he happened to hear about the course and the students' performance on it.

Finally, I would carefully pre-test all of the instruments. A number of students commented that certain questions on the attitude survey were difficult to interpret, and the limited number of answer choices provided did not allow them to make what they considered valid responses. Also, some of the tests (such as the lecture summary) may have been too difficult. Pre-testing the instruments would also have helped us address this problem and balance the quality and quantity of data obtained.

In general, had we spent less time gathering the same kind of information by means of different methods and less time gathering data not related to our basic research question, we could have spent more time refining our primary instruments and preparing the students for the testing experience.

Formats for reporting data, and effects on interpretability

We found it useful to provide examples of student performance at different levels in addition to reporting statistics. This helped audiences relate more directly to the numerical data provided, particularly since only norm-referenced tests were used. For example, a dean at the University of Utah was more concerned with the general level of ability of both experimental and traditional students (as shown by examples of what the students could do with the language) than with what he considered minor (though perhaps significant) differences between the groups (as evidenced by descriptive statistics from the norm-referenced tests used). An even more productive approach would be to develop and use criterion-referenced tests of communicative language ability (Bachman 1989; Bachman and Clark 1987; Bachman and Savignon 1985).

Between-group comparison

Kramer's finding that the control group performed significantly better than the experimental group came as quite a surprise to us. We expected the experimental group to do better. If this single study is considered in isolation, the finding would appear to be rather straightforward evidence against the Input Hypothesis. What this study led to, however, was an investigation of a number of method-comparison studies, all of which dealt with the issue of the relative efficiency of input-based and eclectic instruction (Kramer and Palmer 1990; Palmer 1990). As a result of this investigation, we discovered an interesting pattern of interaction among method of instruction, purity of instruction, and age of students. Briefly, in studies with 'impure' experimental treatments, we found no significant differences. In studies with 'pure' experimental treatments, we found significant differences favoring the experimental (input-intensive) treatment for children, but favoring traditional (eclectic) instruction for adults.

Conclusion

Evaluating input-based language teaching programs is challenging. On the one hand, we want to keep the experimental treatment as pure as possible in order to increase the internal validity of the study. On the other hand, we want to keep the students happy, which may require a more eclectic approach. Thus, we seem to be caught in a tug of war between interpretability and practicality–generalizability: internal and external validity (Beretta 1986a).

Our experience was particularly satisfying because the results we obtained were not necessarily the results we anticipated, so we felt like we had learned something new from the process. Moreover, struggling with the issues of research design, test design, and interpretation helped us clarify some of the problems we faced and suggested some new directions we might take in the future (Kramer and Palmer 1990; Palmer 1990).

The increasing interest in language testing and program evaluation is demonstrated by the enthusiastic participation of large numbers of colleagues in conferences such as the 1986 International Conference on Trends in Language Programme Evaluation in Bangkok, and the 1990 RELC Regional Seminar on Language Testing and Language Programme Evaluation in Singapore. This involvement is likely to bring increased insight into what Alderson (1986) calls 'The nature of the beast.'

References

Alderson, J. C. 1986. The nature of the beast. *Trends in Language Programme Evaluation*. Bangkok: Chulalongkorn University Language Institute.

Asher, J., J. Kusudo and R. de la Torre. 1983. Learning a second language through commands: The Second Field Test. In J. Oller and J. Richard-Amato. *Methods that work: A smorgasbord of ideas for language learners*. Rowley, Mass.: Newbury House, pp. 58–72.

Bachman, L. 1989. The development and use of criterion-referenced tests of language ability in language program evaluation. In R. K. Johnson (Ed.) *The second language curriculum*. Cambridge: Cambridge University Press.

Bachman, L. 1990. *Fundamental considerations in language testing*. Oxford: Oxford University Press.

Bachman, L. and J. Clark. 1987. The measurement of foreign/second language proficiency. ANNALS, AAPSS, 490. March 1987.

Bachman, L. and A. Palmer. 1981. The construct validity of the FSI Oral Interview. *Language Learning* 31(1): 67–86.

Bachman, L. and A. Palmer. 1982. The construct validity of some components of communicative proficiency. *TESOL Quarterly* 16(4): 449–65.

Bachman, L. and A. Palmer. 1989. The construct validation of self ratings of communicative language ability. *Language Testing* 6(1).

Bachman, L. and S. Savignon. 1985. The evaluation of communicative language proficiency: a critique of the ACTFL Oral Interview and suggestions for its revision and development. Paper presented at the 'Perspectives on Proficiency' Forum, 1985 Modern Language Association of America Convention, 29 December 1985, Chicago, Ill.

Beretta, A. 1986a. A case for field experimentation in program evaluation. *Language Learning* 36(3): 295–309.

Beretta, A. 1986b. Program-fair language teaching evaluation. *TESOL Quarterly* 20(3): 431–44.

Brown, J. M. and A. Palmer. 1988. *The Listening Approach: methods and materials for applying Krashen's Input Hypothesis*. New York: Longman Inc.

Brütsch, S. 1979. *Convergent-discriminant validation of prospective teacher proficiency in oral and written French by means of the MLA Cooperative Language Proficiency Test, French direct proficiency tests for teachers (TOP and TWO), and self-ratings*. Unpublished Ph.D. dissertation, University of Minnesota.

Burger, S. 1989. Content-based ESL in a sheltered psychology course: input, output and outcomes. *TESL Canada Journal/Revue TESL du Canada* 6(2): 45–59.

Clifford, R. 1981. Convergent and discriminant validation of integrated and unitary language skills: the need for a research model. In A. S. Palmer, P. Groot and G. Trosper (Eds.) *The construct validation of tests of communicative competence*. Washington, D.C.: Teachers of English to Speakers of Other Languages pp. 62–70.

Edwards, H., M. Wesche, S. Krashen, R. Clement and B. Kruidenier. 1984. Second-language acquisition through subject-matter learning: a study of sheltered psychology classes at the University of Ottawa. *The Canadian Modern Language Review* 41(2): 268–82.

Hauptman, P., M. Wesche and D. Ready. 1988. Second-language acquisition through subject-matter learning: a follow-up study at the University of Ottawa. *Language Learning* 38(3): 433–75.

Kramer, P. 1989. *The classroom acquisition of German and the Input Hypothesis*. Salt Lake City: University of Utah Ph.D Dissertation.

Kramer, P. and A. Palmer. 1990. Comparative program evaluation studies as tests of the Input Hypothesis. Paper presented at the TESOL '90 Convention. San Francisco, March 6–10.

Krashen, S. 1982. *Principles and practice in second language acquisition*. New York: Pergamon Press.

Krashen, S. 1985. *The Input Hypothesis: issues and implications*. New York: Longman.

Krashen, S. and T. Terrell. 1983. *The natural approach: language acquisition in the classroom*. Hayward, California: The Alemany Press.

Krathwohl, D. R., B. S. Bloom, and B. B. Masia. 1956. *Taxonomy of educational objectives*. New York: David McKay Co. Inc.

Lafayette, R. and M. Buscaglia. 1985. Students learn language via a civilization course – a comparison of second language classroom environments. *Studies in Second Language Acquisition* 7(3).

Lightbown, P. 1989. Can they do it themselves? A comprehension-based ESL course for young children. To appear in the proceedings of the Conference on Comprehension-based Second Language Teaching: Current Trends. University of Ottawa, May, 1989.

Oskarsson, M. 1978. *Approaches to self-assessment in foreign language learning*. Oxford: Pergamon Press.

Palmer, A. 1987. An evaluation of student and teacher attitudes toward an input-based program in German. *Trends in Language Programme Evaluation*. Bangkok: Chulalongkorn University Language Institute.

Palmer, A. 1990. The role of language testing in language program evaluation. Paper presented at the RELC Regional Seminar on Language Testing and Language Programme Evaluation. Singapore, April 9–12.

Richards, J. and T. Rodgers. 1986. *Approaches and methods in language teaching: A description and analysis*. Cambridge: Cambridge University Press.

Rodgers, T. 1986. Changing models of language program evaluation: a case study. Paper presented at the CULI First International Conference on Trends in Language Programme Evaluation. Bangkok, Thailand, December 9–11.

Smith, P. and H. Baranyi 1968. *A Comparison Study of the Effectiveness of the Traditional and Audio-lingual Approaches to Foreign Language Instruction Utilizing Laboratory Equipment*. Final Report of USOE Project 7–0133.

Sternfeld, S. 1989. The University of Utah's immersion/multiliteracy program: an example of an area studies approach to the design of first-year college foreign language instruction. *Foreign Language Annals* 22(4): 341–54.

Editors' postscript to Palmer

Palmer's chapter addresses the sorts of dilemmas that evaluators have to face and resolve when designing their studies. The interest and indeed focus of the chapter does not revolve around the results of the particular evaluation, but around the questions that were asked and how they were answered. In this sense, the detailed results of this particular study are perhaps less important, although a study of them might enable the reader to judge for him or herself how useful the data gathered were (a point to which we return below).

The questions that Palmer asks we return to in the final chapter of this volume. Palmer supplies his own answers, and his later reactions to his evaluation study, which will hopefully help the budding evaluator. We will not go into detail here in commenting on the questions or their answers, but refer the reader instead to the final chapter. The value of Palmer's chapter is in the way he asks and answers the questions he was faced with. As he himself says, his aim in producing this chapter is to provide future evaluators with the sort of guidance he wishes he had had before embarking on his evaluation. Hopefully, the final chapter of this book will also provide useful guidance.

A few words are in order, nevertheless, on Palmer's study. He is not merely concerned with evaluating a method, but is even more ambitious: he wishes to evaluate a whole theory of second language acquisition. Now the status and content of that theory – Krashen's 'monitor theory' – have been controversial in the professional literature for some time, yet Palmer decided to see for himself whether it was possible to implement the theoretical ideas and to develop a course based on the theory. In order to do this to his satisfaction, he was obliged to create a potentially artificial situation, where, for example, students were not encouraged to speak before they had 'acquired', since Krashen's theory claims that production follows acquisition, rather than leading to acquisition. This was a bold decision, which may well have led to problems during the course. Formative evaluation, intended to steer the course as it develops, was equally ruled out, since it would potentially soil the purity of the experimental application of Krashen's ideas. In this respect, the study takes on the form of a laboratory experiment and hypothesis verification, rather than an evaluation of a real-life language education project: it is hard to imagine language teachers forcing their students to do things they feel are not appropriate to the developing situation, whereas any attempt to apply a 'pure form' of a theory is obliged at least to attempt this.

Interestingly, however, when designing the evaluation study, Palmer is forced to make compromises between what might be theoretically desirable and what is practical, he consults Bloom *et al.*, and the framework for communicative language ability that he devised with Bachman, and in neither case can he implement the ideas: he is forced back on the need to develop instruments that are easy to develop and administer, and that do not require much training on the part of the administrator. Although this sort of compromise is frequently inevitable in evaluations it must make it difficult to draw conclusions relevant to language acquisition theory from the results of the evaluation.

We are also given an interesting insight into the real-world problems of producing a myriad of instruments for evaluating achievement tests for each skill, plus grammar and vocabulary, plus tutors' ratings and students' self-assessments – and then not being in a position to pre-test the instruments for any design faults or inappropriacies. If those with long experience of test development have problems in designing their instruments, and not having the time or resources to validate them, what chance does the ordinary mortal have of doing the same? Hence, perhaps, evaluators' oft-repeated desires for pre-existing standardised instruments based on an acceptable theory of communicative language ability, which are appropriate for evaluations.

Another interesting confession is that in his concern for coverage, content validity, and the need to encompass unexpected outcomes as well as expected outcomes, Palmer feels he simply gathered more data than he needed, or indeed than he could process. Palmer feels that the evaluation appears to have got out of balance with respect to quantitative compared with qualitative data, and that the different methods used resulted in the same conclusions. We, however, interpret this finding differently, seeing the apparent duplication as a positive result which confirms the validity and robustness of the results. It is, after all, good practice to attempt to triangulate data-gathering methods precisely in order to confirm or disconfirm findings from one method alone. However, given the claim that the different methods resulted in the same conclusions, the reader may feel the need for some indication of the results: which data were most useful, which data were redundant, which instruments did not yield anything insightful or usable? In particular it would have been instructive to know whether data which can be summarised numerically led to conclusions similar to those which were drawn on the basis of qualitative data, or on quotations from such data.

5 Program-defining evaluation in a decade of eclecticism[1]

Steven Ross

Program-defining evaluation in a decade of eclecticism

The spread of the communicative approach to foreign language peda-gogy has been accompanied by a gradual de-emphasis of comparative method studies designed to contrast different pedagogical strategies. The focus of attention in studies of the learning process has instead been placed on comparing the discourse characteristics of teachers and learn-ers in the classroom with that of naturalistic second language acquisition contexts and with the processes initiated by 'innovative' methods. The shift of attention to the process of language learning is partly attributable to the widespread realization that internally valid comparative method studies are extremely difficult to undertake, and that product-focused evaluation often is not directly relevant to theory construction, an activity which has been the primary focus of second language researchers for the past ten years.

Classroom teaching in many EFL contexts mirrors the hiatus on product-centered evaluation. The once ubiquitous discrete-point approach has given way to a more global process-centered approach which comes under the general rubric of communicative language teaching. The concurrent trends of qualitative evaluation and eclectic language teaching have led to a veritable glut of rival techniques, methods and approaches from which the EFL practitioner may freely choose. A *laissez-faire* approach to program administration has, not surprisingly, become a by-product of the communicative movement in foreign language teaching in some countries (e.g. Japan). In any given post-secondary program, unlikely combinations of methods and mater-ials can be found; beta brain rhythm reduction exercises are employed in conjunction with pattern drills, Cuisenaire rods and Jazz Chants™. It is in this sort of context that program evaluation becomes a challenging endeavor. Programs at the college level as manifestations of a single

[1] A word of thanks is due to the participating teachers and observers in this study: Bernard Susser, Norman Angus, Nicolas Halewood, John Beary and Mike Redfield, who all gave freely of their time and expertise. I would also like to thank Bernard Susser and Kevin Gregg for comments on an earlier draft of this paper.

coherent pedagogical approach are a rarity. Evaluation, therefore, needs to be considered at the classroom level since each classroom can be considered a 'program' unto itself.

The study introduced in this chapter addresses the issue of defining the content of second language classrooms with a view to outlining the praxis of language teaching – the amalgamation of techniques, activities and tasks that make up the 'method' – over a seventy-hour course of instruction at a Japanese junior college. As a preliminary to this effort, the context of evaluation in an educational system that has no tradition of product-oriented research is addressed. The choices available to teachers-as-evaluators are examined as are the logistics for organizing the schedule, content and focus of classroom observation.

Evaluation in *laissez-faire* ELT?

The proliferation of language teaching methods and approaches has stemmed not primarily from empirical validation of novel ways of teaching language (Richards 1984), but from two other sources of eclecticism. The humanistic language teaching movement (Stevick 1976; 1980) and implications from second language acquisition research (Krashen and Terrell 1983) have been most influential in fostering an attitude on the part of many language teachers that evaluation is relevant to the extent it displays a similarity of the process of the classroom to the ideals of the humanistic language teaching movement, or to a current SLA 'theory' (cf. Gregg 1986). Given that one of the main aims of the humanistic approaches is to improve the psychological environment in which language is learned, product-oriented approaches have become relatively rare in discussions of the efficacy of learner-centered methods. A consequence of the apparent moratorium on mixing quantitative with process-focused, qualitative evaluation is a growing tendency to rely on the face validity of materials, methods and even techniques as a basic criterion for judging program effectiveness. This inclination to rely on face validity is not limited to classroom practitioners following the latest methodological fad. The newest wave of classroom-centered research, for example, which describes the similarities of interlanguage discourse to naturalistic encounters between native speakers and acquirers (Porter 1985; Duff 1986; Varonis and Gass 1985; cf. Aston 1986) has as a whole conjectured that if interlanguage discourse (i.e. the language used among learners in the classroom) results in a negotiation of meaning resembling the conversational adjustments made by native speakers to non-natives, a major criterion for adopting the task-based approach is satisfied. The rationale for adopting a method for language teaching, be it informed by psychological theories of meaning, or by interlanguage research, is often not necessarily dependent on a coherent set of principles.

The impetus for evaluation of language teaching programs in Japan at the post-secondary level[2] does not typically come from university authorities. It is usually done, if it is done at all, on an in-house basis whereby a member or team of staff members makes provision for observation and formative assessment of the content of classroom lessons. In-house assessment is the method of choice in the Japanese EFL enterprise both because of the widespread policy of *laissez-faire* on the one hand, and of a traditional lack of concern for the ultimate product of language learning at the post-secondary level on the other. Consequently, there has been little interest in the evaluation of ongoing programs, to the extent that coherent programs exist in higher education, and only rarely are there published accounts of small-scale evaluations on the classroom level (for example Dinsmore 1985; Ross and Berwick 1988). When evaluation on any scale takes place, it is most commonly done by the teachers themselves using home-spun instruments with little concern for external validity.

Qualitative or quantitative evaluation?

The diversity of language teaching strategies used at the university level in particular invites both qualitative and quantitative types of evaluation. Given the plethora of theoretically opposed teaching materials and methods used within the walls of the same institution and given the homogeneity of the Japanese student population in higher education, the context for both approaches to evaluation is apparent. The question of which is most appropriate or meaningful for any given context becomes relative when we consider that the evaluation of competitive approaches to EFL pedagogy does not result in the endorsement or rejection of a coherent 'program' anyway. Both qualitative and quantitative types of evaluation can be utilized with a view to defining a program, and as such are better described as program-formative evaluation strategies which may provide alternative views of the same classroom phenomena (Lett and Shaw 1986).

Whichever evaluation approach is chosen, there remains a subtle danger in attempting to directly compare the effects of various materials or methods without first determining whether or not they are being applied in an orthodox way. Long and Sato (1983) have commented on

---

[2] It would be misleading to suggest that the teaching of English as a foreign language in Japan is completely *laissez-faire*. Japanese teachers of English almost without exception rely on cognitive code teaching strategies and grammar translation. Expatriate teachers, on the other hand, are more inclined to following current innovations, or to rely on hybrid forms of the direct method.

the tendency for teachers to claim they are practising a given method while in fact they might be doing something quite different. The teacher variable becomes essential in discussions of comparative method studies and has led to some rather exaggerated attempts to eliminate the teacher from the language lesson altogether (Freedman 1979). But as Beretta (1986) suggests, there is a point at which an attempt to improve internal validity inevitably results in a compromise in the external validity of the experiment.

It may be the case that distinct 'methods' are abstractions to many EFL practitioners. Perhaps even the majority of teachers do not conceptualize and plan their lessons in terms of distinct methodological doctrines at all. Instead, teachers recognize specific teaching techniques, activities, and above all, teaching materials, as concrete manifestations of 'method'. It is the materials – the tapes, texts and videos – which are the tangible tools for the classroom teacher. We can assume, therefore, that comparisons of methods defined *a priori* are likely to be stymied by 'fuzzy' definitions of methodology until there is some provision for describing methods both qualitatively and quantitatively. One approach to doing this starts with defining competitive approaches to EFL teaching in terms of the materials used by the teachers. Through systematic classroom observation and description of the content and focus of the language lessons, the common denominators of classroom processes can be delineated with a view to providing global methodological sketches.

The study described here highlights the quantitative aspects of classroom process differences primarily because the difficulties involved in distilling the insights of five teacher/amateur ethnographers[3] into a coherent whole were considered greater than having to rely on concrete, albeit possibly incomplete, criteria. Since a goal of the project was to include the teachers as participant observers, a coding system was devised. Care was taken to make the contents of the coding scheme as low inference as was practical, while at the same time making it comprehensive enough to capture the dynamics of five different approaches to syllabus organization.

The selection of materials

The materials contrasted in this study were considered representative of the current panorama of alternative approaches to teaching English as a

---

[3] Although there is ample reason for including qualitative sketches of the five classrooms, practical constraints precluded their use in this study. The use of a low inference observation scheme can at least lend itself to some pre-observation norming. Ethnography requires more extensive training and experience. Moreover, by being far more subjective in nature it is susceptible to the biases of a teacher/observer who may defend his/her own approach to teaching by dwelling on the weaknesses of the 'rival' materials and methods observed.

foreign language. With the exception of the audio-lingual materials, the five different classes used materials which had been previously used by the teachers in the study. The selection includes some of the 'best sellers' in Japan, materials which have been highly touted by their publishers and authors.

The materials used in the study are summarized are as follows:

Audio-lingual materials represent 'late' audio-lingualism. Dialogues and comprehension questions are followed by massive pattern drills designed to lead the students from 'mechanical' to 'meaningful' and ultimately 'communicative' ability in English.

Functional-notional materials were selected to represent a literal interpretation of the Council of Europe recommendations for syllabus design. The materials followed a limited set of language functions while at the same time included a structural backbone.

Grammar-based materials follow 'the structure of the day' principle whereby each introductory segment of the lesson, a narrative story, was written to demonstrate a particular grammatical point. Subsequent exercises allow extended practice and review of previously covered grammar points in a cyclical manner.

Self-access pair learning (SAPL) materials apply the principles of Lozanov's suggestopedia (see Stevick 1980; Ferguson 1978, 1981). Emphasis is put on relaxing the students by playing baroque music while they engage themselves in pair work activities. The teacher ('facilitator') intervenes only when there is an apparent problem in an effort to reduce the level of anxiety in the students.

Task-based materials provided a non-text-based alternative to the above mentioned texts. The main characteristic of the task-based lessons is unplanned discourse. An effort was made to create information gap activities (Doughty and Pica 1986) and two-way problem-solving activities (Duff 1986) which required students to create language appropriate for the communicative context. No 'canned' dialogues or patterns were introduced to the students in the seventy hours of instruction.

Strategies for in-house evaluation

In contrast to an emphasis on constructing an evaluation project which will have airtight internal validity (Long 1984), the sort of program-defining evaluation discussed here assumes that a primary goal is generalizability to other Japanese foreign language teaching contexts. Such a strategy precludes the use of 'true' randomization as a basis of assigning students to classes and teachers to materials. Randomization as such would defeat the purpose of the evaluation in that it would not represent language teaching in Japanese higher education. Moreover, it could make for the ridiculous situation in which experienced and dedicated practitioners of a particular set of materials would find themselves asked to try out completely novel materials for the sake of making the randomization process genuine. The happy medium between true experimental design and the need for generalizability is met by allowing teachers to select their own materials[4] and by assigning to each of the participating teachers non-randomized classes composed of students placed alphabetically.

In *laissez-faire* language teaching, the notion of observation strikes fear into the hearts of teachers, especially if the observation is to be done by an evaluator representing an external 'authority'. For this particular reason, involving the teachers in the observation process was considered to both decrease the teachers' anxiety of 'being watched' and allow direct participation by the teacher as both practitioner and observer. The collaborative observation scheme utilized in this study was not necessarily the optimal approach, however. Sampling language lessons by video recording and providing ample practice time for viewing and discussion of the coding of the content of the sample lessons only provided a modicum of observer norming before the actual observation in rotation took place. It could be argued that observation of the classes by external authorities with expert training would provide a more reliable picture of the goings-on of the lessons. Yet in terms of the ecology of the language classes, not to mention the lack of funding for classroom based research, the effort to perfect the internal validity of the evaluation was thought to be of lesser importance.

Devising a coding scheme

The five non-randomized classes included in the study each were assigned a teacher and a set of materials representing current 'state of the art'[5]

---

[4] The project itself was not conceived of as a comparison of methods *per se*. It was rather an attempt to examine the validity of the disparate claims of the numerous 'teacher trainers' who frequent Japan on sales promotional tours aimed at marketing the newest panacea for the woes of foreign language teachers. The purpose of the study was to examine if indeed there are any actual differences among the various materials at the point of delivery to the students in large classes common at Japanese universities.

[5] The inclusion of the audio-lingual materials in the study was not motivated by any endorsement of their effectiveness. Rather, since many current ELT materials appear to revert to crypto-audio-lingual activities, the use of a bona fide audio-lingual text was thought to be a viable approach to exposing its underlying similarities with trendier materials. In fact, some of the more 'successful' private foreign language institutes in Japan synchronize the drills of audio-lingualism into a sort of martial arts method of foreign language learning.

language teaching. Once the individual teachers agreed to participate in the study as both classroom practitioners using their favorite materials and as observers of their colleagues' teaching, a coding scheme was developed which could take into account the need for low inference categories of codings and at the same time be limited to the kinds of activities which were most likely to transpire in the various classes. The coding scheme which evolved encompassed information indicating the main pedagogical strategies employed in the class and at the same time provided information of interest in light of current second language learning models.

The observation scheme resembled a checklist of activity types, which, when marked, led into subcategories of activities designed to provide finer detail about each teaching move and student activity. Four general categories of classroom activity were specified in the observation scheme: student activities, sources of input to students, student behavior and the distribution of classroom time. Within each of the categories a dichotomous coding strategy was employed so as to allow the observer to denote the occurrence or absence of various classroom phenomena during each teaching activity. The totals for each observation were tallied and were subsequently collated with the other observations of the same class at a later date made by a different observer. The result was a set of frequencies for each of the categories and a log of the amount of time that was spent on each. Each activity was also coded as form-focused or message-focused. After collation of the four observations, the set of frequencies was sorted into four main sections which were then used as the basis for comparisons and definitions of 'methods'.

TABLE I FOCUS OF STUDENT ACTIVITY

a)   Message-focused set-up moves; teacher explains tasks to be done
b)   Improvisations and role plays
c)   Information gap activities
d)   Structured listening
e)   Information questions from S to T
f)   Information questions from T to S
g)   Display questions
h)   Comprehension check questions
i)   Dialogue repetition/practice/memorization[6]
j)   Pattern repetition drills
k)   Transformation drills
l)   Substitution drills
m)   Activities with overt correction

The *Focus of student activity* section provides an initial basis for comparison of the observed classes in terms of the type and frequency of aural and oral language practice. The categories also denote the primary focus of the activity, whether designed to allow the student to focus on the meaning of the message the student formulates in a communicative activity with others, or to focus on more formal aspects of language usage.

TABLE 2 SOURCE OF INPUT TO STUDENTS

a)	Student to student
b)	Teacher to class
c)	Audio tape played to class
d)	Teacher to individuals
e)	Small groups
f)	Pairs of students focused on messages
g)	Pairs of students focused on form
h)	Individuals working alone

The second category of codes represented both the source of input to the class and the configuration of the class in each activity. Some materials, for instance, required students to respond to teacher-led drills and display/comprehension questions for some activity types and to work in pairs or small groups in others. The source of input was considered a potentially important characteristic of methods in that it could reveal patterns of consistent types of practice embedded in small-group configurations.

---

6 The distinction made here between display and comprehension questions is centered on the assumption that a display question is asked by the teacher solely for the purpose of examining the form of the student's response. A comprehension question may be asked with the intention of requiring the student to display his/her comprehension of some previously read or heard piece of text. Here, the teacher may anticipate that the student has understood the meaning of the text, but needs to check the degree to which it is understood.

TABLE 3 STUDENT BEHAVIORS

a)   Listening to explanation, lecture or taped material
b)   Repetition of patterns, dialogues or narratives
c)   Questioning drills; all categories of questions
d)   Improvisation
e)   Practice, mimicry or rehearsal of fixed patterns
f)   Problem solving, two-way negotiation of meaning
g)   Listen and respond to cue
h)   Listen and form interrogative
i)   Listen and respond freely
j)   Write, copy dialogue, transcribe or answer questions in writing
k)   Read; silent reading of text

Here the category 'student behaviors' indicates the patterns of activities that the majority of students engaged themselves in. In an ethnographic approach to observation, there might be an estimate about the number of individuals who are not engaged in the intended focus of the activity. Observers of course were aware of the intended focus of the activity when they heard the teacher set up the activity. The third section shares obvious features with the first, the *Focus of student activities*, and the *Student behavior* section provides slightly more detail than the more general first section. The main advantage of having overlapping codings of the types of activities and the actual behavior of the students comes when we wish to compare the relative frequencies of the various codings with a view to determining the internal consistency of the coding instrument. This strategy is a prudent one considering the fact that the observer/teachers had only a few hours to perfect their observation skills and quickly code the rapidly unfolding activities of the classrooms.

TABLE 4 DISTRIBUTION OF CLASSROOM TIME

a)   Total time on form-focused activities
b)   Total time on message-focused activities

As a fundamental concept in communicative language teaching is the exchange of messages, the division of the total time spent in activities into two main classes — form- and message-focus — was an essential step in defining how different configurations of the classes, and the activities introduced in the materials, actually could be considered 'communicative'.

Each activity or teaching move was timed with the use of a stop watch so that the distribution of classroom time could be logged and categorized in terms of time dedicated to pair or group work as opposed to time taken by the teacher. Likewise, the total time spent on message-focused classroom activities could be contrasted with time spent in form-focused pair or small-group activities.

The observation schedule

After an orientation and several practice observation sessions, the five teacher/observers[7] began the classroom observations on a rotational basis. Each group using distinct materials was observed on four separate occasions during the nine-month academic year, each time by a different observer. Six classroom hours out of a total of seventy hours of contact time were observed in this manner. The decision to space the observations across the academic teaching year was made in light of the fact that some of the materials used in the classes incorporated distinct pedagogical strategies which would not be seen if all of the observation was done in consecutive sessions.

Cluster analyses

Individual categories of activities and behaviors in the four sections of the coding scheme were summed for each observation. This approach produced a rectangular matrix of frequencies for each type of activity or behavior occurring in each of the four observations of the five different sets of materials. The matrix was broken down into three separate sections and cluster analyses[8] were done on each of these subsets of data so that classes most like each other would appear as neighbors on the same node of the dendrogram, or 'tree' structure of the observations. Frequencies of discrete classroom activities create 'clusters' which can be used as the basis for a taxonomy of different aspect of 'methods'. For instance, if the frequency of student-to-student interaction is high for all observations of a given set of materials, but is low for all observations of a different set of materials, the two sets of materials will not be found on the same 'branch' of the tree. The cluster analyses thus provided a global picture of the dissimilarity of the independent observations in terms of a latent methodology employed by the five different teachers using five different sets of materials. They also provide some evidence for the

---

[7] Not all five of the teachers were available to observe the other classes because of scheduling conflicts. One 'fill-in' observer made himself available to observe classes that were scheduled when the other teacher/observers were unavailable.

[8] Few observation studies utilizing multivariate data reduction techniques seem to exist. One notable application of cluster analysis on classroom observation is that by Gayle (1980). The clustering method used in the present study was based on dissimilarity coefficients (Euclidean distances) and employed the so-called group average method (see Romesburg 1984).

tendency of certain materials to be realized in a homogeneous method, while suggesting that others may entail a more eclectic methodology.

Cluster analysis of student activities

Two major branches of the tree were identified in this analysis. One major branch split off into two related clusters of observations consisting of the classes that required the students to focus on the form of the foreign language. As each activity observed was coded as either form-focused or message-focused, those which were consistent in the form/message focus aspect became members of clusters in Figure 1. Cluster 2 of Figure 1 shows the observations that were inconsistent in the focus on form dimension. The SAPL materials, for instance, were at the center of the main branch (Cluster 1), and were most related closely to the audio-lingual and grammatical materials. It is interesting to note that all four independent observations of the SAPL and audio-lingual classes should cluster so closely together. These two sets of materials in many ways represent opposing theories of language learning; SAPL materials are designed to allow student practice in an anxiety-free situation. In contrast, the audio-lingual materials require public language practice and immediate correction of errors. Philosophical differences aside, these two sets of materials appear to be quite similar in that they both require students to 'do the text' far more than communicate with the language they already possess.

The second major branch of the student activities cluster analysis was composed of the functional-notional materials and the task-based materials. Three of the four observations of the functional-notional materials appear on this branch while all four of the task-based observations do so.

Figure 1:   Focus of student activities

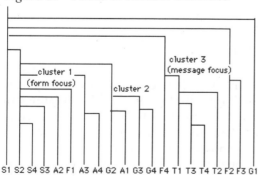

S1 S2 S4 S3 A2 F1 A3 A4 G2 A1 G3 G4 F4 T1 T3 T4 T2 F2 F3 G1

Observations

S1–S4 refer to the four observations of the SAPL class. The other abbreviations refer to the following: A(audiolingual), G(grammar), T(task), F(functional-notional).

The cluster analysis of the input to students (Figure 2) reveals the relative differences in the input format that the different materials utilize. Three main branches appear to differentiate among three main sources of input to the students. The SAPL and task-based materials consistently required the students to work in pairs and groups. The functional-notional materials, on the other hand, initially required students to listen to the audio-recordings before practising on their own for the first three quarters of the year. By the fourth observation the students were apparently set free of the examples of language and were required to improvise on their own. The grammatical materials consistently required the mediation of the teacher as a negotiator of the meaning presented by the text. Although recorded tapes were used with all of the text-based materials, the degree to which the teachers relied on the tape as input to students appears to have varied considerably.

Figure 2:   Input to students

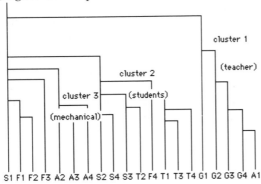

S1 F1 F2 F3 A2 A3 A4 S2 S4 S3 T2 F4 T1 T3 T4 G1 G2 G3 G4 A1

Observations

The teaching materials all required some variation in the kinds of activities the students took part in. The third cluster analysis (Figure 3) summarizes the extent of dissimilarity among the four observations of each group and between the five different sets of materials contrasted in the study. Four main clusters of student activity types were identified. Cluster 1, here labelled 'improvisation', indicates that in the second and third observations of the functional-notional materials group emphasis was put on role play and improvisation of situations in which specific language functions could be used. Cluster 2 represents the primary text-based type of student activity; practice or memorization of dialogues presented as sample language. Cluster 3 appears to be a slight variation of Cluster 2. Here, the focus is definitely still on form, but instead of mouthing fixed sequences of 'canned' language, the students in the grammar-based materials class primarily were engaged in drill activity. Cluster 4 provides more evidence that the task-based materials group were engaged in activities which required the creative use of language.

Figure 3:   Student activity types

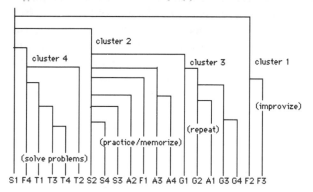

Observations

The three cluster analyses outlined above reveal a number of perspectives on language learning activities actually used in the classrooms. It may be said that there are a number of methodological similarities among the materials in terms of the praxis of language learning. The SAPL materials, audio-lingual materials and grammatically-based materials were overwhelmingly focused on *form*. In contrast, the task-based materials required the creative use of language among the students. The most methodologically versatile materials were the functional-notional, which began with a focus on form and gradually abandoned it in favor of situational improvisation. The variation observed in the functional-notional materials could also indicate the teacher's gradual inclination to 'free-lance' toward the end of the year by asking the students to improvise more than the teacher's guide prescribed.

The primary goal of the cluster analyses is to reduce the ungainly matrix of observation data into a smaller subset of interpretable summaries of the dissimilarities among the observed classes. Although substantial generalization is made possible by this form of data reduction, more precise differences between the materials used in the study are better found in direct comparisons of data gathered in the observation process. It is from the comparison of the most salient differences that hypotheses about how process relates to product can be postulated.

Specific process differences: pair work time

All classroom activities were recorded in real time. This permitted a tally of time taken in each lesson for teacher talk, passive listening and individual work. Pair work was logged into a category encompassing focus on form such as in dialogue repetition, memorization or drills, or into a category for unplanned discourse required in problem solving or information gap activities. The *Pair work time* chart reveals a considerable difference between two classes that spent most of the class time in pair work (dotted bars). The SAPL class primarily worked in pairs, but the content of the activity was overwhelmingly focused on form; on dialogues, or narratives for memorization followed by role-playing which usually resulted in verbatim repetition. In contrast, the task-based class was 'thrown in the deep end' by having to use their own interlanguage for the completion of information gaps, language games, picture completion and the like. The functional-notional class utilized much less pair work than the SAPL class, yet there was considerably more focus on message in the improvisation (note dark bars). This was perhaps because less time was spent in making the students rehearse the short functional dialogues before they were required to extrapolate to a hypothetical situation. Consequently, there was less overt reliance on the forms introduced in the dialogues. As might be expected, both the audio-lingual and grammatical classes required much less pair work per class meeting.

Figure 4:   Pair work time

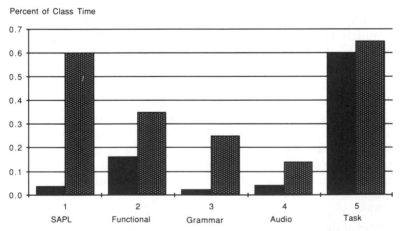

Note: Dotted bars indicate average pair work time. Dark bars indicate pair work which was focused on spontaneous language use, as opposed to drills and dialogue memorization in pairs.

Teacher talk as input

Each distinct activity was cross-referenced with a code signifying the sources of input to the students. A large number of activities involved the students listening to instructions or explanations, as well as listening in specific exercises devised for that purpose in the text. Four principal categories of listening comprehension activities were coded in the observations:

1 Listening to teacher speech or tape-recorded material for note taking, map following, diagram completion, etc.
2 Listening to teacher or tape-recorded cues before completing a 'pair work' speaking task.
3 Listening and responding to set patterns (choral drill).
4 Listening to the tape and questioning another student.

The cumulative frequency of listening activities observed during the six hours of observation in each class provides a basis for comparison of the five groups. Figure 5 shows the extent of differences in listening input to the students in the five classes.

Figure 5:   Total number of listening activities

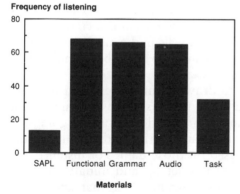

The three most 'teacher-centered' texts involved considerable listening on the part of the students. In contrast, the two groups employing 'student-centered' materials (SAPL and Task) relied primarily on student talk as listening input.

Focus on form

The *Pair work time* chart indicates that pair work *per se* does not necessarily involve unplanned discourse, but can function as an efficient way of organizing the students' focus on form. The *Focus on form* chart incorporates six basic kinds of form focused activities that were used in both the student centered and teacher centered classroom configurations. The figures represent the total frequency of activities focused on form over the six hours of observation for each class.

Figure 6:   Focus on form

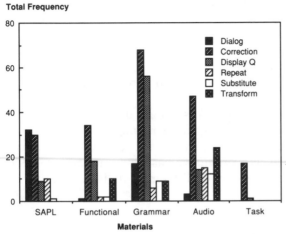

The three charts concur to a great extent with the patterns of clusterings derived from the cluster analyses. The main advantage of examining the relative frequencies of specific classroom activities and foci, in contrast with the global measure of dissimilarity, dwells in the fact that a narrow range of hypotheses about the product can more easily be formulated on the basis of the observations themselves.

Although there are advantages to drawing inferences from the data gathered directly from the observation of the classrooms, it is important to recall that a considerable amount of information about the goings on in each of the classrooms is not included in the original data tallies or the multivariate analyses which are based on those data. For instance, the tallies may indicate that the teacher has set up and initiated a given language-learning activity. It might not show, however, that some of the students have not responded to the 'signals' that a new activity is to be done. They may in fact lag behind for several minutes while the majority of their classmates engage themselves in the activity designated by the teacher. Different types of activities may actually have greater classification reliability in that the low inference codings can be applied cleanly once the teacher signals to the students that a new activity is to be done. Others, such as the more creative non-directive activities, may be more difficult to identify and time. This problem of classification presents a major limitation in abstracting too much information from the low inference observations.

Relating praxis to product

In order to examine the relationship between overt focus on form and the differential sensitivity learners develop to grammar, both in use and in recognition, specific process-to-product hypotheses were formulated.

The observations of the five sets of materials contrasted in this study indicate that there are consistent, identifiable methodological characteristics which may serve as the basis for the formulation of hypotheses about product differences accruing over the seventy-hour course. Hypotheses of greatest interest are those related to current applications of second language acquisition theory to second and foreign language pedagogy. Focus on form, in particular, has been at the center of debate in applied linguistics circles. A number of second language theorists question the validity of assuming that overt *focus on form* will result in the development of more accurate interlanguage. Krashen (1985), Pienemann (1985), Long (1985), Ellis (1986), Faerch (1985) and Higgs (1984) appear to differ in their interpretation of the empirical evidence supporting approaches to language instruction with the focus on form as an essential component.

Hypothesis One

The cluster analysis of the focus of student activities (Figure 1), the relative distribution of pair work time (Figure 4) and the total frequencies of activities with focus on form (Figure 6) together provide sufficient observation data to allow a prediction of the putative effect of focus on form. The observation data suggest that rank ordering of materials requiring learners to focus on the content of the text in the form of grammar drills, dialogs for repetition, supplemented by teacher or peer correction, will lead to a plausible prediction of the outcome. The predicted order is here stated as:

> Grammar materials will have a higher mean score than the audio-lingual materials, which will have a higher mean score than the functional-notional materials, whose mean score will equal the SAPL materials and the task-based materials. In shorthand:

$$G > A > F = S = T$$

Hypothesis Two

An essential component of the communicative language teaching movement has been the emphasis placed on developing the communicative competence[9] of language learners at all stages of the language learning process. In particular, the importance of developing *fluency* has been a central and recurring theme for the past decade. It appears that much of the motivation behind the current craze in ELT overseas to make pair work[10] central in communicative teaching stems from the assumption that it is practice in pairs or small groups that is essential for the development of fluency. There is an implicit 'domino theory' behind fluency; fluent speakers can elicit more comprehensible input and thereby eventually acquire more. A recent series of pair work studies (Pica and Long 1986; Porter 1986) have concluded that some learner dyads can manage very well in fluent and authentic negotiation for meaning without the interference of the teacher. The contrast of pair work time in the observations lends itself to the formulation of a testable hypothesis about the effects of pair work as a crucial ingredient in the making of fluency. If indeed the gross amount of speaking time is the basis of fluency, the observed differences suggest a hierarchical ordering of the outcome measures of fluency. Based on the differences observed in the amount of pair work (see Figure 4) we predict:

SAPL materials will have a mean equal to task-based materials, which will have a higher mean than the functional-notional materials, the grammatical materials and audio-lingual materials. There will be no differences among the last three set of materials. In shorthand:

$$S = T > F = G = A$$

Hypothesis Three

A direct antecedent to the present trend towards pair work for fluency and comprehensible output was the preoccupation with what can be termed the 'listening first' movement (Winitz 1981; Postovsky 1981) and later with 'comprehensible input' (Krashen 1985). Although various classroom techniques were espoused during the height of the 'listening first' movement, the consensus reached was based on the assumption that aural comprehension is the essential starting point for subsequent success in learning to speak. The primacy of listening was interpreted by many classroom practitioners as a rationale for unlimited teacher talk with intermittent display questioning. The 'listening first' movement caused

9   This term seems to encompass basic speaking and listening skills, and not much else.
10 A wide range of activities come under the guise of 'pair and group work'. Many current ELT texts evidently mean 'pair work' to be an efficient way to dialogue memorization. It should be understood that any approach to language teaching, from grammar translation or audio-lingual drills to two-way problem-solving tasks can be accomplished in this particular configuration. Use of the words 'pair work' in this study refers to both pairs and small groups.

substantial modification to the development of language teaching materials as well.

The thirty hours of classroom observations discussed here highlight an essential methodological difference between the text- and teacher-dependent materials, and the student-controlled materials. The contrast of listening activities (Figures 2, 3, and 5) suggests that if the frequency of listening comprehension activities[11] is related to the development of greater listening comprehension skill, we should see a difference in outcome measures of listening comprehension. We state this prediction as:

> Grammar materials will equal functional-notional materials, which will equal audio-lingual materials. The grammar, functional-notional and audio-lingual materials will have higher means than the SAPL materials and the task-based materials. There will be no difference between the SAPL and the task-based materials.

$$G = F = A > S = T$$

Developing outcome measurements

Considering the substantial differences among the types of materials used in the study, no single standardized test was considered appropriate as the criterion for post-instructional differences. Instead, prototypes and alternate forms of measurement instruments were developed and pretested during the academic year preceding the start of instruction for the present study. A number of test types were considered, but four distinct testing instruments were chosen to assess the common product of the materials used in the separate classes. A forty-five item multiple choice grammar test was chosen from among the pool of viable tests. This test was considered useful for assessing the effect of conscious form-focused methods of TEFL. The pretest version had an internal consistency reliability coefficient of .74 (KR-21). Two alternate forms of listening cloze and partial dictation tests were chosen as measures of listening comprehension. The listening cloze and partial dictation tests were considered reasonably representative of the kinds of listening tasks students in the teacher-centered classes were exposed to during the

---

[11] Listening comprehension activities constitute a wide range of planned and unplanned input to the students. The most common form of listening observed was simply the setting up of activities to be done by the class. The functional-notional, grammatical and audio-lingual classes were characterized by short, form-focused activities with relatively long stretches of teacher explanation in between. The grammatical and functional-notional materials also had considerable numbers of listening modules in which students were directed to listen for the gist.

seventy hours of classroom instruction. The partial dictation and listening cloze tests demonstrated reasonable test-retest reliability; .83 and .84 respectively for the pretest versions.

A narrative discourse test (Ross 1987) was also developed as a materials-independent alternative to face-to-face interview techniques. The narrative discourse test involved the viewing of a full-length animated folk tale in the students' L1. Students were then required to retell the story in English as they viewed selected portions of the animation.[12] The resulting 5.25 minute narrative could then be analyzed with holistic ratings of pronunciation, accuracy and fluency. Atomistic scoring techniques were used to assess well formedness (error free T-units), fluency (the total number of T-units spoken) and T-unit length. Inter-rater reliability coefficients for three raters (Kendall's Coefficient of Concordance) were .85 for the holistic ratings (total score), .89 for the T-units and .95 for the error-free T-units. A structured oral interview test[13] was given to forty-four students who had taken the narrative discourse test, but who were not enrolled in any of the groups included in the study. A product–moment correlation of .77 indicated that there was substantial variance overlap between the two measures of basic EFL speaking skills.

Both the SAPL materials and the task-based materials groups utilized extensive pair and group work activities during the course of the academic year. It could therefore be argued that measurements sensitive to the effects of different student learning activities should seek to assess the extent to which learners in these groups benefit from the input they receive from their peers. Unfortunately, tests of Japanese interlanguage comprehension do not exist, and even if they did, they would not satisfy the need for content validity.[14] English in Japan is taught as a vehicle of communication with the 'outside' world and not as a second language for use among Japanese. It is for this reason that the measurements used to assess the product of the seventy hours of classroom instruction were based on standard British and North American norms and not on the students' ability to comprehend Japanese interlanguage.

---

12 Chafe (1979) and Tomlin (1984) note the inclination both native and non-native speakers have toward propositional reduction when narrative discourse is attempted extemporaneously. Effort was made in this study to present the complete story in Japanese so that there would be less of a drift to the type of parataxis that dominates when lower ability speakers are asked to narrate in real time.
13 The John Test (Language Innovations 1974).
14 Localized English, in some sociolinguistic contexts, constitutes a suitable substitute for native-speaker models as a criterion for comprehension. In Singapore or in parts of India, for instance, English is often used as a lingua franca among different linguistic groups. In such circumstances, representative samples of English as it is used as a vehicle of inter-ethnic communication might be made the criterion.

The analytic strategy: identifying moderating variables

The evaluation of the five courses designed for the teaching of spoken English took place concurrently with other courses taught in the English department at the institution. Such a situation has the potential for misleading results about product differences unless effort is made to take into account the content of the concurrently taught courses. Reports from the teachers of the concurrent courses (the Japanese faculty) indicated that there was considerable effort made to standardize both the content and the methodology used in these courses.[15] The only course considered to be a potential moderating variable to the outcome of the courses in spoken English was the language laboratory course. Here again, standardized materials and methodology were used, thus reducing the threat of a concurrently taught course radically influencing the post-test scores.

The opportunities for contact with native speakers of English in major urban centers in Japan have steadily increased in the past decade. A considerable number of students supplement their college language courses with weekly lessons at private foreign language schools. Summer 'home-stay' programs and intensive summer courses also have become popular among college students. The myriad of possible moderating variables makes even a short-term program evaluation difficult without some form of qualification. Given the fact the students were alphabetically assigned to the groups in this study and that there were obvious moderating factors, a quasi-experimental design was utilized (Cook and Campbell 1979). Three covariates were therefore considered vital for statistical 'control'; the pretest scores given before the start of classroom instruction, self-reported extracurricular contact with native speakers during the academic year or summer holidays, and average attendance over the year. The resulting multiple analysis of covariance design (Huitema 1980; Edwards 1985; Cohen and Cohen 1983) thus sought to extract the maximum amount of 'noise' from the comparisons of the effects of the five sets of materials.

The design as a whole lessened the likelihood that spurious differences would be found because multiple measures of each skill were taken, a stringent pair-wise comparison procedure was used only after omnibus non-random ANCOVA F's emerged,[16] and, most crucially, product differences were predicted on the basis of classroom observations.

---

15 One-way analyses of variance were used to assess the extent of LL instructor differences on the listening tests used in this study. No significant differences were found.

16 This approach reduces the likelihood for the so-called type 1 error. No pair-wise contrasts are allowed if the overall ANCOVA significance test does not reach the pre-specified alpha criterion.

The product

Hypothesis One states the predicted ordering of post-test means will match the relative focus on form. To test this hypothesis, two dependent variables were used in separate analyses of covariance (ANCOVA).

TABLE 5 DEPENDENT VARIABLE: MULTIPLE CHOICE GRAMMAR TEST

Covariates	R^2	.271	F= 17.8	p <.001	d.f. 3, 144
Materials	R^2	.316	F= 2.19	p <.08	d.f. 4, 140
Interactions	R^2	.361	F= .78	p <.68	d.f. 12, 128

	Mean scores	
	pre-test	*post-test* (adjusted)
Task-based materials	27.9	30.1
Audio-lingual materials	28.0	31.4
SAPL materials	27.0	28.9
Grammatical materials	27.8	29.8
Functional-notional materials	29.6	28.2

TABLE 6 DEPENDENT VARIABLE: ERROR-FREE T-UNITS ON THE NARRATIVE DISCOURSE TEST

Covariates	R^2	.193	F= 11.4	p <.001	d.f. 3, 144
Materials	R^2	.222	F= 1.34	p <.25	d.f. 4, 140
Interactions	R^2	.288	F= .98	p <.53	d.f. 12,128

	Mean scores	
	pre-test	*post-test* (adjusted)
Task-based materials	4.03	8.07
Audio-lingual materials	4.89	6.76
SAPL materials	5.45	7.53
Grammatical materials	4.77	7.31
Functional-notional materials	5.28	9.73

No support for Hypothesis One was found. In spite of the considerable effort spent on focusing student attention on the structure of the language studied, the form-focused groups did not in the end develop any more grammatical accuracy on either the paper-and-pencil test (F of 2.19 in Table 5) or the narrative discourse test (F of 1.34 in Table 6). A plausible reason why the focus on form observed in the five classes here did not prove to be related to differences between classes could be linked to the fact that the other 'standardized' courses taken by the students were primarily focused on grammar and translation. This would mean, of course, that students in the non-form-focused oral English classes would be getting almost as much grammar practice in their other classes anyway.

Hypothesis Two predicted that groups with more pair and group work time will develop more fluency *vis à vis* the groups with fewer of such opportunities to practice in pairs. It is important to note that there is no distinction made here between pair work involving unplanned discourse and dialogue repetition in pairs in this hypothesis. Two measures of fluency were selected. The holistic rating of fluency on the narrative discourse test made by a native speaker of English and the total number of spoken T-units served as the dependent variables in this test of the fluency hypothesis.

TABLE 7   DEPENDENT VARIABLE: HOLISTIC RATING OF FLUENCY

Covariates	R^2	.316	F= 22.1	p <.001	d.f. 3,144
Materials	R^2	.355	F= 2.16	p <.08	d.f. 4, 140
Interaction	R^2	.442	F= 1.66	p <.09	d.f. 12, 128

	Mean scores	
	pre-test	*post-test* (adjusted)
Task-based materials	2.39	3.53
Audio-lingual materials	2.71	2.85
SAPL materials	2.90	3.27
Grammatical materials	2.77	3.23
Functional-notional materials	2.85	3.44

TABLE 8   DEPENDENT VARIABLE: SPOKEN T-UNITS IN NARRATIVE DISCOURSE TEST

Covariates	R^2	.395	F= 31.3	p <.001	d.f. 3, 144
Materials	R^2	.427	F= 1.95	p <.11	d.f. 4, 140
Interactions	R^2	.485	F= 1.20	p <.30	d.f. 12, 128

	Mean scores	
	pre-test	*post-test* (adjusted)
Task-based materials	17.1	29.3
Audio-lingual materials	17.9	24.9
SAPL materials	19.4	27.4
Grammatical materials	17.7	26.0
Functional-notional materials	19.2	27.6

The analysis of covariance revealed that after the effects of the initial differences and the moderating variables were extracted from the total variance on the post-tests there was no significant difference among the five groups on the holistic rating of fluency (F of 2.16 in Table 7) nor on the total number of T-units uttered in the narration (F of 1.95 in Table 8). Although *post-hoc* comparisons were not attempted, it is nonetheless interesting to note that the predicted hierarchy based on the teacher observation data is quite similar to those seen on both measures of fluency used to test Hypothesis Two. Statistical 'near misses' such as those seen here certainly suggest a trend that needs to be investigated in other contexts with a variety of other methods of assessment.

Hypothesis Three predicted that the groups with the most input from the teacher and the taped materials will benefit in terms of greater gains in listening comprehension. As in the previous two hypotheses, the predicted hierarchy of post-test differences reflects the actual differences seen in the classroom observation data.

TABLE 9   DEPENDENT VARIABLE: LISTENING CLOZE

Covariates	R^2	.276	F= 18.3	p <.001	d.f. 3, 144
Materials	R^2	.353	F= 4.16	p <.01	d.f. 4, 140
Interaction	R^2	.388	F= .61	p <.83	d.f. 12, 128

	Mean scores	
	pre-test	*post-test* (adjusted)
Task-based materials	6.50	8.74
Audio-lingual materials	8.50	10.1
SAPL materials	8.57	7.92
Grammatical materials	9.32	10.2
Functional-notional materials	9.28	9.70

Since the overall test of differences among the groups was significant for listening cloze (F of 4.16 in Table 9) and on the post-test partial dictation (F of 10.8 in Table 11), *post-hoc* comparisons were undertaken. Here Fisher's LSD procedure was employed to make pair-wise contrasts (Huitema 1980). As stated in Hypothesis Three, the predicted order of differences was:

> Grammar materials will equal functional-notional materials, which will equal audio-lingual materials. The grammar, functional-notional and audio-lingual materials will have higher means than the SAPL materials and the task-based materials. There will be no difference between the SAPL and the task-based materials.

TABLE 10 *POST-HOC* TESTS OF LISTENING CLOZE

Predicted	Observed
F A S T	F A S T
G = = > >	G = = > >
F = > >	F = > ?
A > >	A > ?
S =	S =

In this test of Hypothesis Three eight out of the ten predicted mean differences were substantiated. In the above notation > refers to a predicted difference on the *post-hoc* test with a probability of .05. The two predictions that were not supported are marked with a question mark. Specifically, the prediction that the task-based group would have lower listening scores than either the functional-notional group or the audio-lingual group was not upheld.

TABLE 11 DEPENDENT VARIABLE: PARTIAL DICTATION

Covariates	R^2	.170	$F=$ 9.85	$p < .001$	d.f. 3, 144
Materials	R^2	.366	$F=$ 10.8	$p < .001$	d.f. 4, 140
Interaction	R^2	.433	$F=$ 1.26	$p < .25$	d.f. 12, 128

	Mean scores	
	pre-test	*post-test* (adjusted)
Task-based materials	6.35	7.68
Audio-lingual materials	6.60	11.6
SAPL materials	7.36	8.11
Grammatical materials	8.45	10.7
Functional-notional materials	7.28	9.34

Again Fisher's LSD method is applied.

Predicted	Observed
F A S T	F A S T
G = = > >	G ? = > >
F = > >	F ? > >
A > >	A > >
S =	S =

In both sets of pair-wise contrasts only two out of ten significant differences were not predicted on the basis of the classroom observations. A plausible explanation for the fact that the task-based materials obtained similar gains in listening even though there was not much input from the teacher or the taped materials could be that the input from the other students in the pair work exercises required greater attention – and hence deeper processing (Ross and Berwick 1988). In the case of the second dependent variable, partial dictation, there were differences among the functional-notional, grammar and audio-lingual materials that were not predicted. These differences, however, were not part of the hypothesis based on major differences in the quantity of listening input. Perhaps a qualitative analysis of the types of listening activities utilized in these materials would reveal plausible reasons why an equal volume of input did not result in equal gains (see Spada 1987 for a similar conclusion).

Summary

The classroom observation data gathered in this study demonstrate how a longitudinal approach to the evaluation of intact classes can lead to a limited set of testable hypotheses about product differences. In this study, specific hypotheses based on the observations were evaluated with the use of analysis of covariance. No evidence was found to support the position that focus on form results in greater accuracy. Nor was there any clear evidence found to support a pair work-centered method that assumes pair work practice will lead to more fluent speech. The most direct match of process-to-product found was between the incidence of listening input and the development of listening skills in the post-tests.

Although it must be said that many qualitative dimensions to the classes observed don't readily lend themselves to the low-inferential coding schemata used in this study, the results strongly suggest that at least some aspects of language learning product can be inferred from even a restricted coding strategy which accounts for the distribution of class time, the communicative orientation of each activity and the extent of student involvement in pair work activity.

The results of the comparisons of classroom focus and content imply that pair work leads to more practice time. However, contrary to recent claims (for example Ferguson 1978) about the omnipotence of pair work, there is no strong evidence to suggest that pair work which is limited to the manipulation of 'canned' language in the form of dialogues and non-communicative routines will eventually result in a general fluency. In contrast with pair work primarily focused on form, there seems to be considerable potential for other forms of limited pair work which stimulate the students' use of unplanned discourse (Pica 1985; Ellis 1986). The results support the contention that overt focus on language in the form of drills and pattern practice does not directly lead to short-term gains in formal control of either passive grammatical knowledge or integrated knowledge of morphosyntax such as that required in the narrative discourse task.

The consistent fit between the observation data and the results of the listening tests provides ample evidence to endorse an approach to TEFL at the elementary level which seeks to nurture listening comprehension and communication in the classroom at the same time. Such an approach does not necessarily require a steady stream of extemporaneous teacher talk to create on-the-spot comprehensible input. Rather, appropriate listening materials which are calibrated to the interests and abilities of the students are needed for systematic growth in listening skills.

The study demonstrates that program-defining evaluation can take place within an institution by the participant observer/teachers, especially when a collaborative effort to devise a 'local' coding scheme such as that used in this study is made. The orientation in this study was towards the development of reliable low-inferential codings which would lead to quantitative comparisons. These coding schemata provide a basis for defining the actual conduct of classes, of a praxis instead of an idealized process.

The observation schemata used here were designed to provide a limited account of the classes. Other approaches are not precluded, however. There is still an obvious need to supplement this type of approach with a qualitative evaluation strategy, discourse analyses of teacher-to-student interaction and student-to-student interaction as well as diary studies of teachers and students alike. The extent to which such 'micro' level analyses of the affective and linguistic aspects of language learning in the classroom can be utilized in descriptions of differences among rival approaches to language teaching remains to be seen.

References

Aston, G. 1986. Trouble shooting in interaction with learners: the more the merrier? *Applied Linguistics* 7(2): 128–43.

Beretta, A. 1986. Toward a methodology of ESL program evaluation. *TESOL Quarterly* 20(1): 144–55.

Chafe, W. L. 1979. The flow of thought and the flow of language. In T. Givon (Ed.) *Discourse and syntax: syntax and semantics 12*: 159–82. New York, Academic Press.

Cohen, J. and P. Cohen. 1983. *Applied Multiple Regression/Correlation Analysis in the behavioral sciences*. Hillsdale, NJ: Lawrence Erlbaum Associates.

Cook, T. D. and D. T. Campbell. 1979. *Quasi-Experimentation: design and analysis for field settings*. Boston, Mass.: Houghton-Mifflin.

Dinsmore, D. 1985. Waiting for Godot in the EFL classroom. *ELT Journal* 39(4).

Doughty, C. and T. Pica. 1986. Information gaps: do they facilitate language acquisition? *TESOL Quarterly* 20(2): 305–25.

Duff, P. 1986. Another look at interlanguage talk; taking task to task. In R. Day (Ed.) Rowley, Mass: Newbury House 147–81. *Talking to learn.*

Edwards, A. L. 1985. *Multiple Regression and the Analysis of Variance and Covariance.* New York: W. H. Freeman and Co.

Ellis, R. 1986. *Classroom second language development.* Oxford: Pergamon Press.

Faerch, C. 1985. Meta talk in FL classroom discourse. *Studies in Second Language Acquisition* 7(2).

Ferguson, N. 1978. *The Gordian Knot.* Geneva: CEEL.

Ferguson, N. 1981. *Threshold.* Geneva: CEEL.

Freedman, E. S. 1979. Valid research into foreign language teaching – two recent projects. *System* 7(3): 187–99.

Gayle, G. 1980. *A descriptive analysis of second language teaching styles in the oral approach.* Ottawa: University of Ottawa Press.

Gregg, K. 1986. Review of 'The Input Hypothesis: Issues and implications' by S. D. Krashen. *TESOL Quarterly* 20: 66–80.

Higgs, T. 1984. Language teaching and the quest for the holy grail. In T. Higgs (Ed.) *Teaching for proficiency: the organizing principle.* Lincolnwood, Ill.: National Textbook Co.

Huitema, B. 1980. *The Analysis of Covariance and Alternatives.* New York: John Wiley and Sons.

Krashen, S. 1985. *The Input Hypothesis: issues and implications.* London: Longman.

Krashen, S. and T. Terrell. 1983. *The Natural Approach: language acquisition in the classroom.* Hayward, Calif.: The Alemany Press.

Language Innovations. 1974. *The John Test.* New York, N.Y.: Author.

Lett, J. and P. Shaw. 1986. Combining quantitative and qualitative program evaluation: A research report. Paper presented at the 20th annual convention of the Teachers of English to Speakers of Other Languages, March 6, 1986.

Long, M. H. 1984. Process and product in ESL program evaluation. *TESOL Quarterly* 18: 409–25.

Long, M. H. 1985. Input and second language acquisition theory. In S. M. Gass and C. Madden (Eds.) *Input and second language acquisition.* Rowley, Mass.: Newbury House.

Long, M. H. and C. Sato. 1983. Classroom foreigner talk discourse: forms and functions of teacher's questions. In W. H. Seliger and M. H. Long (Eds.) *Classroom oriented research in second language acquisition.* Rowley, Mass.: Newbury House.

Pica, T. 1985. The selective impact of classroom instruction on second language acquisition. *Applied Linguistics* 6(3): 214–22.

Pica, T. and M. H. Long 1986. The linguistic and conversational performance of experienced and inexperienced teachers. In R. Day (Ed.) *Talking to learn.* Rowley, Mass.: Newbury House.

Pienemann, M. 1985. Psychological constraints on the teachability of languages. *Studies in Second Language Acquisition* 6(2).

Porter, P. 1986. How learners talk to each other; input and interaction in task-centered discussion. In R. Day (Ed.) *Talking to learn.* Rowley, Mass.: Newbury House, 200–22.

Postovsky, V. A. 1981. The priority of aural comprehension in the language acquisition process. In H. Winitz (Ed.) *The Comprehension Approach to foreign language instruction*. Rowley, Mass.: Newbury House.

Richards, J. C. 1984. The secret life of methods. *TESOL Quarterly* 18(2): 7–23.

Romesburg, H. C. 1984. *Cluster Analysis for researchers*. Belmont, Calif.: Lifetime Learning Publications.

Ross, S. J. 1987. An experiment with a narrative discourse test. In K. Bailey, T. Dale and R. T. Clifford (Eds.) *Language testing research*. Monterey, Calif.: Defense Language Institute.

Ross, S. J. and Berwick, R. 1988. Scripted and unscripted information exchange tasks: Two approaches to learner negotiation in the foreign language classroom. *PASAA* 18(1): 21–31.

Spada, N. 1987. Relationships between instructional differences and learning outcomes: A process–product study of communicative language teaching. *Applied Linguistics* 8(1): 137–61.

Stevick, E. 1976. *Memory, meaning and method*. Rowley, Mass.: Newbury House.

Stevick, E. 1980. *A Way and Ways*. Rowley, Mass.: Newbury House.

Tomlin, R. S. 1984. The treatment of foreground–background information in the on-line descriptive discourse of second language learners. *Studies in Second Language Acquisition* 6(2): 115–42.

Varonis, E. and S. Gass. 1985. Non-native/non-native conversations: a model for negotiation of meaning. *Applied Linguistics* 6: 71–90.

Winitz, H. 1981. Nonlinear learning and language teaching. In H. Winitz (Ed.). *The Comprehension Approach to foreign language instruction*. Rowley, Mass.: Newbury House.

Editors' postscript to Ross

Ross' chapter discusses an evaluation of foreign language programmes in what he perceives to be a '*laissez-faire*' environment in Japan. He examines five approaches to ESL: audiolingual, functional-notional, grammar-based, self-access pair-learning, and task-based, that are currently popular. He defines the approaches in terms of materials. Here are some of the issues that emerge from the inquiry.

Interestingly, the main goal of the inquiry was to arrive at findings which are generalisable to other Japanese foreign language teaching contexts. It should be pointed out that this goal is a familiar one in modern conceptions of programme evaluation (and a far more achievable one than attempting to make a theoretical statement about language learning). However, it might be worth stressing that even this more modest aim is only achievable if it is conceded at the outset that the generalisation requires a more or less well-reasoned logical leap. Because certain effects may be observed in one time and place under a particular set of circumstances does not mean that they will be observed in another place at another time and under what will necessarily be a different set of circumstances. This is the case both with quantitative and qualitative data, with true-experiment or with ethnography. The generalisation is made on the basis of what is known about the observed situation and the situation the findings might be generalised to: if enough is known about both, and they are both very similar, psychologically, similar findings might be expected to obtain (but there is nothing compelling about this), and the generalisation is weakened as known differences between situations are noted. Thus, in programme evaluation, for generalisation to other contexts to be viable, there is a need for rich descriptive data. So, although Ross points out that quantitative procedures were preferred 'because it was too difficult to distil the insights of five teacher / amateur ethnographers into a coherent reliable whole', it may be that, in view of his goal, such input would have played a useful role.

Another feature of the study worth noting is its attempt to overcome teachers' resistance to being observed. Alderson and Scott (this volume) concerned with utilisation of findings, pay attention to teachers' wishes; Slimani (this volume), not involved in a study where utilisation of findings was an issue, selects a teacher for observation, mentioning that the teacher could hardly refuse without losing face. Ross, conscious that 'observation strikes fear into the hearts of teachers', opts to involve teachers in observing each other. The difficulty here, which Ross alludes to, is that teachers have then to be trained as observers and their coding responses normed. Typically scant resources of time and energy may mean that this stage is not fully accomplished. In the negotiation that takes place prior to an evaluation, such issues would have to be debated.

Finally, Ross helpfully devotes attention to the question of uniformity of treatments, pointing out that teachers typically do not perform in what he calls an 'orthodox' fashion. He reports that considerable efforts had been made to standardise both the content and methodology of the courses. It might be useful to highlight, in regard to standardisation, that it is only achievable if courses and behaviours are so minutely specified that there is no room for ambiguity, and if teachers are so thoroughly (and attritionally) trained that they can eventually work in a totally prescriptive manner. Otherwise, the notion of standardisation becomes very squishy. However, no real-world classroom is ever going to accommodate such extreme rigidity. The question for evaluators is: if our aim is to generalise to other contexts, are we interested in what happens when a programme is implemented in a constrained way or in what occurs when programme implementation varies naturally across teachers and classrooms?

6 Evaluation of classroom interaction

Assia Slimani

Until relatively recently, the tradition in the field of language teaching and learning has been to expect a better understanding of the teaching/ learning phenomenon by making a broad comparison between the learning outcomes and the teacher's plan. The focus was set on the extreme poles of the situation under investigation: those of methods and outcomes. What happened during the implementation of the method was largely ignored when it came to the evaluation of the learning outcomes. This approach is illustrated by the large-scale projects conducted by Scherer and Wertheimer (1964) and Smith (1970), who focused on outcomes and paid relatively little attention to process (see Part I, this volume).

This chapter proposes to analyse and evaluate what is claimed to be learned from classroom interaction. The method, which will be described later, allows a detailed study of the classroom interactive processes in attempting to uncover and evaluate the quality of interaction which leads to learners' claims of uptake. (Uptake is defined as what learners claim to have learned from a particular lesson.)

Importance of the study of classroom interaction

Allwright (1984a) suggests that a high proportion of apparent mismatches between teaching and learning could be explained if instruction is perceived as being the product of both teachers' and learners' contributions. Learning outcomes are not necessarily the reflection of the teacher's plan since, in the process of accomplishing instructional objectives, interactive work takes place among the participants and leads to the creation of a whole range of learning opportunities, many of which are perhaps unexpected.

The observation of language classes typically shows that the discourse is not something prepared beforehand by the teacher and simply implemented with the students. Instead, it is jointly constructed by contributions from both parties so that learners are not just passively fed from the instructor's plan. They can have preoccupations or goals on their personal agendas that they attempt to clarify during interactive work. Teachers know from experience that a lesson does not often take the direction it was planned to take, or, if it does, it might nevertheless include or exclude aspects that neither the teacher nor the learners have anticipated. Problems, queries, perhaps various unexpected teacher's and learners' comments, influenced by the teacher's as well as the learners' psychological and emotional dispositions, arise in the course of the 'planned' lesson and create the learning opportunities from which learners presumably grasp whatever gets learned. Hence, considered from this point of view, lessons are 'co-productions' and 'socially constructed events' brought to existence through the 'co-operative enter-prise' (Corder 1977:2) of both parties. The learners' role in the creation of the co-production is not to be underestimated in comparison with the role played by the instructor. No matter how powerful the latter's influence, 'no teacher teaches without consent' (Corder 1977:66).

The perspective of viewing discourse as a co-production adds a new dimension which ties the teacher, in his/her attempts to make instruction relevant and comprehensible, with the learners, in their attempts to understand instruction and manage their own learning. If the classroom negotiation process is disregarded then what learners get might be different from what the instructor or the researcher had intended (see also Allwright 1984b, 1984c for a fuller discussion of these ideas). In fact, teachers' exclamations of surprise, such as, 'But I taught them that last week!', are only too common in staff rooms. They bear witness to the fact that much more than the investigation of the teacher's plan is needed to provide fuller explanations of the learners' reactions.

Seen from this point of view, it appears quite misleading to predict which linguistic items will be 'uptaken' by learners even before the lesson has taken place. As argued by Allwright (1984a), each lesson is a different lesson for each individual learner as different things are likely to be drawn by different learners from the same event.

Some researchers (Lightbown, 1983; Ellis 1984; Ellis and Rathbone 1987) make prior assumptions about what learners might see as optimal in the input. Hence, choosing to examine the teaching effect on the learners' accuracy of use of the -s morphemes (Lightbown 1983), of WH questions (Ellis 1984), and German word order and verb endings (Ellis and Rathbone 1987) might provide the investigators with the advantage of having a rich description of the developmental stages of such features in first and second language development. However, by predicting the subjects' learning outcomes, such investigators might be missing out on what has actually attracted the learners' attention in discourse.

Therefore, Allwright (1984a) suggested the study of the notion of 'uptake', that is, the investigation of what individual learners claim to have learned from the interactive classroom events which have just preceded. What follows is a discussion of uptake, and of its contribution to a better understanding and evaluation of what gets claimed to be learned during classroom interaction.

Uptake

Learning a language is defined by some proponents of communicative curricula 'as learning how to communicate as a member of a socio cultural group' (Breen and Candlin 1982:91). Hence, it is amply acknowledged that learning a language is not merely a matter of recalling beads of items but rather of coming to grips with the ideational, interpersonal and textual knowledge which is realised through effective communication in the target language. Therefore, one might argue that attempting to measure learning at the end of a lesson implies a narrow definition of what language learning involves. In this paper, it is considered to be the realisation of communicative competence as well as performance in relevant situations.

However, since we are concerned with relating learning outcomes to their immediate and potentially determining environment, it appears rather difficult to think of ways of getting at learning evidence through testing and elicitation procedures as traditionally understood. The interactive process lends itself to the creation of an infinite set of learning opportunities which are not pre-established by the teacher's plan. In such circumstances, it appears to be practically impossible to undertake the complicated task of designing a test to assess the effects of interaction as it occurs, especially since the test has to be administered at the end of the lesson. However, the major problem encountered when attempting to research the issue of the direct impact of interaction on the subjects' claims is that of finding a way to identify and collect the learners' performance data or 'uptake'. Once identified, uptake needs to be related to the classroom environment which might subsequently explain its emergence. To do this, uptake has to be captured some time after the interactive event took place, but before too much could happen to the informants that would obscure the direct impact of the event on the learners' claims.

The problem is not restricted to formal test-based evaluation procedures. SLA elicitation techniques would also fail to meet the objectives of getting unmediated learner data. Elicitation procedures, similar to those used by Lightbown (1983), provide the informants with an obligatory context of use; this enables the researcher to evaluate, under experimental conditions, the informants' accuracy when using the features which are being investigated. By their nature, these procedures assume that one is looking for particular features which are predicted from the teacher's plan. However, what is needed is a way of identifying what learners have got from their experience of being in a particular class session.

The solution eventually adopted to the problem of 'uptake' identification must seem somewhat naive at first sight: simply asking the informants to tell the researcher what they believed they had learned in the lesson they had just attended. It was felt that the advantages of the procedure outweighed its obvious shortcomings.

The great advantage of this approach is that it offers an operational way of getting at what learners perceive they have learned. It makes it possible to relate learning claims to the immediate environment from which they emerged in order to see if it is possible to establish a relationship. The idea of requiring learners to tell us what they thought they had learned would supply the researcher with manageable amounts of data, directly referable to the classroom data. For instance, if some learners claimed that they had learned the difference between 'list' and 'least', the investigator could trace the words back in the transcripts and study the opportunities where 'list' and 'least' arose and scrutinise also the circumstances which might have made those items particularly outstanding to the point of prompting learners to claim them as learned.

It should be acknowledged at this stage that I am dealing here with the learners' perceptions of what they believed they have uptaken rather than with 'facts'. However, in the absence of a satisfactory means of getting at learning in such a way as to relate it to its potentially determining environment, a qualitative approach based on the study of uptake seems to be an interesting phenomenon to guide investigation into a possible relationship between interaction and learning outcomes.

Prior to moving to the description of the method, it is relevant to provide brief information about the participants in the study. They were thirteen Algerian male first year university students at l'Institut National d'Electricité et d'Electronique (INELEC). They were aged between eighteen and twenty. They all spoke Arabic as their mother tongue and French as a second or foreign language. They were on a six-month intensive language program (24 hours per week) to prepare them to undertake their engineering studies in English. To benefit from their language training, the students were put in small groups (in this case thirteen) according to the results of a placement test. Their exposure to English outside their classes was limited to their classroom work and occasionally to listening to folk music. Their instructor was a trained Algerian male teacher.

Method

Uptake

The procedure developed to collect the learners' claims about uptake was to distribute a questionnaire or 'Uptake Recall Chart' at the end of every observed lesson, asking informants to relate, in terms of grammar, words and expressions, pronunciation and spelling, and in as much detail as possible what points they recalled in the events that had just preceded (see Appendix 1 in this chapter for the original layout of the Uptake Recall Chart). After approximately three hours (before too much had happened to them, but after enough had happened to counter immediate recency and primacy effects), each learner was presented with his own uptake recall chart accompanied this time with an 'Uptake Identification Probe' (see Appendix 2 in this chapter for the Uptake Identification Probe). This is another questionnaire asking the participants to annotate their uptake recall charts by clearly dissociating the items they believed they had actually learned in that particular lesson from those they had already seen with other teachers or the same teacher on previous occasions. In this way, I gave the data the strongest possible chance of being relatable to specific interactions in the lesson by asking learners to commit themselves to the things they believed they had encountered and learned for the first time from the preceding events. The three-hour delay allowed the participants to add, if possible, to their first list of items, but above all, it was estimated that the delay allowed time for the learners to absorb what they thought they had learned from today's lesson.

Both instruments, the Uptake Recall Charts and the Uptake Identification Probes, were presented in French, a language with which the researcher and all the learners were familiar.

Learning opportunities

Once uptaken items have been identified, it is necessary to locate them in the relevant interactive events of the lesson in which they occurred. Learners were observed two hours a week during the first six weeks of the term. To carry out the classroom observation procedure a high quality audio-recording of class sessions was crucial to allow the tracing of uptake in the learning opportunities which arose in the lessons. The latter needed to have a good number of instances of interactive work which could be closely studied in an attempt to understand what made learners claim uptake in those particular instances. A monologue where the teacher would be holding the floor during the entire lesson would not have suited the needs of the study. However, a relative lack of interaction seems to be a characteristic of lectures rather than language classes where a fair amount of interactive work generally takes place.

It was felt that the amount of interaction occurring during lessons depended also on the learners' ability level and the subject studied. To produce the right conditions for the project, it was assumed that the teaching of grammar to low intermediate or advanced beginners would offer the most suitable atmosphere. A weak as opposed to a strong group of students might tend to seek more learning opportunities and pay extra attention to what goes on in the classroom in order to improve their language command. It is noted that the subjects of this study were particularly motivated to master the second language. They were expected to take their technical subjects in English at the end of an intensive language programme which served as the setting for this data collection.

Grammar lessons were chosen because discrete points are frequently dealt with in such lessons and it is relatively easy to find out what has become of items in the learners' uptake list. Moreover, it was assumed that it was simpler for the learner to pick up discrete points, such as one might expect to occur during grammar lessons, remember them, and afterwards list them on the charts which would be distributed at the end of the recording.

To investigate the learning opportunities fully, I exhaustively collected all classroom textual materials including all visual and audio aids. I also took notes of what went on the blackboard to help account later for the claims of uptaken items.

Interview

To provide the study with corroborative data, it was felt necessary to interview the subjects twice over the six-week period: once in the middle and once at the end of the data gathering. The idea was to give the researcher a further chance to probe the informants about the possible reasons which made them claim the particular items they reported on their uptake charts. The interview was also believed to allow learners to express other ideas they felt were missing from their uptake charts. As the number of learners was rather small, all thirteen could be interviewed in about one hour, the same day, after the third lesson recording. The subjects were individually asked to answer the researcher's queries while the other learners were outside the room, waiting for their turn to be interviewed.

The interview, conducted in French or in Arabic according to the learners' wishes, was an adaptive structured interview where respondents were free to give details on the five issues which were followed up with all learners during the interview session. The issues could be summarised as follows:

1 Clarifications (if necessary) of self-reported data on the charts distributed at the end of every observed lesson.
2 Rationale for claiming those specific items on today's uptake chart or, if possible, on the uptake charts distributed at the end of the two previous observed lessons.
3 Possibilities for the learners to extend their perceptions of those items.
4 Reactions to the benefits or otherwise of completing the charts at the end of every taped grammar lesson.
5 Feelings about the researcher's presence and the tape-recorder in the back of the classroom during the lesson.

The second question, about the reasons for claiming certain items instead of others, was found to be most problematic to the respondents as some remained evasive while others produced overgeneralised statements as to what made them claim those items. They were unable to tell the researcher the reasons which made any particular item outstanding in their minds. The fact that many of them reacted as if the question was irrelevant or irrational discouraged the researcher from interviewing a second time as this question was the focus of the interview.

The respondents produced responses that were insufficiently precise to be interpreted in relation to what might account for their claims. Because I was observing the same group for the period of six weeks I could have trained the informants by asking perhaps more detailed and specific questions about what most attracted their attention in classroom discourse. However, as I had never even conducted an interview before, I was afraid to put words in the learners' mouths. Moreover, being miles away from any professional consultant, I did not dare meddle with the procedure and run the risk of undermining the data gathering. The interview had to be given within the six observational weeks as the learners' responses had to relate to these precisely observed events.

Method effect

I am aware of the fact that the methodological procedure used to collect the data can strongly raise the subjects' consciousness of the learning process and might, by the same token, pollute the data. This would have been the case if the class observation had lasted over a long period of time. I was however, only thinking of observing two hours a week during six weeks of the informants' timetable, which amounted to twenty-four (24) hours of intensive English lessons per week. It seemed rather unlikely that the methodological procedure would have any major effect on the subjects' behaviour.

However, to confirm this supposition, the results of the Michigan Test were used. This test was already being used, at the beginning of the programme, as a placement test to determine the learners' ability levels. This procedure produced four groups, one of which was the group under study. The other three were, for the purpose of the project, considered as control groups. All four groups were following the same programme, though at their own pace. Without telling the learners in advance, the same test was again administered to the experimental group, as well as to the three control groups, after the six observational periods. The pre- and post-test results were inspected to see whether the study groups' progress had been significantly influenced by the effects of the design.

The following chart summarises the results of the pre- and post-Michigan Tests results (T1 and T2 on the chart).

CHART A: AVERAGE SCORES AND PERCENTAGE INCREASE FOR EACH GROUP

Group 1			Group 2			Group 3*			Group 4		
SS	T1	T2	SS	T1	T2	SS	T1	T2	SS	T1	T2
1	80	88	1	63	70	1	60	85	1	49	73
2	75	83	2	57	73	2	50	72	2	36	81
3	74	84	3	54	79	3	48	68	3	35	63
4	67	83	4	53	78	4	47	83	4	34	71
5	62	76	5	53	68	5	45	82	5	32	78
6	61	78	6	48	75	6	44	74	6	30	37
7	60	75	7	52	63	7	43	66	7	29	63
8	60	64	8	52	76	8	42	84	8	11	54
9	58	75	9	51	70	9	41	77			
10	58	75	10	51	68	10	41	71			
11	57	78	11	50	78	11	41	68			
			12	50	74	12	39	72			
						13	38	70			

Average Scores For Each Group											
T1		T2	T1		T2	T1		T2	T1		T2
64.72		78.09	52.82		72.66	44.53		74.76	32		65

Percentage of Increase For Each Group			
Group 1	Group 2	Group 3	Group 4
20.65%	37.53%	67.88%	103.12%

*group under study

The chart shows the average score obtained by the participants in the study to be slightly higher (74.76) than the one achieved by group 2 (72.66). In comparison, the average score of group 2 does not overtake that of group 1, and neither does group 4 over group 3. It seems rather unreasonable however to attribute this slight improvement wholly to the procedure itself as it was applied on only two hours of instruction out of 24 hours a week. The merit I can see the procedure objectively deriving from this slight increase is that it did not hinder the group in its activities. My presence and the tape-recorder in the back of the room did not seem to have negatively affected the group.

The total percentage increase for each group is a representation, within the whole programme, of the students' language training development in the first six weeks. It appears to happen in an expected way: the lower groups show more progress than group 1 (20.65%) and 2 (37.53%). This increase in language development is quite comprehensible since knowing much less at the outset of the programme, groups 3 (67.88%) and 4 (103.12%) have more room for improvement. The total percentage increase therefore does not display any convincing sign in favour of an interfering methodological design. The learners in group 3, in spite of my demands on them at the end of each of the observed sessions, do not achieve in any markedly different manner than what would be expected from them if one thought that the procedure could have influenced the quantity of their learning.

In summary, two types of data were gathered for the investigation of the issue: learners' specific claims collected through uptake charts and detailed accounts of the learning opportunities obtained through systematic observation of audio-recorded, naturally occurring classroom data. These were supplemented with field notes taken by the author. The interview which was intended to provide corroborative data did not produce responses that were sufficiently precise to be interpreted in relation to what might account for their claims. In the end, the bulk of what might help us find out about the learners' selective attention mechanism would have to arise from a consideration of classroom transcripts in relation to uptake charts as the learners themselves did not seem to be aware of what directed their attention while attending instruction.

Both the teacher and the learners under study were informed in general terms of the goals of the research. Both parties were told that the project was seeking a relationship between what the informants report as 'uptake' and the interactive process in which the class participates. However, I did not go into any further detail with them, not wanting the teacher to give undue emphasis to linguistic items in order for learners to remember as many as possible. It was hoped that the usual teaching and learning situation would not be influenced by alerting the participants' attention to the researcher's focus of interest.

In fact, when filling out the 'uptake charts' at the end of the first observational lesson, it was noticed that some learners tried to peep at their peers' charts to enable them to report more items than they actually could. At this point it was emphasised to the subjects that they should look upon the author as an outsider, a researcher rather than as a teacher, and that whatever reports and comments they made would be entirely confidential. Their reports were not to be shown to the instructor, nor would they have any bearing on their grades.

As it was planned to observe the same teacher with the same group for two hours a week for six weeks, the procedure became routine and my presence was accepted with ease by the learners. The instructor also appeared much more relaxed after the first hour of observation. Prior to deciding which teacher was to be part of the project, I felt some resistance and avoidance on the part of the staff members who alluded to the fact that 'really, not much is going on in our classes right now'. The procedure discussed in this chapter was part of a doctoral project and this made the teachers particularly apprehensive at having their lessons 'dissected' and looked at through 'magnifying' lenses for research purposes. However, I persisted in spite of their anxiety as their refusal could mean the end of my plans. Therefore, I remain indebted to the 'chosen' teacher who, knowing that he could not openly refuse me without losing face, gracefully adjusted to my persistent presence in the back of his classes.

The rest of the chapter will describe some of the tentative findings (see Slimani 1987 for a fuller report) which might help us understand the relationship between the classroom interactive processes and uptake, and their consequences for evaluation studies. Two interesting characteristics of uptake emerged in the investigation of the learners' uptake charts. The first characteristic is that most of the learners' claims were topicalised during instruction. The second is that learners' uptake is strongly idiosyncratic. Both aspects will be discussed in detail below.

Importance of topicalisation on uptake

A thorough study of the informants' Uptake Charts and Uptake Identification Probes showed that a total of 126 items were claimed to have been learned. These items were verbs, nouns, adjectives, adverbs, connectors, auxiliaries, models and some set phrases. Almost all (112 items or 89 per cent) of what the respondents claimed to have seen and learned for the first time in those six observed lessons, had, in one way or another, been focused upon during instruction. 112 out of 126 were given some sort of prominence by being the topic of conversation while the remaining fourteen items or 11 per cent happened as part of classroom interaction with no particular emphasis brought upon them. The following excerpts illustrate the various means used to focus upon or topicalise those items claimed to have been learned: 'least', 'list', 'like', 'look after', 'look like', 'match', 'in order to'.

1 T   *What's the difference between least and list?*
      [pointing at both items written on the board].

2 T   The mother looks after her son at home. *Can you use another word or expression instead of look after?*
  L1 Don't worry.
  L2 Not worried but uh the same uh.
  L3 Uh, take care.

3 T   OK. When I say uh this car is like that one, *what does 'like' mean?*
  L4 Similar.
  L5 Almost the same.
  T   OK. Now, John's new car looks almost the same. *What is 'looks'?*
  L6 To see . . .
  T   To see, uhuh. So, *can you replace 'to look' here by 'to see' and say 'John's new car sees almost the same'?*

4 T   Let's see the instructions given here and see if they match. To match, *that's a new word, I think* [writes it on board]. To match. [A long explanation with attempts to find synonyms follows.]

5 T   OK, in order to. *What does that mean?*

In the above cases the uptaken items have themselves, however briefly, become the ostensible topic of the conversation rather than being simply a part of classroom discourse. The episodes dealing with these particular features are also seen to be terminated by some feedback from the teacher which might be expected to be interpreted by learners as indicating that an item is worth paying attention to.

The difference between the fourteen (11 per cent) and 112 (89 per cent) items claimed to have been learned during the sessions under study is that the latter had, to a greater or lesser extent, been the specific topic of instruction by having their meaning, their spelling, their pronunciation and sometimes two or all three aspects treated by the teacher and/or by the learners. In the case where learners provide their peers with guidance in one or other of the aspects, the teacher is seen to intervene by approving the provision of information.

It must be emphasised however that this does not necessarily mean that the claimed items were intended to be taught prior to the lessons. Many of them, as the following examples show, arose incidentally in the course of events and became topics in discourse terms.

6 L   . . . Bob/bought/five books and George did too.
  T   Bob? What did he do? [Teacher interrupts]

L   Five books
T   What did he do?
L   /bought/
LL   Bought [correct pronunciation]
T   Bought. Which verb is that?
L   To buy.
T   To buy, bought bought

7 T ... OK. Did you like it?
L   Yes, yes, I like it.
T   Yes, I?
L   Yes, I liked it.
T   Yes, I liked it or I did.

It appears, then, that within the limits of the analysis so far of the uptaken items, instruction has exercised a rather positive impact on the subjects since 112 out of the 126 items claimed to have been learned for the first time during those observed lessons have become, however momentarily, teaching points. However, a close examination of the data suggests that the above statement alone is far from establishing the instructor's supremacy as a learning facilitator. A further investigation was necessary to find out the proportion of the topicalised items that are claimed as new acquisitions in relation to those which have apparently been the subject of similar intentions and treatment but which failed to lead to any claims on the part of the subjects.

To evaluate the proportion of what has been claimed to be learned from what has been pedagogically focused upon in some way during those six instructional sessions, the sum total of the topicalised items was counted independently of whether they had been claimed as new or otherwise on the learners' uptake charts. The results are summarised in Table 1 where column 1 indicates the total number of items topicalised in each lesson. Column 2 presents the total number of items which are both focused upon and also claimed by at least one learner to have been learned. Column 3 introduces those which have not led to any positive assertion on the part of the subjects despite the attention paid to them, and column 4 displays the total number of items which have been claimed to be partly or completely familiar already and therefore 'ineligible' for learning claims in the context of this study. The data of the last column were derived from the answers to questions b, c, and d on Uptake Identification Probes which were distributed to help learners dissociate the items they believed they had learned during the observed lessons from those they had already encountered in different circumstances. The observed lessons in which these items occurred again could not fully justify their 'uptaking' as they have already happened in situations which might have facilitated their learning.

TABLE I EFFECT OF TOPICALISATION

LESSONS	1 Total No of topicalised items	2 Topicalised and claimed	3 Topicalised but not claimed	4 Topicalised but known
1	40	17	16	07
2	56	21	23	12
3	31	16	12	03
4	60	31	15	14
5	37	11	19	07
6	32	16	07	09
TOTAL	256	112	92	52
%	100%	43.75%	35.93%	20.31%

Table 1 shows that out of 256 topicalised cases providing learning opportunities for the class, 92 failed to attract the learners' attention and 52 were claimed to be somewhat known as they had already encountered them in earlier events unrelated to this study. In other words, 43.75 per cent focused episodes have 'reached the target', while 35.93 per cent went completely unnoticed and 20.31 per cent were already to some extent familiar to the subjects.

The above figures provide us with a picture of the 'syllabus as reality' as opposed to the 'syllabus as plan'. The former represents what actually happens in the midst of interactive work done by the participants. The on-going interaction leads to the creation of a whole range of learning opportunities, some of which are the results of the teacher's plan; others arise as a by-product of the plan, but some others arise independently of any intentions, perhaps as a by-product of classroom interaction.

No precise comparison can be made with the 'syllabus as plan' which is defined as a syllabus which attempts to predict what is likely to be learned from a planned learning event. I was not, despite my request, provided with very many details about the teacher's objectives. I was given the title of the structure to be taught and the series of exercises in the textbook to practise the grammatical features to be introduced to the group.

Hence, the detailed study of the classroom discourse has revealed that about 44 per cent only of what has been pedagogically topicalised was claimed by the learners. Even though the teacher's objectives were geared toward the teaching of some particular structural features, most of the 44 per cent were lexical items claimed to be seen and learned for the first time in those observed events. Nevertheless it would be misleading to conclude that the lessons were not successful because learners did not claim many of the structural objectives the teacher had on his plan. Although it might be suggested that the shortage of grammatical claims is due to the possibility that it is much easier to report lexis because this does not require the use of metalanguage, in fact, a close perusal of the learners' uptake charts demonstrates that the informants were perfectly capable of reporting what went on during the course of the lessons in terms of grammar. By and large, learners succeeded in accounting for the teacher's structural intentions by reporting the title if not writing the main points of the sessions. Some even illustrated the teacher's focus of instruction by providing examples of sentences to show their comprehension or at least familiarity with what was taught. This suggests that the informants did not lack the means of expressing the structural objectives.

It is believed that one of the reasons why learners did not report as many structural features as lexical ones is that several of these features were already familiar to the class. In fact, it is not surprising that most of the structural features emphasised during instruction were not reported as newly learned because most of them, if not all of them, were part of the syllabus in high school. For instance, only one informant claimed to have seen and learned the passive and active voices for the first time during the observed events. In fact, these affirmations are confirmed by the 20 per cent of topicalised episodes in the lesson which were claimed to be part of the learners' prior knowledge. One could add that after a few hours of teaching, second language instruction becomes very much remedial as structural features are presented and represented for a review.

It looks as if the learners' claims are somewhat different from what the teacher has planned for them. His intentions might have helped learners to rehearse already encountered (if not mastered) structural features. However, in the process of carrying out the plan, the interactive work has lent itself to the creation of a whole range of perhaps unexpected and beneficial events (at least, to some learners if not to all). The learners' claims (44 per cent on Table 1) remain a combination of the teacher's objectives but also their by-product as well as the by-product of the classroom interaction. For these reasons, therefore, attempts to evaluate the learning outcomes against the teacher's plan can be misleading if one does not take into account the mediating interactive processes which characterise classroom interaction.

In view of the data expressed in Table 1 therefore the teacher's influence over the subjects' learning did not reveal itself to be as strong as suggested earlier since approximately 56 per cent of what has been focused upon did not apparently bear any immediate fruit: 20 per cent were claimed to be already familiar and 36 per cent were not, in any way, mentioned by the learners.

It should be pointed out that about 77.45 per cent of the topicalisation was effected by the teacher. This is not particularly surprising in view of the fact that the discourse was unidirectionally controlled by the teacher, who did 45 per cent of the talking. What appears to be strikingly interesting though is that a further analysis of the effect of the teacher's versus the learners' scarce opportunities (22.54 per cent) for topicalisation showed that the latter offered much higher chances for items to be uptaken. Learners benefited much more from their peers' rare instance of topicalisation than from the teacher's.

A close scrutiny of the theme of topicalisation reveals that topics initiated by learners attracted more claims from the learners than the ones initiated by the teacher. The analysis shows that out of 46 items initiated by the learners, 34 (73.9 per cent) were claimed, whereas only 78 (49.4 per cent) out of 158 were claimed when topicalised by the instructor. Thus, the chances for claims are much higher when items are triggered by classmates. A further emphasis on the profitability of the learners' initiation is that it attracts more reporters than when topics are brought up by the teacher.

By limiting to himself the initiative of topicalising most items for instruction, the teacher does not give the learners much opportunity to distinguish between items which are important and those which are not. To this particular teacher everything was relevant. It is therefore possible that the reason why the participants of this study were not affected by the teacher's efforts is that in his attempts to focus their attention on everything, no specific aspect appeared as particularly prominent in his discourse. Having little opportunity to raise topics for instruction, learners might have made some features outstanding to their peers if only for the reason that, coming from learners, topicalisation appeared as a memorable event rather than the routine procedure of the teacher (see Slimani 1989 for further details).

Finally, in this discussion it is worth mentioning that the majority of the unnoticed or 'lost' items (36 per cent) are instances of error treatment provided most often by the teacher. Their analysis has allowed the identification of a limited number of features which differentiate their treatment from that allocated to the topicalised and claimed items (112, or 44 per cent). As the illustrations below show, it appears that absence of metalanguage in the teacher's talk and straight provision, most often by the teacher, of the correct form of the item under focus, without further involvement from the teacher or the learners, characterise the strategies used to deal with these items (see examples 8, 9, 10 below). Cueing by the teacher is another common corrective strategy sometimes followed by the immediate provision of the expected forms by the speaker himself, if he swiftly manages to spot the error (example 11), by his peers (example 12) but less often by the instructor.

8 L ... and uh sometimes uh on Wednesday.
 T And sometimes on Wednesdays. Why on Wednesdays?

9 L ... I looking for my pen.
 T You are looking for your pen.

10 L1 ... [Reading from the book] Bob drink a glass.
 L2 Drinks [Interrupts the speaker].
 L2 Bob drinks a glass of milk every day and George does too.

11 L Pencils have been sharp
 T Sharp?
 L Sharpened
 T Sharpened, yes.

12 L ... The simplest method is by swimming on one side. The rescuer pulls the victim by the /hair/
 LS Hair, hair [correct pronunciation]
 T Yes, hair, by the hair. All right ...

Nearly a third of the lost items consists of corrections of tenses and *-s* morphemes. Informants can, however, be assumed to be already familiar with these features as they have been the explicit content of instruction in other lessons or in high school. Despite previous exposure to explicit explanation of the rules and recurrent repetitions of the correct forms of these features, the subjects of this study persisted in misusing them when using the target language. It is possible that the informants are not ready to learn these structures as part of their interlanguage system and consequently their continued treatment remains pointless, at least, at this stage of their training. It is widely accepted that features such as the use of articles by Arab speakers and some of the *-s* morphemes, for many English as a second language speakers, remain unmastered in oral production till an extremely advanced stage of their training even if these features are explicitly known to the trainees. This situation makes us question the necessity or otherwise of attempting to keep on correcting features which have been persistently dealt with but still remain largely ignored by some learners during verbal interaction (see Slimani 1987 for further quantitative and qualitative analysis of error treatment in this setting).

Learners' idiosyncracies

The second characteristic which emerged from the investigation of the learners' claims is that uptake is highly idiosyncratic. This feature is particularly revealing for evaluation which generally assumes the effect of instruction is somehow uniform for most members of the class. Such evaluation takes as its starting point the teacher's plan which is expected to control what learners would see as optimal in the teaching. Even though the teaching in this particular setting was not differentiated in any obvious way, i.e., in the sense that different learners were given different tasks, it appears that typically only very few learners at any one time happened to take the information in. Table 2 illustrates the extreme individuality with which learners react to instruction. It presents the total number (N) of items or linguistic features (126) reported to have been learned during the observed sessions as well as the percentage of claims associated with them and the number of reporters that each case has attracted.

TABLE 2 PERCENTAGE OF CLAIMS MADE BY REPORTERS ON EACH LINGUISTIC FEATURE

N of items (126)	% of claims	N of reporters
47	37.30%	1
20	15.87	2
27	21.42	3
	Total 74.59%	
7	5.55	4
5	3.96	5
10	7.93	6
3	2.38	7
3	2.38	8
	Total 22.20%	
1	0.79	9
2	1.58	10
1	0.79	11
	Total 3.16%	

The results point to the fact that as many as 74.59 per cent of the total number of claims are reported by no more than three learners at a time, and no fewer than 37.30 per cent of the total are reported by only one person at any one time. A negligible percentage (3.16 per cent) of claims is simultaneously made by nine, ten or eleven subjects. These figures express the high level of 'individuality' and 'autonomy' with which some subjects might face instruction. The figures are particularly striking as the teaching style was not individualised in any sense. It was unidirectionally addressed to the class as a whole. One, therefore, might expect the same items or linguistic features to be claimed by many learners. What happened however is that individual learners reacted individually despite the centrality of the teaching style.

Further evidence that learners show autonomy when undergoing instruction is also clearly illustrated in the 11 per cent or fourteen uptaken items that were mentioned earlier under the heading of the importance of topicalisation. While 112 linguistic features claimed to be learned were the focus of instruction, fourteen happened as a part of the classroom discourse without any specific attention drawn to them. Despite a teaching situation where the classroom discourse is highly controlled by the teacher and does not involve any group work activity, learners have shown considerable individual reaction by claiming items which did not receive any kind of attention in terms of topicalisation, as defined earlier. The above proportion might have been even higher if the teacher had allowed more room for learners to express themselves.

While some of the 11 per cent of the claims were traced back as part of the discourse to deal with classroom routines, some were not found at all in the transcripts. To explain their presence on the learners' uptake charts, one can only assume that what went on during the lessons possibly reinforced some previous learning and brought those particular words back to the learners' minds. The word 'slippers', for instance, remained a complete mystery as I did not even recall the teacher having dealt, however remotely, with a situation which might have led to such a claim on the part of the learner. Moreover, the examination of the learners' charts revealed also the presence of a few examples of appropriate generalisation. For instance, when the words 'thick', 'thickness', and 'thin' were explained, one of the most able learners reported having learned the word 'thinness' even though the latter was not uttered in class. The word 'narrow' was also claimed to have been learned by the same learner in relation to 'thick' and 'thin'.

It is interesting to notice here this learner's tendency to generalise so successfully from a lesson event that he can believe the generalisation was taught. In this respect, it has been suggested that one of the good language learner's attributes is to be able to organise the discrete and disparate information they receive about the target language into coherent and ordered patterns (Rubin 1975; Stern 1975).

Conclusion

The problem of making sense of instruction seems to lie in the difficulty of finding appropriate research techniques capable of evaluating learning outcomes in relation to input. In this paper, input is seen as a co-production by the participants in an instructional setting and therefore renders the task of using traditional testing measures rather difficult. We attempted to find a way of relating the learners' claims to their immediate interactive environment.

The technique used proved to be a useful means of shedding light on what is claimed to be learned from the on-going interactive work which takes place in the classroom. By asking learners to reflect on their perceptions of what they have uptaken, one could see, by examining the interactive work, some of the factors which characterise the emergence of these particular uptaken features.

Most of the learners' claims were topicalised. In this sense, White's (1987) recommendations seem to broadly match the present teacher's behaviour in this particular context. She suggests that

> We should not be afraid occasionally to provide input which is explicitly geared toward ... the form of grammatical teaching, of correction, *or other forms of emphasis on particular structures* [my emphasis]; at worst, it will be ignored and at best, it may trigger change in the acquisition system.
>
> (White 1987:108)

Bringing particular linguistic features to the class's attention appears to be a rather valuable characteristic of uptake as most of the uptaken items were focused upon during instruction. The fact that most of the 'lost' items were error correction does not necessarily contradict the effect of topicalisation. Learners may not be ready to internalise particular structural features despite their persistent explanation and correction. Correction is often seen, in this study, to be provided in an erratic and confusing manner. The study revealed that while some uptaken features were products of the teacher's plan, others were by-products of the plan or perhaps of the classroom interaction.

These uptaken items, which represent 44 per cent of the participants' interactive efforts, are revealed to be highly idiosyncratic. The detailed analysis of the interactive processes has shown that different features of the same event have been uptaken by different learners. Very few items were claimed by all or even most learners. Moreover, while many of the claims could be traced in the transcripts as having received some kind of emphasis on the part of the participants, mostly of the teacher, others merely occurred as part of the classroom interaction or did not feature at all in the text, suggesting that learners reacted with some autonomy to what went on during the interactive event.

H

Viewing input as co-produced by the participants has highlighted idiosyncrasy and topicalisation as particularly relevant to evaluation studies which generally tend to assess learning outcomes on the basis of the teacher's objectives: these objectives are subsequently assumed to be learned by most learners in the class. A test based on the teacher's objectives would have taken into consideration the features which the teacher planned to treat. Such a test would, by its nature, ignore the very many other features which incidentally arose during the actual classroom interaction, some of which learners claimed to have benefited from.

Because of the finding that what actually gets topicalised during the classroom interactive work is different from the teacher's plan, and because uptake is strongly idiosyncratic, it is therefore not helpful to use the teacher's plan as a measuring rod for what has been uptaken from the lesson. In fact, a consideration of the actual classroom interactive work which characterises second language instruction and a study of learner idiosyncrasy might help us gain a better understanding of the complexities of second language teaching and learning. This understanding might subsequently inform the improvement of evaluations of what actually gets learned from language programs.

APPENDIX 1: UPTAKE RECALL CHART

DATE: _____

NAME: _____

QUESTION: WHAT POINTS HAVE COME UP IN TODAY'S LESSON?
Please answer FULLY and in DETAIL. Try to remember EVERYTHING.

1. GRAMMAR: _____

2. WORDS AND PHRASES: _____

3. SPELLING: _____

4. PRONUNCIATION: _____

5. PUNCTUATION: _____

6. WAYS OF USING THE LANGUAGE: _____

7. SUGGESTIONS ABOUT MORE EFFECTIVE INSTRUCTION: _____

8. OTHER(S) . . . (Please specify): _____

Thank you for your cooperation

APPENDIX 2: UPTAKE IDENTIFICATION PROBE

READ CAREFULLY THE FOLLOWING QUESTIONS. MARK
YOUR ANSWERS AS INDICATED ON THE
'UPTAKE RECALL CHART'.

1. Of all the things you wrote on your 'Uptake Recall Chart', which
   do you think you learned today?

       (a) Did you learn anything that was really new to you? If
       yes, circle it.

       (b) Did you learn anything that was not really completely
       new, that you knew partly already? If yes, underline it.

       (c) Was there anything that you did not learn at all because
       you knew it already? If yes, mark it with a zigzag line.

2. Of all the things you wrote, which do you think the teacher most
   wanted you to learn? Mark them with a T.

Thank you for your cooperation.

References

Allwright, R. L. (Ed.) 1975a. Working papers: language teaching classroom research. Department of Language and Linguistics, University of Essex, England.

Allwright, R. L. 1975b. Problems in the study of the teacher's treatment of learner error. In Burt and Dulay: 96–109.

Allwright, R. L. 1983. The nature and function of the syllabus in language teaching and learning. Unpublished mimeograph. Department of Linguistics and Modern English Language, Lancaster University.

Allwright, R. L. 1984a. Why don't learners learn what teachers teach? The interaction hypothesis. In D. M. Singleton and D. G. Little (Eds.) *Language learning in formal and informal contexts*, pp. 3–18. Dublin: IRAAL.

Allwright, R. L. 1984b. The importance of interaction in classroom language learning. *Applied Linguistics*, 52: 156–71.

Allwright, R. L. 1984c. The analysis of discourse in interlanguage studies: the pedagogical evidence. In Davies, Criper and Howatt.

Allwright, R. L. 1988. Autonomy and individualisation in whole-class instruction. In A. Brookes and P. Grundy (Eds.) *Individualization and autonomy in language learning*, pp. 35–44. ELT Documents 131. London: Modern English Publications, British Council.

Breen, M. P. and C. N. Candlin. 1980. The essentials of a communicative curriculum in language teaching. *Applied Linguistics* 1(2): 89–112.

Burt, M. and H. C. Dulay. 1975. *On TESOL '75. New directions in second language, learning, teaching and bilingual education*. Washington, D.C.: TESOL.

Corder, S. P. 1977. Teaching and learning English as a second language: Trends in research and practice. In H. D. Brown, C. A. Yorio, and R. H. Crymes (Eds.) *On TESOL '77. Teaching and learning English as a second language: trends in research and practice*. Washington, D.C.: TESOL.

Davies, A., C. Criper, and A. P. R. Howatt (Eds.) 1984. *Interlanguage*. Edinburgh: Edinburgh University Press.

Ellis, R. 1984. Can syntax be taught?: a study of the effects of formal instruction on the acquisition of WH questions by children. *Applied Linguistics* 5(2): 138–55.

Ellis, R. and M. Rathbone. 1987. The acquisition of German in a classroom context. Unpublished report. Ealing College of Higher Education.

Fanselow, J. 1977. The treatment of learner error in oral work. *Foreign Language Annals* 10: 583–93.

Krashen, S. D. 1980. The theoretical and practical relevance of simple codes in second language acquisition. In R. Scarcella and S. D. Krashen (Eds.) *Research in second language acquisition*, pp. 7–18. Rowley, Mass.: Newbury House.

Krashen, S. D. 1981. *Second language acquisition and second language learning*. Oxford: Pergamon Press.

Krashen, S. D. 1982. *Principles and practice in second language acquisition*. New York: Pergamon.

Lightbown, P. M. 1983. Exploratory relationships between developmental and instructional sequences in L2 acquisition. In H. W. Seliger and M. H. Long (Eds.) *Classroom oriented research in second language acquisition*, pp. 217–45. Rowley, Mass.: Newbury House.

MacFarlane, J. M. 1975. Some types of psychological discussion that help to establish the teacher's treatment of error as a fruitful variable for investigation. In Allwright 1975a, pp. 4–63.

Morray, M. 1976. INELEC: Teamwork in an EST program. In British Council *Team teaching in ESP*. ELT Document 106. ETIC Publications.

Rubin, J. 1975. What the 'good language learner' can teach us. *TESOL Quarterly* 9(1): 41–51.

Scherer, A. and M. Wertheimer. 1964. *A psycholinguistic experiment in foreign language teaching*. New York: McGraw Hill.

Slimani, A. 1987. The teaching-learning relationship: Learning opportunities and learning outcomes. An Algerian case study. Unpublished doctoral dissertation, Lancaster University, England.

Slimani, A. 1989. The role of topicalisation in classroom language learning. *System* 17: 223–34.

Smith, P. D. 1970. A comparison of the cognitive and audiolingual approaches to foreign language instruction: The Pennsylvania Foreign Language Project. Philadelphia, Penn.: The Center for Curriculum Development.

Spada, N. M. 1987. Relationships between instructional differences and learning outcomes: a process–product study of communicative language teaching. *Applied Linguistics* 8(2): 137–61.

Stern, H. H. 1975. What can we learn from the good language learner? *Canadian Modern Language Review* 31: 304–18; also in K. Croft (Ed.) 1980. *Readings on English as a second language: for teachers and teacher trainees*. Second edition. Cambridge, Mass.: Winthrop.

White, L. 1987. Against comprehensible input: the input hypothesis and the development of second language competence. *Applied Linguistics* 8(2): 95–110.

Editors' postscript to Slimani

Slimani's study is not an evaluation of a programme but is rather an examination of a classroom research technique. Its inclusion in a book on programme evaluation is justified because that endeavour very often, if not always, involves some investigation of classroom processes.

The technique is, essentially, to ask learners what they think they have learned from a particular lesson. Examining 'uptake' means trying to relate learning claims to the immediate classroom environment in order to establish the nature of learning opportunities. Directly after a lesson, learners are given uptake charts and asked to say what they recall from the lesson. Three hours later they are given the chart again and asked to fine-tune their responses. After this, the audio-recording of the lesson is scanned for events that could have led to claims that X or Y had been learned. To triangulate findings, learners were interviewed about their claims.

The technique appears, as Slimani is quick to point out, somewhat naive, since the link between data and interpretation is extremely tenuous. Not only does Slimani refrain from glossing over the difficulties, but she deliberately spells them out. The advantages of this are: 1) it shows potential users of the method just what can occur that may not be self-evident; 2) it increases confidence that any findings that *are* reported are well winnowed. The result is a solid account of the merits and shortcomings of the actual use of a technique which might be considered helpful in probing programme effects while the programme is still in progress.

Information gained from this approach is probably only suggestive, but as a programme develops, it is the kind of information that might help to inform decisions. That is to say, the most obvious use of the technique is in formative evaluation, suggesting adjustments during the evolution of a programme.

Anyone thinking of adopting this type of inquiry in an evaluation can turn to Slimani's account and consider how they might overcome some of the problems she highlights. For instance, what might be done about the interviewees' feeling that the interview was absurd? About the tendency for learners simply to glance at their neighbours' uptake charts and pencil in similar claims? Above all, anyone considering the vicissitudes of uptake examination, after reading Slimani's paper, will be in a better position to judge under what circumstances what kind of information can be gathered.

7 Moving the goalposts: project evaluation in practice

Hywel Coleman

Introduction

In this chapter I discuss a KELT (Key English Language Teaching) Project at Hasanuddin University, Indonesia. The discussion falls into two major parts. In the first, the history of the KELT Project is chronicled in some detail. Then, in the second, observations are made on the evaluation of the Project.

In the first part, I have adopted a roughly chronological approach. What began as a Project dealing with the pre-departure language needs of university staff gradually came to concentrate exclusively on the development of the *Risking Fun* study skills programme for first year undergraduates. What emerges is evidence that changes in the Project's objectives came about as the consequence of four different forces. Furthermore, there appears to have been an approximate correlation between the chronological development of the Project and the occurrence of these four different forces.

Now, if it is indeed the case that the fundamental nature of the Project changed over time, then of course it becomes very difficult to know how to evaluate the Project as a whole. As a project changes and its objectives are modified, so, inevitably, the criteria by which it can be evaluated must also change. These are questions which are discussed in the second part of the chapter.

1 The history of the Project

1.1 Prehistory

The Project functioned for just under six years, from October 1980 until the middle of 1986. I was involved in the Project from its beginning until October 1984. However, its origins can be traced as far back as 1978, and at the time of writing (mid-1989) its repercussions are still being felt.

The KELT scheme – now superseded by other agreements – was funded by the Overseas Development Administration and administered on behalf of ODA by the British Council. The procedure for the establishment of a new KELT Project required that a Recruitment Request Form be completed by the institution which was requesting the Project. The form was then countersigned by the British Council's English Language Officer. In practice, the form was sometimes filled in by a British Council official and then presented to the host institution for signature.

A Recruitment Request Form for the post of Senior Lecturer in the Hasanuddin University Language Centre – the post which I was later to hold – was completed in February 1979. The request described the duties of the proposed Senior Lecturer post as being essentially the 'preparation of appropriate course materials to meet the specific target needs of staff ... designated for training overseas'. Several other possible activities were listed in the request, but these were all subordinate to the primary aim of helping the University to prepare its staff for overseas training.

By the spring of 1980, the Hasanuddin University Project had been approved by ODA, and the British Council then began the recruitment process. I was selected and asked to take up the post in October 1980. The emphasis throughout my pre-departure briefing process was on the design of courses and the preparation of materials appropriate to the pre-departure requirements of Indonesian university staff. An important assumption underlying both the initial post description and the briefing process was that the university's Language Centre was sufficiently well staffed to be able to teach all the newly relevant courses which the KELT Senior Lecturer was to provide. (The Recruitment Request Form, for example, estimated that the KELT Officer would need to spend only 9 per cent of his time actually teaching.)

1.2   Arrival at post

However, once I arrived at Hasanuddin University, it became clear that – regardless of what had been said in the formal recruitment request – I was now expected to carry out two duties. The first and by far the more important of these was to help with the *teaching* of a very heavy schedule of TOEFL preparation courses for the staff of universities throughout Eastern Indonesia. The second was to perform an analysis of the English language needs of Hasanuddin University. The function of the KELT Project was therefore seen as being primarily to provide a native speaker teacher of English for intensive pre-departure language training.

How did it come about that, even at this early stage, the Project was so different from what had been planned? Five factors contributed. Considerable funding for the overseas training of university personnel had suddenly become available. There were strict deadlines for the use of this funding. And, contrary to previous assumptions, the Language Centre was suffering from a shortage of staff. A fourth factor was that there is a widespread perception in Indonesian institutions that native speakers of English are more usefully employed as teachers of English than as materials writers.

A fifth factor which played a part in the creation of this situation was my own uncertainty. This was my first experience of working for the British Council, and I wanted to avoid giving the impression of being a troublemaker right from the beginning of the Project. At the same time, I believed that it was necessary for me to display to the university authorities my willingness to co-operate with them.

1.3   Initial needs analysis

The university also expected me to carry out a needs analysis during the first few months. It is not clear where the idea of a needs analysis originated from: there is no mention of it in the recruitment request or in other documents relating to the early period of the Project's history. Nevertheless, for two reasons I responded to this request with enthusiasm. Partly, work on the needs analysis would be a challenging and interesting relief from the drudgery of TOEFL preparation. Partly, also, I foresaw that the needs analysis would provide me with an opportunity to influence the future direction of the Project. In other words, I hoped that any recommendations which I might make as a result of the needs analysis would provide me with an escape route from the teaching of cramming courses.

The needs analysis depended heavily on interviews. I talked to senior and junior staff in every faculty and in many individual departments. I also talked to administrators and to students. I also made considerable use of a range of university documents, in particular a recently completely demographic and attitudinal study of the university's academic staff (Vredenbregt and Roosmalawati 1979).

My report on the analysis was presented in August 1981 (Coleman 1981), and the findings have been summarised more recently (Coleman 1988a). Essentially, the analysis found that the university consisted of numerous administrative units. These units interacted with each other in a way which was both complex and dynamic. The interaction was complex in that the language attitudes and language behaviours of the members of certain units were able to influence the attitudes and behaviours of members of other units. The interaction was dynamic in that, at the end of each academic year, a number of recently graduated students were recruited as lecturers. The attitudes of these people had been influenced by the attitudes and behaviours of their own lecturers. Now they found themselves in a position to influence the attitudes and language behaviours of succeeding generations of students.

These findings had two important implications. Firstly, any input which was intended to solve problems in one particular unit might have repercussions elsewhere in the system. Secondly, input might have repercussions which would not be felt immediately. These implications encouraged me to look at the possibility of developing a global and long-term approach to the university's English language problems.

I reasoned that possibly the most effective way of exploiting the limited resources of the KELT Project would be to concentrate them on two points in the system. The first of these points was the compulsory English language programme for the first year undergraduates of all faculties. The needs analysis had found that most students perceived English merely as a fearfully complicated grammatical system rather than as an instrument which they could exploit in their studies. Consequently, the university libraries, stocked almost exclusively with English language materials, were barely used. Therefore, our first step should be to attempt to modify the attitudes towards English of the university's students and to encourage them to venture into the libraries more frequently. If this could be achieved, then in the long term students would do more reading. Eventually, some of these students would graduate and become lecturers. With their more positive attitudes towards English, and with their wider familiarity with the literature, they would one day have a very positive influence on the students whom they themselves would be teaching.

The second point in the system on which I considered the resources of the Project would best be concentrated was a group of recent graduates from the Faculty of Letters. Because of the severe shortage of ELT staff, these young people were being asked to assist with teaching. They were given the least prestigious work, such as teaching the compulsory English language programme for first year undergraduates. It was these people – rather than the more senior members of the ELT establishment in Hasanuddin University – who each year had direct contact with all new undergraduates. Consequently, it was these people who were in a position to influence the English language learning and the attitudes towards English of all future students. In other words, whatever input was provided at this point in the system was likely to continue to be felt for some considerable time in the future.

The needs analysis therefore indicated that the Project should be paying attention to two areas which were very different from those which had been delineated in the Recruitment Request Form. This change of emphasis was the outcome of a genuine piece of research. At the same time, however, when drawing up the report on the needs analysis, I was not unaware that I was in a position to influence the future direction of the Project. I was out of sympathy with the heavy emphasis on crash courses to prepare members of staff for TOEFL which predominated at the time, and I did not want to spend another two or three years teaching such courses. I could not, and did not, ignore the pre-departure language requirements of university staff in my analysis. But it may be that, subconsciously, I was more diligent in seeking evidence for *other types of need* and that I particularly emphasised these needs in my analysis. This is not to suggest that I deliberately fiddled the results of the needs analysis so that the outcome would be in line with my own interests. After all, the university authorities, with their far greater familiarity with the institution, would soon have picked up on falsified data. Moreover, the replicated needs analysis, carried out eighteen months after I left Hasanuddin University (Pritchard and Ruru 1986), came to almost identical conclusions. Nevertheless, in retrospect, I cannot quite free myself from the suspicion that the analysis of needs was coloured, to put it no more strongly than that, by my wish to avoid any more TOEFL preparation courses.

1.4   Redefinition of aims

Another series of events occurred during May and June 1981, at the time when the TOEFL preparation courses were still under way and when my work on the collection of data for the needs analysis was nearing completion. By this time, the British Council in Jakarta had begun to feel some discomfort at the way in which the KELT Project was developing, with its substantial investment of time in TOEFL preparation teaching. It is likely that the Council was conscious that this might not be to the approval of ODA.

Discussions and correspondence between the British Council in Jakarta and the university authorities took place during this period. These concluded with an agreement that the KELT officer should undertake four types of task: 'i) To continue to work on the General English courses ... ii) English for undergraduates and staff orientation courses ... iii) The training of English teaching staff ... iv) The preparation of language laboratory tapes and of self-access materials' (letter from English Language Officer, Jakarta, to Rector of Hasanuddin University, 1 June 1981).

What seems to have occurred during this period is that the three parties most immediately involved in the KELT Project – the university, the British Council and I – were each trying to assert their own priorities without upsetting one or both of the other parties. The British Council had to ensure that the Project was satisfying the criteria for KELT Projects as laid down by ODA. The university had to try to make use of the resources provided by the Project in order to satisfy their most urgent needs without alienating the body which provided those resources. Finally, my own objective was to ensure that the British Council were sufficiently alarmed by the direction that the Project was taking that they should involve themselves directly and make plain their dissatisfaction to the university, whilst at the same time not alarming the Council to such an extent that they might want to bring the Project to an immediate end. Meanwhile, I wanted the university to appreciate that they could not continue to use me simply as a conspicuous native speaker teacher, but I did not want the university authorities to be alienated to such an extent that they would be unwilling to co-operate with me or the British Council in the future. I was therefore in a peculiar position, midway between the two major parties and with allegiances to both.

1.5 Programme of activities

The revised list of tasks and the later appearance of the needs analysis were followed by a proposed programme of activities for the KELT Project, which I drew up in September 1981. This programme covered the three academic years up to September 1984. In the first year, attention would be focused on the undergraduate English programme; in the second year, attention would be divided equally between undergraduate and staff needs; and in the final year the Project would concentrate on staff training requirements.

This programme was extremely ambitious. Probably it was more accurate as a description of those tasks which needed to be carried out than it was as a forecast of what could be achieved by one person in a period of three years. Nevertheless, it was accepted by both the university authorities and the British Council. Work began according to this programme in October 1981, almost exactly a year after I had arrived at the Project.

Why was the programme so unrealistic and over-ambitious? Part of the answer lies in my own inexperience in long-term project planning. To some extent, also, I was still trying to reconcile the university's desire to have attention paid to the pre-departure language training requirements of its staff with my own growing interest in the study skill needs of undergraduates. Part of the answer also lies in my continuing wish to prove to the British Council that this was indeed a KELT-worthy Project : the more work that could be crammed into the programme of activities the more valid I imagined the Project would appear to be. Indeed, in a review of the Hasanuddin University Project which appeared eighteen months after the proposed programme of activities, I confessed, '... the original programme of activities seriously underestimated the time which would be required for materials writing. ... in my eagerness to prove that the Hasanuddin University KELT Project was a viable one, I was simply over-ambitious when drawing up the programme of activities' (Coleman 1983:3).

1.6   Secondary needs analysis

October 1981 was a turning point for the Project. We had now reached the stage where I was no longer expected to involve myself with TOEFL preparation courses, where a programme of work had been agreed between the university, the British Council and myself, and where I was at last doing the sort of work which I wanted to do and which I believed needed to be done.

In late 1981 I ran a workshop for the young, newly qualified English lecturers who were teaching the compulsory first year undergraduate English programme. During the daytime sessions, we discussed ways of using the set text (*Kernel Lessons Intermediate*). Then, during the evenings, I made frequent observation visits to the classes which these people were teaching.

It was the evening classroom observations which were the most significant aspect of this stage. Whereas in the first stage of the needs analysis (Section 1.3) I was, in effect, identifying the population on whom the energies of the Project were to be focused, during this second stage I was identifying the needs of this population in detail. During this period, I learnt a great deal about normal class size in the university, about conventions of classroom behaviour, and about the students' competence in and attitudes towards English.

1.7   The birth of Risking Fun

Risking Fun was born during the first three months of 1982. In this period I was released from all teaching and teacher training activities, and I was able to concentrate on the preparation of a rationale and set of specifications for the undergraduate study skills programme. I identified four important aspects of the 'total learning-teaching context' (and several less important ones) and I argued that each of these had certain implications for the design of a language course:

1 *The learners' previous experience of reading.* Many students are not familiar with written texts as sources of data. They need to develop a range of study skills.

2 *The learners' attitudes and motivation.* Learners see English merely as a prerequisite for obtaining a degree with no practical utility. They also see it as a complicated grammatical system and are nervous of it. Materials must be relevant and attractive to students.

3 *The teachers.* For various reasons, teachers tend to make little use of the teachers' guides which accompanied published materials. (For a more detailed discussion, see Coleman 1985.) Materials must therefore be explicit so that they can be used without difficulty by

experienced but busy teachers and by younger and less confident teachers.

4 *Class size and the conventions of classroom interaction.* Class size frequently tops 90. English lectures have parallels with ceremonial performances in which students are passive witnesses. (For more details, see Coleman 1986.) Consequently, an interactive methodology is required.

I proposed that the primary objective of the new course – which we called *Risking Fun* – should be to enable students to develop the skills which they would require for reading English language texts in a selective, critical and efficient way, without having to translate word for word. At the same time, the course had to be interactive and usable in very large classes.

1.8   *The introduction of* Risking Fun

In the twelve months following the appearance of these proposals, several events took place. The writing of the first version of *Risking Fun* was finished, the materials were tried out in peer teaching sessions by junior lecturers, and, from February 1983, the course was piloted with 450 students and five teachers. Two in-service workshops for English lecturers, and a new programme of classroom observations was begun. Meanwhile, the KELT Counterpart Officer went to Britain to begin a two-year programme of study leading to an M.A.

In March 1983 I reviewed the progress which had been made so far and detailed the work still needing to be done (Coleman 1983). The tone of this review was exuberant, even though the work of the Project was a long way behind schedule. I was not repentant about this. Indeed, I predicted that things would slip even further behind, because it had become clear that a major rewriting of *Risking Fun* was going to be required.

The most significant aspect which required attention was the deliberate neglect of oral skills in the course. *Risking Fun* had deliberately concentrated on the basic study skills which, it was believed, undergraduates required with some urgency. Once teaching began, though, it soon became apparent that a sizeable minority of students demanded that some attention be given to the development of oral skills, despite the fact that they had no obvious *need*, as such, to speak English. It was clear that, in order to ensure the goodwill and co-operation of this minority, some attention would have to be given to the development of oral skills.

1.9 Full-scale implementation

Risking Fun was introduced as the standard text for all first year undergraduates in August 1983. Approximately 1,300 students used the materials during the first semester of the 1983–4 academic year, and another 830 students used the book during the second semester of the same year. At the same time that the materials were introduced as the standard textbook, I began work on the revisions which had become necessary. However, as the KELT Counterpart was still in Britain, much of my time was taken up with the day-to-day administration of the programme. Moreover, as the programme expanded more people had to be involved in the teaching of the English I course. It was therefore also necessary for me to spend some time working with the teachers who were new to *Risking Fun*.

The developments during this period are chronicled in a series of reports, each of which indicates that previous targets were not being met and that the major revision of the materials which was needed was being pushed further into the future.

1.10 Developments after 1984

Early in 1983 I recommended to the British Council and the university that the KELT Project should be expanded in three directions. I suggested that one KELT Officer should continue to work on the undergraduate materials, that a second KELT should begin to pay attention to the language requirements of the university's staff, and that a third person should spend a couple of years investigating the needs of the under-graduates of other universities in Eastern Indonesia and, if appropriate, adapt *Risking Fun* for use in these institutions. This suggestion sparked off a new round of negotiations between the university and the British Council. Eventually, it was agreed that two of the three posts which I had suggested should be established.

Although only two of the posts which I had proposed were set up, I was able to influence their specifications in that it was I who completed the two Recruitment Request Forms. The duties of the materials writing post were described in the following way:

> To evaluate the existing materials *Risking Fun : Part 1* and to revise and complete where appropriate; to write and trial materials to form *Risking Fun : Part 2*; to run in-service training workshops; to establish a staff development programme; to train a counterpart.

The holders of the two new posts arrived in Ujung Pandang in September 1984; I left shortly afterwards.

I cannot provide a detailed description of the work which was carried out by the new materials writer during his two years at Hasanuddin University. The work which was actually performed seems to differ in certain respects from the job description which was drawn up before the holder of the post began work. But then, as we have seen, this is precisely the same as what happened with my own post.

1.11   Summary

One feature of the Hasanuddin University KELT Project is the fact that documents which in some way were intended to guide or constrain the Project did not in fact achieve that effect.

But the most striking characteristic of the Project is the way in which its objectives changed from time to time. I have tried to indicate that these changes came about as the result of the influence of four factors: negotiation between the parties which had an interest in the Project, increasingly specific information about the needs of the institution and the various constituencies within the institution, interim evaluation, and straightforward slippage or failure to meet deadlines.

A pattern can be discerned in which negotiation of objectives tended to occur at the very beginning of the Project, analysis of needs followed, re-evaluation of objectives occurred during the second half of the history of the Project, and failure to meet deadlines characterised later stages. Admittedly, this pattern is not perfect. But, despite fuzzy boundaries, there is a reasonable correlation between the occurrence of factors influencing change in objectives and historical periods in the development of the Project.

2   The Evaluation of the Project

2.1   Introduction

In the second major part of the chapter, we move in the opposite direction from that in the first part. We begin by looking at ways of evaluating the two most important areas of the Project, the creation of the *Risking Fun* materials and the teacher training activities. Next, we step back to look at the work of the Project from a wider perspective, using some of the documents issued during the first year of the Project's history as reference points for evaluating what was later produced. Finally, we step even further back to consider the implications of any attempt to evaluate the Project with reference to the set of objectives which had been established before the Project actually began to function.

2.2   Risking Fun

Four aspects of the teaching–learning context were identified before the writing of *Risking Fun* started (Section 1.7). In order to determine the extent to which these aspects were successfully catered for, four questions need to be asked. First, were learners better equipped to study through the medium of English after taking the course than they had been previously? Second, did learners have a positive attitude to English at the end of the course? Third, were teachers able to use the materials without difficulty? The final question needs to be asked in two parts: could the materials be used in large classes and was the challenge to the conventions of classroom interaction successful?

TABLE I PRE-COURSE AND POST-COURSE SCORES IN A TEST OF STUDY SKILLS

Semester	N	Pre-test mean %	Post-test mean %	Improvement	Improvement as % of pre-test score
1	557	31.8	66.1	34.3	107.7
2	394	46.8	80.1	33.4	71.3
Total	951	38.0	71.9	33.9	89.2

Essentially, the first question asks whether the learners learned any of those things which *Risking Fun* set out to teach. Students' skills in ordering data, interpreting dictionary entries and relating texts to tables and diagrams were tested at the beginning and at the end of each semester. Test scores are available for both the first and second semesters of the 1983–4 academic year, the first full year of implementation (Section 1.9). More than, 2,100 students took the English I course during this year, and precisely comparable pre-course and post-course results are available for nearly one thousand of these students. These scores are summarised in Table 1. In the first semester more than 500 students, mostly from the natural science and engineering faculties, took the pre-course test and then took the (identical) post-course test sixteen weeks later. On average, these students more than doubled their pre-course scores. During the following semester nearly 400 students, mostly from arts faculties, took the tests. This population achieved post-course scores which were more than 70 per cent higher than their pre-course scores. Overall, the students who participated were able to achieve post-course scores which were very nearly 90 per cent higher than their pre-course scores. Unfortunately, there was no control group of students studying in the conventional way. Nevertheless, there is strong evidence here that by the end of the course students were considerably more adept at performing the tasks which were being tested than they had been at the beginning. Whether these tasks were actually tasks which course participants would have to perform in the course of their student careers is another question, to which we will return below.

The second question which has to be asked is the extent to which learners' attitudes towards English and their self-confidence in the language changed during the course. The initial needs analysis (Section 1.3) had suggested that a major problem was students' apprehensiveness about English. Questionnaires designed to measure students' perceptions of the usefulness and difficulty of the English language were administered during the pilot stage (Appendices 1 and 2 in this chapter) and again during the first semester of full-scale implementation (Appendix 3 in this chapter). The questionnaires also looked at students' evaluations of their own ability in reading, writing, listening and speaking, as a way of uncovering the extent of their self-confidence in the language.

The responses to these questionnaires have been analysed by Hussein and Bazergan (1985) and again by Bazergan (1986). These analyses revealed that, even before teaching started, the great majority of students believed that English was 'very useful'. This immediately contradicts one of the assumptions which underpinned the writing of *Risking Fun*, that is, that learners saw English merely as a prerequisite for obtaining a degree with no practical utility (Section 1.7). It is extremely difficult to reconcile these responses to an objective questionnaire with the perceptions and intuitions which, over a period of four years, I acquired from conversations with students and from the general ambience of the institution. If the questionnaire responses are reliable, then it was probably unnecessary to put so much effort into making the materials and activities relevant to the students and their institution. On the other hand, if my accumulated experience and insights are to be trusted, this suggests that a Hawthorne effect is at work; that is to say, respondents were simply claiming that they believed English to be 'very useful' because they knew that it was their English lecturers who were administering the questionnaire.

The analyses carried out by Bazergan and by Hussein and Bazergan found that, after using *Risking Fun* for one semester, an even larger proportion of respondents (more than 90 per cent) claimed to believe that English was 'very useful'. Furthermore, by the end of the semester, the number of students who felt that English was 'not difficult' was greater than at the beginning of the semester, whilst the number who believed that English was 'very difficult' was smaller. The changes which are recorded here are not dramatic, and, as has been indicated, there are some problems with interpretation of the questionnaire responses. Nevertheless, there is reassurance in these results in that they suggest that the students' attitude to English did not become more negative, while at the same time they gradually became less apprehensive about it.

Bazergan (1986) then looked at the way in which students rated their own ability in the skills of reading, writing, listening and speaking, both before and after taking the English I course. She found that self-evaluation scores for all four skills increased during the semester. The largest increase occurred with regard to writing ability, and the second largest increase occurred in reading. Even though at this stage no attention was being given to oral skills, students still evaluated their oral ability more highly after the course. The difference between pre-course and post-course self-evaluation scores was significantly different for both reading and writing. These results suggest that learners felt more confident in all four skills by the end of the semester, particularly in their reading and writing of English.

The third question concerns the reaction of the teachers. Teachers' opinions were never solicited formally through a questionnaire. Nevertheless, it became clear – through informal discussions, from workshops and seminars, and from classroom observations – that the majority of the teachers enjoyed teaching with *Risking Fun*. The younger ones particularly appreciated the fact that with a highly interactive approach they were no longer the focus of attention and were no longer expected to spend most of their teaching time addressing large numbers of students. At the same time, it was also clear that some lecturers were not happy with the student-centred methodology.

The final question, as we noted, has two parts. Could the materials be used in large classes? And were the conventions of classroom interaction successfully challenged? The first of these questions has been discussed separately in Coleman 1987a, whilst the second is considered in Coleman 1987b.

In addition to these four questions, there is another matter to be considered: what did the students think about *Risking Fun*? In fact, this is the aspect of the Project which has been most extensively studied. To date, the most detailed investigation of learners' opinions of *Risking Fun* is that carried out by Djuraid (1986) using an open-ended questionnaire (reproduced here in Appendix 4). Djuraid found that learners appreciated being able to interact with each other in the classroom, and that the barrier between teacher and students had disappeared. They also claimed to recognise the value of the study skills which they had developed. However, Djuraid found that students had certain reservations concerning the course. These centred on the fact that no grammar is explicitly taught, and on the apparent inappropriacy of some of the activities. Some students from arts faculties were apparently unhappy about tasks which involved the interpretation of tables; these were perceived as tasks appropriate only for science students. Finally, there was a distinct current of dissatisfaction because what had occurred was perceived as being 'not English teaching'.

In addition to the complaints made by Djuraid's students, we would remind ourselves at this point of the problem recorded in Section 1.8. Although every analysis of student needs had indicated that oral skills were not essential, students responding to one of my own course evaluation questionnaires indicated that they wanted to 'learn conversation' in addition to anything more 'relevant' which we wished to provide for them.

Our evalutaion of *Risking Fun* has produced mixed results. The materials satisfied reasonably well the design criteria which had been laid down. But then if the needs analyst, syllabus designer and materials writer are one and the same person, this is perhaps not surprising. Test results show that learners became considerably more skilful at performing certain tasks – but we have still to consider whether those tasks are useful ones. The evidence for changes in attitude and self-confidence is not altogether reliable. If we take the data at face value, students became more positive about English and more confident in English, but this evidence appears not to fit easily with other data concerning students' attitudes and motivation. Finally, evidence from several questionnaire surveys suggests that students enjoyed the new English I course. At the same time, however, they had some reservations about the lack of explicit grammar teaching, the fact that the course did not resemble conventional language teaching programmes, and that there was no teaching of conversation.

2.3   Teacher training

After the creation of the *Risking Fun* materials, the next most important aspect of the Hasanuddin University Project was the teacher training. Some of this activity consisted of formal workshops, but much of it – and perhaps the most influential part – took place in the form of repeated classroom observations of individual lecturers and numerous relatively informal consultations with the same people over a period of several years.

There is relatively little explicit evaluation of teacher training activity in the various documents relating to the Project, although my reports and project reviews include several enthusiastic comments on the young lecturers with whom I was working. I still believe that this enthusiasm was justified. At the same time, it was to be admitted that the Project's teacher training activities were geared towards satisfying the relatively short-term requirements of the university. In particular, much of the teacher training work was aimed at introducing lecturers to the *Risking*

Fun materials. In other words, the emphasis was placed much more heavily on *training* than on *enabling*.

2.4   *Training for revision*

Lecturers who participated in workshops and other training activities were frequently asked to comment on those parts of the *Risking Fun* materials which were currently in preparation. In this way, I felt that I was to some extent achieving the 'ideal integration' recommended by Brumfit and Roberts : 'In an ideal world, training of teachers, development of syllabuses and materials, teaching and inspection would be closely integrated.' (1983:155)

But there is another way of looking at this relationship between materials writing and teacher training. *Risking Fun* was deliberately designed to be suitable for use by the students of a particular university at a particular point in time. It was consequently inevitable that certain aspects of the materials would gradually become outdated and inaccurate. I recognised this fairly early on, but in planning teacher training activities I made no provision for preparing the university's English lecturers themselves to undertake revisions of the materials. Indeed, I undertook the first major revision of the materials myself during 1984 and after I had left Indonesia in 1985.

This deficiency has already been spotted. N. S. Prabhu, commenting on a set of the *Risking Fun* materials, has noted the 'boldness in conception' and 'courageous exclusion of grammar and conversation' of the *Risking Fun* materials (personal communication). Nevertheless, he makes the following comment:

> What I find worrying is the possibility that a course like this can become, in due course, a new form of ritual to replace the old. . . .
> It might well be that there is a choice to be made, in developing any innovative course, between the immediate rewards of thorough specification and possible longer-term benefits of built-in decisions for teachers – between what may be called 'teacher-proofing' and 'teacher-dependence'. . . . The primary purpose of any change should be to enhance the possibility of further change and . . . pedagogy is likely to remain meaningful to the extent there is a process of ongoing/perpetual change.

2.5   *Evaluation of the Project in its own terms*

Having examined the materials writing and teacher training aspects of the Hasanuddin University Project, it is now time to consider its achievements from a wider perspective. In this section we look at the Project 'in its own terms'; that is to say, by judging the extent to which it achieved the objectives which it laid down for itself after it had begun to operate. In Section 2.6 an attempt will be made to judge the Project from an even wider perspective, in the terms of those who established the Project in the first place.

The proposed programme of activities, drawn up in September 1981, provides one particularly useful tool for this evaluation (Section 1.5). This was the first document in which I laid out my own ideas as to the way in which the Project should develop. Among all the Project documentation, it was also unique in that it attempted to map out the work of the Project for the whole of a three-year period.

A comparison between the planned activities and a bald list of those activities which were completed is initially embarrassing. Of the fourteen activities planned for the 1981–2 academic year, one had still not been started by the time I felt the University in 1984. Fewer than half of the twelve activities planned for the 1982–3 academic year were completed. The gradual shift of emphasis from undergraduate to staff needs did not occur, and only about a third of the nine activities outlined for the 1983–4 academic year were completed.

On the other hand, there were many activities which did take place but which had not been planned. The most time-consuming of these were, firstly, extensive teacher training workshops for successive generations of users of *Risking Fun*, and, secondly, the day-to-day administration of the English I programme after the Co-ordinator of the programme went to Britain to study.

These excuses apart, it is clear from this comparison that the nature of that episode in the history of the Project which ended with my departure in October 1984 was ultimately very different from the Project which I myself had planned three years earlier. Originally, the Project was to be a compromise between, on the one hand, the perceived requirements of the institution to have its staff trained so that they could go abroad and, on the other hand, my own belief that the most pressing need was the provision of a study skills programme for undergraduates. As it turned out, the Project concentrated exclusively on the second of these alternatives.

Apart from this rather crude comparison between working schedules and completed tasks, it might be possible to evaluate the Hasanuddin University Project *in its own terms* in two other ways. The first of these concerns the way in which the university's overall needs were analysed in the initial needs analysis. The second relates to the decision to concentrate on study skills improvement.

It will be remembered that the initial needs analysis (Section 1.3) had found that the various administrative units in the university interacted with each other in a way which was both complex and dynamic. This analysis had two implications: that input intended to solve problems in one unit may have repercussions elsewhere in the system, and that input intended to solve problems at one point in time may have repercussions which are not felt immediately. It was this analysis of the situation which had justified my concentration on the development of a study skills programme for undergraduates. If students could be encouraged to use the university libraries and to do more reading of the English language books which the libraries stocked, then they would acquire a more positive attitude towards English. Some of these students would graduate and become lecturers; in turn, their more positive attitudes and their greater familiarity with the literature would have a positive long-term effect on their own students. Now, if we wish to evaluate the accuracy of this initial analysis and of the action which was taken in response to it, then of course we must take a very long-term view of the situation. We will have to wait until those students who have used *Risking Fun* have graduated and until some of these people have themselves begun lecturing before we can make this sort of evaluation.

The second way in which the Project could be evaluated in relation to its own terms of reference is closely connected to the first. This concerns the decision to concentrate on the development of study skills. At the time when I carried out the initial needs analysis I was shocked, in an almost puritanical way, to discover that the university library was relatively underused in comparison with the university libraries with which I was familiar in Britain. It seemed to me a *sine qua non* of university life that one reads and uses libraries as a source of reference. However, as I became more familiar with the workings of the system during my four years at Hasanuddin University I began to suspect that my initial interpretation of what the university was doing – and my prescriptive horror at what it was not doing – had been coloured by an ethnocentric view of the function of academic systems. I began to wonder whether in fact academic systems may have their own (non-explicit) functions which are closely related to and influenced by the wider culture in which they are situated, but which are only superficially and terminologically related to the functions of academic systems situated in other cultures. I gradually began to understand that Hasanuddin University was indeed a system (as I had analysed it from the beginning), but that this system was probably working well if it was interpreted on its own terms instead of being judged by criteria derived from other cultures. This line of thinking has been pursued further in Coleman 1986, Coleman 1988b and Coleman 1989.

If this reasoning is carried to its logical conclusion, then it becomes difficult to justify the decision to concentrate on the development of study skills. It is likely that Hasanuddin University was functioning quite adequately in its own terms and was satisfying the demands made upon it by wider Indonesian society. If this was indeed the case, then there seems to be little justification for trying to make the University do something different even if this 'something different' would be considered useful in, for example, a British university.

2.6   *Evaluation in terms of initial objectives*

We move now to a very brief consideration of the Project from the point of view of those who designed it in the first place. Originally, the preparation of pre-departure courses for staff was to have been the main objective of the Project. A minor aim was to pay attention to 'service English for undergraduate students'. If these original objectives are employed as criteria, then clearly the Project achieved only a fraction – and apparently a relatively insignificant fraction – of what it was intended to do.

However, as we have repeatedly observed, the nature of the Hasanuddin University KELT Project changed radically during the four years that I was associated with it. If the nature of the Project changes, and if its objectives change, then evaluation of the work of the Project in terms of initial criteria inevitably loses most of its value.

3   Conclusions

This article has traced the history of an ELT Project in an Indonesian university over a four-year period. The nature of the Project changed quite radically during this period. These changes were sometimes deliberate and conscious; at other times they happened less conspicuously. For the most part, the various factors which led to those changes occurred at different periods in the Project's history.

Changes in the nature of the Project, and related changes in the objectives of the Project, mean that evaluation of the Project becomes extremely difficult. If we employ the criteria established at the time when the Project was set up, then the outcomes may appear to be largely irrelevant. On the other hand, if we employ micro-level criteria to evaluate the work of the Project, then we may be ignoring a wider perspective. Thus there appear to be two dangers. If we allow ourselves to be constrained by the initial Project description then we lose flexibility and cut ourselves off from the insights which exposure to the situation may bring. On the other hand, if we respond to these insights and constantly update our objectives, it may be difficult to maintain a global perspective of the situation in which the Project is functioning. It may be worth adding that no formal overall evaluation of the Project was ever carried out.

A final point concerns the writing of this article. There is a sense in which this type of analysis of past events allows the author to make sense retrospectively of what was, at the time that it was experienced, a very messy reality. This retrospective making of sense – or, to put it more cynically, the tidying up of history – may be carried out with the *intention* of providing an objective account. Nevertheless, a document of this type presents only one point of view and cannot achieve genuine objectivity. A fuller picture would require parallel descriptions from other individuals and groups who had interests in the Project.

Postscript (June 1990)

Writing the history of a project at any particular point in time is an arbitrary act. Since this paper was written, further developments have occurred. The Hasanuddin University authorities have approached the British Council with a request for assistance in the preparation of a third edition of *Risking Fun*. This request was prompted partly because the second edition is itself now out of date, and partly because other universities in the region wish to adopt the materials but would prefer a neutral version which does not deal specifically with the situation in Hasanuddin University. The British Council has responded positively to this request and in consequence I have made two return visits to the university. It is now planned that a member of the University's ELT staff will spend a year in Britain in 1990–1 rewriting the materials, as part of a master's programme. If this is successful, then the third edition will be introduced in 1992 (that is to say, fourteen years after the Project was first planned, twelve years after it was established, and six years after it formally ceased). These developments underline the difficulty of performing a summative evaluation of a project.

Appendix 1

English translation of pre-course questionnaire for participants in English I programme: February 1983.

This questionnaire consists of 17 questions. All questions should be answered. It is not necessary to put your name on the questionnaire. Ask the lecturer if any questions are not clear. Return the questionnaire to the lecturer when you have answered all the questions. Thank you!

Education before entering Hasanuddin University
1 Type of secondary school where you completed your secondary education:

2 Status of secondary school where you completed your secondary education:
  State/Private

3 Place where you completed your secondary education:

4 When did you receive your School Leaving Certificate?

Study at Hasanuddin University
5 When did you begin to study at Hasanuddin University?

6 Which programme of study are you taking?

Experience of studying English
7 How long did you study English when you were still at secondary school?

8 a Have you ever studied English except in secondary school?
   Yes / No
  b If you have studied English outside secondary school, explain where you studied:

  c How long did you study English outside secondary school?

Ability and attitude
9 Evaluation of your current ability in English:

	fluent	reasonable	not so good	no ability at all
a Reading ability				
b Writing ability				
c Speaking ability				
d Listening ability				

10 In your opinion, studying English is:

very easy   very difficult

1	2	3	4	5	6

11 In your opinion, studying English is:

very useful   not at all useful

1	2	3	4	5	6

12 Explain what you are expecting from the English I programme:

13 In your opinion, why is English included in the Hasanuddin University curriculum?

Personal details
14 Date of birth:

15 Place of birth:

16 First language learned as a child:

17 Sex: Male/Female

Appendix 2

English translation of post-course questionnaire for participants in English I programme; June 1983

I   Your answers to this questionnaire will be very useful to us in our efforts to revise the English teaching materials and to improve the quality of English teaching in Hasanuddin University. You should not feel shy about expressing your opinions in the questionnaire. Do not put your name on the questionnaire.

II This questionnaire consists of 26 questions. Questions 1 to 24 should be answered by all students; questions 25 and 26 are only for those students who began studying at Hasanuddin University before 1982. Choose one of the available answers for all the questions marked *. Other questions should be answered by writing in your own response. Ask the lecturer if any questions are unclear. When you have answered all the questions, return the questionnaire to the lecturer. Thank you.

Ability and attitude

1   Evaluation of your current ability in English:

	fluent	reasonable	not so good	no ability at all
a Reading ability*				
b Writing ability*				
c Speaking ability*				
d Listening ability*				

2   In your opinion, studying English is*:

very easy					very difficult
1	2	3	4	5	6

3   In your opinion, studying English is*:

very useful					not at all useful
1	2	3	4	5	6

4   In your opinion, why is English included in the Hasanuddin University curriculum?

5   What did you expect from the English programme?

6   Have you got what you expected? Yes/No

7   Explain your answer to question 6 above:

Evaluation of teaching materials used during last semester ('Risking Fun')

8   Relevance of 'Risking Fun' (i.e. whether the material used was suitable or not suitable for students' needs)*:

not suitable at all					very suitable
1	2	3	4	5	6

9   Level of difficulty of 'Risking Fun'*:

too easy					too difficult
1	2	3	4	5	6

10   Interest level of 'Risking Fun'*:

very interesting					very boring
1	2	3	4	5	6

11   Cost of handouts*:

too expensive					too cheap
1	2	3	4	5	6

12   Do you think that it is necessary to provide a follow-up English programme with 'Rising Fun Part 2'?

13   Do you have any other comments on 'Risking Fun'?

Evaluation of teaching method used during last semester

14   Use of time in the class*:

very efficient					not efficient
1	2	3	4	5	6

15   Relationships between students and lecturer*:
  a not close, because of the teaching method used
  b not close, but not because of the teaching method used
  c close, because of the teaching method used
  d close, but not because of the teaching method used

16   Relationships between students*:
  a competitive, because of the teaching method used
  b competitive, but not because of the teaching method used
  c co-operative, because of the teaching method used
  d co-operative, but not because of the teaching method used.

17   Do you have any other comments on the teaching method used?

Personal details

18   Date of birth:

19   Place of birth:

20   First language learned as a child:

21   Sex: Male/Female

22   When did you begin studying in Hasanuddin University?

23   Which programme of study are you taking?

24   Do you have any other comments on the teaching of English at Hasanuddin University?

Only for students who have been studying at Hasanuddin University for more than one year

25   What do you think about the 'Risking Fun' materials compared with the English language materials which you used previously?

26   What do you think about the teaching method used during the last semester, compared with the method used for teaching English which you have experienced previously?

Appendix 3

English translation of pre-course questionnaire for participants in English I programme; August 1983.

This questionnaire consists of 11 questions. All questions should be answered. Ask the lecturer if there are any questions which are not clear. Return the questionnaire to the lecturer when you have finished. Your name should not be written on the questionnaire.

Ability and attitude

1 Evaluation of your current ability in English:

	fluent	reasonable	not so good	no ability at all
a Reading ability				
b Writing ability				
c Speaking ability				
d Listening ability				

2 In your opinion, studying English is:

very easy					very difficult
1	2	3	4	5	6

3 In your opinion, why is English included in the Hasanuddin University curriculum?

4 In your opinion, studying English is:

very useful					not at all useful
1	2	3	4	5	6

5 What do you expect from the English I programme?

Personal details

6 Date of birth:

7 Place of birth:

8 First language learned as a child:

9 Sex: Male/Female

10 When did you begin to study at Hasanuddin University?

11 Faculty code:

Faculty name:

Your response to this questionnaire will be very helpful to us in our efforts to revise the English teaching materials and to improve the quality of the teaching of English in Hasanuddin University. Do not put your name on the questionnaire.

Appendix 4

English translation of post-course questionnaire designed by
A.Madjid Djuraid for participants in English I programme,
November 1984.

1 Write about your impressions of studying English using 'Risking Fun':

2 What is the difference between 'Risking Fun' and the learning/teaching
method used at secondary school?

3 What are the advantages of 'Risking Fun'?

4 What are the weaknesses of 'Risking Fun', including the weaknesses of
the lecturer?

5 Suggestions for improving 'Risking Fun':

6 Name and student number:

References

Bazergan, E. 1986. Comparison between changes in students' self-evaluation over a period of time and an objective evaluation of the same students at the end of the same period of time. Unpublished diploma dissertation, Lancaster University.

Brumfit, C. J. and J. T. Roberts. 1983. *An introduction to language and language teaching*. London: Batsford.

Coleman, H. 1981. *English in Hasanuddin University: an analysis of needs.* Unpublished.

Coleman, H. 1983. *ODA-British Council KELT Project at Hasanuddin University, Indonesia: Review of progress, description of work still to be done, and proposals for future developments*. Unpublished.

Coleman, H. 1985. Evaluating teachers' guides: Do teachers' guides guide teachers? In J. Charles Alderson (Ed.) *Evaluation*, pp. 83–96. (Lancaster Practical Papers in English Language Education, 6.) Oxford: Pergamon Press.

Coleman, H. 1986. Interpreting classroom behaviour in its cultural context. Paper presented at the RELC Seminar on Patterns of Classroom Interaction in Southeast Asia, Singapore, 21–25 April 1986.

Coleman, H. 1987a. 'Little tasks make large return': task-based language learning in large crowds. In C. N. Candlin and D. F. Murphy (Eds.), *Language Learning Tasks* pp. 121–45. (Lancaster Practical Papers in English Language Education, 7) London: Prentice-Hall.

Coleman, H. 1987b. Teaching spectacles and learning festivals. *ELT Journal* 41(2): 97–103.

Coleman, H. 1988a. Analysing language needs in large organizations. *English for Specific Purposes* 7: 155–69.

Coleman, H. 1988b. The appropriacy of teaching study skills. Paper presented at the Conference on Studying with English, University of Bristol, 5–6 January 1988.

Coleman, H. 1989. Testing 'appropriate behaviour' in an academic context. In
Verner Bickley (Ed.) *Language teaching and learning styles within and across
cultures.* pp. 361–72. Hong Kong: Institute of Language in Education.

Djuraid, A. M. 1986. Reactions of university students to an interactive course in
study skills. Unpublished diploma dissertation, Lancaster University.

Hussein, B., and E. Bazergan. 1985. *Evaluasi Tentang Sikap dan Kemampuan
Mahasiswa Universitas Hasanuddin, Ujung Pandang, dalam Mempelajari
Bahasa Inggris.* Ujung Pandang: Universitas Hasanuddin.

O'Neill, R., R. Kingsbury, T. Yeadon and R. Scott. 1976. *Kernal Lessons
Intermediate.* Harlow: Longman.

Pritchard, N. and S. Ruru. 1986. *An analysis of English language teaching needs
at Hasanuddin University.* Unpublished.

Vredenbregt, J. and Roosmalawati. 1979. *Persepsi Dosen UNHAS terhadap
Universitas Hasanuddin: Suatu Penelitian Eksploratif.* Ujung Pandang: Universitas Hasanuddin.

Editors' postscript to Coleman

This chapter presents an unusually frank account of the development of a
language education project in the context of 'overseas aid for developing
countries' and is highly relevant to current concerns in the English
language teaching world about and interests in the role and nature of
management in ELT, particularly the management of ELT projects in
overseas settings. Although confessional reports of projects like the
Indonesian KELT project are relatively rare in the applied linguistic
literature, Coleman's experience is by no means unique as the reactions
of many current and former Project Officers testify, and the chapter bears
telling witness to the often conflicting aims and objectives (and loyalties?)
of the various parties to such aid projects, as well as to the varying
perceptions that can result. Any attempt at evaluation of or by objectives
must address the issue of whose objectives are to be evaluated, and it
should also seek to identify any different or even opposed objectives and
desires. It is important to note, in this context, that the chapter is written
by one of the parties in the project, presenting his own perceptions, albeit
frankly, and that we do not have any independent record of the
perceptions of the project – or the evaluations of it – by the British
Council, the British Overseas Development Administration (ODA) or by
the university itself. It is therefore a partial view in both senses of the
word. One of the main points of Coleman's chapter is that any view is
necessarily partial: evaluation can never be comprehensive.

Coleman also clearly documents the role of the insider – one of the
agents of change – in influencing the directions of the project and its
change of objectives. Is it reasonable, as often happens in projects like
this, to expect the Project Officer him- or herself to be neutral with

respect to the objectives and direction of the project by whose success she or he will be judged? Clearly not, as it is not reasonable to expect such officers to stand by as a project rolls into disaster because of inappropriate aims, but how far can such an officer be allowed to 'subvert' the aims of the project, and how and by whom is that officer to be held accountable? It is, of course, also clearly the case that other individuals employed as project officers might have chosen different objectives for the project, or might have decided upon different means of achieving the same objectives: Coleman decided to concentrate upon first-year undergraduates as a means of achieving the broad objectives, yet his successors or other professionals might not agree. Who is in the best position to decide and can this be known in advance, rather than by means of that most exact science: *post-hoc* rationalisation? In addition, Coleman draws our attention to a poignant aspect of the insider's dilemma: his own career prospects may be affected by the failure of the project, judged according to someone else's (inappropriate) objectives! And as if that were not enough, he sees himself obliged to exaggerate the needs of the situation and the activities of the project well beyond what is feasible, simply in order to convince agencies that the project is 'aid-worthy': that it should be funded by outside agencies. An honest account of what could be achieved in the circumstances might well have seemed trivial. Yet by overstating the needs and activities, he makes himself liable to accusations of inefficiency when he fails to achieve the impossible, or of unprofessionalism in advocating the impossible.

However, such apparent ambitiousness may not be the result of innocent duplicity or even of inexperience: it may simply be the result of changing circumstances. What seems feasible at the beginning of a project very often appears optimistic in the light of experience. Revisions of timescales and deadlines are relatively common experiences in projects such as this, and flexibility and accommodation are important elements to build into project plans. Can an evaluation identify the existence of or the need for such flexibility, or will it interpret delays as evidence of incompetence? Overambitious aims and objectives may be an inescapable consequence of setting up objectives at the beginning of the project, rather than establishing the objectives after a project has been completed. Once the project has been implemented, the statement of objectives can be descriptive, and thus reflect reality, rather than being prospective and risking unreality. It is, after all, not uncommon in the curriculum design world to advocate the use of objectives for reflection upon a curriculum rather than for guiding its development. It is, of course, also the aim of evaluation to provide feedback upon the appropriateness of the objectives in the light of experience – to ask, in other words, not simply: were the objectives achieved? but rather: what was achieved, was what was achieved intended, and were the intentions appropriate?

A common approach to the establishment of objectives for projects such as this is to conduct a 'needs analysis' in order to determine what is required, and indeed this happened on Coleman's project, too. Yet it is worth a brief reflection on what might have happened, how might the project's objectives have been influenced, if Coleman had not paid attention to the infrastructure of the university. He would have over-looked what he plausibly argues to be a dynamic and complex interaction among administrative units, such that they are mutually influential in interesting and important ways which arguably affect the long-term health of the project. A different needs analysis, focusing perhaps upon the terminal behaviours of graduates in their target situations, would almost certainly have missed this insight, and the project would have developed in very different directions whilst still pursuing plausible objectives.

The identification of long-term goals that resulted from this 'needs analysis' itself creates problems hinted at by Coleman: when can the success of such a project be evaluated? Almost certainly long after the funding agencies have ceased to support the project, yet it is surely unrealistic to expect the attainment of such goals to be evident within the life of a typical KELT Project. This realisation has implications not only for the nature and timing of evaluation, but crucially for funding agencies and the horizons to which they plan and evaluate. It is interesting to note in this context that only recently has the university approached the overseas agencies for assistance in the revision of the teaching materials – after the Project had ended. If one takes such a request as evidence for the success of the project, when can the project be said to have finished? What is the end, rather than the result, of projects?

The evaluation that Coleman reports is of two kinds. Here we are thinking not of the micro and macro levels – the materials and the project and its ecology – but of the difference between the data gathered by Coleman and his colleagues with respect to the materials – empirical evidence of the effect of the materials – and the reflection and confession that Coleman engages in about the history of the project. Both methodologies have their place, and both benefit from the other. Reasoned argument and the exposition of values and perceptions on the part of participants are essential input to an evaluation. They do not dispense with the need for the collection of evidence about the effects of intentions, actions and implementations. It is also worth reflecting briefly on the value of the data that Coleman *et al.* collected: the need for a change of objectives for the *Risking Fun* materials – from study skills to oral communication – only emerged during the trials and materials evaluation phases. A deterministic approach to evaluation, evaluating the materials only in terms of their original objectives, would likely have missed the need for change and adjustment, and would thus have been partial. The evaluator is nevertheless placed in another dilemma: does he believe the results of the original needs analysis – as Coleman tends to – or does he accept the emerging opinions that contradict such an analysis, at least in part? What, one occasionally wonders, is the truth value of the students' opinions: did they really find the language learning experience useful, or were they engaged in telling the evaluators what they believed they wished to hear? When does one stop believing the responses and begin believing one's own intuitions and perceptions instead?

Which brings us back full circle to where we began: the variety of perspectives, perceptions, aims, goals and objectives in this project and in many like it, and the need for evaluation to recognise this, to be clear about whose values and perceptions it is addressing, whilst acknowledging that others exist.

8 What can be learned from the Bangalore Evaluation

Alan Beretta

Introduction

The purpose of the present chapter is to provide an account of the evaluation of a program, not so much so that the program may be judged but in order to document the shifting perspectives, false starts, design alterations, obstacles, and difficulties of interpretation that often characterise evaluations.

Evaluation reports that give the impression of a smooth, professional operation that went off without a hitch are far from the mark. Current thinking in evaluation would deny the validity of such impressions. Discussion with other evaluators, my own experience, and established perspectives in the evaluation literature (e.g. Cronbach *et al.* 1980) suggest that a more realistic picture would present a messy, chaotic series of compromises, where classic research designs disintegrate, where vain hopes of contributing to certain kinds of learning theory are soon dispelled, and where all that lies between the pragmatic evaluator and scholarly perdition is a sense of disciplined inquiry, whether it relates to quasi-experimental research, to a host of naturalistic approaches, or to policy analysis.

The intention of this chapter is to provide food for thought not only for would-be evaluators, but for L2 program developers too, who can assist substantially in the evaluation process in ways that will hopefully become evident in the course of the present account.

In the mid-1980s, I conducted an evaluation of an English language project in Bangalore, India. In this chapter, I will use this evaluation as a focus for discussion as it features many of the issues that are of interest to evaluators. I shall begin with an overview of the two main phases of the evaluation of the Bangalore Project. This will be followed by an introspective account of why the inquiry took the turns it did, including a consideration of 1) the purpose of the evaluation, 2) the point-of-entry problem, 3) a lost opportunity for richer evaluation, 4) an attempt to broaden the scope of the study, 5) an if-I-knew-then discussion.

The purpose here is only to give a very general idea of the kinds of inquiry that were undertaken and of the results. For a full account of the studies, see the three published papers (Beretta and Davies 1985; Beretta 1989; Beretta 1990a) and the archive document (Beretta 1987).

Before proceeding to discuss the evaluation, a brief account of the project itself may be helpful.

Brief description of the project

The Bangalore Project, also known as the Communicational Teaching Project (CTP), ran from 1979 to 1984. It was based on the familiar precept that language form can be learnt in the classroom entirely through a focus on meaning and that grammar-construction by the learner is an unconscious process. In this respect, it has much in common with the Natural Approach (Krashen and Terrell 1983). Generalisations about language structure are thought to interfere with unconscious development. A methodology was assembled through trial-and-error in the early stages of the project's life, and resulted in a set of problem-solving activities which foster a concern with the task at hand, attention to language itself being relegated to incidental status. The problem-solving activities eventually formed a task-based syllabus.

Although this description is necessarily brief, there are more detailed accounts. The early development of the project is recorded in the Newsletters and Bulletins put out by the Regional Institute of English in Bangalore, but these are not readily available. More available is the project director's personal view of second language acquisition which, although (unlike Krashen's) it pays little attention to SLA research, is based on experience with the project (Prabhu 1987), and thus may be regarded as the major reference. Also of interest are a couple of articles that have commented on the project, notably Brumfit (1984) and Johnson (1982).

The first phase of the evaluation, in the last months of the project's life, involved testing experimental and control groups. The second phase, after the project had come to an end, was a retrospective study focusing on 1) levels of implementation, 2) teachers' stages of concern, and 3) the treatment of error. These elements are discussed in turn.

Phase 1 Evaluation

Interpreting results is fraught with danger in all social science inquiry, but comparing programs on a range of tests has had a particularly difficult passage. Testing comparisons suggest to the unwary that some kind of 'no-nonsense' rigor has entered the debate when, in fact, this can be quite specious. The first phase of the Bangalore evaluation is a good example of such a comparison.

During the last months of the project, CTP students were compared with peer groups in the same schools who had received instruction in the prevailing structure-based approach. A range of tests was used: two achievement tests, 1) structure-based and 2) task-based, and three (ostensibly syllabus-neutral) proficiency measures, 3) dictation, 4) contextualised grammar and 5) a communicative listening/reading test. (For samples of these tests, see Appendix 1 in this chapter.)

Although the results of these comparisons suggested that the CTP students fared better than their peers, it was noted that there were several factors which could account for this, such as test-content bias, more highly motivated and qualified teachers, and the fact that treatments may have overlapped.

Evidence has since been found confirming that the latter two considerations may constitute competing explanations of the results.

There is a distinct possibility that the treatments overlapped and that therefore distinctions were blurred. This is suggested by the testimony of visitors to the project who recorded that CTP staff who were regular teachers in the schools tended to revert to a focus on form (Brumfit 1984; Davies 1983). Reported overlap was only in this direction. This is further substantiated by the CTP teachers themselves, including the non-regular teachers who were drafted in from the British Council, teacher training colleges and universities. In their written accounts of their experience during the project, several acknowledged that they consciously taught grammar. One teacher, for example, concerned that her less able students were falling behind, observed that she gave special extra-curricular grammar teaching to one of the CTP groups used in the phase 1 evaluation. Finally, an analysis of the 21 CTP transcripts that were made available to the author showed that even the initiator of the project could slip into form-focused teaching (see *Phase 2 Evaluation*, below). Since implementation of the CTP was not monitored, it is not possible to know to what extent there was overlap, and therefore, to be certain that this constitutes a rival explanation for CTP test performance; but all of the indications are that CTP students possibly experienced both structural and CTP teaching, and it is reasonable to infer that this may have been an advantage for CTP students on the testing comparison.

As for the superior qualifications and motivation of the CTP teachers, there is little room for doubt that this was a major factor behind the CTP learners' superior performance. Most of the CTP teachers were non-regular teachers: they had earned MAs in TEFL in the UK, while the peer-group teachers were all locally educated to lower levels. Also, as we will see below, the phase 2 evaluation demonstrated that the non-regular teachers were exceptionally highly motivated.

Phase 2 Evaluation

Levels of implementation

The phase 1 evaluation, focusing as it did solely on student performance on tests, clearly suffered from a fatal flaw shared by a great number of evaluations. This common flaw is a failure to adequately document the *independent* variable, that is, what happened in the classroom between the inception of a program and its termination (e.g. Scherer and Wertheimer 1964; Smith 1970).

Over the last fifteen years, a large number of studies have been undertaken which have focused on measuring implementation of programs (Wang *et al.* 1984; Stallings 1975), but most of these inquiries have monitored the program while it was in operation. This was an avenue not open to the evaluation of the Bangalore Project since the opportunity for collecting such data had passed, that is, the project ended as soon as the testing was over.

However, Cronbach's (1982) association of program evaluation with historical research and his description of the value of retrospective accounts appeared to offer a means of rescuing the evaluation.

The Hall and Loucks (1977) concept of levels of use of an innovation was taken as a starting point and a model of three levels of implementation was developed to accommodate the Bangalore Project. Teachers were requested to write detailed narrative accounts of their experience with the CTP. These accounts were then rated according to such criteria as 'knowledge' and 'performance' (based on a close reading of the Bangalore literature) and individual teachers were assigned to one of three levels: 1) orientation (when teachers are still coming to terms with the demands of the project), 2) routine (when teachers are operating comfortably with the project), and 3) renewal (when teachers are looking for ways of improving the project). (For details of categories, see Appendix 2 in this chapter.)

No pattern could be discerned in the findings except that 75 per cent of the regular teachers (i.e. those who were teaching in the project schools on a full-time basis) were at the lowest (orientation) level of implementation whereas 73 per cent of the non-regular teachers (i.e. those who were not full-time teachers in the project schools but were teacher trainers, British Council staff, university professors who taught on a temporary, part-time basis) were at the second (routine) and third (renewal) levels. There were two factors which explained the more successful implementation of the non-regular teachers: 1) they were far more highly qualified in TESL and 2) they were far more highly motivated.

That they were better qualified is clear from biodata forms the CTP teachers completed as part of the evaluation, and the motivation is evident in the long narrative accounts. Non-regular teachers talked of a 'CTP team' and of 'our fold', and perceived themselves as 'pioneer teachers'; one observation was that 'we – the members of the CTP – constructed the method bit by bit'. As far as they were concerned, the CTP belonged to them.

For the regular teachers, by contrast, recruitment simply meant that the project arrived at their school, as their accounts testify.

From the perspective of external validity, it would be germane to note that implementation of the project cannot be expected from regular teachers. Thus, if the CTP were transplanted to other parts of India, regular, local teachers would probably struggle to come to terms with the demands of the project and would most likely revert to a focus of form.

Teachers' stages of concern

Another way of gathering retrospective information is through the use of questionnaires.

Since, by this stage of the evaluation, the interest had shifted from a focus on whether the CTP was 'better' than the structural approach to broader questions of extrapolation (i.e. the extent to which the evaluation might help in determining whether or not similar projects could be set up elsewhere), it was clearly valuable to know which teacher concerns were uppermost at different periods of the project's life. The emergence of different concerns at different times is likely to have a bearing on the way an innovative program is implemented. In the educational literature, a lot of work has been done on the various concerns of teachers at different stages of implementation, and a reasonably well-validated questionnaire has been devised by Hall, George and Rutherford (1977). This *Stages of Concern Questionnaire* (SoCQ) was selected as an appropriate tool and modified for the purposes of the evaluation (see Appendix 3 in this chapter).

SoCQ is based upon the idea, which has empirical support (Fuller 1969), that beginning teachers move from initial concerns about 'self' (ability to cope), through 'task' (day-to-day management issues) to 'impact' (effects on learners). Hall *et al.* (1977) found the same movement of concerns applied to teachers involved in innovations.

The picture that emerged from the results of this questionnaire is that regular teachers manifest far greater concern altogether than non-regular teachers. This indicates that regular teachers never became completely comfortable with the CTP. Secondly, the non-regular teachers' early concerns with coping fade as concerns with the effects of the CTP on students' learning gain prominence. For regular teachers, on the other hand, there is no clear development, and early concerns actually increase appreciably.

Overall, the indications are reasonably clear: first, the discrepancies between regular teachers and non-regular teachers evidenced by SoCQ results increase confidence in the finding that regular teachers remained at the orientation level; second, the non-regular teachers' sense of 'ownership' of the program was accompanied by a reduction in anxiety about adequacy to cope and a greater interest in the consequences for learners.

Attention to form or meaning? Error treatment in the Bangalore Project

The CTP rejects a focus on form because of the belief upon which it is founded that a focus on form interferes with the learner's developing internal grammar. As a result, lessons were supposed to focus on meaning and not on form. The question was: how could one distinguish, when observing a lesson (or examining transcripts), whether the teacher was attending to form or to meaning? A lesson transcript (in Regional Institute of English 1980 Bulletin 4 (i):44–53) illustrates the problem. Some participants in a seminar held in Bangalore in 1980 judged the transcript to be a clear example of a focus on form. For Prabhu, by contrast, it was just as clearly a focus on meaning. Fortunately, it was possible to investigate this question because Prabhu (1982:5–6; 1987: 62–3) had offered reasonably precise accounts of how both linguistic and content errors should be treated. Certain kinds of teacher reaction to linguistic error are considered to be appropriate to a focus on language form (e.g. generalisation, exemplification, and explanation – rephrasing and ignoring are thought to be acceptable ways for the teacher to react) while others are considered appropriate to a focus on meaning (correcting content errors).

Twenty-one CTP lesson transcripts were analysed 1) for the relative incidence of content and linguistic error treatments, 2) to determine whether the statements against the use of generalisation, exemplification and explanation were strictly observed, 3) to provide a descriptive account of CTP error treatment and 4) to explore the possibility that certain variables might explain the incidence of different treatment types. (The analysis was based on slightly modified categories of error treatment devised by Chaudron 1977; see Appendix 4 in this chapter.)

It should be pointed out that eighteen of the twenty-one transcripts were of Prabhu and his closest associate, and that there were no transcripts of any of the regular teachers' lessons. It was already known from observers' reports (Davies 1983; Brumfit 1984) that the regular teachers reverted to form-focused teaching, so the interest here was in the non-regular teachers.

It was found that there was significantly greater attention to treatment of content error than there was to linguistic error. This finding is consonant with the CTP focus on meaning rather than on form.

From the descriptive analysis of the lesson transcripts, it transpired that the majority of treatments for linguistic error involved minimal intervention or none at all. Content errors, by contrast, were treated in a wide variety of ways, indicating that more sustained attempts were made to secure the correct answers to problems. The descriptive analysis thus broadly supported the stated CTP approaches to error correction. However, the stipulation that explanation, generalisation and exemplification be avoided was not strictly observed, and the fact that non-regular teachers could slip into focus on form was noted.

Examining variables that might contribute to treatment type, the most salient finding was in the relationship between location in time and error treatment. Prabhu (personal communication) judged that the CTP methodology had settled by 1982, so it was pertinent to look at this variable since earlier lessons might be judged on criteria that only emerged later on. It transpired that there was very little error treatment post-1982. This was due to the simple fact that there was very little error in the students' classroom performance, which could be explained neither by the length of the recordings nor teacher style.

The best explanation seemed to be that certain *tasks* were more highly associated with linguistic error than others and that these tasks occurred only in the earlier period. Considering the nature of the tasks, it emerged that the tasks associated with little linguistic error called for physical responses and extremely limited verbal responses. The earlier tasks required greater verbal production. Early tasks like Lecturettes and Letter-writing are not even mentioned in Prabhu's later (1987:138–43) list of task types.

The implication of these findings appears to be that task types that called for production were phased out and only those that stressed reception were retained. When this interpretation is considered along with one teacher's testimony that the CTP did not attend sufficiently to production ('generally our tasks were cognitively very challenging, but linguistically did not make adequate demands on the learners' productive abilities'), confidence in this interpretation is increased.

Prabhu argued from the beginning of the project that CTP practice is based on a belief that reception comes before production and that a period of incubation is to be reckoned with, i.e. production will occur when the learner is ready for it (1980:21). All of the lessons in this study post-date these statements and yet the differences between the 1981 set and the 1983/4 set are clear. But in any case, there is presumably a difference between 'forcing' production (which Prabhu disapproves of) and 'permitting' production (which is markedly truer of the 1981 lessons than the later ones).

Bearing in mind the limitations of the data and analysis, the following tentative findings are suggested by the study of error treatment. On the whole, the treatment of error conforms with the fairly precise attitudes stated by Prabhu. However, while the *treatment* of error may be consonant with CTP prescriptions, in the later years of the project, selection of task type virtually precluded even the possibility that learners might make linguistic error, in turn precluding the possibility that the teacher's correction might focus on form.

In short, what this part of the evaluation showed is that attention to form can indeed be distinguished from attention to meaning in classroom practice. However, in the specific case of the Bangalore Project, there appears to have been an unacknowledged and possibly unconscious move to eliminate the *possibility* of linguistic error and the attendant possibility of a focus on form via mode of correction. Thus, there is an important question from this study for teachers involved in content-based curricula and who are interested in changing their planning and correction habits. The question is: Are they prepared to engage only in tasks which inhibit learner production in order to ensure that form does not become a focus?

Looking back

The above outline of the evaluation as it has been reported in the literature and in my PhD thesis does not tell what it was like to be involved in the evaluation: by examining the data, the various steps in analysis and the interpretations, it is possible for the reader to judge the adequacy of the various lines of inquiry. However, the nature of evaluation is not illuminated by these reports because it is not clear from them why the evaluator selected certain areas for inquiry rather than others. In experimental research, when a researcher uses a weaker design rather than a more powerful one, it is not necessary for an explanation to be offered because it is taken for granted that the more powerful design would have been chosen had the researcher been given the choice. But what is the most powerful design for an evaluation? Since the purpose of an evaluation is primarily to contribute to practice and not to theory, and since every evaluation has different goals, different audiences, and different scope, it is difficult to gauge the value of any particular design. The evaluator can serve a useful purpose by conveying the very real forces that determine the design of evaluations to the research community at large and to would-be evaluators reading for guidance.

What follows, then, is an introspective account presented in five sections: 1) the purpose of the evaluation, 2) the point-of-entry problem, 3) a lost opportunity for richer evaluation, 4) an attempt to broaden the scope of the study, and 5) an if-I-knew-then wrap-up and discussion.

The purpose of the evaluation

When the author was asked to carry out the Bangalore evaluation, it was considered that the study could usefully be reported in a doctoral thesis, under the tutorship of Dr Alan Davies (who was invited to direct the evaluation), at Edinburgh University. It was decided that the author should travel to India in January 1984 under the auspices of the British Council, who were the principal funders. Thus, in the months available to the author, initial preparations were made for the evaluation. The evaluation literature indicated that the first step was to obtain a clear brief detailing the *purposes* of the evaluation. Prabhu, the Bangalore project director, was asked for this and his reply was:

> 1   To assess, through appropriate tests, whether there is any demonstrable difference in terms of attainment in English between (i) classes of children (one each in Madras, Cuddalore and Bangalore) who have been taught (from the beginning level) on the CT project and their peers who have received normal instruction in the respective schools; (ii) a class of children (in Madras) who have been taught on the CTP for about a year (in their 4th year of English at the school) and another class in the same school which has been deliberately/carefully taught for the same period on the lines expected by the state system (i.e. the 'structural' control group).

One reaction to this would be to point out that this was not a statement of purposes (addressing the question 'why?'), but a statement for the form the evaluation would take (addressing the question 'how', which was not asked). However, the ambiguity of the term 'purpose' would perhaps explain this. What can be learned from exchanges such as this, however they may be interpreted, is that simple but profound misunderstandings reinforce the conviction that thorough negotiation must take place before an evaluation begins (a point taken up in the section *If I had known then* ... below).

However, regarding the form of the evaluation, a method comparison in the tradition of the Pennsylvania Project was formally requested (Prabhu explains, personal communication, June 1989, that he and Alan Davies had already agreed on this informally). Communication was by mail and the letter stating the 'purposes' of the evaluation, written on December 15, arrived only shortly before the evaluation was due to begin. There seemed to be no possibility of delay because the project was due to finish in the spring after the visit. It appeared to the author that there was no time to enter into further dialogue. It is recalled, however, that at the time, the L2 literature had not focused on the problems of testing comparisons, or on the need to negotiate fully the purposes of the evaluation and to let the purposes dictate the form of the inquiry. Also, the author was more familiar with 'how-to' manuals than 'why-bother?' critiques.

There was a further 'purpose' stated by Prabhu:

> 2 To examine (to the extent possible and warranted), whether the modes of assessment used in 1 above might have failed to capture adequately the learning that has taken place in the children (in either category) as indicated by classroom observation, children's class work, teachers' and observers' impressions etc.

It is reasonable in an evaluation to ask for observation and more subjective appraisal to augment other data. However, to ask for a testing comparison and then to seek to establish a further tribunal *if warranted*, adds an additional complexity. The obvious difficulty was: who decides, and on what basis, whether the tests fail to capture the learning that has taken place? In the worst scenario, proponents of the competing approaches are able to claim that the tests were biased, if the results are not to their liking. So the terms of reference given to the evaluator were : Provide us with a testing comparison, but we reserve the right to dispute the results. And why not? As argued elsewhere (Beretta 1986), it is virtually impossible to design tests that are program-fair. But the clear danger was that no matter what the results, nothing would be gained from the evaluation. Clearly, the evaluator would have been wiser to begin (instead of ending) negotiation at this stage (see Beretta 1990b), anticipating outcomes, considering what-if scenarios, debating the use that can be made of findings, and so on (cf. *If I had known then* ...). In the event, the results, although very difficult to interpret, appeared to favour the CTP, and Prabhu included the report (Beretta and Davies 1985) in his book (Prabhu 1987).

With regard to the appeal to alternative sources of enlightenment, i.e. classroom observation, no systematic recording of lessons had actually taken place, in spite, as will be seen, of advice to gather such data. However, such scattered recordings as had been made, along with teachers' and other observers' impressions, were available for use by the evaluator in phase 2 of the evaluation.

So what *was* the reason for the evaluation? One reason (and one understandably often nurtured by program directors) may have been that external evaluation would lend credibility to the project. After all, not everyone would take the statements of the proponents of methods on faith. Crookes, for example, looking at the problems of judging the value of the CTP, says that 'a point which even sympathetic commentators such as Brumfit have noted, is the lack of hard information about the success of the project' (1986:25). Richards selects the CTP as a classic example of 'the need for rigorous evaluation procedures in planning methodological innovations' (1984:19). He inveighs against the inattention to evidence:

> Unfortunately, in the Prabhu study neither objectives nor evaluation was incorporated into the program design. This makes any serious consideration of his claims impossible. Carefully designed research takes neither more nor less time and effort to conduct than poorly designed research.
>
> (Richards 1984:20)

Long (1985), in an article about task-based language teaching, simply does not mention the CTP.

Uncertainty regarding the purpose of the project itself may well have produced ambiguity about the purpose of the evaluation. This uncertainty may be characterised as follows: on the one hand, the CTP claims not to see itself as an attempt at propagation, at usurping the dominant position of structural teaching in South India; CTP teachers were ostensibly free to accept or reject or modify the approach according to a personal sense of plausibility. On the other hand, in a public debate about the CTP, an extract from a CTP lesson provokes a reaction from some seminar participants to the effect that the lesson seemed just like a structural lesson; Prabhu ripostes that 'in that case our burden of retraining is likely to be reduced' (1980:50), thereby fuelling fears of a 'takeover bid' (i.e. that the CTP aspired to be an official method).

Although they are only impressions, and not data, Davies (1983) and Brumfit (1984) both express doubts as to the intentions of the project, which the author's own visit was not able to resolve. Similarly, one of the CTP teachers recalled (cf. Beretta 1987) that she and her colleagues saw the CTP as a model offered for dissemination, and comments that this must have appeared threatening to many.

This uncertainty about what the CTP intended to achieve is reflected in the discussions of evaluation in the RIE Newsletters and Bulletins:

> what we expect at the end of this project is ... suggestions for evaluation criteria and methods, if the approach being tried out should ever be implemented on a large scale.
>
> (RIE 1979, Vol. 1 No 1:3)

Evaluation here is clearly associated with some form of future large-scale implementation. Later, in a discussion about summative evaluation, the role of conventional language tests is explored in connection with the CTP:

> Our view is that this type of evidence, while not necessary for us
> ... will probably have a role in convincing the language teacher of
> the effectiveness of our approach. We suggest, therefore, that until
> language teachers are confident of the value of the method, such
> evidence may be collected.
>
> (RIE 1980, Vol. 1 No. 4.29)

and, in the same discussion:

> 'General English' tests have some value. They will not be
> particularly difficult for our pupils, and although their overall
> validity as a test of language use is limited, such items are useful to
> persuade the 'hardened language teacher' of the effectiveness of the
> method.
>
> (RIE 1980, Vol. 1 No. 4:32)

From these two extracts, testing within a summative framework was clearly being considered from the perspective of persuading others of the effectiveness of the CTP, directly contradicting an earlier statement that 'this is a searching exercise, not a selling one; an attempt at self-assurance, not at persuading others' (Prabhu, in RIE 1979, Vol. 1 No. 2:21). In 1979 and 1980, summative evaluation appears to have been entertained, at least in part, as a means of 'persuasion' and large-scale implementation.

S. Pit Corder visited the project and was under the impression that evaluation was to be linked to propagation:

> If this approach is to gain general recognition and eventually
> perhaps be adopted as an official teaching method then it is
> necessary to be able to show to the satisfaction of those who make
> the decisions that learning as or more relevant and effective takes
> place as a result of the teaching than occurs under the present
> generally practised 'structural' approach.
>
> (Corder 1982:3)

This would suggest that Corder did not totally exclude the possibility that the CTP aspired to the role of an 'official teaching method' for large-scale implementation.

If 'self-assurance' were all that is of interest to program directors, internal evaluation would normally suffice. However, in this case, summative evaluation for the purpose of winning over doubting teachers appears also to have been a matter of interest and concern.

Thus it is likely that the inconsistencies concerning the intentions of the project were reflected in the inconsistencies evident in the attitudes towards and aspirations for the evaluation.

As will be discussed in the section, *If I had known then* ... the onus is on the evaluator to ensure (through negotiation) that such critical ambiguities are resolved *before* the evaluation begins.

The point-of-entry problem

The point-of-entry problem has been identified by Scriven (1981) and Stufflebeam (1985) as the problem of *when* a client calls for an evaluation. Typically, the evaluator is called in at the eleventh hour and is expected to work a miracle since the opportunity for most of the data collection has already passed. Just as statisticians complain that they frequently have to carry out salvage operations because they were not approached to help design a study but only to take a *post hoc* look at the figures, so evaluators can do a far better job if they can influence the way a project is set up and arrange for data collection that will be most illuminative and have the most leverage.

Bangalore is a good example of the point-of-entry problem. The project ran for five years and it was agreed by the project director, the British Council and the University of Edinburgh that the author would be engaged and sent out for the last few months of the project's life. Thus, there were no baseline data, there was no plan for systematic data collection or for ethnographic inquiry. Indeed, it became apparent on the author's arrival in India that a large number of the students who had been taught by CTP teachers had dispersed; there were four classes of children to whom a variety of things could have happened in and out of class while they were supposedly being exposed to CTP teaching; there were a small number of scattered recordings of individual lessons (which did not include regular teachers).

It could be argued that the CTP evolved through a process of trial-and-error and that the attentions of evaluators would have prematurely frozen its development. This is a fair point. However, once the project had arrived at a point where its principles and methodology were reasonably stable, if it wanted evaluation, that would have been an opportune time to seek it. Such a point, as will be seen in the following section, was in fact identified.

A lost opportunity for richer evaluation

Given that the CTP required free rein to develop its methodology, external evaluation, if required at all, would have to wait until this was perceived to be settled. Then, if external evaluation were desired, it would be most useful if the program were to start afresh in new schools so that baseline data could be collected and implementation monitored (but this would depend on the purposes of the evaluation).

One of the visitors to the project in 1982, Douglas Barnes, made recommendations very much along these lines. The CTP, he said, 'now seems to be ready to move to a more explicit account of itself' (1982:4). He advised setting the project up in new and different kinds of schools for at least four years; in addition, he recommended that detailed illuminative and summative evaluations be set in motion. The duration, the range of schools and the illuminative elements of the evaluation would promote extrapolation by potential users of the project, while the summative element would attempt to offer a more objective appraisal (for potential administrators, for instance).

Barnes clearly had in mind a rather large operation and much of his proposal may have been unfeasible. In the event, although the project did continue with four fresh schools, none of his recommendations was implemented. Even in four schools, they would have been worth following. Whatever the reasons, from the point of view of evaluation, an opportunity was missed at this juncture.

An attempt to broaden the scope of the study

When phase 1 of the evaluation was completed, a second phase was considered, as a testing comparison alone was clearly inadequate. An initial proposal for an observational study, which involved re-activating the project, was simply not viable. Since there were some data extant in the form of transcripts, and since the project teachers could still be reached, it was decided that such avenues should be explored. Thus the phase 2 studies reported above were conceived.

Phase 1 was sought by the project director; phase 2 by the evaluator who wished to ensure that the evaluation was more complete.

If I had known then ...

... what I know now, how would I have conducted the Bangalore evaluation? On the grounds that the timing was too late and the purpose too ambiguous, I might have politely declined.

But if I had accepted, and if I had known then what I know now, I would probably have tried to persuade the CTP team that a far more substantial evaluation could be carried out if the project teaching were started afresh at new schools (re-presenting much of Barnes' advice). This would permit such data as could serve a useful purpose to be collected (baseline information, changing attitudes, systematic observation, and so on).

But all of this would depend on the pre-evaluation negotiation. First of all, I would have ensured that the purposes of the evaluation were not left in doubt. I would have oriented the initial discussion to a consideration of what *use* could be made of the findings. Even if it had meant that I arrived in India with no brief and two or three months to accomplish it, I would still have pursued the pre-evaluation discussion in order to arrive at a clearly articulated agreement about the use that was to be made of findings (and thus what kinds of information would have leverage and whether or not such data could be collected), about who the audience was, about who would be affected by the evaluation (i.e. who the stakeholders were), and about deadlines for reports.

I would have stressed the need for funders, director, teachers, school principals, proponents of structural teaching, and other stakeholders to discuss quite what they wanted from an evaluation. The aim would have been to arrive at a point where everyone knew precisely what they were going to get, when they were going to get it, in what form, from whom, and exactly what they were going to do with it. There would be no mystery, no surprises. And there would be no remaining ambiguity about the reasons for the evaluation ever having taken place.

The question of a testing comparison would probably have been abandoned, particularly since implementation of neither program had been monitored in any principled fashion. It would have been explained that results from such an inquiry would not be very helpful. They would neither indicate that a teaching approach worked, nor even that the teaching approach existed. After all, there were many rival plausible explanations for any differences in student performance and there was no longer any way of knowing if the CTP was implemented (to what degree, if at all, by whom, etc.).

However, this is not to say that outcomes would have been of no interest. For instance, if the project had wished to specify goals, it would have been possible to use those goals in constructing criterion-referenced tests.

I would have made clear to all concerned that no theory of language learning was going to be enhanced by the evaluation. In itself, this may have been enough to shift attention to more constructive debate about what an evaluation *can* achieve and what is desired in any particular case.

If the Bangalore evaluation teaches one thing above all, it is that in an evaluation capable of being utilised, the real action takes place before anyone lifts a finger to collect data.

Program developers can assist in the evaluation enterprise by taking the pre-evaluation seriously and by calling for evaluation either at the design stage or at a time when the program is clearly articulated. The terms of reference which emerge from such pre-evaluation ensure a *clearly stated purpose* for the evaluation, a clear use to which the findings can be put and by whom, and ensure that the principal stakeholders' interests are those which are served.

Evaluators, like all researchers, can maximise the utilisation of findings by focusing attention on the design and scope of the inquiry *a priori* rather than making it up as we go along.

Of course, partisan discord can never be silenced (Cronbach *et al.* 1980:9). Evaluations take place in the real world and not in laboratories, and thus the results are always tentative, judgmental and incomplete; they can never remotely approach inescapable conclusions. Evaluation cannot snuff out controversy; partisanship is not endangered in the slightest. However, if all sides agree to a well-negotiated charter, findings are more likely to be utilised, and evaluation has played its part.

Appendix 1

Sample items from the five tests used in Phase I of the evaluation

1 *Structure*: This test consisted of a series of multiple-choice items. The structures were drawn from the Karnataka and Tamil Nadu State syllabuses. Example:

> We ＿＿＿ going to school today. It's Sunday.
> a. aren't   b. not   c. isn't   d. don't

2 *Contextualised grammar*: This comprised items where the testee was required to fill in the blank with one word. Example:

> Through the window I can see my father. He can't see me because he ＿＿＿ looking at the road. He is going to the market.

3 *Dictation*: A short passage was dictated in the following way:

> (i) reading of whole passage at conversational speed; e.g.
> I have two brothers and three sisters. We all go to the same school. Sometimes we take the bus. Today we are going by bus. After school we will walk home.
>
> (ii) one reading only of each segment at conversational speed;
>
> (iii) final reading of whole passage at conversational speed.

4 *Listening/reading comprehension*: This required testees to read, for example, a hotel advertisement and to write answers to spoken questions. Example:

> Hotel Ashok: One room only Rs 150 a day! Bring your family! In our grounds you can enjoy cricket, football, and Kabbadi. We have a good restaurant. English and Indian meals. Film show every night

at 8 p.m. Write to: Hotel Ashok, 74 Ghandi Street, Delhi. Tel: 883921.

Instructions: Listen carefully to the questions. You will hear each question twice. Answer the questions, using the information from the advertisement. E.g. (spoken question): Where is the hotel?

5 *Task-based*: The test was a representative sample of the tasks used in CTP lessons. For example, solving problems related to a timetable and to a calendar.

Appendix 2

CTP Teacher Implementation Categories

The CTP Teacher Implementation Categories, based on a close reading of the CTP literature and the Levels of Use chart (in Loucks, Newlove and Hall 1975), are as follows:

KNOWLEDGE: What the teacher knows about the nature of the CTP.
Level 1: Has only limited general knowledge of the CTP.
Level 2: Has sufficient knowledge of the CTP for appropriate and stable use.
Level 3: Has sufficient knowledge to evaluate the use of the CTP and to seek modifications.

ACQUIRING INFORMATION: The teacher solicits information about the CTP in a variety of ways, including discussion, review of published descriptions and commentaries, sharing plans and problems.

Level 1: Makes little attempt to find out more about the CTP; discusses the CTP only with the director; discusses only discipline and classroom management; asks for ready-made materials.
Level 2: Reads the Newsletters and Bulletins relating to the CTP; attends seminars; discusses with other CTP teachers; discusses the effects of the CTP and the development of own materials; observes other CTP classes.
Level 3: Tries to find out ways of improving the CTP; discusses with both CTP and non-CTP teachers; discusses possible modifications of the CTP; compares strengths and weaknesses of own (and others') teaching and seeks modifications to improve pupil learning.

ASSESSING: Examines the effects of use of the CTP; this could be an informal mental assessment or actual data collection.

Level 1: Only informal reports of the impact of the CTP on students' attitudes and linguistic performance.

Level 2: Checks the impact of the CTP through in-house achievement tests.

Level 3: Examines the strengths and weaknesses of the CTP through some form of comparative testing (not just achievement testing).

PERFORMING: Describes personal use of the CTP.

Level 1: Does not develop own materials; perceives CTP as requiring a great deal of time and effort; finds the transition from structural to CTP teaching difficult; is confused about the treatment of error; evinces a tendency to focus on language form; simply goes through ready-made tasks with little sense of planning.

Level 2: Develops own materials with reference to a 'model'; feels no great effort or stress in implementing the CTP; puts into practice perceptions of CTP principles out of a sense of conviction, or discipleship, or concern about experimental contamination; treats error according to published CTP perceptions; planning involves constant modification of the challenge level of the tasks based on daily feedback from students.

Level 3: Develops own materials, consciously deviating from the 'model'; develops pedagogic procedures, introducing own ideas; tries out modification of the CTP to improve pupil learning.

Appendix 3

Modified Stages of Concern Questionnaire (SoCQ)

1 I was concerned about learners' attitudes towards the CTP.
2 I knew of some other approaches that might have worked better.
3 I did not know anything about the CTP.
4 I was concerned about not having enough time to organise myself each day.
5 I wanted to help other teachers in their use of the CTP.
6 I had very limited knowledge of the CTP.
7 I wanted to know what effect the CTP would have on my professional status.
8 I was concerned about keeping all of the learners involved.
9 I was concerned about revising my use of the CTP.

10 I wanted to develop working relationships with other teachers using the CTP.
11 I was concerned about how the CTP would affect learners.
12 I was not interested in the CTP.
13 I wanted to know whether my involvement with the CTP would help or hinder my career.
14 I wanted to discuss the possibility of using the CTP.
15 I wanted to know what materials and training would be available if I decided to adopt the CTP.
16 I was concerned about my inability to manage all that the CTP required.
17 I wanted to know how my teaching was supposed to change.
18 I wanted to familiarise other teachers or schools with the benefits of the CTP.
19 I was concerned about evaluating my impact on learners.
20 I wanted to revise the CTP's instructional approach.
21 I was completely occupied with other things.
22 I wanted to modify my use of the CTP in view of the effect it was having on my learners.
23 Although I did not know anything about the CTP, I was interested in teaching methods in general.
24 I wanted to get my learners enthusiastic about their involvement in the CTP.
25 I was concerned about discipline and organisation in the classroom.
26 I wanted to know what using the CTP would require in the immediate future.
27 I wanted to co-ordinate my effort with others in order to maximise the effects of the CTP.
28 I wanted to have more information on time and energy commitments required by the CTP.
29 I wanted to know how other people were using the CTP.
30 I was not interested in learning more about the CTP.
31 I want to know how to supplement or enhance the CTP.
32 I wanted to use feedback from learners to change the CTP.
33 I wanted to know how my role would change when using the CTP.
34 Preparing for CTP lessons was taking too much of my time.
35 I wanted to know how the CTP was better than structural teaching.

Appendix 4

Treatment categories based on Chaudron's (1977) framework

IGNORE: Teacher ignores learner's error and goes on to another topic.

ACCEPTANCE: Simple approving or accepting word (often as a sign of reception of the utterance), but teacher may proceed to correct an error.

ATTENTION: An attention getter, like 'think'.

NEGATION: Teacher shows rejection of part or all of learned utterance.

PROVIDE: Teacher provides the correct answer when learner has been unable to or when no response is offered.

REPETITION with NO CHANGE: Teacher repeats learner utterance with no change of error nor omission of error.

REPETITION with CHANGE and EMPHASIS: Teacher repeats learner utterance with no change of error, but emphasis locates or indicates fact of error.

REPETITION with CHANGE: Usually, teacher simply adds correction and continues to other topics.

REPETITION with CHANGE and EMPHASIS: Teacher adds emphasis to stress location of error and its correct formulation.

EXPLANATION: Teacher provides information as to cause of error, possibly including a generalisation of the type of error.

REPEAT: Teacher requests learner to repeat utterance with the intention of having the learner self-correct.

LOOP: Teacher honestly needs a replay of learner utterance due to lack of clarity or certainty of its form.

PROMPT: Teacher uses a lead-in cue to get learner to repeat utterance, possibly at point of error; possible slight rising intonation.

CLUE: Teacher reaction provides learner with isolation of type of error, or the nature of its immediate correction, without actually providing the correction. E.g. further examples of the same error type may be given.

ORIGINAL QUESTION: Teacher repeats the original question that led to the incorrect response.

ALTERED QUESTION: Teacher alters original question syntactically but not semantically.

QUESTIONS: Numerous ways of asking for a new response, but not just original or altered questions, i.e. when error occurs, a new line of questioning is taken up.

TRANSFER: Teacher asks another student or group of students to provide correction.

ACCEPTANCE*: Teacher shows approval of learner utterance and then repeats the error apparently confirming that it is correct.

VERIFICATION: Teacher attempts to make sure that the class has understood the correction.

References

Barnes, D. 1982. *Report to British Council on a visit to Madras and Bangalore.* Mimeo, British Council, London.

Beretta, A. 1986. Program-fair language teaching evaluation. *TESOL Quarterly* 20(3): 431–44.

Beretta, A. 1987. Evaluation of a language-teaching project in South India. Ph.D. thesis, University of Edinburgh.

Beretta, A. 1989. Attention to form or meaning?: error treatment in the Bangalore Project. *TESOL Quarterly* 23: 283–303.

Beretta, A. 1990a. Implementation of the Bangalore Project. *Applied Linguistics* 11: 321–37.

Beretta, A. 1990b. The program evaluator: the ESL researcher without portfolio. *Applied Linguistics* 11: 1–15.

Beretta, A. and A. Davies. 1985. Evaluation of the Bangalore Project. *English Language Teaching Journal* 39: 121–7.

Brumfit, C. J. 1984. The Bangalore procedural syllabus. *English Language Teaching Journal* 38(4). 233–41.

Chaudron, C. 1977. A descriptive model of discourse in the corrective treatment of learners' errors. *Language Learning* 27: 29–46.

Corder, S. P. 1982. Report on visit to Madras. Mimeo, British Council, London.

Cronbach, L. J. 1982. *Designing evaluations of educational and social programs.* San Francisco: Jossey Bass.

Cronbach, L. J., S. R. Ambron, S. M. Dornbusch, R. D. Hess, R. C. Hornik, D. C. Phillips, D. F. Walker and S. S. Weiner. 1980. *Toward reform of program evaluation.* San Francisco: Jossey-Bass.

Crookes, G. 1986. Task classification: a cross-disciplinary review. Technical Report No. 4, University of Hawaii at Manoa.

Davies, A. 1983. Evaluation and the Bangalore/Madras Communicational Teaching Project. Unpublished manuscript, University of Edinburgh, Department of Applied Linguistics.

Fuller, F. F. 1969. Concerns of teachers: a developmental conceptualisation. *American Educational Research Journal* 6(2): 207–26.

Hall, G. E. and S. F. Loucks. 1977. A developmental model for determining whether the treatment is actually implemented. *American Educational Research Journal* 14 (3): 263–76.

Hall, G. E., A. George and W. W. Rutherford, 1977. Measuring stages of concern about the innovation: a manual for use of the SoC questionnaire. Austin, Texas: Research and Development Center for Teacher Education, University of Texas. (ERIC Document Reproduction Service No. ED 147 342)

Johnson, K. 1982. *Communicative syllabus design and methodology.* Oxford: Pergamon Press.

Krashen, S. D. and T. D. Terrell. 1983. *The Natural Approach: language acquisition in the classroom.* Oxford: Pergamon Press.

Long, M. H. 1985. A role for instruction in second language acquisition: task-based language teaching. In K. Hyltenstam and M. Pienemann (Eds.) *Modelling and assessing second language acquisition.* London: Multilingual Matters.

Loucks, S. F., B. W. Newlove, and G. E. Hall. 1975. *Measuring levels of use of the innovation: a manual for trainers, interviewers and raters.* Austin, Texas: The Research and Development Center for Teacher Education, University of Texas.

Prabhu, N. S. 1980. Theoretical background to the Bangalore project. In RIE Bulletin 4 (1): 17–26.

Prabhu, N. S. 1982. The Communicational Teaching Project, South India. Mimeo, British Council, Madras.

Prabhu, N. S. 1987. *Second language pedagogy.* Oxford: Oxford University Press.

Richards, J. C. 1984. The secret life of methods. *TESOL Quarterly* 18: 7–23.

RIE (Regional Institute of English, South India). 1979. *Newsletter. Vol. 1. No. 2.* Bangalore: Author.

RIE (Regional Institute of English, South India). 1980. *Newsletter. Vol. 1, No. 4.* Bangalore: Author.

RIE (Regional Institute of English, South India). 1980. *Bulletin. Vol. 4. No. 1.* Bangalore: Author.

Scherer, G. A. C. and M. Wertheimer. 1964. *A psycholinguistic experiment in foreign language teaching.* New York: McGraw-Hill.

Scriven, M. S. 1981. *Evaluation Thesaurus.* Inverness, CA: Edgepress. 3rd ed.

Smith, P. D. 1970. *A comparison of the cognitive and audio-lingual approaches to foreign language instruction: the Pennsylvania Foreign Language Project.* Philadelphia: The Center for Curriculum Development, Inc.

Stallings, J. 1975. Implications and child effects of teaching practices in Follow Through classrooms. *Monographs of the Society for Research in Child Development* 40, No. 7–8 (Serial no. 163).

Stufflebeam, D. L. 1985. Coping with the point of entry problem in evaluating projects. *Studies in Educational Evaluation* 11: 123–9.

Wang, M. C., M. Nojan, C. D. Strom and H. J. Walberg. 1984. The utility of degree of implementation measures in program implementation and evaluation research. *Curriculum Inquiry* 14 (3): 249–86.

Woods, A., P. Fletcher and A. Hughes. 1986. *Statistics in language studies.* Cambridge: Cambridge University Press.

Editors' postscript to Beretta

Alan Beretta's chapter is interesting for a number of reasons. The first is because it provides an account of an attempted evaluation of a project – the Bangalore Communicational Teaching Project – that had achieved considerable fame in the early to mid 1980s. This fame was partly a result of the stream of visitors from the UK and elsewhere who wrote articles describing the project and extolling its achievements and potential. It was also at least partly because the project was widely (at least in applied linguistics circles) regarded as being a bold experiment in applying theoretical principles in a practical language teaching setting. Yet, as Beretta illustrates, the project was criticised for not attempting a thoroughgoing evaluation of its work. Thus, any evaluation of a project that had received considerable 'media' attention must be important, and Beretta does not disappoint, precisely because he attempts a 'warts-and-all' account of the evaluation.

Which brings us to the second reason why the chapter is of interest: as Beretta himself says, most evaluation reports give the impression of a flawless design, problemless administration and the production of a non-controversial report. Yet most evaluations are simply not like that: in the real, messy, political, ever-changing world of education, educational politics and personalities, compromises are the order of the day, where ideal designs for evaluation studies have to be sacrificed at the altar of undefined aims, where hopes and fears abound, and where evaluation methodologies and foci are arrived at all too often 'on the hoof' – in a rush, without deliberation or negotiation and in some confusion. Hindsight is not only the most exact science; it is also the discipline best able to give the impression of order, rationality and careful planning.

The real world is less organised, more vague, less detached and more evangelical. In the real world, innovations are often the result of individual vision, energy and commitment, not rational planning and experimentation. Which brings us to the third reason why this chapter is so valuable. It reveals a real world in which evaluation is not built into a curricular innovation from its inception, where the aims of the evaluation that is eventually established appear to be undefined and contradictory, and where it is no surprise to discover that misunderstandings, missed opportunities, missing information and problematic evaluation designs appear to prevail. However, the reader should be perfectly clear that this is not a criticism of a particular project: this is, in the experience of very many, what evaluation looks like 'out there', rather than in the sanitised reports and theories of 'experts'. Beretta recounts his experience, and provides useful 'lessons' that he has learned, especially with respect to the need to clarify aims, objectives, methods and content of evaluations before they get under way.

This theme returns in the final chapter of the book, but it is perhaps salutary to remind ourselves that the proposed negotiation and hoped-for eventual agreement does not always emerge from preliminary discussions about an evaluation project. In the real, messy world, the evaluator may be forced to compromise, to agree to undertake an evaluation with no clear contract, no clear idea of what is required and why, nor any useful guidelines from the sponsors themselves. This is often simply because the sponsors – and other stakeholders – do not necessarily know what they want, which is why they brought in an 'expert' in the first place. It may be that what they want is for the evaluation to reveal what they themselves believe to be the case: that the project is a success, and adverse comment is certainly not expected. Even if they give the impression of not knowing exactly what they want of an evaluation, they often *do* know what they do *not* want, and that is: exposure, public criticism, blame, accusations and the like. So an evaluation that questions the beliefs of stakeholders about achievement may be perceived as unwarranted criticism and intrusion: in such circumstances, another evaluator is sent for!

To believe that this will not occur is naive: egos and time and effort are invested in curricular innovation and development, and only an insensitive evaluator would not expect defensiveness on the part of those being evaluated. Evaluation, quite simply, can be face-threatening, and we need to take every opportunity to reduce its threatening nature, and make it more acceptable to all concerned.

A fourth reason why Beretta's chapter is of importance is because it shows reasonably clearly how important it is that evaluations scratch below the surface of their 'results'. In the Bangalore context, the finding that CTP teachers did not correct error appears to be an impressive result, until one is told that more probing study showed that the children were simply not given the opportunity to produce errors, hence there was less error treatment. Similarly with respect to the enquiry into teacher commitment and understanding: a less sensitive evaluation would not have investigated these variables and might have concluded, because the test evidence showed an apparent advantage for the CTP, that one might be justified in recommending a wider adoption of a CTP-type programme. Yet such a recommendation would have been misguided, since further analysis appears to show that the 'success' of the project may owe at least as much to the commitment, evangelical zeal almost, of the non-regular teachers. Regular teachers, uncommitted to the particular project, show more anxiety and confusion, less commitment, and less understanding, than the atypical non-regular teachers. Any attempt to introduce the CTP more widely, without taking account of these special circumstances, could be inviting disaster on a large scale.

Beretta's chapter is, therefore, central to the theme of this volume, which is that evaluation is important, and needs to be taken into account from the beginning of a project; yet at the same time it is not an exact science; it is exposed to accusations of interference, lack of understanding of circumstances, and partiality of method and interpretation if the results are not as expected. Above all, the brief of the evaluation needs to be carefully and fully discussed, contingency plans need to be laid in the event of unexpected problems and developments, and the purpose and likely outcomes of an evaluation should be as clearly defined, and agreed, as possible in advance of the study itself.

PART III

Guidelines for the evaluation of language education

J. Charles Alderson

The aim of this final chapter is to bring together the various threads running through the book on what might be or are more and less appropriate ways to conduct evaluations of language education. In addition, it is hoped that it will provide would-be evaluators with guidance on how to go about designing and implementing an evaluation (the sort of guidance that Palmer – this volume – wishes had been available to him). The chapter aims to suggest answers to the perennial WH questions in evaluation: who, what, when, how, how long, to evaluate and to point the way forward to further developments (and hopefully improvements) in the methodology and practice of language education evaluation.

The organisation of the chapter follows the usual and logical stages in the conduct of an evaluation: planning, implementing, interpreting, reporting, using, evaluating. Inevitably, the first section, on the planning of an evaluation, is the longest, since this is the most important stage: it is difficult to adjust later for mistakes or omissions at this stage. However, as this chapter is intended to provide practical guidance, to relate to the real, imperfect and under-resourced world in which evaluations are usually conducted, it will be recognised that perfect planning and design are both rare and unlikely, and therefore attention will also be paid to how imperfections in design can be catered for at later stages.

The reader should, however, beware of concluding from this chapter that there is One Best Way of conducting an evaluation. There is not. Much depends upon the purposes of the evaluation, the nature of the programme or project being evaluated, the individuals involved – their personalities and their interrelationships – and on the timescales and resources involved. This emphatically does not mean that 'anything goes': it is essential that evaluations be conducted in a principled, systematic and explicit manner. The reader should also be warned that evaluations will not reveal The Truth about a programme or project. It is the belief of this author (Alderson 1986a and 1986b) that there is no One Truth waiting to be discovered by evaluation. Rather, a multitude of 'truths' or interpretations can be constructed and presented for inspection by interested parties, and this can be done more or less thoroughly, convincingly or impartially. It also follows from this that the search for a completely 'objective' evaluation is fruitless. No evaluation is ever objective: the evaluators, their sponsors and the objects of the evaluation all have perspectives and understandings which are subjective. These will inevitably influence the design, implementation and interpretation of any evaluation. The best we can hope for is pooled intersubjectivity and reduced or neutralised partiality.

Planning an evaluation

Purpose: Why?

Evaluations are requested for a variety of reasons, and the most important question that has to be addressed at this stage (and not lost sight of at others) is: *Why is this evaluation required?*

The aim might be to convince a sceptical language teaching profession that a particular method 'works' and should be introduced more widely. The aim might be to investigate whether a project has produced 'value for money' – to satisfy government that taxpayers' money has been wisely spent. Or the aim might be to contribute to institutional decisions on whether to discard or continue a programme/ methodology etc.

It is impossible to provide guidance to would-be evaluators in this area. It would be unduly arrogant to assert that evaluations must have one of a fixed set of purposes. It is, however, possible to indicate the sorts of purposes that evaluations might have, or have had in some past project, or that evaluations 'typically' have. It is, for example, possibly instructive to reflect upon the purposes of the case studies in this book:

The purpose of Palmer's study was to show whether a particular theory of language learning was correct.

The purpose of Ross's study was to establish which of a rival set of language teaching methodologies was most successful.

The purpose of Mitchell's study was to discover whether a particular approach to bilingual education should be continued and extended.

The purpose of Coleman's study was to establish whether the needs of a given set of students had been met by a particular innovation.

The purpose of Alderson and Scott's study was to identify the effects of a particular approach to second language education and to inform decisions on its future nature.

The purpose of Beretta's study was initially to compare the value and effects of an innovative approach to language education over more traditional approaches, and later to provide information that might be useful to anyone interested in implementing similar approaches.

It is arguable that purposes which assess more specific and less global questions or issues are more likely to gather usable, interpretable information than more general purposes. Evaluations that purport to evaluate language teaching methods in general are more likely to result in uninterpretable results than those which investigate the outcomes of particular programmes, with particular teachers and materials and in specific settings. The purposes of the latter kind of evaluation are more likely to be easily defined, and therefore easier to evaluate. In general, one could argue that evaluations which are intended to gather information which will help decision makers decide on the allocation of resources are, other things being equal (which of course they never are), more utilisable than evaluations aiming to substantiate claims about the superiority of particular approaches or methods. Nevertheless, many evaluations, as this book bears witness, do indeed attempt to investigate or justify one approach or another. Given the frequency with which the language teaching profession is bombarded with claims for one approach or another, there is clearly a need for the evaluation of such claims, if only in order to establish clearly that wide-ranging, global claims are hopelessly naive or harmful, in that they ignore the complexity of the interaction of a host of variables in the implementation of any method.

Bearing in mind this word of caution, one might in general terms wish to say that a list of purposes for evaluations might look something like this:
to decide whether a programme has had the intended effect
to identify what effect a programme has had
to determine whether a programme has provided value for money
to vindicate a decision
to justify future courses of action
to compare approaches/ methodologies/ textbooks/ etc.
to identify areas for improvement in an ongoing programme
to show the positive achievements of teachers and pupils
to motivate teachers
to allay suspicions among parents or sponsors

Such are the 'official' purposes of evaluations. However, there are other, more hidden agendas that are often discernible, even in the case studies in this volume:
One party is determined to show that they/he/she have been justified in advocating and implementing a particular course of action.
The initiator of the project being evaluated may wish to advertise his/her project by having the evaluation proclaim its achievements.
The sponsor may need to show others that earlier decisions were correct, or those of predecessors incorrect.

The would-be evaluator clearly needs to be wary of the existence of such hidden agendas, and would be well advised to attempt to discern their nature. However, it may also be the case that the evaluator might have hidden agendas: he or she might be conducting the evaluation in order to earn a PhD, or in order to earn or develop a reputation as a competent evaluator, or in order to earn money, to travel, or to publish articles and further his/her career. In such cases, other stakeholders need to be on their guard, too.

The point is that some purposes will be more evident than others. Those designing an evaluation must be alert to the fact that there will be more and less explicit purposes for an evaluation. It is always wise to attempt to discover the 'hidden agendas' as early in one's evaluation as possible, although evidently it will equally be difficult to make these explicit or to confirm that one's interpretation of others' purposes is indeed correct.

However, it should be emphasised that even when one has identified the purpose of a particular evaluation, explicit and implicit, it is not the case that a given course of action, a particular evaluation design, will flow from that purpose. Clearly, some purposes require particular evaluation designs. Comparing two or more methodologies will require data to be gathered on each of the methodologies involved, and identifying value for money will involve the identification of suitable econometric criteria. However, although purpose is important, there is no one-to-one relationship between the purpose of an evaluation and the form the evaluation should or could take. This will appear frustrating to the novice (and indeed experienced) evaluator, and the purpose of this chapter is to suggest ways in which evaluations might be carried out more rather than less satisfactorily. But what follows from an identification of purpose will depend upon other factors discussed in this chapter, as well as from the evaluator's own skills, personality and preferences, and on the outcome of the negotiations that should take place between the various parties to an evaluation.

Although it is a truism to declare that one's purpose determines one's decisions and actions, it is somewhat naive to assume that this is always true. In a rational world, this might be the case, but in the real, emotional world in which we live, purposes are not always reflected in action. This may be because purposes are unrealistic – requiring more resources than are available, depending upon greater knowledge than is currently possessed – or misguided – ignorant of developments and understandings achieved elsewhere, ignorant of (legitimate or illegitimate) constraints from predictable or unpredictable sources.

Audience: Who For?

It is clearly the case that different parties involved in what is being evaluated – the 'stakeholders' – may have different purposes. Those financing the evaluation may wish to show value for money, or may be convinced and intend that a particular outcome will result, or that a particular course of action should follow the evaluation. For example, sponsors may have already decided to prolong a project in a particular form in advance of the evaluation, and require the evaluation to confirm the wisdom of their decision. Teachers, however, may wish to show that the project being evaluated has had a clear negative effect, and that it should therefore cease.

In other words, *who the evaluation is for* is a key consideration at the planning stage. It is common to assert that 'he who pays the piper calls the tune', and to argue that those who are financing the evaluation (and most evaluations are financed, directly or indirectly) should determine the nature of the evaluation. However, life is rarely so simple and there are also important ethical issues that evaluators have to face. Is it in fact the case that those in financial control have the right to control how an evaluation should be carried out and what aspects of content will be investigated? If the sponsors' purposes conflict with the purposes of others involved, is there not a need to resolve such conflicts, or at least to make all parties involved aware of their existence? Pragmatically, if some parties disagree with the aims of the evaluation as imposed by the sponsors, they may simply refuse to co-operate with the planning, the data gathering or the interpretation. They are also likely to ignore or frustrate any recommendations resulting from the evaluation with which they disagree.

A disagreement may extend beyond the purposes of the evaluation. The sponsors may have no ideas on how or what to evaluate, or may be reluctant to reveal them. However, they may also have very strong views on these topics, yet the evaluator may feel that the sponsor's views are too narrow, misinformed or too naive. She or he may feel that the evaluation should also aim to educate the sponsor in the possibility, acceptability or desirability of other methods of evaluation, or of other purposes for evaluations. This may also be true for other parties in an evaluation: the evaluators may feel that teachers are also misguided in their views on how or what to evaluate, or are unduly defensive about being observed in class, or having their learners take tests.

The views and values of the different stakeholders in an evaluation may vary considerably, and must therefore be reconciled to some extent. It will usually be the case that compromise is necessary to resolve potential conflict, but it is usually wisest, if at all possible, to identify such potential sources of conflict as early as possible in the design stage, and to seek through negotiation to get agreement on the nature and use of the evaluation. Later sections of this chapter address the issue of how reconciliation might be achieved but it will always be the case that each evaluation has to reach its own unique compromise in the light of the prevailing circumstances.

The Evaluator: Who?

So far, we have used the term 'evaluator(s)' without defining who is to be involved. However, this is an issue that needs some discussion. In some settings, it may be the case that only one person is to evaluate a programme. However, it is frequently the case that more than one person is involved, and that a team of evaluators or associated staff is required. In both cases, however, the issue arises: who is to evaluate? In particular, is the evaluation to be conducted by someone from within the programme, or by an outsider?

Alderson and Scott (this volume) address this issue, and make it clear that they believe that both insiders and outsiders should be involved collaboratively in conducting evaluations, and this at all stages in the process. They also acknowledge the difficulties presented by such an approach. However, one can certainly envisage situations in which it is simply not acceptable that an outsider be asked to evaluate a programme – because there are particular sensitivities involved which cannot or ought not to be revealed to outsiders. Equally, one can envisage situations in which the contribution of an outsider alone is crucial – perhaps because insiders are deeply divided amongst themselves as to the benefits of a programme, or because an impartial view is required, or because the requisite expertise does not exist within a programme. (It is, however, the experience of this author that not all outsiders asked to evaluate programmes possess the requisite expertise either, and that insiders often have an unacknowledged expertise, not necessarily in the technicalities of evaluation, but in relevant and related areas.) What is indisputable is that insiders have an experience and a knowledge of a programme that can be invaluable to an evaluation.

The commonest reasons given for involving outsiders alone in an evaluation are that only then can objectivity be guaranteed, or that they are perceived as having greater credibility, or that they may offer a 'fresh' perspective. It may indeed be the case that outsiders can have great professional or public credibility and may see the issues in a different (not necessarily clearer) light than those on the inside. This different perspective can often be very valuable to insiders. However, it will be clear to the reader that the present author does not believe that objectivity is ever guaranteed: all the decisions involved in conducting an evaluation require judgements to be made, and these judgements are inevitably subjective, however well informed by expertise and experience and however impartial with respect to the particular evaluation being conducted. Some indeed believe, as we have seen in Part I, that even impartiality is impossible, and that therefore the most honest solution to the issue of who is to evaluate is to select a number of evaluators, who have known biases or stances, and require them to argue for their

K

particular interpretation and recommendations. This is known as the 'advocacy' method of evaluation, and its rationale would imply that there is a strong case for including insiders in an evaluation, as advocates of a particular perspective.

Interestingly, a version of advocacy evaluation seems to be being practised when a further evaluation is commissioned after one evaluation study has been submitted, and its findings need to be confirmed or disconfirmed. This is a common practice in British-funded ELT projects overseas, when one evaluator's (or JIJOE's – Alderson and Scott, this volume) report is followed by a further visit to a project by other evaluators from the British Council, from the Overseas Development Administration or from other outside evaluators.

Another issue related to the question of 'who conducts the evaluation' is: what expertise is required of an evaluator and his or her team? The argument for including insiders in an evaluation is that they possess particular knowledge of the programme. What qualifies an outsider, especially if that person has no knowledge of the programme?

Knowledge or experience of similar programmes in similar settings (educational, social, cultural, geographical) would clearly be of value. Expertise in the particular methods of evaluation thought to be needed in a specific evaluation might be thought to be important. (Thus, if language tests were to be used, a language testing 'expert' might be of use. If classrooms needed to be observed, someone with expertise in that area would be of advantage.) Experience in evaluating programmes or projects in general would certainly be relevant, as would some academic or professional qualification in the area of language education evaluation. However, perhaps equally important would be an established track-record of successful evaluations: that is (and we will return to this later), evaluations that were delivered on time, were relevant, commanded general agreement and whose recommendations were acted upon. Known sympathy with or hostility towards the philosophy, aims or methods might be of particular importance in some settings. Experience and qualifications in language education or applied linguistics would be an advantage. All too frequently, however, being a recognised 'figure' in the field of language education generally is taken to be the sole criterion for the selection of an evaluator. Certainly such a reputation would add weight to the findings and may well influence utilisation, but it is no guarantee of their validity.

In addition, the evaluation team may well need expertise in other fields: the present author has been involved in evaluations of language education that have included people with expertise in management, economics, and sociology. Statistical or ethnographic skills may be needed, as may particular linguistic abilities, or the ability to communicate well in reports or in public relations, as well as attributes like persuasiveness, diplomacy and tact. There will certainly be a need for people with secretarial and administrative skills, and in a relatively large project there may also be a need for people with the skills of leadership and person management.

Content: What?

There is a wide range of content that an evaluation can focus on, from the learning outcomes of the programme, in terms of the knowledge or behaviour of the learners, to attitudes to the language, its speakers and culture; from attitudes to aspects of the programme itself, to general aptitude for further study; from the cost of a programme, to a programme's impact on its institutional or social setting. In general terms, the content of any evaluation must relate to its purpose, and also to the objectives of the particular programme. Indeed, it used to be a commonplace to assert that an evaluator must assess the extent to which a programme's objectives have been achieved. As was discussed in Part I, it is currently usual for evaluators to take a less dogmatic, indeed sceptical attitude to the evaluation of objectives. Some objectives may be more observable or measurable than others. Some objectives may have proved to be inappropriate and were therefore abandoned, whilst others were developed during the programme. Most programmes are dynamic, which means that objectives are likely to become more or less important through the life of a programme. Finally, focusing upon objectives stated in a programme document may lead the evaluator to overlook important outcomes which were unexpected.

Despite these reservations about the value of focusing exclusively upon a programme's objectives, it is likely to be the case that any evaluator will have to identify the objectives of a programme (bearing in mind that different stakeholders might well have different objectives) and will at least have to bear them in mind when drawing up a list of areas to be evaluated.

The list of possible areas of content is very long (as well as different for different programmes). The list in Celani *et al.* (1988), referred to briefly in Alderson and Scott's chapter, is an example of such a long list that in practice proved to be too long. However, it is perhaps useful to identify general areas that are likely to need evaluating on most evaluations:

What were the outcomes of the programme? (e.g. what did students learn? how did behaviours change?) What were the attitudes and opinions of the participants (teachers and administrators as well as students)? Did these change?

What impact did the programme have on the context it was intended to influence? (e.g. did students gain more or better employment?) Were the community's attitudes to language education of importance? What was the suitability of the programme to its educational and social context? (Was it a foreign implant based on an alien or inappropriate educational philosophy? Was it locally derived, emerging from the needs and perceptions of teachers/ students/ parents/ administrators?)

What was the process of the programme? (What actually happened in classrooms? Was the proposed programme actually implemented, or did it look rather different in practice from the intentions of its designers, and rather similar to other, supposedly different programmes? What materials were developed and how were they used or adapted? What activities were devised?)

What were the teacher-training implications and achievements? (Were teachers well qualified and experienced? Did they need and receive special preparation/enthusiasm/skills for the programme?)

What were the resource implications of the programme, and were these recognised and the resources supplied? (Money for teacher training, materials, access to facilities, travel to seminars etc.) Were libraries/ resource centres/equipment needed and supplied?

What was the relationship between the cost of the programme (to each and all stakeholders) and the benefit derived (again, by each and all stakeholders and participants)? Was value for money achieved? Did the effort exceed the value of the outcomes?

It is hopefully clear that a complete list is likely to be rather long, and the evaluator will have to exercise judgement in deciding which areas are more or less central to the purpose of the evaluation, more or less observable, more or less likely to be identifiable at the point in time or the period in which the evaluation is being carried out. In other words, an evaluator will have to select aspects of content to concentrate on: in the real world, it is impossible for an evaluation to cover all possible areas of content. During the planning phase, the evaluator will need to decide, hopefully as a result of discussions and negotiations with stakeholders, what content will be selected.

Method: How?

One of the most vexed questions in evaluation about which would-be evaluators feel unsure is how is the evaluation to be conducted. Clearly, *how* one is to evaluate will depend upon *what* is to be evaluated: if learning outcomes are to be measured, then it is likely that language tests will be needed. If attitudes and opinions are important to the evaluation, then doubtless questionnaires or some form of interview (structured or unstructured) or group discussion would seem to be called for. Nevertheless, as might be expected, there is no one-to-one relationship between the content and the method of evaluation, and a key issue in the planning of an evaluation is what method or methods are to be used.

Several of the case studies in this volume address this issue: Lynch in particular gives details of a range of possible options. It is often said that the choice is between quantitative and qualitative methods, between the gathering of measurable, countable data – test results, questionnaire surveys, bio-data, costs, numbers of publications, and so on – and the observation, recording and interpretation of events, activities, thoughts and feelings of participants. However, this dichotomy should not be accepted at face value. Researchers in language education are, for example, increasingly interested in developing ways of quantifying the results of so-called qualitative methods like introspective think-aloud protocols, free-wheeling discussion groups, or learner diaries, and evaluators are well advised to pay attention to developments in this area relevant to their own methodologies. Although often research methodologies are simply too elaborate or too time-consuming for use with the resources available to the average evaluator, evaluation methodologies can be adapted to take advantage of the increased insights that developing methodologies might offer.

A further issue debated in the evaluation literature is the need for experimentation and control (see Part I). A common evaluation paradigm for language education in the 1960s and 1970s was to identify a suitable set of groups of learners, to match them with appropriate control students, to administer a treatment to the experimental group and compare the results of such an experiment with the outcomes from the control group. As is pointed out in Part I, the results of such experimental methodologies were less than encouraging, and it is claimed (Beretta 1986) that such approaches are inappropriate to programme evaluations. Indeed, many such studies might more realistically be called research studies than evaluation studies: although their aims were clearly evaluative in nature, their time span, the nature of the questions being addressed and the resources invested in the projects make them appear less relevant to the sorts of evaluations that are typically commissioned, and which are exemplified in this volume. Nevertheless, as is hopefully becoming clear through this chapter, the view of this author is that it is impossible and indeed harmful to assert that any method or paradigm should *never* be used. Although particular methods may not be recommended, there may be occasions when they are inevitable. An obvious example is when a sponsor requires a comparison of approaches. In such circumstances, some variation of an experimental/control paradigm may be highly desirable, however difficult – and the evaluator has a responsibility to point out in negotiations the problems associated with particular methods or designs. Nevertheless, in many circumstances, the reality of the situation is more likely to be relevant to the paradigm chosen for an evaluation than its theoretical desirability, and the fact is that for most language education programmes it is simply impossible to identify groups of students who can be matched with the experimental groups, and subjected to either different or no treatments. Such, surely, is the lesson of Beretta's and Palmer's chapters in this volume. Although constraints from the real world can be resisted or adapted in some circumstances, it is inevitable that they will strongly influence the evaluation methodology that will be adopted.

One common misconception about evaluation which has implications for its methodology is that evaluation is synonymous with testing. This leads to the assumption that any evaluation of language education needs to use language tests. In fact, of course, language tests form only one set of instruments for evaluation. Evaluation can be carried out without tests, and no doubt often should be. Indeed, in recent years (see, for example, Beretta 1986) there has been a tendency to question the automatic inclusion of language tests in the evaluation of language education. Testing has many opponents and critics, and it is common to argue that since tests cannot tell one everything one might wish to know about learning, they should not be used at all. The problem with this sort of argument is that it rarely if ever suggests how language learning outcomes can be identified, if not measured, if language tests are not to be used.

Traditionally, language testing researchers have tended to neglect the difficult question of the measurement of achievement, preferring instead to concentrate on the measurement of proficiency (see Alderson 1990). One consequence of this is that the tests that are available, especially in ESL/EFL, even if standardised, are relatively inappropriate for use on evaluation studies. In those evaluation designs where pre- and post-tests are required, it is typically the case that proficiency tests do not reveal much improvement. Yet if tailor-made achievement tests related to the particular syllabus/method/institution do not exist, or where they are of dubious validity and reliability, there is a temptation, difficult to resist, to use ready-made tests, which tend to be proficiency tests.

A further problem is that sponsors often require language test data, understandably enough if they are interested in outcomes, yet lack the professional expertise to recognise the appropriacy of instruments, the misapplication of tests, or to interpret test results with suitable caution. Tests yield figures, figures look like hard data, and tend to be believed, naively. However, the way out of this dilemma is not to refuse to use language tests, or to use quick-and-dirty methods like cloze procedures for test construction, but to ensure that sponsors are aware that the construction of good tests (as well as other instruments) requires time and resources, to take the responsibility of devising appropriate instruments rather than asserting that tests cannot in principle be appropriate, and to construct the best and most appropriate tests that resources will allow. Having done that, it is equally important to seek to triangulate data on outcomes achieved through tests with other methods – observations, self reports, teacher reports, more qualitative examination of written work and so on.

The notion of triangulation is particularly important in evaluation. Given that there is No One Best Method for evaluation, it makes good sense to gather data from a variety of sources and with a variety of methods, so that the evaluator can confirm findings across methods. But in evaluation, outcomes and effects are often contentious, and the perception of these may vary considerably depending upon the perspective, vested interest or even personality of the participants. In addition, the views of stakeholders as to the appropriacy of particular methods for evaluation typically also differ radically. In such settings, it does not seem sensible to rely on one method for the purposes of data gathering, but rather to try to complement or neutralise one method with another. Thus, a generalisable recommendation for evaluations would be that they should wherever possible plan to triangulate in method.

Interestingly, there is a tendency in many evaluations for the sponsor to go to the opposite extreme to triangulation by requiring what Alderson and Scott (this volume) call 'an inspection' rather than an evaluation. This might be best thought of as one particular method of evaluation. It consists of an 'expert' in language education being asked to visit a project or programme for a short period of time, to prepare him or herself by reading background documentation, once on site to talk to relevant (and irrelevant) people, typically including officials and teachers, but more rarely involving learners, and then being expected to deliver him or herself of a set of judgements and recommendations about the project or evaluation either at the end of the visit, or shortly thereafter. This is what Alderson and Scott rather tendentiously term the JIJOE approach. Although this may be a relatively common evaluation method, it is not one which is particularly recommended by the present author, nor, interestingly, is it one on which the standard textbooks on educational evaluation or research design offer much advice.

There are, however, many sources of advice in the educational, sociological and general social science literature, as well as specifically in the evaluation literature, on evaluation methodologies, and it is not the aim of this chapter to repeat or even to summarise what is more than adequately available elsewhere. The interested reader is referred to the following reference works for further information on particular research and evaluation methodologies:

Oppenheim (1966); Moser and Kalton (1972); Bradburn, Sudman *et al.* (1979); Briggs (1986); Erickson and Simon (1980); Faerch and Kasper (1987); Hughes (1989); Gronlund (1976); Bachman (1990); Allwright (1988); Cohen and Manion (1985); Seliger and Shohamy (1989); Cook and Reichardt (1979); Hughes (1976); Burgess (1984, 1985a, 1985b); Nash (1973); Walker and Adelman (1975).

We will return to the issue of evaluation methodologies in subsequent sections. However, it is perhaps finally worth mentioning one method of evaluation that is particularly relevant to the planning phase in an evaluation study, and which is perhaps particularly important in the JIJOE-type evaluations referred to above, and that is: document analysis.

It is particularly important in the initial phases of planning an evaluation that the would-be evaluator consult, understand, interpret and where possible discuss as much documentation relevant to the programme or project being evaluated as possible. Sadly, not many sponsors are aware of the need for, or are prepared to fund, an adequate briefing period during the planning phase, where the evaluator becomes as familiar as possible with the background to and the nature of the project and programme to be evaluated. Yet reading a programme's planning documents, descriptions of its operation, reports written by participants, administrators or other evaluators, is crucial to achieving an adequate overview of what is to be evaluated. Indeed, the need will usually become apparent during such a reading period for interaction with stakeholders and participants as well as sponsors, in order to clarify facts, opinions and issues, before the final form of the evaluation is decided upon. This interaction may take the form of correspondence, telephone or face-to-face discussions, and may need to be protracted. It is essential that the evaluator be familiar in some sense with techniques for document analysis and for the analysis of conversations, and the historical sciences may well be useful sources of information on appropriate methodologies.

Timing: When to evaluate?

There are a number of different aspects to this question, which will be addressed separately.

The first is the question of when should an evaluation start. Typically in descriptions of the nature of curriculum development, evaluation is identified as the last element in the cycle (Aims: Content: Method: Evaluation is one popular model, see Breen and Candlin 1980). Yet if evaluation is left until the end of development, it loses any opportunity to inform and influence the nature of that development. If it comes at the end of the process, it is frequently argued, it simply comes too late. Much more desirable is to plan for evaluation at the same time as the programme or project is being evaluated. Indeed, one might argue that the best way to *begin* planning a programme is by asking, 'How will we know that it has been a success?' Thus a 'good' project will build evaluation in from the beginning: evaluation will start with the start of the project, and will shadow and inform the development of the project.

There will, however, be circumstances when it will be important to begin an evaluation *before* a project has begun, and for further evaluative data to be gathered *after* the project has finished. If the evaluation is intended to estimate the impact of a project, then it is desirable to attempt to establish what things were like before the project began. This necessitates the gathering of *baseline* data. Such data will need to relate to the predicted outcomes of the programme – and will obviously be subject to the same dangers of shifting foci and priorities for educational programmes as are educational objectives. Nevertheless, a carefully designed baseline study can collect information about the state of affairs before an innovation or intervention which will enable subsequent study of the impact of a programme. Interest in this aspect of language education is increasing, and more systematic attempts at describing the '*status quo ante*' explicitly, rather than relying on or referring to anecdotal or assertive accounts of situations, are very much to be welcomed.

Similarly, there has been growing interest in the notion of follow-up studies, where evaluative data are gathered on the performance/attitudes of participants or stakeholders some time after a programme has finished (for an early attempt at this form of evaluation and a discussion of the problems involved, see Alderson 1985). Here the intention is to determine whether a programme has had effects that have lasted beyond the immediate timescale of the programme itself or, indeed, whether the programme has had effects that have only become evident some time after the programme has terminated. Given the present state of ignorance about likely 'gestation periods' for learning or attitude/behaviour changes as a result of a language education programme, it is impossible to recommend when might be an appropriate period after the end of a programme for an evaluator to expect effects to be evident. That educational programmes are intended to achieve lasting effects is beyond question. Whether they do, is debatable, and there is clearly a need for systematic study over a period of time of the nature of latent programme effects that might become discernible.

Furthermore, it is likely that different purposes for evaluation will determine what point in time an evaluation will focus on. A formative evaluation (Scriven 1967) will be concerned to evaluate during the lifetime of the project, since its primary aim is to provide information that will contribute to the project's development, whereas a summative evaluation will concentrate upon the end of a project – if end there be – in order to focus upon the achievements of the project over time, to enable relatively definitive statements to be made about a project's worth, rather than contributing to the development of the project.

Which brings us to a third question: how long should the evaluation last? Part I has already referred to the problem of 'educational commando raids' (Eisner 1984), and the previous section mentioned the tendency for JIJOEs to make relatively short evaluation visits. The implication in both cases is that 'short is bad'. In other words, the longer the period that an evaluation covers, the better. Or, to put it more realistically in a world of limited resources, 'the longer, the better'. The problem, as with a piece of string, is in deciding how long is enough. In part, this depends upon what sort of results can be expected over what period of time. Is it reasonable to expect change in behaviour, attitudes or learning over a period of two or three weeks? Typically, in language education, this is unrealistic. However, we have little idea of what sort of learning, and how much, it is reasonable to expect to be observable/measurable over any given period of time, with any given intensity of programme. Lacking this information, it is currently impossible to give any better guidelines about length of evaluation than to repeat: the longer the better.

Finally, when planning an evaluation, it is also important to ask about the timescale of the whole evaluation process, from design to reporting and implementation of findings. It is a common experience, and Mitchell's chapter is an eloquent testimony to the problem, that evaluators typically underestimate the length of time needed in each phase of the process. Gathering data can involve various complications which lead to a need for extra time and resources. The data analysis can reveal unexpected complications and problems – often, sadly, in the way in which the data were gathered (which is why pilot studies are so essential, even in evaluation studies). But somewhat unexpectedly, and yet commonly in the experience of the author, the phase in which the results of the evaluation have to be written up and reported in accessible form to a variety of audiences is typically underestimated. Experience shows that it takes a considerable amount of time to present results and the ensuing recommendations and conclusions to the sponsors, stakeholders and other interested parties. Yet time saved at this stage is emphatically time lost: if an evaluation is to have an impact and to lead to decisions and actions on the basis of the findings, it is crucial that the results and recommendations be presented convincingly, clearly and comprehensively. All too many evaluation studies gather dust on shelves, and no action results. All too often this is because not enough time and effort have gone into planning and preparing the publication of the results. Any planning for the timescale of an evaluation project should err on the generous side when deciding how much time to devote to report writing. It will nevertheless likely be discovered that not enough time was devoted to this phase.

Initial negotiations

It is relatively commonplace and superficially sensible to recommend that before an evaluation begins all stakeholders should be clear about what is to be done and why. Indeed in some settings it is normal to draw up a contract between sponsor and evaluator which explicitly states the conditions under which the evaluation is being conducted. As far as possible, discussions should be held in the planning phase to ensure that the various stakeholders have the opportunity to present their requirements or wishes about the nature of the forthcoming evaluation, and disagreements should be resolved in negotiations which result in an agreed document specifying what will be done, when and how, by whom and how the results will be presented.

Nevertheless, it is the experience of this author that such negotiations are not always possible. In some cases, the sponsors are simply not interested in discussing the details of an evaluation, and expect the evaluator as an 'expert' to go ahead and do what she or he thinks fit. Or stakeholders may be unwilling to reveal their own views and priorities, despite the evaluators' attempts, and refuse to take part in negotiations. Or one or other of the stakeholders may prove adamant that their position is correct, and should prevail. In such circumstances negotiations may prove very difficult, if not impossible, and the evaluator will need to decide whether his or her own reasons for undertaking the evaluation outweigh the disadvantages, or indeed whether it will prove possible and justifiable to subvert the evaluation in some way – by ignoring or differently interpreting the views of stakeholders.

It is also germane to bear in mind that however much agreement there may be at the outset of an evaluation, events may change such that the previous agreement becomes obsolete. Personnel may change, resources may suddenly cease to be available, data gathered may reveal unexpected results, methodologies may prove impossible to implement, reports may take much longer to write than expected. Indeed, the audience of the evaluation may itself change. Agreement reached at the design stage needs to be flexible enough to adjust to changing circumstances, or at least to allow for a renegotiation of plans if the need becomes apparent (Coleman's chapter in this book is an example of how things can change unexpectedly).

Deadlines, deliverables and dust: What happens to an evaluation report?

It is of the utmost importance that evaluators and stakeholders should reach agreement on what is to be delivered by the evaluation study, and when. It is also of great importance that consideration be given at the planning stage to the dangers of the evaluation report simply gathering dust after it has been submitted: every effort must be expended to ensure that the evaluation that is planned is one that will be acted upon, that the findings reached will be used in the decision-making process. An evaluation that is not used is a waste of time and resources, and all involved in the planning have a responsibility to ensure 'utilisation', as the evaluation jargon calls it.

To this end, the planning stage should not conclude without agreement among the parties on deadlines. It is a platitude to observe that these should be realistic but firm: inevitably slippage will occur for unexpected reasons, but such delays should obviously be minimised and should not be allowed to affect key decisions that will be taken on the basis of the evaluation study. So, deadlines need to be drawn up with regard to those points in time when decisions have to be taken for which the evaluation is crucial. These might be the date when a key participant's contract is due to expire or be renewed; when further resources have to be committed to the programme; when admissions decisions, or decisions with regard to the purchase of teaching materials, or the establishment of in-service training programmes for affected teachers, have to be made. The deadlines agreed upon should allow for possible slippage, but should be regarded as firm by all parties. It may be that some deadlines can be identified as being more flexible than others, but those that are not – i.e. those that are related to the timing of key decisions – must be identified as such. The use of analytic tools like Critical Path Analysis is recommended when complex projects are being evaluated, or when time is particularly at a premium.

It is also important in the planning stage to identify 'deliverables': what exactly is to be handed over to the sponsors and other parties? Fairly obviously a final report will be required on the study, but its nature may need consideration during the planning: will all the data gathered be included, or only summaries? Are statistical analyses needed, or only the interpretations that result? How much of the documentation is to be treated as confidential, how important is anonymity of informants? Are different reports required for different audiences, and of what will the differences consist? What will be the policy over publication of reports and associated conference papers and articles?

Will interim reports – pilot study reports, progress reports, and the like – be required? If the evaluation has an overseeing body, or a steering committee, how will the project report to that body? Are information sheets/newsletters/updates needed for those affected by the evaluation (teachers/students/administrators)?

What will the status be of instruments devised by the evaluation? Will the sponsors wish to vet them, and if so, at what stage? Who retains ownership of such instruments, and of equipment and facilities needed by the evaluation?

How will the financial accounting of the evaluation be handled, and how often will budgets be drawn up, invoices presented, and expenditure reported? How will cost over-runs be handled, and will further funding be possible to cover underestimation of costs?

Project frameworks: Planning documents

There may be occasions when the planning process of an evaluation is greatly facilitated by the prior existence of documents that relate to the programme or project. This is, for example, increasingly the case in projects funded by the British Overseas Development Administration (ODA). The ODA has relatively recently instituted what are called 'Project Frameworks' which are intended to guide and govern the development of a project, including projects in language education.

Typically, such project frameworks set out, in varying degrees of detail, the objectives of a project, how these will be achieved, and how their achievement will be monitored and evaluated. Deyes (1988) gives the following outline of a typical framework:

FIGURE I: PROJECT FRAMEWORK (DEYES 1988)

	Project narrative	*Indicators of achievement*	*Means of verification*	*Important assumptions*
Wider objectives Immediate objectives Outputs Inputs				

As language education becomes increasingly aware of the benefits to be gained from the introduction of management tools from other areas of educational, commercial, industrial or developmental enterprises, it is likely that similar documents and techniques will become more widely accepted and adapted for use in the context of language education.

However, since they will conceivably have a substantial effect on the way in which evaluations are designed and implemented, it is clearly important that those experienced and knowledgeable in the area of language education be consulted when the documents are drawn up or the techniques and tools are decided upon, *even though the evaluation study itself may not be being planned at that stage.*

Implementing an evaluation

The preceding section has emphasised that it is important that plans and designs for evaluation should be practical, realistic and flexible. Projects are dynamic entities, constantly changing and adjusting to new circumstances, and it is inevitable that plans will themselves need to be adjusted to take account of this dynamism. The implementation of an evaluation is rarely straightforward, and intentions will need to take account of the developing reality. This issue could be addressed as 'What might go wrong?' but such a question carries an implication of deviation, rather than a normal state of affairs. A better question might be, 'How might the evaluation develop?'

A major factor in the development of an evaluation is the people involved. Staff engaged in the evaluation may fall ill, be transferred or otherwise become unavailable to the evaluation, and adjustments may need to be made to design, instrumentation or timescales and resources in the light of such developments.

Those who are to be evaluated or who are to be the sources of data may simply refuse to co-operate, on the grounds that the evaluation is intrusive. More frequently, they may half co-operate – responding to data collection, but only partially – with some information but not all, with half truths rather than their 'real' perceptions, and so on. Poor response rates to surveys may not be deliberate obstruction, but lack of interest, or lack of time, or forgetfulness. Those to be tested may fail to turn up on time, or at all, or only some may turn up. Students' attendance at class may fluctuate, such that a full longitudinal record may be impossible. People may drop out of classes and programmes, and become extremely difficult to trace. Almost inevitably the evaluators will need to expend more time and effort than expected in chasing potential respondents in order to complete the required datasets, yet the importance of acquiring an adequate (even if not technically representative) dataset cannot be overemphasised.

The instruments being used for the collection of data may themselves be opaque and therefore difficult for respondents to respond to. This possibility entails that all data collection instruments should be piloted and adjusted in the light of the pilots before being used in the data collection. And yet all too frequently this does not happen, for reasons of time, resources or the lack of a willing or representative pilot population. If piloting is indeed impossible (even if planned for), then either pre-tested instruments or procedures will need to be substituted or adapted for the evaluation, or the results of the data collection should be analysed for the adequacy of the instruments, and data analysis and interpretation adjusted accordingly.

Even when instruments are adequately piloted, it will almost certainly be the case that both too much and too little data will be gathered. Either respondents will misinterpret the instruments and questions, and their responses become unusable, or it may turn out that many of the intended answers are in the event uninterpretable or in some other way unusable (for example, because there is inadequate time to analyse them, especially in relation to other data). It is a common experience that a mass of data is collected and much of it has eventually to be ignored, for lack of time and resources. It is also a common experience that as projects develop and change in direction, content, method or whatever, data that were potentially relevant become irrelevant, and will need to be discarded. In all such cases, evaluators will have to make judgements about what can be used and what must be ignored.

In order to improve the usability of the data that are being gathered, it therefore becomes important not to wait until all the data have been collected before one begins to analyse them. Data analysis frequently results in two sorts of insights: one, that the data are in some way deficient and the instruments or procedures used need to be adjusted in order to gather adequate data, or two, that unexpectedly interesting insights have shown up, and need to be pursued, possibly involving a change in procedures, subjects, timescales, or whatever.

Given the inevitability of the variation of implementation from inten-tion, it is often important, especially in longer term evaluations (say of more than six months' duration) that some form of steering committee exist to which the evaluator or evaluation team can report. Such a body would be informed on an ongoing basis of the development of the evaluation, and could decide on necessary adjustments in the light of the project's experience and recommendations. This would involve decisions about priorities which it is difficult for the evaluator to make alone, and which it is as important to negotiate over as is the original evaluation plan or contract.

Although this section has so far laid emphasis on the fact that many unexpected things can occur during the implementation of an evaluation, it should also be stressed that evaluations cannot be infinitely adaptable. Resources and time are finite, and therefore difficult decisions will need to be faced and taken as to how much adaptation to plans is acceptable. The tendency is usually to wish to prolong the timescale and to request increased resources, but the pressures from elsewhere, especially the sponsors, are equally important. An evaluation that takes too long is likely to be overtaken by events, and therefore to become irrelevant: decisions about projects may have to be taken without full results, and it is usually better that these decisions are taken with partial information than with no information at all. If evaluation is to be of practical use, it must be delivered more or less on time and in the form that was agreed, whatever the problems and weaknesses of what has been achieved. Deadlines and deliverables have to be respected if humanly possible. Given that the final report is likely to be the most important source of information as to the result of the evaluation, it is crucial that the time allotted to the writing of a suitably readable and explicit report not be skimped. During the implementation of an evaluation, there are many pressures to extend the data collection and analysis and therefore to cut down on the time available for the final stages of report writing. These pressures must be resisted, as the interim and final reports are likely to be key documents. This recognition argues for the establishment of and adherence to some form of Critical Path Analysis, in which key points in and periods of time are clearly indicated. Such a Critical Path can be of great assistance in the adjustments to plans that are inevitable in implementing an evaluation.

Interpretation and reporting

This section is clearly linked to the previous section on implementation, in that both interpretation and reporting of results are part of the design of an evaluation and therefore part of its implementation. One could equally well have identified other aspects of the implementation to be the subject of special consideration, and indeed other aspects are often given considerable attention: the evaluation methods, instruments and the nature of the sample consulted are frequently the subject of lengthy sections in evaluation reports. The nature of the interpretive process, and of how reports are actually written tend to be somewhat neglected in accounts of evaluations. Yet they are key factors affecting how or whether an evaluation study is ever utilised. They have therefore been selected for special treatment in this chapter.

The interpretation of data

It is an increasingly accepted fact in language education that the interpretation of texts and data will vary with the purposes, knowledge, interests and perspectives of the interpreter. This is as true of the results of evaluation studies as it is of other text types and collections of data. The first section of this chapter attempted to take this fact into account by stressing the importance of a triangulation of opinions and interpretations and the need for multiple perspectives on events, as well as for a prior negotiation of the design of an evaluation in order that the different perspectives of stakeholders could be adequately represented. Nevertheless, despite a general recognition that different people will have different perspectives and hence interpretations of events, it is relatively unusual for this to be acknowledged in the way in which different interpretations of an evaluation are triangulated by being invited or accommodated.

Yet if it is important to represent or accommodate the perspectives, interests and so on of the various stakeholders in design, it is surely inconsistent to leave the interpretation of data and its analysis up to an 'expert' evaluator.

Indeed, of course, what usually happens in practice is that reports are submitted to the various stakeholders, and are interpreted in different ways by different readers. Some might choose to accept the evaluator's interpretation, others to reject it. Some might choose to focus upon the main recommendations made, while others might be more interested in unexpected and arguably peripheral insights that have emerged, which suit their particular interests or prejudices. Given that the interpretation of results is a judgemental matter, it would indeed be surprising if there were not areas of disagreement or emphasis in interpretation. Yet all too often this variation in interpretation is inexplicit: that is, the different stakeholders may make their own interpretations, yet not make them available to others for discussion and possible resolution of differences. The argument here is that this is unfortunate, because insights from evaluations are more likely to be enriched by a sharing of differing interpretations of evidence than they are to be confused.

All too often, the evaluator is given an *apparently* privileged position with respect to interpretation: he or she is allowed, indeed expected, to be in some sense omniscient with respect to interpreting the data. He or she is endowed with special qualities, that imply a superior set of insights, interpretive abilities or critical faculties. This privileged position is apparent, in that the evaluator/report writer is usually the only party to an evaluation whose interpretation is reported.

Yet at the same time, other stakeholders have a more *powerful*, and therefore actually more *privileged*, position with respect to interpretation, in that they – particularly the sponsors and decision makers – are the parties who receive the report, interpret its results and have the responsibility of implementing or ignoring its findings. In other words, some parties to an evaluation will have their interpretations made public – in the report – and others will not necessarily.

It is the contention of this author that the reason many evaluation studies are not, in the event, utilised is because one or more parties, typically but not only stakeholders, do not agree with the interpretation of events and results that have been presented publicly. Since, however, there has been no expectation that such stakeholders would make their interpretations explicit or public, they are relatively free to disagree privately and therefore not to account for their subsequent decisions or actions. In other words, if you disagree, all you have to do is ignore. This would appear to invalidate, or at best to devalue, the evaluation that has been carried out.

Now, it may be the case that some parties and stakeholders would prefer that their interpretation remain inexplicit, or covert. There may indeed be strong political reasons for some points of view not to be uncovered, especially where these are in sensitive areas like personalities and personal relationships. However, it is important that evaluations be as comprehensive and explicit as possible, in order to inform decision makers appropriately, and this need for comprehensiveness and explicitness should where possible include the various interpretations that might be or have been made of results.

It would therefore seem to be important for the evaluator to devise ways in which the different interpretations of data that are both theoretically inevitable and practically and politically important can be gathered as part of the evaluation. This implies either that the various stakeholders need to be presented with evaluation results, and asked to interpret them from their own perspectives, or, minimally, that the evaluators present their interpretations of the data and request other stakeholders to comment on and modify those interpretations where appropriate.

Practicality, explicitness and confidentiality

This recommended course of action is, of course, a potentially lengthy process, and some stakeholders may be very busy people, or may indeed not feel that they have the expertise or experience to make public interpretations. Since it seems likely that judgements and interpretations of evaluations will be made anyway, the design of an evaluation study should wherever possible include a stage during which alternative interpretations can be sought from stakeholders, and incorporated into the final report wherever appropriate.

It should perhaps be added that the definition of stakeholders here includes students and teachers – insiders – as well as administrators, decision makers and outsiders. Students' and teachers' interpretations of data that have been gathered from them may well provide extremely valuable insights into the nature of the data, the programme or the evaluation. Although they may not be as immediately influential as the interpretations of other stakeholders, they may ultimately be crucial to the success of the project or programme being evaluated, and should therefore be made as explicit as possible.

Certainly, issues of confidentiality and the status of some of the information gathered is important. Evaluation is typically carried out in areas that may be sensitive, personalities are often involved in the way decisions are taken and the way programmes and projects develop. The extent to which information and interpretations must remain confidential is obviously important. Ideally this topic will have been thought out in advance, during the planning stage, but like many other aspects of evaluation, it may be the case that aspects of programmes are revealed that are unexpectedly confidential. Certain individuals may turn out to be unusually obstructive, or unusually influential in the development of a programme; certain facts or opinions may have been conveniently overlooked or distorted at some point, data may be commercially or politically sensitive, and so on. In such cases, difficult decisions will need to be taken about what can be published in reports, what must not be revealed, and what must be known, in order that appropriate action can be taken, without being published in reports. Clearly, no guidelines can be given since such matters depend upon particular circumstances, but the lack of guidelines should not obscure the importance of this issue and its satisfactory resolution.

The report

It has already been pointed out in previous sections that the report of the evaluation is a crucial document, since it is frequently the only product that stakeholders might see. The need was therefore stressed for adequate time and resources to be devoted to the production of an appropriate report. It was also pointed out that different reports may be necessary for different audiences, and that the needs of different audiences for different sorts of reports, recommendations, interpretations and indeed data, may well vary considerably.

Evaluations are carried out in order for decisions to be taken, for actions to follow. Therefore, the sorts of decisions that different audiences are likely to take, the nature of the actions that they are able or likely to engage in, need to be considered. For example, some readers may need detailed information on what aspects of the programme need to be adjusted when the programme is repeated – the content of materials or tests, the nature of administrative procedures, the registration and certification process, and so on. Sponsors, on the other hand, are unlikely to need such information as they will 'merely' have to decide whether to fund a continuation or modification of a programme. Thus the report writers need to determine what information, interpretations and recommendations are needed by which stakeholders, and to adjust the report accordingly.

It may well be the case, after due consideration of such issues, that different reports will be needed for different audiences, and it is indeed often the case that reports are divided into different sections, of varying length, detail and content, for different audiences, with the busiest or more senior stakeholders receiving only summaries, or generalised recommendations, and those intimately involved in the project receiving justifications for positions taken, detailed recommendations for adjustment and so on.

A common format for an evaluation report is for a summary of recommendations to be contained in one volume, and the Main Report, with details of the study and justifications for recommendations, to be published separately. Recommendations may be printed in **bold** type, to assist certain readers, and detailed information may be placed in appendices which are only available for certain needs, or which may be offered to other readers in order for them to arrive at possible alternative interpretations and recommendations for action.

Whatever the detail of the format of the reports – and many different formats are possible and justifiable – the substantial general point is that the report is a very important piece of communication, and it behoves language educators in particular to pay special attention to the effectiveness and appropriacy of their communication if they are to achieve the desired effects.

Using and evaluating evaluations

Evaluations are perhaps best distinguished from 'research' in that they are intended to serve practical ends, to inform decision makers as to appropriate courses of action, and, above all, to be *useful* and to be *used*. An evaluation that is not used is in some important sense a failure. It may have employed an elaborate design, the data collection instruments may have been well designed and appropriate to needs, there may have been appropriate planning of timescales and resources, and so on. Yet if the results and recommendations are ignored, the efforts that have gone into the evaluation are wasted. The evaluators' main concern must be to obtain results that can be used, and to make recommendations that can be followed.

There is, of course, a danger that this might be interpreted as getting action at all costs, and that therefore one is justified in telling decision makers what they want to hear in order to ensure action. This would almost certainly be taking to extremes the notion that evaluation reports must be user-friendly. But it is also true that unpalatable recommendations are less likely to be acted upon, unless there is good evidence and strong justifications. Ultimately, judgements have to be made as to the nature of the inevitable compromise between 'telling the truth' and 'getting action'. ('Truth', after all, is considered in this chapter to be relative, not absolute.) This does also argue for the pre-eminence of 'utilisation' as a criterion for the success of an evaluation. Since evaluations that are not relevant are also unlikely to be used, the relevance of an evaluation is an important criterion against which it must be judged.

In order to stand a chance of being used, an evaluation must not only be relevant, but it also needs to be the result of a negotiation process between the stakeholders at the outset; it needs to be adequately resourced and implemented; deadlines and deliverables must be kept to; the results and recommendations must be adequately interpreted in terms of educational policy and be adequately reported. In other words, at the risk of sounding Utopian, in order to increase the likelihood of utilisation, the evaluation should seek to follow the guidelines and principles set out in this chapter, and elsewhere in this volume.

But even that is not sufficient. As was pointed out in the opening section, evaluation needs to be reflexive. It needs not only to illuminate the nature of programme design, development and implementation; it also and importantly needs to offer insights into the nature of the evaluation process itself. It is important to evaluate the effect of following recommendations made. Did they prove to be sensible recommendations? What were the results of following the recommendations, and could these have been foreseen or improved? If competing conclusions are reached by parallel evaluations, which was more justified or effective and why? Were the recommendations adapted or modified in some way before being followed and why? What was the effect of such adaptation? Is it possible to replicate particular evaluation methods, procedures and indeed recommendations, and if not, why not? Was the evaluation used, and if not why not?

Clearly there are many questions that need to be asked about the usefulness and effectiveness of evaluations. Evaluation can only benefit from the experiences of evaluators, who need consciously to reflect upon the value of what they have achieved, and seek the causes of that achievement. If evaluators can evaluate evaluations, they can help improve the evaluation process, and thus contribute to the usefulness and relevance of evaluations.

Appendix A

PROJECT TITLE: PROJECT FRAMEWORK

PERIOD OF FUNDING
FROM F/Y   TO F/Y
TOTAL ODA FUNDING: £
DATE FRAMEWORK PREPARED/REVISED

PROJECT STRUCTURE	INDICATORS OF ACHIEVEMENT	HOW INDICATORS CAN BE QUANTIFIED OR ASSESSED	IMPORTANT ASSUMPTIONS
WIDER (ie Sector or National Objectives) What are the wider problems which the project will help.	What are the quantitative ways of measuring, or qualitative ways of judging, whether these broad objectives have been achieved?	What sources of information exist or can be provided cost-effectively.	What conditions external to the project, are necessary if the project's immediate Objectives are to contribute to the Wider Objectives?
IMMEDIATE OBJECTIVES What are the intended immediate effects on the project area or target group? What are the expected benefits (or disbenefits) and to whom will they go? What improvements or changes will the project bring about?	What are the quantitative measures (including the realised Internal rate of return), or qualitative evidence, by which achievement and distribution of effects and benefits can be judged?	What sources of information exist or can be provided cost-effectively? Does provision for collection need to be made?	What are the factors not within the control of the project which, if not present, are liable to restrict progress from Outputs to achievement of Immediate Objectives?
OUTPUTS What ouputs (kind, quantity and by when) are to be produced by the project in order to achieve the immediate Objectives? Eg teaching institution, miles of road built or rehabilitated, irrigation systems and associated management installed, persons trained.		What are the sources of information?	What external factors must be realised to obtain planned Outputs on schedule?
INPUTS What materials/equipment or services (personnel trained etc) are to be provided at what cost, over what period, by: – ODA – other donors – recipient?		What are sources of information?	What decisions or actions outside control of ODA are necessary for inception of project?

Appendix B

PROJECT TITLE: Bergenian Curriculum Development   **PROJECT FRAMEWORK**   **PERIOD OF ODA FUNDING**

PROJECT STRUCTURE	INDICATORS OF ACHIEVEMENT	HOW INDICATORS CAN BE QUANTIFIED OR ASSESSED	IMPORTANT ASSUMPTIONS
WIDER OBJECTIVES To help develop an educated work-force, which will contribute to the socio-economic development of Bergenia, particularly in agriculture, mining and tourism.	1. From 1994, those leaving school with brevet will enter the labour market/further training with adequate English communication skills. 2. From 1997, those leaving school with baccalaureat will enter the labour market/tertiary education with adequate English communication skills.	1. A satisfactory pass-rate in the new English examination. 2. Judgement of employers in priority areas. 3. Tracer studies of employability.	1. Continuation of present Bergenian policy on socio-economic development. 2. Continued use of English in priority fields. 3. Continued employability of school leavers in priority areas. 4. No increase in school drop-out rate.
IMMEDIATE OBJECTIVES To provide students leaving secondary school at both short- and long-cycle levels with adequate English communication skills by: 1. The establishment of an English teaching Unit in the IPN. 2. Revision of the English language syllabuses and examinations. 3. Appropriate in-service training of teachers.	1. From 1994, 5,000 school leavers per annum at brevet level will have English communication skills appropriate to Bergenian needs. 2. From 1997, 1,000 school leavers per annum at baccalaureat level will have English communications skills appropriate to Bergenian needs. 3. By Oct 1988, an ETU will have been established. 4. From 1991 the first part of new English syllabus will have been implemented. 5. In 1991, the new English exam will be introduced at short-cycle level. 6. By 1994, English teachers from all schools will have received in-service training in the use of the new syllabus.	1. Reports from: Ministry of Education Head of IPN Head of ETU In-service training tutor Testing consultant ELT Adviser 2. Year marks and exam results. 3. Teacher feedback. 4. BETA feedback.	1. Reports forthcoming and on time. 2. Availability of appropriate staff. 3. Availability of facilities and supplies. 4. An efficient and clearly defined relationship between the ETU and other Sections of the Ministry. 5. English textbooks produced by IPN will not be inconsistent with the aims of the project. 6. Commitmen to time-scales by all parties.

PROJECT STRUCTURE	INDICATORS OF ACHIEVEMENT	HOW INDICATORS CAN BE QUANTIFIED OR ASSESSED	IMPORTANT ASSUMPTIONS
OUTPUTS 1 The English Teaching Unit within IPN. 2 A revised English syllabus for short- and long-cycles. 3 Revised exams at brevet and baccalaureat levels. 4 In-service training courses for teachers. 5 School leavers with English communication skills appropriate to Bergenian needs.	– by October 1988 – by 1991/by 1994 – by 1994/by 1997 – from 1990-94 – from 1994	As for Immediate Objectives	The arrival of equipment and supplies on time. Availability of support staff at appropriate times.
INPUTS Bergenia Personnel: Head of ETU 4 ETU ELO staff 1 Project Secretary 1 Typist 1 Messenger/Cleaner 1 Library Assistant Services: Travel Budget Maintenance contracts Materials: Premises for ETU Typewriters (2) Air-conditioning Office furniture	ODA 1 ELT Adviser 1 Testing Consultant (to establish a pattern of continuing consultation services 1 In-service tutor (3 weeks x 3 years) MA Training Awards (2 in 1989–90; 2 in 1990–91) Seminar Budget Word Processor Photocopier Reference Books (BBP) Cassette Recorder	'Visual verification'	Greater efficiency in provision of UK support services.

References

Alderson, J. C. 1985. 'Is there life after the course?' In J. C. Alderson (Ed.) *Evaluation* Volume Six of Lancaster Practical Papers in English Language Education. Oxford: Pergamon Press.

Alderson, J. C. 1986a. The nature of evaluation. Plenary address to National ESP Seminar, Embu, Brazil, November 1986.

Alderson, J. C. 1986b. Evaluation: the nature of the beast. In A. Wangostorn *et al. Trends in language programme evaluation.* Bangkok: Chulalongkorn University Language Institute.

Alderson, J. C. 1990. Language testing in the 1990s: How far have we come? How much further must we go? Plenary address at the Seminar on Testing and Evaluation, RELC, April 1990.

Allwright, R. L. 1988. *Observation in the language classroom.* London: Longman.

Bachman, L. 1990. *Fundamental considerations in language testing.* Oxford: Oxford University Press.

Beretta, A. 1986. Program-fair language teaching program evaluation. *TESOL Quarterly* 20 (3): 431–44.

Bradburn, N. M., S. Sudman and Associates. 1979. *Improving interview method and questionnaire design.* San Francisco: Jossey-Bass.

Breen, M. P. and C. N. Candlin. 1980. The essentials of a communicative curriculum in language teaching. *Applied Linguistics* 1(2): 89–112.

Briggs, C. L. 1986. *Learning to ask.* Cambridge: Cambridge University Press.

Burgess, R. G. (Ed.) 1984. *The research process.* Lewes: The Falmer Press.

Burgess, R. G. (Ed.) 1985a. *Field methods in the study of education.* Lewes: The Falmer Press.

Burgess, R. G. (Ed.) 1985b. *Strategies of educational research: qualitative methods.* Lewes: The Falmer Press.

Celani, M. A. A., J. L. Holmes, R. C. G. Ramos and M. R. Scott. 1988. *The Brazilian ESP Project: an evaluation.* São Paulo: Editora da PUC–SP.

Cohen, L. and L. Manion. 1985. *Research methods in education.* London: Routledge.

Cook, T. D. and C. S. Reichardt (Eds.) 1979. *Qualitative and quantitative methods in evaluation research.* Beverly Hills: Sage.

Deyes, A. 1988. 'A Framework for the design of English language projects'. Paper presented at the 22nd TESOL Convention, Chicago, March 8–13.

Eisner, E. W. 1984. Can educational research inform educational practice? *Phi Delta Kappan* 65 (7): 447–52.

Erickson, K. A. and H. A. Simon. 1980. Verbal reports as data. *Psychological Review* 87: 215–51.

Faerch, C. and G. Kasper. 1987. *Introspection in second language research.* Clevedon, Avon: Multilingual Matters.

Gronlund, N. E. 1976. *Measurement and evaluation in teaching.* London: Collier Macmillan. 3rd ed.

Hughes, A. 1989. *Testing for language teachers.* Cambridge: Cambridge University Press.

Hughes, J. A. 1976. *Sociological analysis: methods of discovery.* London: Nelson.

Moser, C. A. and G. Kalton 1972. *Survey methods in social investigation.* New York: Basic Books, 2nd ed.

Nash, R. 1973. *Classrooms observed*. London: Routledge and Kegan Paul.

Oppenheim, A. N. 1966. *Questionnaire design and attitude measurement*. London: Heinemann.

Scriven, M. 1967. The methodology of evaluation. In R. Tyler, R. Gagne and M. Scriven (Eds.). *Perspectives of curriculum evaluation*. Chicago: Rand McNally.

Seliger, H. W. and E. Shohamy. 1989. *Second language research methods*. Oxford: Oxford University Press.

Walker, R. and C. Adelman. 1975. *A guide to classroom observation*. London: Methuen.

Appendix: Evaluation materials

Note   Materials not directly referred to in the text have been collected here. Appendices 1–10, pp. 306–49, refer to Alderson and Scott. Figures in parentheses in Appendices 6, 7 and 9 are percentages. Note that in some cases in Appendices 6 and 7 totals are more than 100% because respondents could answer more than one alternative.

The *Test instruments* on pp. 350–66 refer to Lynch.

Appendix 1: Original Evaluation Framework

This document was drafted in November 1985 by the central Project team, working with Charles Alderson. It was then sent to all universities taking part in the Project in January 1986 for discussion and suggestions concerning the content of this document. This then served as a basis for the development of the research instruments and the questionnaire items at the National Seminar in May 1986.

PROPOSED PROJECT EVALUATION:
    AIMS, CONTENT, METHODS AND PROCEDURES

1.0 AIMS OF THE EVALUATION

1. To attempt to carry out an evaluation which will be participatory and informative in nature.
2. To help the Project participants, – Brazilian teachers of ESP - to become more aware and self-critical; to see themselves as agents and not patients.
3. To help similar projects do well, (or better!)- e.g. can our experience with the Resource Centre be used or improved?
4. To help understand the nature of innovation by monitoring developments and guiding them by the provision of feedback.
5. To show how we have investigated ourselves and to investigate the evaluative process itself. Could this evaluation be a possible model for other projects?
6. To encourage project funders and personnel to take evaluation more seriously and to build it into the design, ab initio, of projects of this type.
7. To show supporting agencies what has been achieved:
    What progress has been made
    How the project could have been more efficient
    What remains to be done
    What the funding implications for the future are.
    What 'value for money' has been gained
8. To have defences in case of possible criticism

2.0 CONTENT OF THE EVALUATION
What is to be evaluated in detail

2.1 Effectiveness of the Resource Centre
a. Attitudes to the Resource Centre. Is it useful?
b. Atttitudes to others in the Project using your own materials. Does there exist:
    a fear of exposure through 'imperfect' materials?
    possessiveness after so much effort in producing materials?
    fear of credit not given to authors by other users?
    inhibition due to intention to publish?
c. Why do teachers (not) submit their materials?
d. Why do teachers (not) request materials in writing?

e. Which would you prefer: an occasional visit from a KELT specialist (with attendant cost) or opportunity to request materials from the Resource Centre?

f. Can a Resource Centre functioning on a national basis replace a KELT specialist/teacher trainer?

g. How would you go about setting up a new ESP course? What steps would you take?

h. What is the relationship between local and national Resource Centres? Once a local Resource Centre is established do requests to CEPRIL for materials and for the review of home produced materials naturally decline?

i. What do teachers expect from the Resource Centre?

j. How would teachers like a Resource Centre to operate?

k. How do teachers see the Resource Centre as best helping them?

l. Is the classification system at present in operation usable?

m. Does the classification system relate to what happens in classes and to how teachers see their materials?

n. Has the classification system achieved its teacher training aims:
   to make teachers more aware of bases for course design?
   to encourage greater use of resources?

o. Has the classification system resulted in greater retrievability?

p. Has the Resource Centre resulted in the identification of gaps in exercises/materials which can be filled by, e.g. resource packages?

q. What is the nature and use of the Resource Centre:
   Number of materials retrieved and their origin.
   Number and nature of books, articles, course materials in the archive.
   Requests and their origin: national/international

r. Administration of the Resource Centre: are there problems in receiving materials or publications?
   How many requests were not met/partially met?
   If not met, what were the reasons?

s. How much of what is produced locally is submitted to the Resource Centre?

t. What is the effect of the Resource Centre on the status/image of the Project?

u. How can the Resource Centre best be used as a data base for research?

v. What is the role/function of Resource Centre research assistants in the administration of the Resource Centre? Is it suitable or improvable?

2.2 The Approach and Methodology

a. What do participants think the ESP Approach consists of?

b. Did the Project evolve in relation to specific Brazilian necessities or was it imposed from outside?

c. Was the approach presented as Eternal (God-given) Truth, or by rational argument, with reference to evidence?

d. Did teachers simply accept the project approach word for word or did they approach it critically and understand the underlying principles?

e. Is there perceived to be an 'ESP Approach' or a variety of personally evolved ESP approaches

f. Is the approach appropriate according to students and teachers?

g. What resistance has the approach met up to now?

h. Do teachers understand that the principles/approach can be realized in the classroom or in materials in a variety of equally valid ways?

i. Do teachers see the difference between technique and principle? ('We tried ESP and it doesn't work')

2.3 Learning Outcomes (of Students)

a. What do students learn, in terms of:
   language use?
   knowledge of language?
   skills?
   awareness of the reading process?
   awareness of the nature of learning?
   attitudes to reading: unknown words, strategies, 'meaning'?

b. Do students learn what is intended to be learned? i.e. is reading ability improved in English or in Portuguese?

c. Do students become independent readers/learners?

d. Do they read more in English after the course?

e. Do they read more fluently, faster, more confidently etc, after the course?

f. Do students make more references to English bibliography after the course?

g. Do they think they could if they had to?

2.4 Attitudes

a. What are the attitudes of students, ex-students, Project teachers, non-Project teachers, administrators, subject specialist teachers, employers, etc.? Do these attitudes vary within the categories, according to age, experience, and other factors?

b. What are the reactions of the above to the aspects listed below, and any changes which occur:

   The Project: regional and national seminars, local events, publications (Working Papers, ESPecialist etc.)

   The Resource Centre

   The Approach: is ESP a preparation for a consumer society?

   The language, is English a tool of imperialist domination?

   Reading in a foreign language (References and Bibliography)

   Reading for academic purposes, (rather than newspapers)

   Materials: teachers' anxiety for perfection.

   Previous foreign language learning.

2.5 Relevance and Impact on Outsiders

a. Are students more employable after successfully completing an ESP course?

b. Do employers feel that students are better equipped than formerly?

c. What is the effect on ELT colleagues within the 'Letras' department, but who are outside the Project?

d. What is the effect of teachers of Literature and Linguistics within the same department?

e. What is the effect on ELT colleagues in other universities, in technical schools, in secondary schools?

f. What is the effect on professional institutions for teachers of EFL in Brazil?

g. What is the effect on the course content of academic departments?

h. Has the Project had an effect on authorities and institutions in Brazil or the U.K.?

2.6 Materials

a. What sources do teachers use for texts, or published materials used in the ESP course?

b. What are the sources of materials sent to the Resource Centre?

c. How much time is spent preparing and modifying materials?

d. Do certain types of materials result in better outcomes?

e. What are students' attitudes to materials?

f. Are students' reactions systematically gathered and incorporated into the revision of materials?

g. Do the materials reflect the Approach? Could we use published materials analysis checklists to evaluate this?

h. Is the Resource Centre's questionnaire for materials evaluation returned to the Resource Centre, analyzed and returned to the authors of the materials?

i. Is this feedback useful to the authors of materials?

2.7 Classroom Management

a. Is there a common set of practices within the Project which can be identified as peculiar to the Project?

b. Does classroom practice reflect the approach?

c. Are students treated in an adult manner?

d. Is the ESP class different from the subject specialist classes? If so/not so, is this a positive or negative factor?

e. Is a variety of techniques used or is the class relatively monotonous?

f. Is a Project different from a non-Project class in terms of:

exposition or discussion?

negotiation of course content and methodology?

teacher-student relations?

language used (L₁ or L₂)?

student participation?

awareness of reasons for content or methodology?

attentiveness?

g. Have classes changed as a result of the introduction of the Project?

2.8 In-Service Training
a. What is the perceived value in terms of in-service training of the following:
   Local, regional and national seminars
   Intensive courses, e.g. at PUC
   Visiting speakers from the UK
   Short courses abroad e.g. Lancaster, Aston
   M.A. and Ph.D. programmes in Brazil and abroad
   KELT-led training, (e.g. with research assistants)
b. How many recipients of the above training programmes?
c. What is the origin of these recipients and what is the distribution of scholarships and training events in terms of regions and institutions?
d. What further in-service training is needed?

2.9 Administration of the Project

a.   How   do   the   Project   participants   see   the appropriateness of the:
   roles of the KELTs?
   location of the KELTs?
   transfer of responsibilities to Brazilian teachers and the encouragement of this transfer process?
   structure and organograms of national coordination, local voluntary coordinations etc.?
   training for responsibility?
   loose federation i.e. the local responsibility for participation and action, freedom to elect or change coordinators and team members to communicate with the National Project?
   way in which universities were enrolled in the Project, -or not, - by invitation.
   role of the Resource Centre?
   role and functions of research assistants at the Resource Centre?
   the Project's conception of 'counterparting'?
   links with the PUC M.A. programme?
   reporting and feedback system, e.g. seminar reports?
   role and relevance of visiting speakers?
   mailing and communication system?
   relations and communication with sponsors?

2.10 Publications
a. Who reads them?
b. What do they do with the publications and the ideas contained in them?
c. What effect do the publications have on attitudes and classroom practice?
d. How readily available are the publications?
e. Are other types of publications needed?
f. Are changes to existing publications needed?
g. Who contributes to publications?
h. Who are publications aimed at?

i. What is the purpose of the publications and is this achieved?

2.11 Research
a. What has been done?
b. How much has been voluntary or informal and how much has been formal (i.e. in order to obtain an academic qualification)?
c. Who has done research and who has not?
d. Is UK/Brazil joint research ever contemplated or done?
e. What effect has research had on the Project?
f. How was research structured? Could it have been better structured?
g. How was research encouraged in the first place?
h. What research awareness is there?
i. Do teachers read research reports?
j. Do teachers feel that it is important to carry out research?
k. Do teachers feel interest and confidence in carrying out research?
l. Do teachers question what they are doing? Is there any critical open-ness?
m. What will be the role of research in later phases of the Project?

3.0 METHODOLOGY FOR THE EVALUATION RESEARCH

1. Need for Project participants to help with the design at all stages.
2. Need for genuine team effort and general agreement on content and method.
3. Need for the evaluation to be seen as research.
4. Evaluation must have the following characteristics:
    Non-threatening, we must not accuse anyone.
    Not a white-wash.
    It must constitute a learning experience.
    Must be publishable as documentation.
    It must not be seen as an 'Alderson and KELTs' evaluation but as a 'Project Evaluation'
5. The size of Brazil must be taken into consideration; it could be that a national steering committee for the evaluation might be desirable.
6. Need for triangulation to confirm and complete the picture.

4.0 PROCEDURES
1. Each local university to conduct structured interviews and discussions with students, former students, ELT teachers and subject specialist teachers.
2. National coordination to advise on procedures with guidelines after consultation with local coordinators.
3. Nationally administered questionnaires to be developed with local input, coordinated by central team.
4. Each local university team to be encouraged to select an area for investigation within the evaluation research framework and to develop plans, gather data locally and

present results nationally for discussion of implications. This could include many types of action research including quasi-experimental design with controls and pre/post test impact research.
5. Test results from local university projects to be collated nationally at PUC for evaluation of usefulness of the data and possible refinement of the design.
6. An interim report with initial results to be aimed at for extensive discussion so that we can suggest if any modification is required and identify additional investigation needed.
7. Full use to be made of the seminar and coordination network to discuss and present plans, communicate results and discuss further procedural steps when necessary.

Appendix 2: Results of Materials Survey

An analysis of materials received by CEPRIL during the period 1984-86 was carried out by the CEPRIL research assistants.

There were some problems in identifying materials produced in this period due to faulty CEPRIL records and the absence of dates in the materials.

They were analysed in the form they were received in, either as packages of isolated units or as complete courses. The checklist was set up in accordance with items in the questionnaires, to help comparison with teachers´ and students´ answers to those questionnaires. The

Total number of courses analyzed: 15. This includes sets of materials which appeared as collections of isolated units and also those which appeared as complete courses.

Checklist for Sets of Materials

1. Unit

How was the material in question sent to the Resource Centre? As an isolated unit? Group of units? Complete course?

Isolated single unit	4
Group of units	7
Complete course	4

2. Teachers´ notes

Are they included? Complete or sketchy?

No teachers´ notes at all	14
Complete teachers´ notes	1
"Sketchy" notes	0

3. Objectives of Unit

Are they explicitly mentioned?

Not mentioned	9
Mentioned	6

4. Objectives of Exercises

Are they indicated?

Not indicated	75
Indicated	4

5. Course Components (N of exercises containing:)

(a) Conscientização	4
(b) Reading Strategies	28
(c) Translation	7
(d) Trad. Grammar	5
(e) Rhetorical Functions	2
(f) Critical Reading	3
(g) Dictionary Use	3
(h) Vocabulary	19
(i) Text Structure	2
(j) Connectives	0
(k) Word Formation	5
(l) Skills other than reading	0
(m) Other	0

6.   Classroom Management

Can you encounter in the materials, or teachers´ notes, any
evidence for the following?   (N of exercises
                                                containing:)
      (a) Use of English for explanations   4
      (b) Open-ended discussion   4
      (c) Group Work   2
      (d) Negotiation of content   1
      (e) Individualized work   0
      (f) Flexible course design   1
      (g) Grammar tests   0
Any other features that you could identify and which are of
interest? Exercises in the same unit with some instructions in
English and others in Portuguese (one instance).

7.   Texts

How would you categorise the texts used?
      (a) Authentic   7
      (b) Taken from EFL textbooks   1
      (c) Adapted   7
Any other features, e.g. can you identify the source?
      Source identified: 8
      Source not indicated: 7

Some Conclusions

This is only a small sample so we are unable to say that
these are characteristic of all Project materials, used
throughout the country, but we have analysed a high proportion of
the materials sent to the Resource Centre during the period 1984-
1986.
Some findings are very much as expected. For example, no-one
is surprised to find the vast majority of exercises dealing with
reading strategies. The second most popular topic, however, is
vocabulary, with 27 examples, if we include word formation and
dictionary work.
This contrasts with other items "characteristic" of the
Project, such as conscientização and critical reading, which
appear relatively low in the order.
The presence of so many exercises involving translation may
refer to the activity involved rather than the objective of the
exercise, but may help to explain more why students indicated
translation as an important feature of the courses.
Other surprising features may be the following:
Only 6 examples out of 15 sets of materials explicitly
stated the objectives of units, and we had 4 examples of
exercises with the objectives stated as opposed to 75 without any
explicit objective.
Only 7 out of 15 texts were authentic and un-adapted, and 7
texts had no source indicated. This suggests that teachers were
still reluctant to use authentic source materials or did not have
easy access to them.
The absence of group work and alternative exercises may
indicate that materials were somewhat inflexible and that there
probably occurred very little negotiation of course content which

teachers, but not students, said is typical of ESP methodology.

We must take into account the fact that teachers may tend to send in "polished" and "teacher-proof" materials rather than more flexible and open-ended materials requiring more creativity, inventiveness and advance preparation on the part of the teacher. In other words, the materials may not be typical. The most striking feature here is that the analysis of these materials matches better the students´ opinions than those of the teachers in the questionnaire items on course content and classroom procedure.

Appendix 3: Instructions given to Coordinators

For Subject Specialist Questionnaire

1.   Coordinators make contact with subject specialists and fill in identification data at the beginning of questionnaire.
2.   Interviewer when visiting the specialist, offers clarification, waits while the questionnaire is filled in, or else fills it in as in an interview.
3.   The possibility of using the questionnaire for a telephone interview is not excluded, if it seems more practical.
4.   The aim is to reach at least one specialist per specialism.

For ESP Teacher Interview

1.   The interview is to be carried out <u>after the ESP Teacher Questionnaire has been answered</u>.
2.   As many interviewers as are available should be used.
3.   The interviewers should themselves be interviewed.
4.   The interviewer should write a report of at least one page, and ideally check it with the interviewee.
5.   The report should specify whether the interviewee is or is not considered an active member of the National Project, but the teacher's name should not be included.
6.   Ideally, the ESP Teacher's Questionnaire should be returned to the interviewer and stapled to the interview report.
7.   Telephone interviews are not excluded, if necessary.

For ESP Teacher Questionnaire

1.   In order to get the greatest possible response, it is suggested that:
    a) a meeting is arranged for the teachers in the ESP team to fill in the questionnaires, individually;
    b) for teachers who are not engaged in the Project, that the questionnaires be handed out and at the same time an appointment be agreed for the interview, when the questionnaires will be returned at the same time.
2.   It is important that all ESP teachers answer the questionnaire.

For Student Questionnaire

1.   The questionnaires should be handed out by teachers in class.
2.   Teachers should be familiar with the content of the questionnaire.
3.   It is essential that the class ("turma") the students belong to should be clearly indentifiable. If there are classes with the same code at different times of day, it is necessary to specify which time (morning, afternoon, evening).
4.   It is important to ask students to reply with total frankness, emphasizing that their anonymity will be guaranteed.
5.   Emphasize the importance of the evaluation.

For Student Class Discussion

1.   In the first class of the week, hand out questionnaires to be answered at home.
2.   In the second class:
    a. Students keep their questionnaires until the end of the session.
    b. Explain the list of topics for discussion:
        (i)   What are the positive aspects of this course?
        (ii)   What are the negative aspects of this course?
        (iii) What are your suggestions for improvement of the course?
        (iv)   What is your opinion about the course testing system?
    c. Ask one student to take notes of the whole final discussion and write up a short report (at least one page).
    d. Ask students to discuss the topics in small groups (4 or 5 students) for about 20 minutes.
    e. Organize a plenary discussion, during which the selected student and the teacher both take notes.
    f. As soon as possible after the discussion, write up the report.
    g. Hand in the two (2) reports to your ESP Coordinator.

Appendix 4: Summarized Results of Student Interviews

The questions were: what is going well, and what are the problems in your ESP course, what do you think of the testing system, and what suggestions would you make?
     The number of reports clearly identifiable as having come from students was 77: all figures therefore relate to that number. The categories are the ones which were retained after they had been successfully refined in reading the reports. The columns indicate numbers of Positive, favourable comments made, Negative, critical comments, and comments about the Importance of particular categories, where there is no clear indication of criticism or praise. The last section reports the suggestions made, in order of frequency.

	Positive	Negative	Importance
Attitude and Motivation			
interest	16	6	
confidence	8	1	
clarity	9		
participation	23	5	
Language			
a foundation of English	7	2	10
vocabulary	28	5	1
grammar	7	27	
text structure	16	1	
affixes	3		
teaching of language	3	1	
rhetorical functions	1		
Reading Strategies			
usefulness	43		
novelty	2		
applicability to Portuguese	6		
liberating effect of	13		
teaching of reading strategies	28	1	
use of dictionary	23	6	
"Conscientização" (Awareness)			
"conscientização"	2	1	1
teaching of conscientização	11	1	1
Text Selection			
quality of texts in general	13	7	
specific texts	10	18	14
general texts	3	2	1
variety	6	5	2
freedom to choose		1	1
up-to-date	13		2
informative	5	1	
appearance	1	7	

	Positive	Negative	Importance
Classroom Management			
discussion	8	3	1
use of time		3	
teacher's behaviour	7	5	
students' behaviour	7	1	
group work	7	1	2
homework	1	1	1
teacher-student relationship	23	4	
Methodology/Approach			
materials	12	17	
learning	12	2	
text-book	4	1	1
Comprehension			
literal translation	2	2	3
English-Portuguese translation	23	1	1
Needs			
real needs		4	
oral skills	2	14	2
writing in English		4	4
reading	7	1	
specific subject discipline	4	2	13
Administration			
obligatory course	1	13	2
optional course	8	3	3
large classes		5	
mixed-ability classes	1	17	
duration of the course	1	31	
Department administration		3	
condition of classroom		3	
equipment	1	2	
stage in degree at which ESP taught	1	3	
timetabling	1	24	
ESP Project			
student as guinea pig		1	
national dimension	1		
evaluation: usefulness	5		
evaluation: value to student	5		
Testing			
length of tests: too long 1, too short 1			
number of tests: too few 2, okay 3			
coherence with the course	31	5	1
collective testing			3
assignments instead of tests			9
classroom participation/performance			16
testing system	39	10	2
Other			
ideology	5	1	

```
Suggestions
use of subject-specific texts          33
study of grammar                       23
course should last longer              21
use of audiovisual techniques          16
oral activities in class               13
course should be optional              13
classes organized by specific subject  11
study of use of dictionary              9
study of vocabulary                     8
classes streamed by level of English    7
teaching materials should be improved    7
music in class                          6
course should be shorter                5
course should be more dynamic           5
texts should be more up-to-date         4
more awareness ("conscientização")      4
better texts wanted                     4
translation should be taught            4
```

suggestions with a frequency of three or less were:

use of language lab, use of games in class, more homework, course should be obligatory, seminar skills should be taught, texts should increase in difficulty as course progresses, texts to be selected by the student, summary skills to be taught, tests should be answered in English, there should be more discussions, texts should have more illustrations and cognates, teacher-student relationship could be improved, writing should be taught, attention paid to motivation, new strategies taught, texts should deal with regional conditions, fewer students per class, better teacher punctuality, keep same teacher, drama, listening comprehension, changes in the curriculum, tests should be more consistent with course objectives, use of the computer, more publicity about the ESP course, use of group work.

Appendix 5: Summarized Results of ESP Teacher Interviews

The number of interviews received was 50. All figures are
therefore out of 50. The answers are ordered by frequency and
follow the order of the questions.

1. What is for you, the approach proposed by the National
    Project?
Reading strategies	(30)
Text comprehension	(15)
Student needs	(12)
Global comprehension/Skimming	(5)
Teacher as facilitator approach	(3)
Language as instrument	(3)
Related to Brazilian conditions	(3)

    Develop students´ ability, Elitist, Student as active
    agent, Teacher´s change of approach, Don´t know (1)

2. Do you believe the approach commended by the Project has
    shown itself to be efficient or inefficient? Why?
Efficient	(28)
Very efficient	(9)
Efficient but ...	(8)
Not efficient	(1)

3. What do you think of the Resource Centre?
Positive as a source of material	(16)
Important role in the Project	(12)
Failures in interchange/communications	(6)

4. What suggestions could you make to improve it?
More exchange of information	(9)
More publicity	(8)
More exchange of materials	(6)
Acquisition of new material	(5)
More efficient services	(3)
Creation of local Resource Centres	(2)
Explanation of classification system	(2)
Free materials	(2)
More Federal resources	(1)
No suggestion	(10)

5. What do you take into account when choosing, preparing and
    using teaching materials?
Student interest/motivation/needs	(44)
Course objectives	(10)
Text that is good to work with	(9)
Students´ level of English	(9)
Specificity	(9)
Text quality	(6)
Difficulty of language	(4)
Students´ reality	(3)
Facility of acquiring materials	(3)
Up-to-date texts	(2)
Social/intellectual level	(1)

6. Of the Project's teacher-training activities (local, regional and national seminars, intensive courses abroad, etc.) which do you consider most useful and which least useful and why?

        Local Seminars   Very useful   (12)
                                 Useful   (23)
                                 Not very useful   (2)
                                 Not useful   (3)

why? against: Repetitive, Couldn't attend, Different needs, Same teachers participating
for: Exchange of materials, Direct training

        Regional Seminars   Very useful   (10)
                                 Useful   (17)
                                 Not very useful   (2)
                                 Not useful   (0)

        National Seminars   Very useful   (4)
                                 Useful   (19)
                                 Not very useful   (2)
                                 Not useful   (1)

why? against: Too many different people with different needs, Couldn't attend
for: Integration & evaluation of Project work, Contact with other universities, Contact with speakers, with new ideas, Exchange of experience.

        Courses   Very useful   (3)
                                 Useful   (11)
                                 Not very useful   (1)
                                 Not useful   (2)

why? for: Theory is applicable to practice.

        Courses abroad   Very useful   (10)
                                 Useful   (18)
                                 Not very useful   (1)
                                 Not useful   (0)

why? against: Approach different from our reality
for: Improved fluency, improvements in theory and practice, Contact with different teachers.

        KELT visits   Very useful   (2)
                                 Useful   (7)
                                 Not very useful   (1)
                                 Not useful   (0)

7. As far as you have been able to see, what impact has the Project had on your colleagues who teach Language, Literature, Linguistics?

        Language teachers Yes (15)   No (1)
        Literature   (2)   (7)
        BA programme teachers (2)   (0)
        Other FL teachers   (2)   (0)
        Linguistics   (3)   (3)
        ESP teachers   (2)   (0)
        No impact   (2)

```
            Causes impact              ( 9)
            Colleagues in general      ( 3)
            All teachers               ( 3)
            Some teachers interested, others not (3)
```

8. Have you seen any changes in the National Project since you
    joined it? (If so,) what were they?
    Yes (34)   No (15)
    Not involved in Project   (7)
    New to Project   (2)
    Changes: Normal development,"More suitable to the
    circumstances and less ´rigid´ in its rules",Developing
    the method of reading strategies,More receptivity/More
    teacher motivation

9. Have your methodology or classroom performance changed
    because of the Project?
    Yes (35)   No (5)
    Use of materials   (4)
    Classroom methodology   (10)
    General/Specific English   (1)
    Reading techniques   (1)

10. What would you like to say about the Project publications,
    considering their quality and effects?
    Working Papers   Very good   (1)
                         Good   (4)

    Resource Packages   Efficient   (1)
                         Very good   (1)
                         Good   (2)

    The ESPecialist   Good   (3)

    Publications in general:
                         Efficient   (4)
                         Very good   (10)
                         Good   (13)

11. What sort of research could be done to help you as a
    teacher?
    No Answer   (8)
    Testing   (7)
    Lexical analysis   (4)
    Text analysis   (3)
    Reading   (3)
    Learning outcomes   (3)
    Writing   (2)
    Discourse analysis   (2)
    Don´t know   (2)
    Regional differences   (2)
    Other skills   (2)
    Use of ESP in BA course   (2)
    Needs/Wants analysis   (2)
    Tertiary/Secondary relation   (1)
    Error analysis   (1)
    True/False beginners   (1)
```
```

12.   Which items of the written questionnaire would you like
      clarified, questioned, added, criticised?
        Nothing to say   (28)
        Too long   (5)
        Specific questions   (5)
        Good   (1)
        Too repetitive   (1)

13. When teachers return from regional or national seminars, what
     kind of subsequent work is carried out?
        Presentations on what happened   (28)
        Discussions   (12)
        New ideas on ESP   (4)
        Suggestions   (3)
        No answer   (5)
        Nothing is done   (2)
        Put into practice   (1)

Appendix 6: Results of Student Questionnaire

Brazilian National ESP Project   STUDENT p. 1

Dear Student,

This questionnaire was drawn up by teachers in the Brazilian National ESP Project. Its purpose is to evaluate the work carried out to date, as well as to work out proposals for reformulations and improvements.

We ask for your valuable help by filling this questionnaire in as accurately as possible. It is not necessary to sign it. However, we are always ready to discuss any of the topics mentioned in it.

Thank you in advance for your cooperation.

1. University   : ....N = 2066................
2. Course: ....N = 1945................
3. Level: Undergraduate (66) "Básico"
                      (23) "Profissional"   N = 1941
         Postgraduate (11)
4. Code (number or letter(s)) of your ESP class :.......................

***   Mark <u>one</u> of the alternatives.   ***

5. Does this course meet your needs regarding use of the English language?

   (17) a.   a lot
   (56) b.   adequately   N = 2051
   (24) c.   not much
   (3) d.   not at all

6. Your receptivity to the materials used on the course:

   (12) a.   indifferent
   (70) b.   high   N = 2054
   (18) c.   very high

7. Do you have a chance to contribute in class with your specific knowledge and personal experience?

   (13)   Always
   (35)   Usually   N = 2047
   (45)   Seldom
   (7)   Never

8. Do you feel more independent now, to read texts in English better?

   (68)   Yes
   (32)   No   N = 2040

9. At the end of the course do you think you will be able to use more texts in English?

   (58)   Yes
   (9)   No   N = 2060
   (34)   Don't Know

10. This course is helping to improve your reading ability:

   (52) a.   in English
   (35) b.   in English and Portuguese   N = 2054
   (3) c.   in Portuguese
   (10) d.   neither in English nor in Portuguese

11. When you entered the course, your knowledge of English was:

    (1) a.   excellent
    (20) b.   good   N = 2056
    (41) c.   regular
    (35) d.   weak
    (3) e.   none

12. After attending the course you think your English:

    (16) a.   improved a lot
    (67) b.   improved a bit   N = 2053
    (16) c.   stayed the same
    (1) d.   got worse

13. In your opinion, in your course curriculum, ESP should:

    (42)   appear as an obligatory course
    (55)   appear as an optional course   N = 2043
    (4)   not appear in the curriculum

***   Mark with an X, <u>one</u> or <u>more</u> alternatives if necessary.   ***

14. In an ESP course, which of the following objectives do you consider most appropriate to meet your needs:

    (30) a.   understanding spoken English   N = 2055
    (44) b.   knowing the grammatical structures of the language
    (73) c.   developing reading strategies
    (42) d.   perceiving the organization of texts
    (23) e.   speaking English
    (30) f.   writing in English
    (6) g.   other. Please specify ....

15. In your opinion the objectives of this course are:

    (8) a.   improving your writing skill
    (45) b.   translating texts into Portuguese N = 2055
    (23) c.   improving your knowledge of grammar
    (48) d.   increasing your vocabulary
    (91) e.   developing the skill of comprehending texts
    (9) f.   improving the speaking skill
    (2) g.   other. Please specify ....

16. You think that this course

    (46) a.   changes your way of reading in English
    (9) b.   changes your way of reading in Portuguese
    (17) c.   helps you to read only for academic purposes
    (63) d.   helps you develop your provious knowledge of English
    (10) e.   increases your chance of a better job
    (14) f.   doesn't help much   N = 2050

17. You think that as a result of this course you manage to:

    (38) a.   select texts which interest you
    (34) b.   select topics of interest to you N = 2043
    (78) c.   get the gist of a text
    (32) d.   find relevant information
    (27) e.   make summaries
    (53) f.   use reading strategies
    (30) g.   use the dictionary
    (26) h.   develop your own way of reading
    (34) i.   get to know the English language better
    (4) j.   none of the above
    (1) k.   other. Please specify ....

18. In your opinion the materials used in class

    (4) a.   de-motivate
    (53) b.   arouse interest   N = 2034
    (12) c.   are not interesting
    (21) d.   are selected carefully
    (26) e.   are related to your area of interest
    (13) f.   are irrelevant to your area of specialization
    (50) g   are useful

19. You believe this course encourages

    (41) a.   the teacher-student relationship
    (29) b.   discussion   N = 2046
    (54) c.   student participation
    (32) d   student awareness of the programme and of the methodology
    (28) e.   student attention/concentration in class
    (18) f.   negotiation of the programme and course methodology
              between teacher and student

20. Taking into account your knowledge when you started this course, do you
    believe that you read and understand English texts:

    (3) a.   with more difficulty
    (65) b.   more easily   N = 2037
    (22) c.   faster
    (2) d.   with less confidence
    (46) e.   with more confidence
    (15) f.   none of the above

21. Learning ESP seems to you to be:

    (12) a.   preparation to meet the needs of the consumer society
    (8) b.   a means for spreading the imperialist domination of other
              nations   N = 2008
    (16) c.   a way of getting to know other peoples
    (49) d.   a means of access to the specific bibliography in your area
    (60) e.   a means of access to any text in English
    (10) f.   useful for getting a job
    (3) g.   other(s). Please specify ....

22. Which of the following items appeared in your present ESP course?

    (83) a.   strategies for approaching a text (using cognates, guessing
              new words, etc.)   N = 2041
    (45) b.   awareness of the process involved in reading
    (55) c.   translation from English to Portuguese
    (33) d.   explanation and practice in grammar
    (26) e.   text functions (description, classification etc.)
    (31) f.   critical reading
    (49) g.   using the dictionary
    (43) h   exercises to increase vocabulary
    (53) i.   connectives (because, however, etc.)
    (77) j.   text structure (locating main ideas, etc.)
    (65) k.   word formation (prefixes, suffixes)

23. Of the items you marked in question 22, which are the 3 (three) which
    most helped you to develop your reading skill:

    (a,j,c)   (the most useful)   N = 1773
    (j,a,c)   (the second most useful)   N = 1748
    (k,j,a)   (the third most useful)   N = 1717

Many thanks.

Appendix 7: Results of ex-Students' Questionnaire

Brazilian National ESP Project   EX-STUDENT p. 1

Questionnaire for Ex-Students of ESP

This questionnaire was drawn up by teachers in the Brazilian National ESP Project. Its purpose is to evaluate the work carried to date, as well as to work out proposals for reformulations and improvements.

We ask for your valuable help by filling this questionnaire in as accurately as possible. It is not necessary to sign it. However, we are always ready to discuss any of the topics mentioned in it.

Thank you in advance for your cooperation.

1. University : ....N = 233......

2. What is your current academic situation:

    (82) a.   taking undergraduate courses
    (12) b.   taking postgraduate courses   N = 227
    (1) c.   taking an extra-mural course
    (5) d.   other. Please specify ....

3. If you work, what is your present occupation ? ....N = 56......

4. When you did the ESP course were you:

    (83) a.   taking undergraduate courses
    (10) b.   taking postgraduate courses   N = 228
    (7) c.   taking an extra-mural course
    (1) d.   other. Please specify ....

5. In which <u>semester</u> of which <u>year</u> did you begin the ESP course
   at the University?

    .... / 19 ..   N = 212

6. What was the duration of your ESP course?

    (33) a.   one semester
    (60) b.   two semesters   N = 228
    (8) c.   three of more semesters

7. The duration of the ESP course was:

    (32) a.   sufficient
    (68) b.   insufficient   N = 226

8. In your opinion, in your course curriculum, ESP should

    (46)   appear as an obligatory course
    (48)   appear as an optional course   N = 231
    (7)   not appear in the curriculum

9. When you entered the course, your knowledge of English was

    (2) a.   excellent
    (23) b.   good   N = 231
    (37) c.   regular
    (33) d.   weak
    (6) e.   none at all

EX-STUDENT p. 2

10. Considering your answer to question 10, do you think this level was adequate for your ESP course?

    (74) a.   yes
    (26) b.   no   N = 228

11. In your opinion, at what stage should the ESP course be provided for optimum results?

    (72) a.   at the beginning of your course
    (21) b.   half-way through your course   N = 224
    (7) c.   at the end of your course

12. Were the ESP classes different from other English language classes you have had?

    (87) a.   yes. In what way ?...
    (5) b.   no. In what way ? (sic) ....N = 226.......
    (8) c.   I have never had other English classes

13. If you answered <u>yes</u> to question 12, do you consider this difference

    (81) a.   positive
    (13) b.   negative   N = 201
    (6) c.   unimportant

***   **Mark with an X, <u>one</u> or <u>more</u> alternatives if necessary.**   ***

14. Which were the most important objectives of your ESP course:

    (11) a.   improving your writing skill
    (65) b.   translating texts into Portuguese   N = 233
    (14) c.   improving your knowledge of grammar
    (50) d.   increasing your vocabulary
    (81) e.   developing the skill of comprehending texts
    (9) f.   improving the speaking skill
    (3) g.   other. Please specify ....

15. Do you wish other skill(s) had been developed?

    (57) a.   listening to and understanding spoken English
    (40) b.   speaking   N = 233
    (52) c.   reading and understanding texts
    (23) d.   writing in general
    (25) e.   writing summaries and abstracts
    (30) f.   translating into Portuguese
    (3) g.   none of the above
    (3) h.   other. Please specify ....

16. You think that as a result of this course you managed to:

    (32) a.   select texts which interest you
    (23) b.   select topics of interest to you   N = 233
    (68) c.   get the gist of a text
    (33) d.   find relevant information
    (16) e.   make summaries
    (35) f.   use reading strategies
    (19) g.   develop your own way of reading
    (28) h.   get to know the English language better
    (9) i.   none of the above
    (2) j.   other. Please specify ....

17. If you had practice in reading/comprehension, what did it aim to emphasize:

    (40) a.   vocabulary
    (58) b.   reading strategies   N = 236
    (15) c.   grammatical aspects
    (23) d.   critical reading
    (5) e.   other(s). Please specify ....

18. If the emphasis on your ESP course was reading and comprehension, did this help you to read and understand a text in English with greater fluency and self-confidence ?

    (82) a.   yes
    (9) b.   no   N = 218
    (9) c.   does not apply to my case

19. In the ESP course,

	good	regular	weak	don't recall	N
a. your interest in the content of the texts was	(56)	(38)	(4)	(2)	229
b. the layout of the texts was	(46)	(30)	(9)	(7)	223
c. the connection between the texts and your specific field was	(54)	(26)	(17)	(3)	228

20. Do you think the ESP course:

    (39) a.   changed your way of reading in English
    (9) b.   changed your way of reading in Portuguese   N = 218
    (23) c.   helped you to read only for academic purposes
    (43) d.   helped you develop your previous knowledge of English
    (6) e.   increased your chance of a better job
    (25) f.   didn't help much

21. Learning ESP seems to you to be:

    (13) a.   preparation to meet the needs of the consumer society
    (7) b.   a means for spreading the imperialist domination of other
              nations
    (10) c.   a way of getting to know other peoples   N = 224
    (66) d.   a means of access to the specific bibliography in your area
    (46) e.   a means of access to any text in English
    (12) f.   useful for getting a job
    (2) g.   other(s). Please specify ....

22. How do you consider the ESP course in relation to your profession ?

    (84) a.   relevant
    (4) b.   irrelevant   N = 229
    (12) c.   indifferent

23. At the moment, you use English for:

    (66) a.   reading in your field
    (5) b.   writing reports, etc.   N = 227
    (10) c.   spoken communication
    (26) d.   none of the above
    (7) e.   other. Please specify ....

Many thanks

Appendix 8: Results of Teachers' Questionnaire

PRELIMINARY INFORMATION

Dear Colleague,
   This questionnaire has as its objective the evaluation
of some aspects of the Brazilian Universities' ESP
Project. Your cooperation would be of great help for the
success of the task we have set ourselves. We thank you in
advance for your collaboration

1. University:
      (121 reponses)

2. Are you at present teaching on an ESP course in this
first semester of 1986?
      YES _70%_   NO _30%_
                  (N = 120)

3 (a) If the answer is YES, in what subject areas are you
working?
      _____
      _____
      _____

   (b) Level:
      Undergraduate:
                     'Basico'   _46%_
                     ' Profissional' _25%_
      Postgraduate: _12%_
                  (N = 121)
   (c) Reference code numbers of your ESP classes:
      _____
      _____

4. If you are not teaching ESP at the moment in which year
did you teach your most recent ESP class?
      _1985 (52%)_
            (N = 38)
5. In which year did you teach your first ESP course?

         (1979, 1980, 1981)
            (N = 111)

6. How many classes have you taught since then?
         (Average: 10.3)
         (N = 102)

7. Do you consider yourself an 'active member' of the
Brazilian National ESP Project?
      YES _71%_   NO _29%_
            (N = 120)

NOTE The percentages given below correspond to Project teachers (PT's) and Non-Project teachers (Non-PT's) according to the answers given in Question 7 above.

1. Do you think that the approach as presented by the Project, differs much from that which you were using?

         YES 84% (PT's)   NO   16% (PT's)
              85% (Non-PT's)   15% (Non-PT's)
                   (N = 120)

2. If your answer was YES, what does this new approach consist of?

    Indicate one or more of the alternatives below:

PT's	Non-PT's		
97%	91%	(a)	Introduction to strategies/ new ways of using texts (skimming, scanning etc.)
94%	87%	(b)	Wider view of processes involved in reading
3%	9%	(c)	Explicit study of grammar
37%	35%	(d)	Increasing vocabulary
76%	74%	(e)	Strategies for guessing the meaning of lexical items
77%	78%	(f)	Developing a critical sense
71%	61%	(g)	Acquisition of a minimum contextual grammar for text comprehension
0%	0%	(h)	Developing oral skills
3%	0%	(i)	Developing essay writing skills
66%	74%	(j)	Developing the ability to summarize
10%	13%	(k)	Translation into Portuguese
84%	78%	(l)	Concentration on reading skills
39%	52%	(m)	Use of Portuguese in the classroom
7%	0%	(n)	Others. Please specify

                   (N = 70 (PT's); N = 23 (Non-PT's))

3. What type of problems do you think the Project encountered?

PT's	Non-PT's		
20%	9%	(a)	Failed attempts to apply the approach
43%	18%	(b)	Rejection of anything new
43%	35%	(c)	Doubts as to the relevance of the objectives
64%	41%	(d)	Difficulites in getting hold of suitable texts
44%	32%	(e)	Lack of familiarity with the approach
5%	6%	(f)	Others. Please specify

                   (N = 84 (PT's); N = 34 (Non-PT's))

4. The Project was presented as:
PT's   Non-PT's
33%   21%   (a) The best option
 1%   6%   (b) The only option
26%   21%   (c) One of several options
58%   29%   (d) Something which could be adapted to local
                   circumstances
48%   32%   (e) A desirable and viable choice for all
                   universities
 2%   0%   (f) Something which would have to be followed
                   without adaptation in order to
                   function best
 1%   0%   (g) Others. Specify: _____
               (N = 84 (PT's); N = 34 (Non-PT's))

5. In your opinion the Project approach showed itself to
be:
PT's   Non-PT's
79%   29%   (a) Suitable for Brazilian conditions
 7%   3%   (b) Difficult to put into practice
 1%   0%   (c) Of little relevance to English teaching
 0%   0%   (d) A passing fashion
11%   21%   (e) Excessively restricted to teaching
                   strategies
               (N = 84 (PT's); N = 34 (Non-PT's))

6. In an ESP course, which of the objectives below meet
the needs of your students:
PT's   Non-PT's
 7%   15%   (a) Understand spoken English
17%   44%   (b) Get to know the grammatical structures
68%   59%   (c) Recognize text organization
85%   74%   (d) Develop reading strategies
 5%   6%   (e) Speak English
 2%   3%   (f) None of the above
14%   12%   (g) Others. Please specifiy

7. In your opinion, the objectives of your course are:
PT's   Non-PT's
 1%   6%   (a) Develop the writing ability
 5%   18%   (b) Translate texts into Portuguese
 6%   24%   (c) Improve knowledge of grammar
48%   62%   (d) Increase vocabulary
100%   85%   (e) Develop the ability to understand texts
 2%   6%   (f) Develop the ability of oral expression
 4%   3%   (g) Others. Please specify
               (N = 84 (PT's); N = 34 (Non-PT's))

8. After the ESP course, the student manages to:

PT's	Non-PT's	
56%	53%	(a) Select texts that interest him
56%	44%	(b) Select interesting topics
92%	85%	(c) Get the meaning of a text
77%	74%	(d) Seek out relevant information
62%	47%	(e) Summarize
87%	74%	(f) Make use of reading strategies
63%	56%	(g) Use the dictionary
60%	32%	(h) develop his own reading method
48%	44%	(i) Get to know English better
0%	3%	(j) None of the above alternatives
4%	3%	(g) Others. Please specify

(N = 84 (PT's); N = 34 (Non-PT's))

9. Which of the following items is included in your course

PT's	Non-PT's	
99%	85%	(a) Explanation of strategies for tackling a text (using cognates, guessing new words, etc.)
87%	71%	(b) Awareness of processes in reading
25%	41%	(c) Translation from English to Portuguese
27%	44%	(d) Grammar explanation and practice
61%	50%	(e) Text functions (description, classification, etc)
75%	62%	(f) Critical reading
71%	65%	(g) Using the dictionary
54%	41%	(h) Exercises to increase vocabulary
71%	47%	(i) Work on connectives
96%	47%	(j) Text structure (finding main ideas etc)
87%	71%	(k) Word formation (prefixes, suffixes etc)
4%	3%	(g) Others. Please specify

(N = 84 (PT's); N = 34 (Non-PT's))

10. In your opinion, the teaching of ESP seems to be:

PT's	Non-PT's	
8%	6%	(a) Preparation to fit the interests of a consumer-based society
5%	0%	(b) A means for extending imperialist domination by other countries
75%	71%	(c) Means of access to any reading matter in English
20%	15%	(d) Means of getting to know other peoples
85%	91%	(e) Means of access to specific bibliography
20%	18%	(f) Help in getting a job
4%	3%	(g) Others. Please specify

(N = 84 (PT's); N = 34 (Non-PT's))

11. From the groups mentioned below, do you know of anyone
in your town who has been influenced by the National ESP
Project?

PT's   Non-PT's
76%   62%   (a) Teachers of English language
27%   12%   (b) Teachers of English literature
43%   18%   (c) Teachers of other foreign languages
12%   3%   (d) Teachers of linguistics
55%   29%   (e) English teachers in Technical Schools
29%   15%   (f) English teachers in primary schools
43%   21%   (g) English teachers in secondary schools
        (N = 84 (PT's), N = 34 (Non-PT's))

12. Has the Brazilian National ESP Project brought about
changes in the syllabus of the 'Letras' course at your
university?
        YES _68%_(PT's)   NO _32%_(PT's)
            _57%_(Non-PT's)   _43%_(Non-PT's)
        (N = 76 (PT's); N = 28 (Non-PT's))

13. Has the Brazilian National ESP Project helped to bring
about a closer approximation between university and the
local community?
        YES _78%_(PT's)   NO _22%_(PT's)
            _56%_(Non-PT's)   _44%_(Non-PT's)
        (N = 81 (PT's); N = 25 (Non-PT's))

14. If the answer is YES, in what way?
PT's   Non-PT's
87%   57%   (a) By means of extra-mural courses
60%   28%   (b) By means of seminars
37%   29%   (c) Advice and consultation
 4%   3%   (g) Others. Please specify
        (N = 63 (PT's); N = 14 (Non-PT's))

15. In your university is any work being done with primary
and secondary schools?
        YES _30%_(PT's)   NO _56%_(PT's)
            _26%_(Non-PT's)   _39%_(Non-PT's)
        DON'T KNOW_14%_(PT's)
                  _36%_(Non-PT's)
        (N = 78 (PT's); N = 31 (Non-PT's))

16. In your university is any work being done with Federal
Technical High Schools?
        YES _42%_(PT's)   NO _49%_(PT's)
            _20%_(Non-PT's)   _47%_(Non-PT's)
        DON'T KNOW_9%_(PT's)
                  _33%_(Non-PT's)
        (N = 81 (PT's); N = 33 (Non-PT's))

17. What is the source for the texts you use?
PT's   Non-PT's
71%   79%   (a) Books from the specific areas
24%   35%   (b) EFL textbooks
93%   79%   (c) Newspapers and magazines of general
                    interest
74%   62%   (d) Academic journals
 2%   6%   (g) Others. Please specify
        (N = 84 (PT's); N = 34 (Non-PT's))

18. Where do you find the texts you use?
PT's   Non-PT's
52%   50%   (a) Specialized section of library
49%   21%   (b) National Project resource centre
21%   3%   (c) Exchange with other universities
55%   47%   (d) Departmental bank of texts
75%   74%   (e) Personal collection
 6%   3%   (g) Others. Please specify
        (N = 84 (PT's); N = 34 (Non-PT's))

19. Who chooses the texts?
PT's   Non-PT's
67%   39%   (a) The ESP team
18%   15%   (b) Subject specialist teachers
68%   62%   (c) You yourself
33%   21%   (d) Your students
38%   35%   (e) You with your students
        (N = 84 (PT's); N = 34 (Non-PT's))

20. Regarding materials you have mainly used:
PT's   Non-PT's
81%   74%   (a) Material prepared by yourself
39%   9%   (b) Material from other universities
36%   29%   (c) Materials from the National ESP Project
                    Resource Centre
39%   56%   (d) Material taken from language textbooks
75%   59%   (e) Materials prepared jointly with
                    colleagues
        (N = 84 (PT's); N = 34 (Non-PT's))

21. Once you have prepared the material, is it modified?
        YES _90%_(PT's)   NO _10%_(PT's)
            _76%_(Non-PT's)   _24%_(Non-PT's)
        (N = 73 (PT's); N = 29 (Non-PT's))

22. If your answer was YES indicate the reason(s):
PT's   Non-PT's
90%   85%   (a) Classroom use of material indicated the
                    existence of some weaknesses
57%   48%   (b) Topic of texts out of date
61%   57%   (c) Suggestions provided by students
59%   52%   (d) Suggestions provided by colleagues
54%   74%   (e) Habit of renewal
        (N = 84 (PT's); N = 34 (Non-PT's))

23. Are you satisfied with the materials you use?
    YES 90% (PT's)   NO   10% (PT's)
         76% (Non-PT's)   24% (Non-PT's)
    (N = 73 (PT's); N = 29 (Non-PT's))

24. If you answered NO, indicate the reasons:
PT's   Non-PT's
29%   57%   (a) Above the students' level
57%   14%   (b) Not relevant to specialist area
14%   14%   (c) Content out of date
14%   0%   (d) Lack of teachers' notes
14%   0%   (e) Objectives not relevant
43%   29%   (f) Others. Please specify
        (N = 7 (PT's); N = 7 (Non-PT's))

25. Can you identify some classroom procedures which are
specific to ESP and which are reflected in your own
classroom practice?
        YES 99% (PT's)   NO   1% (PT's)
            100% (Non-PT's)   0% (Non-PT's)
        (N = 76 (PT's); N = 30 (Non-PT's))

26. If your answer is YES which are the aspects that in
your opinion characterize an ESP class?
PT's   Non-PT's
15%   10%   (a) Seating arrangements
56%   47%   (b) Discussion
67%   60%   (c) Teacher/student relation
64%   53%   (d) Language used in the classroom
72%   73%   (e) Student participation
76%   80%   (f) Making students aware of objectives and
                    method
37%   30%   (g) Negotiation of course design with
                    students
79%   73%   (h) Enriching class with students' experience
 1%   10%   (i) Others. specify
        (N = 75 (PT's); N = 30 (Non-PT's))

27. Of the activities given below, which do you use
frequently?
PT's   Non-PT's
11%   12%   (a) Games, competitions etc
10%   9%   (b) Songs etc.
16%   12%   (c) Library visits
94%   91%   (d) Group work
10%   0%   (e) Projects
82%   65%   (f) Discussions
10%   0%   (f) Role play
11%   6%   (g) Others. Please specify
        (N = 84 (PT's); N = 34 (Non-PT's))

28. Have changes occured in the techniques which you used
in the classroom due to your contact with the Project?
     YES _96%_ (PT's)   NO _4%_ (PT's)
         _91%_ (Non-PT's)   _9%_ (Non-PT's)
     (N = 82 (PT's); N = 23 (Non-PT's))

29. On the left indicate the   On the right indicate the
    number of times you part-   usefulness of the event.
    icipated in the event.
    No. of times   Type of event   Usefulness

    *NOTE Here we gave a tabulation of the results
    rather than an attempt to reproduce the original
    format of the questionnaire. The latter alternative
    would be too confusing.*

(A) LOCAL SEMINARS   (B) REGIONAL SEMINARS

No. times	PT's	Non-PT's
0	8%	18%
1	14%	21%
2	24%	24%
3	18%	6%
4	19%	0%
5	5%	3%
6	1%	0%
8	0%	3%
30+	0%	3%

(N=75(PT's); N=26(Non-PT's))

No. times	PT's	Non-PT's
0	7%	21%
1	31%	24%
2	24%	12%
3	11%	6%
4	10%	0%
5	1%	0%
6	4%	0%
7	1%	0%

(N=84(PT's); N=34(Non-PT's))

(C) NATIONAL SEMINARS

No. of times	PT's	Non-PT's
0	16%	21%
1	33%	27%
2	16%	6%
3	7%	0%
4	1%	3%
6	0%	3%

(N = 61 (PT's); N = 20 (Non-PT's))

USEFULNESS: A = LOCAL SEMINARS
             B = REGIONAL SEMINARS
             C = NATIONAL SEMINARS
             D = TERM COURSE IN THE U.K.
             E = MASTER'S PROGRAMME IN BRAZIL
             F = MASTER'S PROGRAMME ABROAD

	VERY USEFUL		USEFUL		INDIFFERENT	
	PT's	Non-PT's	PT's	Non-PT's	PT's	Non-PT's
A.	67%	21%	33%	38%	0%	10%
B.	61%	53%	37%	43%	1%	0%
C.	77%	80%	23%	13%	0%	7%
D.	90%	67%	10%	33%	0%	0%
E.	75%	92%	21%	8%	4%	0%
F.	72%	89%	28%	11%	0%	0%

Numbers responding:
```
A.     (N = 67 (PT's); N = 21 (Non-PT's))
B.     (N = 70 (PT's); N = 15 (Non-PT's))
C.     (N = 48 (PT's); N = 15 (Non-PT's))
D.     (N = 50 (PT's); N = 15 (Non-PT's))
E.     (N = 48 (PT's); N = 12 (Non-PT's))
F.     (N = 36 (PT's); N =  9 (Non-PT's))
```

Specify the seminars and courses you mentioned above

30. Of the items you answered in question 29, give below
the   two   which   most   helped   with   your   professional
development.

	MOST USEFUL		2ND MOST USEFUL	
	PT's	Non-PT's	PT's	Non-PT's
A.	30%	29%	18%	33%
B.	23%	7%	54%	50%
C.	18%	14%	14%	0%
D.	21%	7%	12%	0%
E.	7%	21%	2%	8%
F.	0%	21%	0%	8%

MOST USEFUL: (N = 56 (PT's); N = 14 (Non-PT's))
2ND MOST USEFUL: (N = 50 (PT's); N = 12 (Non-PT's))

31. Local seminars helped you to:
```
PT's   Non-PT's
75%    53%      (a) Prepare your materials
23%     6%      (b) Build up your team
64%    44%      (c) Define your course objectives better
37%    35%      (d) Prepare tests
48%    29%      (e) Use a greater variety of activities in
                    your classroom
67%    47%      (f) Choose more suitable texts
49%    35%      (g) Relate theory to practice
 0%    12%      (h) None of the above
 1%     3%      (i) Others. Please specify
                (N = 84 (PT's); N = 34 (Non-PT's))
```

32. What were the main problems encountered in local
seminars:
```
PT's   Non-PT's
12%%    9%      (a) It was difficult to apply the ideas to
                    your own situation
 2%     6%      (b) They didn't present anything new
 6%     6%      (c) They didn't contribute to your
                    professional development
 1%     3%      (d) They were monotonous and boring
11%     3%      (e) The group interaction wasn't successful
 0%     3%      (f) The ideas were out of date
                (N = 84 (PT's); N = 34 (Non-PT's))
```

33. Have you already had the opportunity to train teachers of your own or any other institution?
YES __44%__ (PT's)   NO __56%__ (PT's)
    __23%__ (Non-PT's)   __77%__ (Non-PT's)
(N = 75 (PT's); N = 26 (Non-PT's))

34. If you answered YES, this training was, or is being given at the level of:
PT's   Non-PT's
42%   33%%   Primary school
64%   67%   Secondary school
58%   17%   University level
18%   0%   Federal Technical High School
(N = 33 (PT's); N = 6 (Non-PT's))

35. In your opinion, what topics should be dealt with in the next local seminars?
_____

36. Should the administration of the project continue to be situated at PUC São Paulo?
YES __71%__ (PT's)   NO __8%__ (PT's)
    __43%__ (Non-PT's)   __7%__ (Non-PT's)
DON'T KNOW __22%__ (PT's)
           __50%__ (Non-PT's)
(N = 79 (PT's); N = 30 (Non-PT's))

37. Should the Project be de-centralized?- -i.e. each university should have its own project completely independent from the National Project?
YES __1%__ (PT's)   NO __86%__ (PT's)
    __12%__ (Non-PT's)   __61%__ (Non-PT's)
DON'T KNOW __13%__ (PT's)
           __27%__ (Non-PT's)
(N = 77 (PT's); N = 33 (Non-PT's))

38. The Project should be made up of local projects with their own characteristics, but without losing the integration and central orientation from a National Coordination.
YES __72%__ (PT's)   NO __17%__ (PT's)
    __77%__ (Non-PT's)   __3%__ (Non-PT's)
DON'T KNOW __11%__ (PT's)
           __19%__ (Non-PT's)
(N = 76 (PT's); N = 31 (Non-PT's))

39. Do you agree with the organizational structure of the Project, represented by a national coordinating committee, local coordination and several teams of participating teachers?

YES __95%__ (PT's)   NO __3%__ (PT's)
    __72%__ (Non-PT's)   __24%__ (Non-PT's)
DON'T KNOW __3%__ (PT's)
      __24%__ (Non-PT's)
(N = 77 (PT's); N = 29 (Non-PT's))

40. Do you think that the eventual creation of a regional coordinating committee would be advisable?

YES __54%__ (PT's)   NO __28%__ (PT's)
    __67%__ (Non-PT's)   __7%__ (Non-PT's)
DON'T KNOW __18%__ (PT's)
      __24%__ (Non-PT's)
(N = 78 (PT's); N = 24 (Non-PT's))

41. Indicate your opinion with regard to communication:

A. = Communication between the national project and local coordination
B. = Communication system between local coordination and local teacher.
C. = Communication among various local coordinations
D. = Availability of KELT specialists.

	Inefficient		Efficient		Don't Know	
	PT's	Non-PT's	PT's	Non-PT's	PT's	Non-PT's
A.	18%	19%	67%	31%	15%	50%
B.	21%	31%	77%	54%	1%	15%
C.	47%	36%	25%	9%	20%	55%
D.	21%	18%	54%	18%	25%	64%

A. (N = 76 (PT's); N = 26 (Non-PT's))
B. (N = 75 (PT's); N = 26 (Non-PT's))
C. (N = 60 (PT's); N = 22 (Non-PT's))
D. (N = 76 (PT's); N = 22 (Non-PT's))

42. Do you think the Project received an excessive influence from the U.K. specialists?

YES __14%__ (PT's)   NO __68%__ (PT's)
    __28%__ (Non-PT's)   __38%__ (Non-PT's)
DON'T KNOW __18%__ (PT's)
      __35%__ (Non-PT's)
(N = 77 (PT's); N = 29 (Non-PT's))

43. Do you think that from now on the involvement of the U.K. specialists should be reduced?

YES __12%__ (PT's)   NO __74%__ (PT's)
    __14%__ (Non-PT's)   __55%__ (Non-PT's)
DON'T KNOW __14%__ (PT's)
      __31%__ (Non-PT's)
(N = 78 (PT's); N = 29 (Non-PT's))

44. Are you familiar with the project publications?
    MOST __55__ (PT's)   SOME __47%__ (PT's)
        __22%__ (Non-PT's)   __69%__ (Non-PT's)
    NONE OF THEM __0%__ (PT's)
                  __9%__ (Non-PT's)
    (N = 83 (PT's); N = 37 (Non-PT's))

45. Do you have access to the Project publications?
    YES __100%__ (PT's)   NO __0%__ (PT's)
        __89%__ (Non-PT's)   __12%__ (Non-PT's)
    (N = 76 (PT's); N = 26 (Non-PT's))

46. Has the National Project produced a satisfactory number of publications?
    YES __76%__ (PT's)   NO __10%__ (PT's)
        __29%__ (Non-PT's)   __7%__ (Non-PT's)
    DON'T KNOW __15%__ (PT's)
               __65%__ (Non-PT's)
    (N = 82 (PT's); N = 31 (Non-PT's))

47. What is done with the publications received by the local coordinator?
PT's   Non-PT's
46%   24%   (a) They are consulted on an individual basis by each Project member
23%   15%   (b) They are read and discussed in meetings with the local team
79%   47%   (c) They are placed at the disposal of the teachers in the department
6%   12%   (d) Others. Please specify
    (N = 84 (PT's); N = 34 (Non-PT's))

48. How have these publications influenced your work?
PT's   Non-PT's
44%   21%   (a) Classroom management
79%   47%   (b) Preparation of teaching material
48%   15%   (c) In your research
63%   42%   (d) In providing a theoretical base
4%   15%%   (e) They haven't influenced you
0%   3%   (f) Others. Please specify
    (N = 84 (PT's); N = 34 (Non-PT's))

49. What changes would you like to see in the Project publications?
PT's   Non-PT's
71%   41%   (a) More reports of teaching experiences
57%   27%   (b) Reactions of students with regard to activities or materials
62%   27%   (c) Critical reviews of published materials
48%   24%   (d) Critical reviews of articles
1%   6%   (e) Others. Please specify
    (N = 84 (PT's); N = 34 (Non-PT's))

50. Evaluate the following publications according to their usefulness:

	The ESPecialist		Working Papers	
	PT's	Non-PT's	PT's	Non-PT's
Very useful	58%	64%	65%	39%
Useful	40%	28%	32%	39%
Indifferent	3%	4%	1%	4%
Don't know	0%	4%	3%	22%

	Resource packages		Newsletter	
	PT's	Non-PT's	PT's	Non-PT's
Very useful	60%	21%	17%	29%
Useful	27%	32%	61%	33%
Indifferent	3%	0%	10%	47%
Don't know	10%	47%	5%	24%

```
ESPecialist:          (N = 81 (PT's); N = 25 (Non-PT's))
Working papers:       (N = 79 (PT's); N = 23 (Non-PT's))
Resource packages:    (N = 77 (PT's); N = 19 (Non-PT's))
Newsletter:           (N = 76 (PT's); N = 21 (Non-PT's))
```

51. What other types of publications do you think that the Project should consider?

_____

52. Have you personally carried out research in ESP?
YES 53% (PT's)   NO   48% (PT's)
     36% (Non-PT's)   64% (Non-PT's)
(N = 80 (PT's); N = 33 (Non-PT's))

53. If you answered YES what was the topic of your research?

_____

54. Your research has been:

PT's	Non-PT's		
17%	18%	(a)	Individual and informal without intention to circulate results or publish
24%	12%	(b)	Individual and informal but with intention to circulate results and publish
2%	3%	(c)	Compulsory, demanded by the department
0%	0%	(d)	Demanded by specialist department
2%	0%	(e)	In conjunction with other ESP teams
16%	9%	(f)	Others. Please specify

(N = 84 (PT's); N = 34 (Non-PT's))

M

55 If you answered NO to question 53, why?
PT's   Non-PT's
61%   48%   (a) Lack of free time
29%   5%   (b) Lack of training in research
26%   10%   (c) Lack of theoretical basis
 3%   5%   (d) Lack of interest
37%   0%   (e) Lack of resources
34%   0%   (f) Lack of incentive
 3%   0%   (g) Lack of confidence
13%   43%   (h) Others. Please specify.
        (N = 38 (PT's); N = 21 (Non-PT's))

56. Have you been keeping up with the research carried out
by the Project?
        YES _56%_(PT's)   NO   _44%_(PT's)
            _21%_(Non-PT's)   _79%_(Non-PT's)
        (N = 84 (PT's); N = 34 (Non-PT's))

57. The research that has been reported has influenced:
PT's   Non-PT's
20%   12%   (a) Your way of thinking
36%   15%   (b) Your motivation to carry out your own
                    research
30%   18%   (c) Your own conduct in the classroom
        (N = 84 (PT's); N = 34 (Non-PT's))

58. Indicate an area of research that would be useful to
the Project:
    _____

59. Have you ever made use of CEPRIL? (The resource centre
of the National Project)
        YES _49%_(PT's)   NO   _51%_(PT's)
            _6%_(Non-PT's)   _94%_(Non-PT's)
        (N = 79 (PT's); N = 33 (Non-PT's))

60. If you answered NO, why?
PT's   Non-PT's
 5%   32%   (a) Didn't know of CEPRIL's existence
20%   19%   (b) Not familar with the materials
                    classification system
43%   29%   (c) Lack of information about the material
                    available
53%   42%   (d) Due to factors such as distance, lack of
                    time and resources which could hamper
                    the prompt delivery of material
33%   16%   (e) Preference for use of own material
        (N = 40 (PT's); N = 31 (Non-PT's))

    *Since you have not had any contact with CEPRIL it
    is not necessary to answer the remainder of this
    questionnaire*

61. If you answered YES, for what reasons?
PT's   Non-PT's
39%   0%   (a) The material requested meets our local
                    immediate needs
15%   0%   (b) Due to the lack of individual practice in
                    preparing material
74%   50%   (c) T⌐ offer greater variety, alternating
                    with local material
49%   0%   (d) To keep up to date with work done by
                    other Project teams
18%   0%   (e) Due to difficulty in getting hold of
                    resource materials for courses
13%   0%   (f) To ask for advice in materials
                    preparation
33%   0%   (g) To ask for bibliographical material for
                    research or other work
41%   0%   (h) To set up new ESP courses
15%   0%   (i) To ask for orientation from the U.K.
                    KELT specialists
        (N = 39 (PT's); N = 2 (Non-PT's))

62. Have you already sent material to CEPRIL?
        YES __64%_(PT's)   NO   __36%_(PT's)
            _0%_(Non-PT's)   _100%_(Non-PT's)
        (N = 44 (PT's); N = 6 (Non-PT's))

63. If your answer is YES, why?
PT's   Non-PT's
56%   0% (a) To contribute to CEPRIL's collection
50%   0% (b) To submit material to comments from KELTs
42%   0% (c) Intention of including in Project
               publications
 0%   0% (d) Others. Please specify
        (N = 24 (PT's); N = 0 (Non-PT's))

64. If you answered NO, why?
PT's   Non-PT's
 0%   0% (a) No interest in showing materials
43%   0% (b) Doubts as to suitablity of material
 0%   0% (c) Fear that authorship of materials will not
               be recognized by those who re-use them
50%   100% (d) Because of not having an opportunity to
               produce own material
 0%   0% (e) Others. Please specify.
        (N = 14 (PT's); N = 1 (Non-PT's))

65. Which means do you use to get in touch with CEPRIL?
PT's   Non-PT's
12%   0%   (a) Telephone
30%   0%   (b) Letter
10%   0%   (c) CEPRIL request form
32%   100%   (d) Visit to CEPRIL
        (N = 84 (PT's); N = 34 (Non-PT's))

66. Does the material arrive in time to be used?
PT's   Non-PT's
64%   100%   ALWAYS
33%   0%   SOMETIMES
 3%   0%   NEVER
        (N = 39 (PT's); N = 1 (Non-PT's))

67 If you answered NO, what were the reasons?
PT's   Non-PT's
 0%   0%   (a) Unclear requests
100%   0%   (b) Material requested not available
 0%   0%   (c) Deadline too short for material to arrive
                   in time
 0%   0%   (d) Others. Please specify
        (N = 1 (PT's); N = 0 (Non-PT's))

68. Does your making use of CEPRIL result in your filling
the gaps thsat exist in your ESP course?
        YES _64%_(PT's)   NO _16%_(PT's)
           _100%_(Non-PT's)   _0%_(Non-PT's)
        (N = 31 (PT's); N = 1 (Non-PT's))

69. Do you think that the existence of a local resource
centre:
PT's   Non-PT's
33%   6%   (a) Would help local materials production
 6%   0%   (b) Would reduce requests for material from
                   CEPRIL
20%   3%   (c) Would require a visit to give advice from
                   a U.K. KELT specialist
 6%   0%   (d) Would not be viable due to lack of local
                   resources.
31%   9%   (e) Would be necessary
 1%   0%   (f) Would be redundant
        (N = 84 (PT's); N = 34 (Non-PT's))

70. How would you like CEPRIL to operate?
PT's   Non-PT's
26%   3%   (a) Sending correspondence/publications to
                   you individually
16%   3%   (b) Sending correspondence/publications to
                   your department
37%   12%   (c) Sending correspondence/publications to
                   your coordinator
 1%   0%   (d) Others. Please specify
        (N = 84 (PT's); N = 34 (Non-PT's))

Appendix 9: Results of Subject Specialist Questionnaire

Brazilian National ESP Project   SUBJECT SPECIALIST p. 1

Dear Teacher,

This questionnaire was drawn up by teachers in the Brazilian National ESP Project. Its purpose is to evaluate the work carried out to date, as well as to work out proposals for reformulations and improvements.

We ask for your valuable help by filling this questionnaire in as accurately as possible. It is not necessary to sign it. However, we are always ready to discuss any of the topics mentioned in it.

Thank you in advance for your cooperation.

1. University : ....N = 143.................................
2. Departament (in full) ....
3. Course (in full) ....N = 136.........................
4. At which level(s) do you teach: Undergraduate (50)
                        N = 141   Postgraduate (14)
                            (both : 36)
5. Do you consider a knowledge of English important for good academic performance in your discipline?
                                              yes   (97,5)
                        N = 141   no   (2,5)

If your answer was in the negative, it is not necessary to go on answering this questionnaire, but please return it to the person who handed it to you for statistical purposes.

6. What contribution should English make to good academic performance in your area, with regard to:

	important	regular	insignificant	N
a. access to bibliography in the area	(91)	(10)	(0)	137
b. preparing summaries and abstracts	(44)	(34)	(22)	128
c. following classes in English	(31)	(30)	(39)	129
d. discussion with foreign specialists	(44)	(31)	(26)	133
e. translating texts into Portuguese	(74)	(19)	(7)	133

7. In the last five years, have you seen any evidence that your students:

	often	sometimes	rarely	never	N
a. used bibliography in English	(40)	(18)	(36)	(7)	135
b. wrote their own summaries	(6)	(22)	(24)	(47)	127
c. understood talks in English	(4)	(25)	(40)	(31)	124
d. expressed themselves in English	(2)	(12)	(37)	(50)	125
e. stopped using translators	(12)	(21)	(32)	(35)	123

8. Over the past five years have you spotted any significant changes in your students with regard to:

	no	yes: improved	got worse	N
a. using bibliography in English	(48)	(43)	(9)	129
b. writing their own summaries	(78)	(13)	(8)	119
c. understanding talks in English	(65)	(30)	(6)	121
d. expressing themselves in English	(78)	(17)	(5)	113
e. stopping using translators	(69)	(25)	(6)	118

9. If you think there has been a change <u>for the better</u>, to what can it be attributed: (Mark more tha·i one alternative if necessary)

    a. study programmes abroad   N = 67   (10)
    b. participation in classes given by foreign teachers   (16)
    c. regular attendance by the student at ESP courses at the University   (57)
    d. requirement on the part of teachers in your area that students consult bibliography in English   (87)
    e. growing needs to consult sources in English, because of the development of the field   (9)
    f. other(s). Please specify ....

10. If you believe there has been <u>no change</u>, what can this be attributed to: (Mark more than one alternative if necessary)

    a. ineffectiveness of the teaching of English at the University   (43)
    b. shortage of time dedicated to the teaching of English   (54)
    c. little or no connection between the study of English and that of your specific subject   N = 72   (33)
    d. existence of adequate bibliography in Portuguese in your field   (42)
    e. other(s). Please specify ....26.

11. Have you been forced to alter the content of your course due to:

    a. a lack of knowledge of English on the part of the students

                                            yes   (29)
                      N = 124   no   (71)

    b. an improvement in the students' knowledge of English

                                            yes   (12)
                      N = 90   no   (88)

12. In your courses, do you refrain from recommending texts in English because of the difficulties students would have in understanding ?

                                          yes   (46)
                      N = 125   no   (54)

13. If you answered <u>affirmatively</u> to question 12, what type(s) of text:

    a. textbooks   (61)
    b. highly specialized journals   N = 66   (61)
    c. less specialized journals   (29)
    d. reference books   (47)
    e. manuals   (24)
    f. other(s). Please specify ....5.

14. In your opinion, is a knowledge of English a favourable factor in the competition in the labour market in your field?

                                          yes   (88)
                      N = 137   no   (6)
                                don't know   (7)

15. Have you noted whether a knowledge of English has helped your students in getting a job?

                                          yes   (38)
                      N = 136   no   (20)
                                  don't know   (43)

Many thanks.

Appendix 10: Universities involved in the Evaluation

North/North-East

Universidade Federal de Alagoas	Maceió
Universidade do Amazonas	Manaus
Universidade Federal da Paraíba Campus I	João Pessoa
Universidade Federal da Paraíba Campus II	Campina Grande
Universidade Federal de Pernambuco	Recife
Universidade Federal do Piauí	Teresina
Universidade Federal do Rio Grande do Norte	Natal

Centre-West

Universidade Federal da Bahia	Salvador
Universidade de Brasília	Brasília
Universidade Federal do Espírito Santo	Vitória
Universidade Federal de Goiás	Goiânia
Universidade Federal de Mato Grosso	Cuiabá
Universidade Federal de Minas Gerais	Belo Horizonte
Universidade Federal de Uberlândia	Uberlândia
Universidade Federal de Viçosa	Viçosa

South

Universidade Estadual de Londrina	Londrina
Universidade Federal do Paraná	Curitiba
Universidade Federal do Rio Grande do Sul	Porto Alegre
Universidade Federal de Santa Catarina	Florianópolis
Universidade Federal de Santa Maria	Santa Maria
Pontifícia Universidade Católica de São Paulo	São Paulo

Appendix to Lynch – Test instruments

ESLPE, GUADALAJARA, 1986, FORM A   BOOKLET NO........

DO NOT MARK IN THIS TEST BOOKLET

PART ONE: LISTENING
DO NOT TURN THIS PAGE UNTIL TOLD TO DO SO

DIRECTIONS: In this part of the test you will hear
two short passages. Each passage will be read aloud
two times. Your task will be to remember the passage
and to choose the best answer (A, B, C, or D) to the
questions. Mark your answers on the answer sheet, not
in this test booklet.

LISTEN TO THE PASSAGE.
Do not turn this page or begin answering the
questions until after you have heard the passage two
times.

STOP!
DO NOT TURN THIS PAGE UNTIL TOLD TO DO SO.

ANSWER ITEMS 1-10 ON THE BASIS OF THE PASSAGE YOU JUST HEARD.

1. An attitude of purism causes...
    A. word taboos.   C. cultural bias.
    B. language errors.   D. unkindness.

2. Taboos are usually related to...
    A. sex.   C. obscenities.
    B. cultural errors.   D. inappropriate words.

3. Word choice is much more important for addressing...
    A. cultural groups.   C. vocational groups.
    B. sexual matters.   D. none of these.

4. Taboos fill particular...
    A. glossaries.   C. vocational groups.
    B. cultures.   D. minority groups.

5. The penalty for violating a taboo is...
    A. swift revenge.   C. anger.
    B. fear.   D. social disapproval.

6. Taboo substitutes are usually...
    A. soft.   C. harsh.
    B. offensive.   D. rare.

7. Supposedly, things that sound good...
    A. may not be good.   C. are good.
    B. are deceptive.   D. are limited.

8. The passage mentions...
    A. politics.   C. obscenity.
    B. archaeology.   D. geography.

9. Euphemisms...
    A. lack approval.   C. are in short supply.
    B. ease the sting.   D. outnumber taboos.

10. There were less taboos...
    A. in the 1880s.   C. in the 1980s.
    B. in the 1920s.   D. at no time.

STOP!
NOW LISTEN TO THE NEXT PASSAGE.
DO NOT TURN THIS PAGE UNTIL TOLD TO DO SO.

ANSWER ITEMS 11-20 ON THE BASIS OF THE PASSAGE YOU
JUST HEARD.

11. Psychology is a science because it...
    A. is a systematic study.   C. studies mental activities.
    B. studies what people do   D. is a study of behavior.

12. Behavior refers to...
    A. objects we study.   C. observation and description.
    B. things that we do.   D. the study of aggression.

13. An example of mental behavior is...
    A. aggression.   C. experiencing.
    B. talking.   D. moving.

14. An example of an activity of the body is...
    A. experiencing.   C. observation.
    B. dreaming.   D. talking.

15. Psychology has studied the relationship between TV violence
    and...
    A. aggression in children.   C. dreaming in children.
    B. aggression in adults.   D. dreaming in adults.

16. One example of a behavior that psychology studies is...
    A. sleep.   C. aggression.
    B. television.   D. accidents.

17. Another example of a behavior that psychology studies is...
    A. college life.   C. waking.
    B. dreaming.   D. children's games.

18. In a recent study, 16 college students were shown a...
    A. stressful film.   C. violent TV program.
    B. picture of an accident.   D. film about war.

19. In the same study, the 16 college students...
    A. became aggressive adults   C. slept in a laboratory.
    B. suffered an accident.   D. went to dreaming classes.

20. Studies show that dreams often...
    A. use waking experience.   C. relieve daily tension.
    B. make aggressive behavior. D. show a person's behavior

CONTINUE ON TO THE NEXT PART OF THE TEST.

PART TWO: READING COMPREHENSION

DIRECTIONS: Read the following passages and select the correct answers to the questions. Choose your answers only on the basis of the information in the passages. Mark your answers on the answer sheet. DO NOT WRITE IN THE TEST BOOKLET.

Passage 1

The smallest but most intense of all known storms is the tornado. It seems to be a typically American storm, since it is most frequent and violent in the United States. Tornadoes also occur in Australia in substantial numbers and are reported occasionally in other places in midlatitudes.

The tornado is a small, intense cyclone in which the air is spiralling at tremendous speed. It appears as a dark funnel cloud hanging from a cumulonimbus cloud. At its lower end the funnel may be 300 to 1500 feet (90 to 460 meters) in diameter. The funnel appears dark because of the density of condensing moisture, dust, and debris swept up by the wind.

Wind speeds in a tornado exceed anything known in other storms. Estimates of wind speed run as high as 250 miles (400 km.) per hour. As the tornado moves across the country, the funnel writhes and twists. The end of the funnel cloud may alternately sweep the ground, causing complete destruction of anything in its path, and rise in the air to leave the ground below unharmed.

21. An appropriate title for this passage is...
    A. Varieties of Storms   C. Wind Speed
    B. Tornadoes   D. Cloud Formations

22. Among storms, the tornado is said to be the...
    A. largest   C. most widespread
    B. smallest   D. least intense

23. Tornadoes occur primarily in...
    A. Australia   C. America
    B. higher latitudes   D. lower latitudes

24. Tornadoes resemble a dark funnel proceeding from...
    A. an intense cyclone   C. a cloudy sky
    B. writhing and twisting   D. dust and debris

25. The darkness of a tornado's appearance is due to...
    A. cloud type   C. debris density
    B. wind speed   D. cloud cover

26. Wind speeds of a tornado are known to reach...
    A. 400 miles per hour   C. 460 meters per second
    B. 250 miles per hour   D. 1500 feet per minute

CONTINUE ON TO THE NEXT PAGE.

Passage 2

Geography, though its effect is often overrated, has some bearing especially on architecture. First, the site chosen for a building may determine its direction and character. Except for the prevailing incidence of sun or wind, a structure on a plain might face in any direction. A sloping plot restricts such freedom. Moreover, a design suited to the great plains may be inappropriate for wooded, mountainous terrain.

Second, where an architecture is indigenous, we might expect to find a high pitched roof in countries with cold climates, a low pitched roof in others with warmer climates. The gentle slope of the roof of the Parthenon suffices to void any rainfall, but would be less suitable if snow were a serious consideration. The steep roof of the Parson Capen House in Topsfield, Massachusetts, implies the rigorous New England climate. Architecture in a desert exhibits a flat roof, as in the Indian pueblos of the Southwest or in Egyptian temples. However, so many other considerations exist, such as the wind, the type and materials of construction, or the transmission of an architectural type from one region to another, that precipitation is not a paramount factor.

27. An appropriate title for this passage is...
     A. Reasons for Sloping Roofs   C. International Building
     B. Architectural Geography   D. Appropriate Construction

28. The direction a structure faces may stem from...
     A. plot slope   C. wind velocity
     B. constructions materials   D. precipitation

29. The architectural effect of a sloping plot is to...
     A. enhance beauty   C. introduce rigor
     B. withstand the elements   D. restrict freedom

30. Countries with warmer climates are characterized by...
     A. higher pitched roofs   C. lower pitched roofs
     B. less rainfall   D. Parthenon structures

31. The Parson Capen House was constructed so as to...
     A. keep an architectural type C. withstand a harsh climate
     B. utilize a sloping plot   D. fit a mountainous area

32. Egyptian temples share an architectural feature with the...
     A. Parson Capen House   C. Parthenon
     B. Indian pueblos   D. great plains buildings

CONTINUE ON TO THE NEXT PAGE.

Passage 3

Soldering is generally required to assure permanent electrical connections. Wires, or wires and terminals, are wrapped or twisted together, then solder is melted into the heated joint. When the heat is removed, the solder and wire cool, making the solder joint look like a solid piece of metal. It is not possible, after proper soldering, to separate the wires at a joint except by breaking them or by unsoldering them.

Solder is an alloy of lead and tin. It has a low melting point and comes in wire form for electronics use. Electronics solder is made up of 60 percent tin and 40 percent lead, though the composition may vary for certain applications. Rosin core solder is used for soldering electronics components. The rosin is a flux which flows onto the surface to be soldered, assuring a more perfect union. Acid and soldering paste should not be used in electronics.

The solder must not come in direct contact with the tip of the soldering iron or soldering gun because it will melt too readily. If the wires or terminals to be soldered have not been preheated sufficiently, the molten solder will not adhere to their surface. The joint may look well soldered, but the chances are that it is not. Cold solder joints provide poor electrical contact. Defects arising from poor soldering are difficult to discover when troubleshooting.

33. The best title for this passage is...
    A. The Composition of Solder C. Electrical Soldering
    B. Soldering Wires   D. Electrical Wiring

34. When solder comes in contact with the tip of the soldering iron, it will...
    A. melt   C. burn the wires
    B. separate the wires   D. assure permanent connection

35. The wires should be preheated so that the...
    A. wires may be separated   C. rosin will flow
    B. solder will melt   D. solder will adhere

36. Solder is made up of...
    A. rosin   C. wires
    B. lead and tin   D. heated joints

37. To separate soldered wires, they must be...
    A. electronically soldered   C. broken or unsoldered
    B. reheated   D. wire-wrapped connections

38. Rosin-core solder is used for...
    A. preventing poor soldering C. acid base soldering
    B. wire-wrap connections   D. electrical soldering

CONTINUE ON TO THE NEXT PART OF THE TEST.

PART THREE: GRAMMAR

DIRECTIONS: Choose the best answer to complete the following
sentences. Mark your answers on your answer sheet.

39. If my professor had not said it, I...............it.
    A. would never have believed C. never have believed
    B. had never believed   D. never believed

40. If you........... this food, you will probably get sick.
    A. would eat   C. can eat
    B. eat   D. had eaten

41. If we continue present research activities, the knowledge of
mankind ....
    A. increases   C. has increased
    B. increased   D. will increase

42. Until this century, no one .... Mt Everest.
    A. climbed ever   C. ever has climbed
    B. has ever climbed   D. had ever climbed

43. Long-term memory .... information which can be recalled
many days or weeks later.
    A. contained   C. has contained
    B. contains   D. had contained

44. It has been estimated that it ...... at least five years for
the effects of the recent oil spill on fishing to disappear.
    A. has to take   C. might have taken
    B. could have taken   D. could take

45. The earth .... to be round.
    A. he says   C. is said
    B. they say   D. it is said

46. Many plans .... by the committee.
    A. was studied   C. were studied
    B. studied   D. have studied

47. ...., Mary learned geometry quickly.
    A. Her being intelligent C. Her not being stupid
    B. Because intelligent   D. Being intelligent

48. Damage which .... often has lasting effects.
    A. the brain has suffered it C. has suffered the brain
    B. the brain has suffered   D. been suffered by the brain

49. Alfred Hitchcock had made over 100 films ....
the time he died.
    A. for   C. since
    B. by   D. on

50. .... oil supply of the world is limited.
    A. 0 C. An
    B. The D. Some

51. You tell time by looking .... your wristwatch.
    A. on C. in
    B. to D. at

52. If .... speed of an object is great enough, it will
    be consumed by heat due to atmospheric friction.
    A. 0 C. the
    B. a D. some

53. He knows ....
    A. to go where C. where to go
    B. where going D. going where

54. John worked very hard; .... he got a good grade.
    A. however C. therefore
    B. in spite of D. accordingly

55. Mary tried her best; ...., she did not succeed.
    A. however C. therefore
    B. in spite of D. accordingly

56. Joseph said .... it.
    A. that I see C. I see
    B. he had seen D. that he seen

57. Of all the tests I have taken, the one last week was
    .... of all.
    A. most difficult C. the more difficult
    B. more difficult D. the most difficult

58. I don't want to drive to San Francisco. ....about 400
    miles from Los Angeles.
    A. It is C. There's
    B. There are D. There is

CONTINUE ON TO THE NEXT PART OF THE TEST.

PART FOUR: VOCABULARY

DIRECTIONS: Choose the word with the same meaning as the
underlined word. Mark your answers on the answer sheet.

59. They broadcast the results immediately.
    A. announced C. determined
    B. censored D. interpreted

60. He heightened my hopes.
    A. raised C. fulfilled
    B. lowered D. discovered

61. Please don't <u>hinder</u> me.
    A. help   C. talk about
    B. delay   D. force

62. He was <u>obstructing</u> justice.
    A. delivering   C. studying
    B. impeding   D. constructing

63. We tried to <u>suppress</u> his writings.
    A. reprint   C. restrict
    B. emphasize   D. certify

64. He must <u>relay</u> the information to his boss.
    A. return   C. race
    B. transfer   D. mail

65. He <u>retrieved</u> his money.
    A. recovered   C. invested
    B. stole   D. spent

66. The president tried to <u>maintain</u> his position.
    A. renounce   C. share
    B. keep   D. buy

67. Sarah was not likely to <u>perpetrate</u> a crime.
    A. report   C. have
    B. commit   D. prevent

68. He was very <u>animated</u>.
    A. crude   C. brusque
    B. beastly   D. energetic

69. His <u>prolific</u> contributions made him famous.
    A. scholarly   C. prestigious
    B. copious   D. kind

70. He seems to be <u>brutal</u>.
    A. cowardly   C. impolite
    B. corrupt   D. violent

71. The government was <u>autonomous</u>.
    A. oppressive   C. dictatorial
    B. modernized   D. independent

72. His ideas were <u>conventional</u>.
    A. commonplace   C. embarrassing
    B. famous   D. political

73. Andrew had several <u>pernicious</u> habits.
    A. physical   C. helpful
    B. ridiculous   D. destructive

74. They stood at the <u>rim</u> of the canyon.
    A. side   C. edge
    B. bottom   D. crest

75. The <u>wording</u> of the paper was too difficult.
    A. choice of words   C. spelling
    B. sentence length   D. punctuation

76. His work was a <u>challenge</u>.
    A. difficult   C. boring
    B. threatening   D. physical

77. Some people use <u>lard</u> in cooking.
    A. animal fat   C. spice
    B. fire   D. salt

78. The conductor used a <u>podium</u>.
    A. rod   C. platform
    B. costume   D. chair

          CONTINUE ON TO THE NEXT PART OF THE TEST.

          PART FIVE: WRITING ERROR DETECTION

DIRECTIONS: Each of the following items has <u>only one</u> error.
Find which part of the sentence has the error (A,B,C, or D).
Mark your answer on your answer sheet.

                    Passage 1
                A   B   C
79. Since computer was invented / science and technology / have
              D
    made / amazing progress.
              A   B   C
80. In the beginning / people only used / computers to do /
                 D
    complicated scientifical calculations.
                A   B
81. Now, science and technology / use computer robots / to
        C   D
    replace / the manpower.
              A   B   C
82. Even supermarkets / they use / computers to speed up / the
              D
    checkout process.
                 A   B   C
83. Maybe some day, / the professor / which answers your
                                  D
    questions / will be an intelligent computer.

Passage 2

```
            A                   B                        C
84. Comets / which none of them / are exactly alike / are
            D
    strange objects in the sky.
                         A                    B
85. Appearing without warning, / they remain visible / for a few
               C                    D
    weeks or month / and then disappear.
            A                    B                        C
86. They moved / in elliptical paths / returning periodically /
            D
    into view.
            A                    B                        C
87. One example / would be Halley's Comet / which return / every
            D
    77 years.
                    A                         B
88. Because characters / of comets are different, / it is
                C                         D
    difficult to describe them / as a group.
```

Passage 3

```
                      A                         B
89. The emphasis on career education / in the 1970s / had a
                C                         D
    profound effect / at the American educational system.
              A                B                C            D
90. They affected / other countries / in the world / as well.
                    A                              B
91. The purpose of this paper / is to compare these changes / in
                    C                              D
    the educational systems / of United States and Brazil.
              A                              B
92. Americans and Brazilians / regarded career educational / as
                          C                              D
    the solution to the oldest of problems: / education for the

    poor.
              A                         B
93. The necessity / to having better skills / to work in
    C                    D
    industry / is critical for them.
```

Passage 4

```
           A                            B
94. The Greenhouse Effect / is a condition which occurs /
                  C                            D
    because atmosphere thermal blanket / reflects heat to earth.
          A               B                    C
95. It is caused / by many dangerous / things which happens, /
                       D
    such as industrial pollution.
          A                B                         C
96. In the first place / it will rise / the temperature of the
                       D
    world / around 3-9 degrees annually.
               A                      B
97. Although it might be possible / that this effect / will keep
                  C                            D
    the rate of temperature increase / rising more and more.
          A                B            C
98. The modern world / may become / too hot for / human beings

    living.
```

THE END.

BE SURE YOUR NAME IS ON YOUR ANSWER SHEET.
RAISE YOUR HAND WHEN YOU ARE FINISHED.

Multiple Choice Cloze Test – 'Dissecting Air'

Lungs extract oxygen from air; gills glean the same life-giving gas from water. For years scientists have tried to weave artificial membranes that could purify gases and liquids in the same way lungs and gills do. Some (1) .... are moving

        a. researchers
        b. readers
        c. therefore
        d. however

closer to that goal. (2) .... efforts could make it easier to

        a. Science
        b. Our
        c. Oxygen
        d. Their

(3) ......,, oxygen-enriched air to hospitals, high-altitude

    a. send
    b. liquid
    c. create
    d. lung

(4) .... and aquaculture centers; to supply

    a. oceans
    b. leads
    c. purifies
    d. observatories

concentrated (5) .... of nitrogen and oxygen to industry,

        a. organisms
        b. streams
        c. operate
        d. fortify

(6) .... to purify natural gas and other hydrocarbon-based

    a. science
    b. water
    c. but
    d. and

fuels.

    One 'artificial (7) ....', developed by the Dow

        a. lung
        b. reads
        c. animal
        d. conserves

Chemical Co. of Midland, Mich., (8) .... 10,000 miles long,
         a. membrane
         b. instructs
         c. letter
         d. is

(9) .... it could fit into a large mailbox. The membrane
a. but
b. thus
c. sending
d. positioning

system, called Generon, (10) .... of 10 four-by one-foot
         a. and
         b. consists
         c. therefore
         d. researches

(11)............ packed with prodigious lengths of tiny hollow
  a. and
  b. tubes
  c. because
  d. minerals

plastic (12) .... finer than a human hair. The tubes have
       a. fibers
       b. lungs
       c. consists
       d. subsists

filtered, compressed air fed into (13) ....
        a. investigating
        b. purifying
        c. them
        d. it

(14) ...., oxygen molecules permeate the fibres and
  a. These
  b. However
  c. As a result
  d. Tubes and air

(15) ..... through a pipe at the end of each tube. (16)........,
  a. send   a. Fibers
  b. flow   b. Therefore
  c. tubes   c. By permeating
  d. gases   d. At the same time

hydrogen and other gases repelled by the membrane (17) ....

    a. result
    b. wall
    c. door
    d. exit

through an auxiliary pipe on the side of the unit. (18) ....

    a. His
    b. This
    c. Lung
    d. Purifying

process, which has no moving parts, yields an air stream that is 35 percent oxygen - nearly twice the concentration of oxygen in normal air. (19) ...., another Generon system uses a gas

    a. Similarly
    b. Industry
    c. As a result
    d. Fibers and tubes

stream that is 95 to 99 percent nitrogen. (20) .... can then

    a. Fibers
    b. They
    c. It
    d. Water

be sold to industry to protect volatile materials and preserve agricultural produce.

    (21) .... pioneer in hollow-filter-membrane
    a. The
    b. Another
    c. Science
    d. Investigation

(22) ...., the Monsanto Co. of St Louis, Mo., is marketing

    a. thus
    b. gases
    c. however
    d. technology

separators that filter out hydrogen, carbon dioxoide, helium and other gases. One system (23) .... hydrogen from methane

    a. investigator
    b. eliminates
    c. proposes
    d. reader

fuels; (24) .... extracts CO_2, used to enhance recovery of
      a. it
      b. then
      c. another
      d. similarly

heavy crude oils. A similar process recycles helium breathed by
deep-sea divers; (25) ....
      a. it
      b. then
      c. another
      d. however

is being tested by Statoil, the Norwegian state-owned oil
company.

Where is Planet X?

Uranus and Neptune misbehave constantly. The orbits they follow around the sun are irregular, and many astromoners think they know why. They believe an unknown body is ....(1)...... in the solar system and that ....(2)......... gravity disturbs the movement of the ....(3)...... planets.They call this body Planet X. ....(4)......... all they have to do is.......(5)...... it.

Astromoners have been looking for Planet ....(6)...... for more than half a century. ....(7)..... far this mysterious object has eluded ......(8)..... . The first person to mount a ....(9)..... search was a skilled amateur ......(10)...... Clyde Tombaugh. In 1930 he found ....(11)......... planet X candidate, but it turned ......(12)...... to be much too small to ......(13)..... the orbits of Uranus and Neptune. ....(14)..... discovery was named Pluto, the ninth ....(15)......... of the solar system.

Tombaugh spent 14 ......(16)..... patiently continuing the search for ......(17)...... transplutonian planet, using the same ......(18)......... that helped him find Pluto: comparing ......(19)..... plates of the night sky taken ......(20)..... or even years apart. By 'blinking' ......(21)...... plates in a device called a comparator, which ......(22)...... him a quick look first ......(23)... one plate and then at ......(24)..... same view taken at a later ......(25)..........., he hoped to spot a moving ......(26)...... that might be a new planet. '......(27)......... searched more than 70% of ......(28)...... sky,' Tombaugh, now in his 80's, ...(29)...... . 'I blinked plates to the extreme limit, ...(30)...... at objects four to five times fainter than Pluto was when I found it.' Tombaugh's quest turned up nothing.

Author index

Subject index

References in italics indicate tables or figures. References followed by 'n', e.g. '176n', indicate references to notes at the bottom of pages.